ISBN 978-1-331-66185-6
PIBN 10219455

English
Français
Deutsche
Italiano
Español
Português

www.forgottenbooks.com

Mythology Photography **Fiction**
Fishing Christianity **Art** Cooking
Essays Buddhism Freemasonry
Medicine **Biology** Music **Ancient
Egypt** Evolution Carpentry Physics
Dance Geology **Mathematics** Fitness
Shakespeare **Folklore** Yoga Marketing
Confidence Immortality Biographies
Poetry **Psychology** Witchcraft
Electronics Chemistry History **Law**
Accounting **Philosophy** Anthropology
Alchemy Drama Quantum Mechanics
Atheism Sexual Health **Ancient History**
Entrepreneurship Languages Sport
Paleontology Needlework Islam
Metaphysics Investment Archaeology
Parenting Statistics Criminology
Motivational

Love 3:16
God's love is unconditional
not based on F.E.

Agape   Kind, Selfless
        unconditional
        immeasurable, incomparable

Witnesses of the Father and the Son.
Reveals and teaches the truth of all things.

Communicates to my Spirit Soul.
Guides, protects from physical harm.
Gives His Gifts to me.
Parent and Comforter
Fill me with hope and Love.
Teach the peaceable things of the Kingdom.
His power sanctify as I repent, Receive the
ordinances of baptism and confirmation
and remain true to all covenants.
He is the Holy Spirit of promise.
Lead me to Jesu christ and the Gospel.
Constant Companionship of Holy Spirit, member
of the Godhead, Rafah Keep God's commands.
Help me God Jehovah to do flat, Amen.

Asceticism; renounce worldly pleasures that distract from
        Spiritual growth.
                                        m 5:48
Monasticism: Jesus' teaching on perfection. Celibacy math
                                                    19:10-12
        and poverty m 19:16-22. Controlled environment
        and surround Nuns/themselves with like minded
        devotees. Elijah, John the Baptist, Jesus Himself.

Poverty has many attributes: it instills patience, courage,
            obedience, no desire for worldly things, or
        relationships.
obedience: Jn 8:51 Keep my Word and be faithful.
chastity: Celibacy, secluded from the World, Virtue, fasting.

Benedictus Dominus:

A

COURSE OF MEDITATIONS

FOR

EVERY DAY OF THE YEAR.

BY

R. M. BENSON, M.A.,

STUDENT OF CHRIST CHURCH: SUPERIOR OF THE SOCIETY OF
S. JOHN THE EVANGELIST, COWLEY.

Blessed be the Lord God of Israel.
Rafah Khulud's Book from God, Amen.
Jesus grants me His good [many] will, grace.

LONDON:
J. T. HAYES, 17 HENRIETTA STREET,
COVENT GARDEN.

1900₂

TO

THE MEMBERS

OF

THE SOCIETY OF THE APOSTOLIC RULE

AND

IN ESPECIAL REMEMBRANCE

OF

SUSANNA BATLEY,

FOUNDRESS OF THAT SOCIETY,

THESE MEDITATIONS,

ORIGINALLY DRAWN UP FOR THEIR USE,

ARE AFFECTIONATELY INSCRIBED.

PREFACE.

THESE brief heads of Meditation were at first drawn up for the use of a small Society, in order that its members, though outwardly separated from one another and living in the world, might feel the bond of union which is formed by such devotional agreement. The Meditative Life is that whereby the soul abides in union with God; and the practice of Meditation upon the same subjects daily is one great means of binding together those who are held back by the necessities of external society from much personal fellowship. Even the pursuit of some accidental object of natural science forms a link between many who have never met, although the object contemplated has no power of giving any life to the student. Much more does the contemplation of Divine Truth. For Divine Truth is not merely Truth which lives, but the Living Truth gives Life to those who dwell upon its contemplation. A common Faith in the Living God is therefore a common Life; and the exercise of such Faith, according to common modes of worship, is a development of that Life in common, according to the fulness of Divine Love.

Hence arises, indeed, the great value of common forms of Devotion throughout the Church. They are

not merely an appointment of arbitrary devotion by
authority, but in making such appointment, the Church
is accepting, hallowing, developing, utilising, a law of
our human nature.   The law of sympathy in contemplation was given to us by God for this very purpose.
Mankind was formed to find delight in Truth ; not
merely after the manner of individual intelligences, but
with the consciousness of common joy in one Life-
giving object.   And thus we were not only to find our
Life in the knowledge and Love of God, but in the
Love of one another, which that knowledge sustains
and purifies.

The Antiphons belonging to the Benedictus have
been chosen as the basis of these Meditations, and the
opening words of that Canticle seem to supply a fitting
name for the series.   Surely we ought to approach our
Meditation constantly with an utterance of Blessing
and Praise to our Covenant God.   It is hoped that
this Book will thus have a particular interest and use-
fulness for those who are in the habit of reciting the
Canonical Hours.

It will not be the less serviceable for Churchmen at
large.   These Antiphons are themselves generally culled
from the Scriptures which occur for use in the Communion Service of the day, and are of course suitable
in themselves for the particular season at which they
are found.

In our Meditation-books we require helps of varying
length.   Some persons like a good deal of reading to

prepare them for their Meditation. Those in this book are all brief, and rigidly restricted to one page.

Such brief heads are useful both for persons of much business, as requiring less time to master, and also for persons of much devotional energy, as leaving them more free to meditate according to the impulse of their own inspiration.

In meditating we shall often find that we are helped most, when we are helped least. Meditation is an energy of the soul in Communion with God; and prolonged lections often tend to hinder this, as they keep the soul passive in the grasp of the author's mind rather than in that blessed control of the Holy Spirit which, while it does render us intensely quiescent beneath the power of His all-comprehending operation, does nevertheless raise us to an intensity of spiritual energy far surpassing anything which can be derived from any human guide.

The few words in which the various Heads are given, may of course be developed as a Meditation for any length of time, according to the desire of each individual. Occasionally it will be found that more is suggested than is required for use upon any one occasion. The reader will then not feel himself bound to use more than he finds desirable.

Some leading Affections suitable for each Meditation are put down; and those who use this book ought to try and expand the several points in such a manner as to make acts of devotion expressive of these affections.

At the bottom of the page there is a short Collect, which sums up the thought of the preceding exercise. It will not take the place of the extemporaneous colloquies of the soul with God, which are the most important part of the Meditation, but it supplies a key-note for them.

May God of His mercy bless this little book to the edification of many of His people.

Those who use it, are entreated of their charity to pray for the writer.

CONTENTS.

CONTENTS.

NOTE.—*The Meditations for Feasts of the Holy Apostles, for St. Matthew, and for All Saints', may be used on those days of Apostles and Evangelists for which nothing special is appointed.*

INTRODUCTORY REMARKS.

MEDITATION is the exercise of all the powers of the soul in the apprehension of God. It is the means by which we cling to God. By the Sacraments God takes hold upon us, and works invisibly in us. By Meditation we take hold upon His invisible Presence, feed upon Him in our souls, receive the illumination of His Holy Spirit, grow in grace, and become perfectly united to Him. By it we exercise Faith, which is the substance of things hoped for, the evidence of things not seen. Without Meditation we cannot exercise Faith; that is, we cannot know the things of God to be such realities as can outweigh the things of sense. It is not wonderful that there is so little Love of God in the world, because there is so little Meditation. Without it the Brightness and Joy of God must remain hidden from the consciousness of the soul: for we see the scenery of the outer world merely by the faculty of sense, without any act of the will; but we do not see the things of the world to come unless we choose to gaze upon them. There must be an effort of the will, otherwise we shall never know them. And yet people are content to go on without making this effort. The consequence is, that even many persons of the most cultivated intellect are quite void of any love or knowledge of God. The application of the intellect to other matters does not

b

fit people to know God any the more. God must be known by the effort of the whole soul acting in correspondence with the Holy Spirit of illumination. God's spiritual gifts, and man's highest natural faculties, avail not to lead us onward in the Love of God, unless we are using them in combination.

For want of Meditation, therefore, prayer is often ineffectual, Sacraments are profitless, the reading of Holy Scripture uninstructive, the knowledge of the true Faith void of unction. A lower measure of gifts used with meditative delight is of more value than any large measure, if it be not thus spiritually exercised.

Great is the necessity of Meditation, and not less great is its joy. Other exercises lead on to future joy; but the joy of meditation is as immediate as it is lasting. True, indeed, there will often be in meditation seasons of great dryness and desolation; but the faithful soul is able to accept them with a supernatural love. There is a dryness which arises from the imperfection wherewith we meditate. This is generally to be known by the fretfulness and distress which it occasions. This, however, is a result of our own sluggishness. If we would rise out of it, we must learn to meditate better. But it will also happen that those who are loving God the most, feel great desolation when they practise their spiritual exercises. These chosen souls do not fret at the discipline to which God subjects them. They know His Love, and they can say, "Though He slay me, yet will I trust in Him." There is a mysterious joy in the midst of such sorrow. The soul knows the nearness of God, although He hides Himself. The words spoken on Calvary gather up such souls into their holy questioning: "My God, my God, why hast

Thou forsaken me?" The faithful soul is sustained so as to utter the confident acknowledgment, "Thou continuest Holy, O Thou worship of Israel."

When, however, persons complain of not having power to meditate, the fault is commonly with themselves. They come to it unprepared, and how can they expect to enjoy the peace of Heaven when the din of earthly excitement is making their whole nature vibrate in sympathy with its unholy strife? Or else they try to meditate merely in the strength of the natural reason, and then they weary themselves to no purpose: for the natural heart understandeth not the things of the Spirit of God.

In order to meditate upon Divine Truth, we ought to come to the act of meditation with composure, expectation, and delight.

Composure must be obtained in two ways. First and chiefly, by the habitual repose of the soul in God. We must be living in continual fellowship with God. This *habitual preparation* is of the utmost consequence. If we are strangers to the Life of God, we cannot put ourselves, nor expect to be drawn, into the Life of God suddenly. Watchfulness in daily life helps us to contemplate God, and the habit of looking up to Him helps us to be watchful.

The *immediate preparation* consists in determining certain points as the heads of our meditation, so that we may not be perplexed when we come to perform our exercise. The preparation of ourselves, and the preparation of our subject, are both of them most necessary.

It is well to have the Heads of Meditation made out over night, so that we may give our minds without effort to the thought of them. Happy it is if we wake with our Meditation for the day clearly before the mind, and speak thereon with God as early in the day as possible, before other occupations disturb the memory.

There is no form of introduction which can surpass the *Veni Creator*. We should always invite the Holy Ghost when preparing to meditate.

In the outline provided in this book there is first *one prelude*, consisting of some words of Holy Scripture, except in a very few instances, and this brings forward the whole subject.

The *second Prelude* is commonly called a Composition of place. It is an act of imagination, by which we seek to give greater vividness to the words previously recited, by picturing to ourselves the speaker, and the circumstances under which they were spoken, or some object selected from the things of sense as a symbol of the abstract Truth which we desire to consider.

God has given us this gift of imagination not merely for our own gratification but as a means of approach to Himself. We must be careful not to exercise this faculty rashly, for then we become its dupes. Clearness of imagination deceives many, for they cannot realize the falsity of their conception, and yet it is only the creation of their own minds. What they see with so much clearness they believe to be a necessary truth, and then they set about constructing their theological system so as to make room for it. But the imagination is an excellent servant, although it is a most pernicious master. By the aid thereof we are able to apprehend verities of the faith which are beyond the grasp of our natural reason. The imagination, when under discipline of the faith, does not fill the vacant mind with idle notions of its own, but portrays, under forms of its own experience, the things unseen which God reveals.

Our nature is formed to learn truth by means of analogy. Imagination uses the outer world as symbolizing moral truth, and moral truth as being truly akin to what is spiritual. Hence our Lord's teaching was so frequently by Parables. It is a great gift of God to learn lessons from nature in this way. The highest poetry is the simplest Primer of Eternal Truth.

We should not dwell upon the Preludes, but we ought to have them constantly in remembrance, so as to bring them forward in the Meditation at many points. They should constitute the framework upon which our minds shall weave the thoughts that have to be developed.

Having the scheme of Meditation thus symbolically before us, we should make a final act of self-surrender to Almighty God. We are not only coming to think *about* God, but to speak *with* God.

In brief ejaculations, humbling ourselves before Him, we ought to express both our distrust of ourselves and our confidence in His Love.

So then, expectation is important. We must hope that God means to speak with us. It were an insult to Him to come to speak with Him, and to think that He would be dumb. Many persons think that God is dumb towards them, because they only care to listen to themselves. Those persons will not meditate well, who feel that they can tell God what He ought to say to them. We come to Meditation in order that we may listen and learn. "Speak, Lord, for Thy servant heareth."

This introductory part should be summed up with the *Lord's Prayer;* and having said this, we are to feel that we are alone with God to hear what He will say

concerning us. We are given over to Him, and He
may speak to us in such way as seemeth Him good.
O how great should be the delight of this filial self-
surrender, to love as we are loved !

These brief acts being done, we come to the *Points
of Meditation*. In this Book there are generally three
Points and three subdivisions. It is by no means necessary always to go through all of these. Sometimes one
Point will be enough. We ought to use more or less
according to the guidance of God's Holy Spirit.

If the Meditation has been read over the night
before, the *memory* will recall, by an almost instan-
taneous act, the whole scheme of thought. It is now
for the *understanding* to investigate whatever is presented to it. Divine Truth is not given to us in order
to check the exercise of the understanding, but to
develop it. Only we must exercise it with caution. It
is not for us to imagine that we can fathom all the
rationale of the works, much less of the nature, of
God. Our understanding gains strength from patiently
following as the Spirit of God speaks. By habitual
intercourse with heavenly things, a supernatural
instinct is gained. Alas, that people are so content to
live without it !

The understanding must not be exerted too labori-
ously. When we apply our understanding alone to
Divine Truth, we call it study. Meditation is something more than this. The understanding is trans-
ported by the Divine inspiration beyond its natural
limits. The unction which we have received of God
teacheth us all things when we thus seek to be taught;
not, that is, to be taught anything new, but to be
taught so that the old truth may shine out before us

with a new lustre, and continual freshness, and an individual correspondence of life.

We should pass on as soon as we can from the work of the understanding to that of the *will.* The great object of meditation is to be found in the development of the affections. He that loveth not, knoweth not God, for God is love. The exercise of the understanding comes short of God unless the will reaches out after God, and so the affections must be rapt into the energy of God. The understanding may teach us to admire, but we cannot truly know, unless we do more than this. We must love. The understanding does but supply the data upon which the affections are to act.

Every effort, therefore, of the understanding, whatever its result may be, should lead us to love. If God reveal some truth to the understanding, we cannot but love it. If God leave the understanding in darkness, still we must be absorbed in Love, holy, aspiring Love, whereby we long the more to see, because we are left without any gift of vision. We know God wants to show Himself to us. Oh! it is often blessed to end a meditation with the simple desire,—Lord, show me Thy glory.

For we must always remember that the meditation has not merely to do with vague truth. We meditate, in order to come to the Personal Truth, to God. As He is Love, it is only in the act of Love that we can come to Him.

Various affections ought therefore to be elicited in meditating upon the points which are given. The Holy Spirit will develop these, if we give ourselves up to His guidance. He teaches us the things of God

more truly by leading us to proper affections towards
God, than by giving us clear intuitions of what
God is.

Constant aspirations, and devout acknowledgments
uttered throughout the time of meditation, in sweet
colloquy with God, are the really important part of
the meditation. Sometimes, perhaps, these find their
strongest utterance in the profound silence with which
the soul waits upon God. God hears when we are
silent, if our silence is the silence of Love.

It is not well to force ourselves to put into words
what we would address to God. To pray thus is blamed
by our Lord as being vain repetition, the much speaking of the Pharisees. The words thus uttered are apt
to be unreal. Instead of producing joy and comfort in
the soul, such an effort throws the soul back upon its
own incapacity, and makes it only despair of getting to
God. If we will be content to look to Him as little
children, He will draw out the powers of our intelligence to grasp His living Truth by the inspiration of
His Holy Love.

But then, that look must not be the mere look of
vacancy or idleness. We must know what we worship.
We must rest upon the simple Truths of the Creed.
We do not throw ourselves into an abyss of sentimen-
tality when we fall down before God Who is Love.
He welcomes us. However little joy we may feel in
coming to Him, we must praise that Love whereby He
rejoices to welcome us. The more we can thus feel
ourselves to be passively correspondent with the Love
of God in meditation, the better it will be for us. By
giving ourselves up to hear Him speak, we gain the
mysterious power of His Voice speaking within us.

This is called in Holy Scripture, " praying in the Holy Ghost," and thus it is that we should " build ourselves up in our most Holy Faith."

At the close of the Meditation it is well to use a Collect, which may sum up what has gone before. It is also very customary to conclude with the following Hymn as an act of intense unitive praise to Jesus :—

> " Soul of Christ, sanctify me ;
> Body of Christ, save me ;
> Blood of Christ, inebriate me ;
> Water from the side of Christ, wash me ;
> Passion of Christ, strengthen me ;
> O Good Jesu, hear me ;
> In the hour of my death call me ;
> And suffer me not to be separated from Thee ;
> That with Thy Saints I may praise Thee ;
> For ever and ever.   Amen."

We thus seek to have our whole nature sanctified by the operation of the nature of Christ. We are members of His Body, of His Flesh, and of His Bones. We live with His Life, not merely because He has obtained for us life which we had forfeited, but because He has given us His own. We live in Him. We have the Mind of Christ, and therefore it is that we are able to meditate. The Wisdom, which is from above, is given to us, and our own natural faculties of thought are elevated thereby.

This elevation of the mind by the power of the Spirit is a knowledge of Divine things, which, as we have seen, carries an elevation of the heart along with it. Knowledge and Love are but differing expressions for the same act of Divine apprehension.

The word " inebriate " is intended to imply this

rapture of the consciousness. Physical inebriation is the destruction of human consciousness by an exhilaration which degrades as it carries the soul out of itself into a world of factitious energy. The Blood of Christ inebriates by filling the soul with the joy of the Holy Ghost. The Blood is the medium of exhilaration, and the Blood of Christ, wherein is the Life, *i.e.*, the Holy Ghost, operates immediately upon our own Blood wherein is our Life, *i.e.*, our soul; and thus " our souls are washed through His most precious Blood." If we yield ourselves truly to this influence, we lose our own consciousness, and are lifted up into the fellowship of His Mind. This inebriation is that state of which S. Paul speaks as " being beside ourselves." In his own experience he describes it, saying, "Whether in the body I cannot tell, or out of the body I cannot tell." The intensity of his rapture differs from what we may hope for; but in kind it was the very same as we ought to seek in meditation.

By this rapture we hear unspeakable words, which it is not lawful for man to utter. The glory of Divine Truth shines upon the soul in a manner which no human words can convey. The Holy Ghost thus teaches the regenerate soul by His own interior power, according to the promise in the New Covenant, that " they shall be all taught of God."

The utterances, the prophesyings, of the early Christians were doubtless the unfolding of Divine Truth by such Spiritual Exercise. S. Paul says, " We speak Wisdom among them that are perfect, the Wisdom which the Holy Ghost teacheth." We ought to seek for this prophetic Wisdom, this Spiritual intuition, this handling of the Word of Life as a substantive reality.

When we meditate, we ought to set before ourselves this high aim. Otherwise we shall not reach it. But then we can only reach it by the power of the Holy Ghost; and that is given to us by the Blood of Jesus Christ, circulating in our veins as an exhilarating principle of transporting delight, opening the eye of our soul to the sight of objects beyond this world, making us to see Heaven opened.

The difference between real rapture and the delusions of fanatics is manifest. They are for the purpose of satisfying curiosity, nourishing pride, conveying spiritual knowledge carnally to others. This rapture, on the other hand, is for the edification in the faith already received, conveying knowledge that is new, not in matter but in kind; involving the humiliation of those who receive it—for without humility none can receive it— and leading others onward, not by any merely intellectual process, but by the sympathy of Divine Joy. S. Paul speaks thus of being comforted together with his disciples, "by the mutual faith both of you and me."

The fanatic is always liable to be deceived, for he trusts in himself as a test of Truth. The faithful, in all their raptures, are subject to the received law of Truth. The self-will of fanatics leads only to renewed schism. Every freshly invented dogma becomes an occasion of separation. The rapture of the faithful soul by the power of the Holy Ghost leads to a greater appreciation of unity, a truer exercise of the One Life which fills the whole of the undivided Body. "Came the Word of God out from you? or came It unto you only?" Truth can never be the proud possession of the individual soul. It is the Light shining throughout the whole consciousness of the Body of Christ, and the more we see thereof, the more must we lose ourselves in the Communion of Saints. So should meditation help all Christians to dwell together in unity; for it is the exercise of the One Faith which is the Life of the One Body in the power of the One Spirit.

After meditation we ought to examine ourselves, whether we have been acting in union with God throughout it. We ought to humble ourselves for our failures, and praise Him for His goodness. It is a great insult to Almighty God to come to Him and go away without any acknowledgment of the help which He has given. One great reason why people experience so much dryness in meditation is probably because they are so little accustomed to thankfulness after meditation. The Church closes her Daily Office with a Collect of thankfulness to our Lord Jesus Christ, " Who has given us grace at this time with one accord to make our common supplications unto Him." It is a great act of grace which enables us to pray, and we ought not to take it as a matter of course. If we do so, it shows that we have been praying in our own natural strength, and that is equivalent to not praying at all.

We ought to form certain *resolutions* as the result of our meditation. These need not be new every time. If they have been made before, perhaps often made and often broken, they should be made with increasing self-humiliation, self-distrust, self-sacrifice, and a corresponding increase of reliance upon God, hope in God, and delight in God.

Meditation must not make us dreamy and unpractical, for then it could not be true. If by meditation we come to see more of the Life of God, our meditations will lead us to show forth in our lives more truly the Life of God.

Some text of Scripture is useful to us as a *memorial* of the meditation, to be frequently repeated as an ejaculatory prayer until the next meditation. Our inner Life thus gains a continuity of Divine energy, without which it cannot develop itself in a healthy manner. The effect of our meditations upon our lives very much depends upon cherishing the result of each meditation at once, before it has, so to speak, got cold. The memorial, which is sometimes called by a beautiful metaphor, the Spiritual Nosegay, gathered in the Paradise of Meditation, will often be a refreshment amidst the weariness of the day which follows. One thought of it will recall to our hearts the invigorating fragrance of our intercourse with God in all the power of His Love.

Thus should our meditations, time after time, be leading us onwards, according to the words of the Psalmist, "They will go from strength to strength ; and unto the God of gods appeareth every one of them in Sion."

MEDITATIONS.

First Sunday in Advent.

THE INCARNATION BY THE POWER OF THE HOLY GHOST.

PRELUDE. i. *The Holy Ghost shall come upon thee, Mary; fear not : thou shalt conceive in thy womb the Son of God. Alleluia.*—S. Luke i. 35, 30, 31.

ii. The Dove, as the emblem of the Holy Ghost, hovering over the Blessed Virgin whilst she kneels in prayer, and making a glorious Light of Divine Presence to surround her.

POINT I. *Consider the Son of God coming down from the Father.*

    a. Consubstantial with the Father in the eternal unity of Godhead.

    b. Exercising the energy of Divine Life by the eternal procession of the Holy Ghost.

    c. Effecting all His work in creation by the power of the Holy Ghost, Who thus proceeds eternally from Himself and from the Father in the undivided energy of Godhead.

POINT II. *Consider the Holy Ghost sanctifying the Creature.*

    a. Consubstantial with the Father and the Son in the unity of Godhead.

    b. Expressing eternally in His own Person the Holy Joy of the Father and the Son.

    c. Making the power of Godhead to be felt outside of the Divine Being, by moving upon that which He has created.

POINT III. *Consider the Holy Ghost communicating Divine Life.*

    a. No life true life, save the Life whereby God lives.

    b. No holiness to be found, save in the participation of this Life.

    c. No possession of this Life, save by the life of the Holy Ghost, so that that which lives thereby is verily and indeed the Son of God.

AFFECTIONS. Worship of the Triune God. Gratitude for the manifestation of Divine Life. Self-surrender to the quickening influence of the Holy Ghost. Desire for Christ to be revealed in our own selves by the same power.

PRAYER.

O Lord Jesu Christ, Who ever dwellest in the Glory of the Father, and yet didst vouchsafe to take upon Thyself our earthly nature by the power of the Holy Ghost, grant me by the inspiration of the same Eternal Spirit constantly to remember Thy Holy Incarnation, and to live no longer in the life of the flesh, but in that better Life which Thou hast brought unto us ; that so Thy Life in the flesh may be my salvation, and the life which I live in the flesh may be to Thy Glory, Who with the Father and the Holy Ghost ever abidest one God, world without end. Amen.

B

THE HUMANITY ASSUMED.

PRELUDE. i. *The Angel of the Lord appeared unto Mary: and she conceived of the Holy Ghost. Alleluia.*

ii. The Blessed Virgin bowing down beneath the Light of the Divine glory with her face to the earth and saying, Be it unto me according to the Word of the Most High.

POINT I. *Consider the reality of the nature assumed.*

a. The very Humanity of Adam, which was formed originally in God's Image, remaining essentially complete.

b. The very Humanity which fell from union with God by Adam's sin, and which had passed through such degradation of sin in many intervening generations.

c. The very Humanity to which the promise of restoration was given, for that which should triumph over Satan, was the very seed of the first woman, the humanity taken from Adam's side.

POINT II. *Consider the completeness of the nature assumed.*

a. Body, perfect in sanctity by the interior Presence of God, although assumed in a condition external to the manifestation of Divine beatitude.

b. Soul, glorious with the Light of God's Presence, and ruling the flesh in the perfection of truth, although feeling its exile and its emptiness.—Phil. ii. 7.

c. Spirit, rejoicing in communion with the Divine Nature according to the original purpose of God, but in a higher degree of supernatural fellowship than Adam forfeited.

POINT III. *Consider the three faculties of the soul as constituting the Divine Image wherein this Humanity is fashioned.*

a. Memory, accepting the law of the Father as the motive of all actions, even as He is one with the Father in the eternal Divine Energy.

b. Understanding, gazing in the perfection of Divine Wisdom upon the Divine purpose, and rejoicing to know Himself as the Eternal Word.

c. Will, rejoicing to do the will of God in the unity of the Holy Ghost, not by mere human excellence, but by Divine Power.

AFFECTIONS. Wonder at the greatness of God's love to man. Trust in God's promises. Desire to consecrate all human faculties to His service. Glory to Jesus for calling us in Himself to the supernatural life.

PRAYER.

O my Jesu, Who hast assumed the nature of Man as the instrument wherein the fulness of the Father's purpose may be accomplished, grant that I may so meditate upon Thy Holy actions, that here I may act in Thy strength, and hereafter may share in Thy reward, Who art my only Mediator and Advocate. Amen.

THE INCARNATION A HEALING.

PRELUDE. i. *O Jerusalem, lift up thine eyes, and behold the might of thy King. Lo, thy Saviour cometh to cure thee of thy wound.*—Hos. v. 13.

ii. The Body of Christ in the midst of the Humanity whence it was taken, as a coal red with fire in the midst of ashes that have lost their light.

POINT I. *Consider the deadness of human nature.*

  a. From the moment of Adam's sin, when he forfeited the life of God, which was his supernatural health.

  b. Increasing in manifestations of decay, as especially in many of the wicked kings of Judah and Israel, from whom nevertheless Christ was born.

  c. Continuing irremediably up to the moment of the Incarnation, when the Word in Whom was Life, was Himself made Flesh.

POINT II. *Consider the new Life of Humanity in the Person of Christ.*

  a. Decay arrested. Outside of Christ, man must become worse and worse.

  b. Strength renewed. The renewal of organized life, so that all faculties operate in their true subordination to the reason, while the rational will is true to the Will of God.

  c. Glory communicated. The joyous energy of healthy action while serving God.

POINT III. *Consider the spread of Life from the Humanity of Jesus to those who are incorporated therein.*

  a. The need of this Life. Christ does not save the dead in their death, but He saves them by giving them Life.

  b. The necessity of incorporation into Christ. Christ taking our nature does not regenerate us, even though we were as closely allied to Him as the Blessed Virgin Mary; but we must obtain Life by being taken into His Nature.—S. Luke ii. 28.

  c. The propagation of this Life. Our state of decay does not hinder the fulness of God's purpose in sending us health and a cure in His Only-begotten Son.

AFFECTIONS. Thankfulness. Lamentation over our continuing deadness. Hopefulness in seeking the health which Christ brings.

PRAYER.

O Jesu Christ, Who givest health to us, although by nature perishing in corruption, grant me so thankfully to accept the strength which Thou givest, that I may stedfastly resist the power of sin, and may rise to serve Thee with faculties renewed in the power of Thine endless Life, Who reignest with the Father in the unity of the Holy Ghost, God for ever and ever. Amen.

B 2

THE INCARNATION A LAW.

PRELUDE.　i. *The Law shall go forth of Sion, and the Word of the Lord from Jerusalem.—Micah iv. 2.*

ii. The Body of Christ as the Organ of Divine utterance, through which the Word of God speaks to the world.

POINT I.　*Consider the Word of God revealed to man in Jesus Christ.*

　　a. The utterance of speech. He speaks a language which man can understand.

　　b. The utterance of sympathy. Men can appreciate the words of a fellow-sufferer.

　　c. The utterance of example. Jesus spake by His actions, calling us to follow His steps.

POINT II.　*Consider the holiness of this Law.*

　　a. Adapted by the eternal purpose of the Father to perfect the Creation in moral completeness.

　　b. Manifested in the obedience of the Son triumphing over every solicitation of evil.

　　c. Glorified by the supernatural co-operation of the Holy Ghost, by Whom He presented Himself without spot to God.

POINT III.　*Consider the universality of this Law.*

　　a. As proceeding from the Father of all. The fixity of the laws of creation a result of the unchangeableness of the Will of the Creator operating according to an unalterable analogy in every department of His works.

　　b.　As manifested by the Son, Who has taken upon Himself the nature of all men, and requires all to be conformed to Himself.

　　c. As intended to bring mankind to the same beatitude of moral perception in Divine Life.

AFFECTIONS.　Joy in surrendering the will to God. Cheerfulness in following Christ's example. Rapture in the consciousness of His sympathy.

PRAYER.

O Lord Jesu Christ, Who hast made known to us the Will of the Father, as a law of righteousness to which we must be conformed, and a law of grace whereby we may be strengthened, grant that I may so accept Thy revelation, that I may know Thy Gospel as the Power of God bringing me to salvation through the communication of Thy Truth. Amen.

THE INCARNATION A BLESSING.

PRELUDE. i. *Blessed art thou among women; and blessed is the Fruit of thy womb.*—S. Luke i. 28, 42.

ii. The Blessed Virgin, praising God for the gift of His Son to be her Child.

POINT I. *Consider the dignity of Humanity by reason of the Incarnation.*

    a. The angels worshipping the Incarnate God.

    b. Creation finding itself perfected by the Son of Man.

    c. The Divine glory treasured up in Jesus, waiting for the manifestation of the Great Day.

POINT II. *Consider the remedy for sorrow provided in the Incarnation.*

    a. Blessed is the sorrow which leads to such a Divine gift.

    b. Blessed is the Son of Man in Whom that gift is given.

    c. Blessed is the soul to whom Christ comes in proportion to the closeness of union with Him.

POINT III. *Consider the Divine fruition to which man is called by the Incarnation.*

    a. Grace is the earnest of a glory to be revealed hereafter.

    b. Fellowship with Christ in suffering shall be recompensed with the participation of His triumph.

    c. To experience the power of Jesus is to know the Love of God.

AFFECTIONS. Humiliation before the power of God. Exultation at the nearness of God. Encouragement by the invitation of God.

PRAYER.

O Lord Jesu Christ, how can I praise Thee for the blessing which Thou dost vouchsafe to me in Thyself! Teach me so to meditate upon the mysteries of eternal joy which Thou dost make known to all who share Thy Life by suffering, that I may experience in every moment of need the all-sufficiency of Thy beatific sweetness. Amen.

First Friday in Advent.

THE INCARNATION AN ENTHRONEMENT.

PRELUDE. i. *Behold, He that is God and Man shall come forth from the House of David: to sit upon His Throne. Alleluia.*—Acts ii. 30.

ii. The Child Jesus with a crown of glory round His Head seated upon His mother's knees.

POINT I. *Consider the throne of creation, vacant before the Incarnation.*

 a. Man fallen from the Sovereignty for which He was created.

 b. No man worthy to reign as Head over the human race.

 c. No creature worthy to claim the allegiance of the universe.

POINT II. *Consider the ancient promise of a King.*

 a. The seed of the woman Who should bruise the Serpent's head.

 b. The Son of David Who should raise the House of Israel.

 c. The High Priestly King Who should sit on the Right Hand of God.—Zech. vi. 13.

POINT III. *Consider the Sovereignty of God manifest in the flesh.*

 a. As Redeemer of mankind who must own Him as King of this world, and have Him as Saviour.

 b. As King of Angels who wait upon His bidding.

 c. As Conqueror of Devils, who tremble at His Presence.

AFFECTIONS. Confidence in Jesus. Readiness to obey Him. Delight in being called by Him to give any token of loyalty by act or suffering, in thought, word, or deed.

PRAYER.

O Lord Jesu Christ, Who comest to reign over mankind, grant that I may so continually bear in mind Thy sovereign power, that I may yield Thee hearty obedience, and own it as the glory of my life to be ever united unto Thee my King, whether in suffering or in joy. Amen.

THE INCARNATION A DELIVERANCE.

PRELUDE.   i. *Fear not, daughter of Sion ; behold, thy King cometh.*—S. John xii. 15.

ii. The Child Jesus putting His Hand upon thy Head and making a mark of light to rest thereon, so that the power of darkness may lose his hold upon thee.

POINT I.   *Consider the security of Christ's Kingdom.*

    a. The Divine warrant. God hath established it.

    b. The overthrow of enemies. All must be brought before the King for judgment.

    c. The glory of the faithful. Those who have glorified Him as their King shall be glorified with Him in His Kingdom.

POINT II.   *Consider the destruction of the world outside.*

    a. The antagonism between the kingdom of Satan and the Kingdom of Christ.

    b. The hopelessness of creation in the grasp of the tyrant.

    c. The Manifestation of Christ personally driving away the evil from before His Face.

POINT III.   *Consider the personal welcome which the Incarnate God vouchsafes to thee.*

    a. The escape from the tyrant's power into His loving embrace.

    b. The covenant of close following wherein He rejoices to bind thee to Himself.

    c. The bright mark of Love which the Prince of Darkness cannot but recognize in thy regenerate soul, as long as thou abidest in union with Jesus.

AFFECTIONS.   Loving gratitude to thy Deliverer. Stedfast purpose of cherishing His gift of freedom. Reliance upon Jesus in every threatening difficulty.

PRAYER.

O Jesu, grant that I may never be unmindful of the deliverance which Thou hast wrought, but help Thou me to praise Thee for that which Thou hast done, by faithfully exercising the freedom of holiness wherein Thou callest me with Thyself to serve the Father in the power of the Holy Ghost. Amen.

THE KINGDOM OF CHRIST ETERNAL.

PRELUDE i. *Upon the Throne of David and upon His King-dom shall He sit : for ever and ever. Alleluia.*—Isa. ix. 7.

ii. The Throne of Christ shining with the eternal glory of God.

POINT I. *Consider the promise of God to David.*

  a. What God has promised shall surely come to pass in spite of all vicissitudes that may intervene.

  b. What God has promised shall be fulfilled, not only to the requirements of the letter, but so as to overflow with the glory of the Divine Character.

  c. What God has promised shall have no merely transitory accomplishment, but shall live in God's eternal Truth.

POINT II. *Consider the Divine Life of the King.*

  a. Jesus does not receive glory from the Throne of David, but He gives glory by coming.

  b. As Jesus is the Potentate Who only hath immortality, He cannot forfeit the Kingdom of which He has taken possession.

  c. Jesus gives eternal life to all who enter into His Kingdom.

POINT III. *Consider the communication of this glory to the Kingdom wherein He reigns.*

  a. The whole Kingdom is indestructible. Other kingdoms are not worthy to last. Jesus gives His glory to His Church that she may never fail.

  b. Each individual is united to the King in the reality of Spiritual bonds, so as truly to live with eternal life in Him.

  c. The Divine glory shines round about this Kingdom increasingly. Death does not stifle Divine glory, but rather awakens the soul to the consciousness of its glory.

AFFECTIONS. Earnest expectation of Divine promises. Largeness of hope proportionate to our perception of God's glory. Solicitude that we may be found worthy to bear our final portion in this Kingdom.

PRAYER.

O Lord Jesu, strengthen me with Thy grace, that I may walk worthy of Thy Kingdom and glory ; and as Thy gifts are unfailing so replenish me with grace, that I may worthily glorify Thee through the ages of the future. **Amen.**

THE KINGDOM OF CHRIST FROM HEAVEN.

PRELUDE. i. *From Heaven shall the mighty Lord come: and in His Hand is power and might.*—1 Chron. xxix. 12.

ii. The multitude of Angels bowing down before the Son of God, as He passes unseen through the midst of them, to become Incarnate in the nature of man beneath their ranks.

POINT I. *Consider the Divine Glory of the Kingdom of the Incarnate.*

a. Inalienable. It is not dependent upon external accident, but inherent in the Sovereign.

b. Invisible. By reason of its Divinity, it cannot be seen in itself by any who are not gathered into the fellowship of the Divine Nature.

c. Manifested in the Incarnate form. The Hosts of Heaven rejoice with the faithful upon earth in recognizing the Glory of God in the Person of Jesus Christ.

POINT II. *Consider the interest of the Heavenly Host in the Kingdom of Christ.*

a. They have ever been waiting to welcome with worship the Only-begotten when He should come into the world.—Heb. i. 6.

b. They have looked forward with intense desire for the manifestation of those glories which His Incarnation would teach them.—1 S. Peter i. 12.

c. They recognize a glory spreading through their own ranks by this Presence of God in the midst of His creatures.—Ps. xxiv. 7 ; Col. i. 20.

POINT III. *Consider the Heavenly Power of this Kingdom.*

a. The Angel Hosts receive their power from Jesus while they wait around.

b. The powers of darkness will tremble at the manifestation of a Power greater than any power hitherto known in Heaven, as soon as they recognize in the Person of Jesus the presence of the Conqueror.

c. This Kingdom operates on earth by Heavenly power. None can share its power save by entering into its Life. To the unbelieving it is hidden.

AFFECTIONS. Spirituality of desire in contemplating the development of this Kingdom. Detachment from earthly means of confidence. Praise to God for causing us to live in the Light of this revelation.

PRAYER.

O Lord *Jesu Christ,* open *Thou mine eyes to see the Heavenly Glory of Thy Kingdom, that I may indeed delight therein, and welcome Thee as Thou comest into the world, by preparing my heart for the participation of those Heavenly joys, to which in Thy wondrous mercy Thou callest me.* Amen.

THE KINGDOM OF CHRIST WITH GLORY.

PRELUDE. i. *The Lord shall arise upon thee, O Jerusalem! and His Glory shall be seen upon thee.*—Isa. lx. 2.

ii. The Light of Jesus shining upon the elect, as they are seen mysteriously rising out of the darkness of the future, according to the purpose of the Divine Predestination.

POINT I. *Consider the Glory of Jesus as a glory of promise.*

　　a. Worthy of Him that makes the promise. It is indeed the very Glory of God Himself to be communicated to men.

　　b. Fitted for those who shall receive it. However much it be beyond us, yet even now we have a capacity of hoping for it, and our nature is formed for the purpose of developing into those energies which this Kingdom requires.

　　c. Full of promise to the end. Although we have received the gift, yet its true value remains to be made known.

POINT II. *Consider the Glory of Jesus as a Resurrection Glory.*

　　a. The Lifegiving Light. The nature is renewed and elevated thereby.

　　b. The forthshining of the Eternal. It is the Glory of God which rises upon the darkness of the fallen creature.

　　c. The transforming Light. Those on whom it shines are brought out of their old condition of being.

　　d. The abiding Light. The Glory of God is a day which never comes to a close.

POINT III. *Consider the Glory of Jesus as an individual glory.*

　　a. Individual admission into this Kingdom. The baptized soul receives glorious gifts which it cannot communicate to others.

　　b. Individual consciousness of glory. We need to cherish in our hearts the experience of this Divine gift.

　　c. Individual manifestation of this glory. Each soul on whom this Light shines must not only live therein, but show forth its operative power.

AFFECTIONS. Joy in the Divine Light. Hearty correspondence with present gifts of grace. Gratitude in the consciousness of increasing transformation. Individual appropriation of the glory to which each is called in the common inheritance of the Kingdom.

PRAYER.

O Lord Jesu Christ, grant that I may so recognize the Glory of Thy Kingdom, that I may find myself strengthened thereby to praise Thee, and may be conformed to Thy likeness by Thy lifegiving power in the fellowship of all Thy Saints. Amen.

Second Wednesday in Advent.

THE KINGDOM OF CHRIST PREPARED. ✓

PRELUDE. i. *Behold, I will send My Messenger: and he shall prepare the way before Thee.*—Mal. iii. 1.

ii. S. John the Baptist warning the multitudes at Jordan of the coming of One greater than himself.

POINT I. *Consider the necessity of preparation in order to see this Kingdom.*

    a. The preparation of the heart. Sensuality holds the fleshly heart in darkness, so that it can only see the objects of darkness.

    b. The preparation of the mind. Earthly reasonings hold the natural understanding enchained, so that it is incapable of appreciating the higher Truth of God.

POINT II. *Consider the necessity of preparation in order to welcome this Kingdom.* *body need to be holy, living saclifice, godliness*

    a. The Body. We cannot welcome things from above, unless we are weaned by holy discipline from the love of pleasures which are from beneath.

    b. The Soul. The faculties of the soul must learn the unsatisfactory character of earthly wisdom. True philosophy confesses its ignorance. Pride frets at it, and hates that revelation which a purified spirit of philosophy desires. *worldly Comforts, Pleasures, fame, status & chatting.*

    c. The Spirit. Our higher nature is often fascinated by the foul delights which evil spirits can inject; and must be purified in order to rejoice in Communion with God. *Surrender to Jesus only. Commit to Jesus*

POINT III. *Consider the necessity of preparation in order to live in this kingdom.*

    a. It demands action. Divine Life is not a dead treasure but an active power. It acts not merely upon us, but in us.

    b. It demands capacity. God can in a moment change the material universe, but not the moral nature; for it would involve the destruction of our personal responsibility. He therefore prepares His people to welcome His advent. *Help God.*

    c. It demands will. No one can plead incapacity of moral nature, for the very fact of pleading it evidences a will which might be given to God, and which needs discipline on our part to correspond with proffered grace. *good will.* *Jesus Help*

AFFECTIONS. To empty the soul of earthly objects. Resolution to bring your whole nature into discipline for Christ. *Yes, Please.*

Keep New Covenant of christ the blood and water **PRAYER.** *christ + Holy spirit. I do.*

O Lord Jesu Christ, as Thou didst send Thy messenger to prepare Thy people of old, even so now grant me Thy Holy Spirit, that I may be ready to welcome Thee in every form wherein Thou appearest to me, and may follow Thee in obedience to Thy call. **Amen.**

Have the things what I need to keep self healthy, fit, Spiritual. Do not burden self or haem self, but love self because Rafah's property of Jesus. Amen

THE KINGDOM OF CHRIST BRINGING SALVATION.

PRELUDE. i. *Thou art He that should come : for Whom we look to save Thy people.*—S. Luke vii. 20.

ii. The faithful as a multitude of captives, and Christ entering into the prison-house of the world to deliver them.

POINT I. *Consider the power of Satan.*

a. Its vastness. All mankind needing a deliverer.

b. Its intensity. The Law could not set men free, although it might awake the desire of freedom as it communicated some knowledge of truth.

c. Its duration. It would last until a conqueror came, who should bind Satan.

POINT II. *Consider the expectation of the faithful.*

a. The intimation of Prophecy. The whole history of the world is based upon the expectation which the coming of Christ alone fulfils. The promise to Adam was constantly renewed and developed.

b. The anticipations of Nature. Man would be formed for nothing but disappointment, if it were not for Christ's better Kingdom. Hope in the human breast would be nothing but a mockery.

c. The discipline of the Ceremonial Law. The Covenant which God established with His ancient people, although it did not bring the deliverance which man needed, served nevertheless to prepare them for the organization of that glorious kingdom of grace in which deliverance should be given.

POINT III. *Consider the joy of knowing that Christ is come.*

a. Look to Him for the work of salvation. No one else but He can bruise the Serpent's head or free mankind. Universal Redemption is His work.

b. Look to Him for the terms of salvation. We cannot profit by this Redemption except according to the terms of the Covenant which God makes with us in Christ.

c. Look to Him for the power of salvation. The Gospel of Christ is the power of God unto salvation. Through the Sacraments He works invisibly but effectually upon us, and we must recognize this power if we are to profit by it.

AFFECTIONS. Gratitude. Carefulness in observing the terms of this Covenant. Wonder at deliverance effected. Hope for sanctification to be completed.

PRAYER.

O Blessed Jesu, great is Thy mercy Who hast provided the kingdom of grace wherein I may find salvation from the tyranny of the Evil One. O teach me to praise Thee for Thy goodness, and to walk in that freedom wherewith Thou hast made me free, that by the salvation which Thou hast given I may attain to that which Thou hast promised. Amen.

THE KINGDOM OF CHRIST REQUIRING FAITH.

PRELUDE. i. *Say to them that are of a fearful heart, Be strong, fear not ; behold, your God will come.*—Isa. xxxv. 4.

ii. An angel calling mankind to recognize the presence of an unseen power Almighty to save.

POINT I. *Consider the salvation offered to all, not forced upon any.*

a. A call to the fearful. We do not come to Christ because we feel our security, but because we feel the need of it.

b. A call to be strong. We cannot come to Christ and remain in our feebleness.

c. A call to union with God. God comes to us, and we must come to Him.

POINT II. *Consider the terrors of evil still remaining all around.*

a. We must not look at things as they seem. Satan makes things look hopeless, so that we can see no way of escape.

b. We must expect fresh causes of fear to arise continually. Our faith needs to be proved and perfected by growing difficulties which meet us on all sides.

c. We must rise out of the fear of Satan in order to experience the Divine deliverance. We are saved from Satan's tyranny by the strength which is given us to quit it.

POINT III. *Consider the necessity of appropriating the offer of grace ere it be withdrawn.*

a. The Kingdom of Christ requires violence on our part, if we would appropriate it. Our own will must act. Those who cannot shake off their fears cannot follow in the battle.

b. We cannot enter into the Kingdom, save by having hold on Christ the King. We must acknowledge the all-sufficiency of His Love.

c. We cannot hold faithfully to Christ unless we are conscious of our peril under the tyranny of Satan. To delay is to perish.

AFFECTIONS. Eagerness in following Christ. Boldness in reliance upon His word.

PRAYER.

O sweet Jesu, be merciful unto me, so miserably perishing under Satan's dominion, and grant me the power of Thy grace, that with fulness of faith I may draw near to lay hold upon Thee, and in the fellowship of Thy Body may find the glory of Thy Spirit of Peace. **Amen.**

THE KINGDOM OF CHRIST GATHERING ALL NATIONS.

PRELUDE. i. *He shall set up an ensign for the nations: and shall assemble the outcasts of Israel.*—Isa. xi. 12.

ii. The Son of God calling all the nations of the world around Him, to fight against Satan and his hosts.

POINT I. *Consider the enemies.*

  a. The world. The sign of the Son of Man will always be the special object of hatred to the world.

  b. The flesh. The ensign of Jesus is set up amongst the dead, and none can rally round it save by dying. Therefore we are baptized into His death. The flesh must die.

  c. The Devil. He knows that Jesus triumphed on the Cross, and he trembles at the sign of the victorious Kingdom.

POINT II. *Consider how the nations gather round Him.*

  a. By repentance, conscious of their own misery.

  b. By faith, relying upon His power.

  c. By taking up their Cross, yielding themselves to follow Him.

POINT III. *Consider the Grace which He gives.*

  a. The power of the Holy Ghost. The Spirit of Christ dwells in His people, that they may accomplish His work.

  b. Under the form of Sacraments. The Sacraments both symbolize and contain the grace which they convey.

  c. It necessitates a change of life. We cannot be following Jesus, and be friends with the world which put Him to death.

AFFECTIONS. Boldness to struggle against evil. Hope of final victory by the power of the Spirit of Christ. Readiness to endure all things while the struggle remains.

PRAYER.

O Jesu, Who hast called us in our Baptism to fight manfully against the world, the flesh, and the Devil, grant that I may take up the Cross whereat Thine enemies tremble, and follow Thee in the victory of faith. **Amen.**

THE INQUIRY OF THE FORERUNNER.

PRELUDE. i. *When John had heard in the prison the works of Christ, he sent two of his disciples, and said unto Him : Art Thou He that should come, or do we look for another ?*—S. Matt. xi. 23.

ii. The Forerunner with his disciples, conscious of his own approaching end, anxious to leave them with Jesus.

POINT I. *Consider the eagerness of S. John for the manifestation of Jesus.*

    a. His long preparation in the wilderness. The Holy Ghost had been guiding him during many years of solitude.

    b. His witness of the Descent of the Holy Ghost. This manifestation of Jesus by the Voice of the Father was the great object for which he lived.

    c. His confidence in Christ's mission. He feared not to suffer the loss of popular following, by announcing the truth of Christ.

POINT II. *Consider the patience with which he waits.*

    a. His consciousness of his own decrease. He had trained his disciples for the time of his departure.

    b. His enduring witness to moral truth. He had to feel the full pressure of moral evil, while calling men to repentance that they might receive Christ.

    c. His expectation of Christ as a Restorer of holiness. He called men to repentance, but he felt himself powerless to remove the evil from which they suffered.

POINT III. *Consider his anxiety to provide for his disciples.*

    a. His witness of their fear at the approach of his end, as they gathered round him in his prison, and felt him no longer able to superintend them.

    b. His trust in Jesus to make Himself known to them. He could only point to Jesus as the Christ, but it was the power of the Holy Ghost and the call of Jesus Himself which must really draw them fully onward to Him.

    c. His readiness to hand them over to Jesus. He did not form this company to keep them for his own interest, but for the very purpose of leading them to cling to One greater than himself ; and he rejoiced that his work was done.

AFFECTIONS. Expectation of Jesus. Joy in surrendering everything to Him. Trust in Jesus for all future needs.

PRAYER.

O Blessed Jesu, all earthly things fail, but Thou remainest. Help me to know Thee with increasing experience, that I may rest in the contemplation of Thy goodness, and seek no other love but Thine. Amen.

THE WORLD-WIDE PROMISE.

PRELUDE. i. *There shall come forth a Rod out of the stem of Jesse, and all the earth shall be filled with the knowledge of the glory of the* Lord: *and all flesh shall see the salvation of God.*— Isa. xi. 1, 9; Hab. ii. 14; S. Luke iii. 6.

ii. The Tree of Life spreading its branches and dropping its roots over all the earth, so that all which is covered with its shadow springs into fruitfulness.

POINT I. *Consider the wide-spreading character of the Incarnation.*

    a. Christ dwells upon the earth not only as a Person, but much more as a race, a new family amongst mankind.— 1 Cor. xii. 12.

    b. Wherever Christ is found, He is a spreading power, a principle of missionary zeal, a germ of expansive energy.

    c. The Divine Promise rests upon Christ, so that no earthly power can stop the growth of the Tree of Life.—Is. xi. 1, 2.

POINT II. *Consider the universal claim of this Revelation.*

    a. The Presence of Christ carries with it the Revelation of God as a Divine power claiming allegiance wherever it is made known.

    b. The gift of Christ satisfies the longings of all hearts, so that none can reject the moral claim of its tenderness.

    c. The glory which fills all lands is a Divine and not an earthly glory. However widely it spreads it loses none of the Divinity of its origin. It never exhausts itself.

POINT III. *Consider the individual offer of salvation.*

    a. The Manifestation is universal, but the acceptance is individual.

    b. The Word made flesh makes no general utterances, but speaks individually to each that comes.

    c. If we would see the glory, it can only be by accepting His salvation. To know Him without praising Him as a Saviour —our own Saviour—is not to know Him at all.

AFFECTIONS. Thankfulness for Revelation. Living in its power. Waiting for its further manifestations.

PRAYER.

O Lord Jesu Christ, grant me so to meditate upon the extension of Thy glorious kingdom, that I may rejoice in the operation of grace transforming me according to Thy Will. Amen.

THE PREDESTINED PLACE OF BIRTH.

PRELUDE. i. *And thou, Bethlehem, in the land of Juda, art not the least among the princes of Juda : for out of thee shall come a Governor, that shall rule my people Israel.*—S. Matt. ii. 6.

ii. Angels and men coming to Bethlehem in honour of the Birth of Christ.

POINT I. *Consider the choice of David.*

a. Altogether unexpected. God calls not by reason of any fitness which we can foresee.—1 Sam. xvi.

b. At the time of sacrifice. God calls individuals in connexion with official acts of worship.—Acts xiii. 2.

c. Manifest. If God calls us to any work, He will not suffer us to live in doubt.

POINT II. *Consider the sure mercies of David.*

a. Proved during so many years of a life of sorrow. God ever loved him, and ever kept him stedfast.

b. Transmitted through many generations in love, even though they seemed to have failed, and showing the power of God at the last.

c. Abounding in Divine glory, according to the capacity of the receiver, and perfect in Christ, since in Him the human nature derived from David was perfected by hypostatic union with the Son of God.

POINT III. *Consider the City of David.*

a. Its smallness. The coming honour and the remembrance of the past did not raise it from its humble position, but made that smallness the more conspicuous.

b. Its significance—the House of Bread. Though small in itself, it was to be the place whence all the world should be nourished.

c. Its glory. Although so little to be valued by men, the angels could recognize therein the hidden glory of the Incarnate God, the Saviour of mankind.

AFFECTIONS. Patience and reliance upon God. Mistrust of natural anticipation. Praise for God's covenanted promises. Comfort amidst the outward reverses of Christendom.

PRAYER.

O Jesu, Who wast born according to the word of prophecy, in the City of David, grant that my heart, however unworthy, may be nevertheless the place of Thy manifestation, since Thou hast called me to dwell in the Covenant of Thy Love. Amen.

c

THE VIRGIN MOTHER.

PRELUDE. i. *The Angel Gabriel was sent from God to a Virgin espoused to a man whose name was Joseph: and the Virgin's name was Mary.*—S. Luke i. 26, 27.

ii. The Angel coming to the Blessed Virgin, finds her in prayer.

POINT I. *Consider the retirement of the Virgin's life.*
- *a.* With none around to understand her. It is often in the most uncongenial places that God trains souls to do His special work.
- *b.* Conscious of the Eye of God resting upon her, and prepared to receive the visit of the Angel, although in solitude.
- *c.* Finding in solitude an occasion of elevation of heart rather than depression of spirit.

POINT II. *Consider the detachment of the Virgin's heart.*
- *a.* Espoused to Joseph, so as to live under the care of that aged man in separation from the world.
- *b.* Free from expectation in the simplicity of love wherewith she rested in God.
- *c.* Quick to behold the supernatural character of the maternity to which she was called, and assured that " this shall be" in some manner consistent with a dedicated virginity.

POINT III. *Consider the Angel Messenger.*
- *a.* Sent by God. The truest results of holy lives are such as come not by natural consequence from our actions, but by Divine Benediction as supernatural communications from His glory.
- *b.* The individuality of the worshipper. God sends His angels at certain occasions of public fitness marked out for His Church, but to individual souls.
- *c.* Gabriel, " the Power of God." All who would do God's will must lose themselves in the confession of God's Power.

AFFECTIONS. Love of retirement. Detachment from earthly hopes and earthly means of power. Communion in solitude with the unseen world, waiting upon God.

PRAYER.

O God, Who didst send thine Angel to announce the Incarnation of Thy well-beloved Son to the Blessed Virgin, grant that we, being detached from all worldly thoughts, may so rest in Thy Love that we may be able to accomplish whatsoever Thou, by Thy mighty power, callest us to do; through the same Jesus Christ our Lord. Amen.

Third Thursday in Advent.

THE PREPARED HEART.

PRELUDE. i. *The Lord our God is at hand : watch ye therefore in your hearts.*—Phil. iv. 5 ; S. Matt. xxiv. 42.

ii. The people of God as an army who know that their King is in the midst of them although concealed, whilst all around are bidden to be on the look out for Him to manifest himself.

POINT I. *Consider the nearness of God.*
- a. His power surrounding us. The Blessed Virgin was living in the full faith that God could effect His will without natural means. So should we live.
- b. His Majesty claiming our homage. We must live in a continual habit of prostration before His adorable Presence.
- c. His glory ready to show itself. His action towards us in His manifestation is not under our own control. His manifestation of His glorious power is subject only to the limitations of His own Sovereign Will.

POINT II. *Consider the necessity of watching for Him.*
- a. It is due to Him. When we are forgetful of His nearness we are insulting His Majesty, which though unseen, is ever near.
- b. It is necessary for our own safety, for we must give account not only of occasional acts of worship, but of the continual habit of worship whereby we have acknowledged Him.
- c. It is elevating to the character. To live in the consciousness of God raises up the soul to rejoice in the likeness of God.

POINT III. *Consider the characteristics of true watching.*
- a. Its absorbing interest. We must watch for God as the one object drawing us unto Himself, so that in comparison with Him all earthly things are as nothing.
- b. Its intense delight. This watchfulness not wearisome. The more we watch the less can we be weary.
- c. Its action true. It leads to acts of present communion with Him, Whom as yet we see not.

AFFECTIONS. Adoration. Elevation of purpose. Longing to behold God. Habitual dignity in solitude.

PRAYER.

O Lord Jesu, enable me so to realize Thy Presence while I watch for Thy Manifestation, that in the fellowship of Thy Love I may rejoice to accomplish Thy will and prepare for Thy glory. Amen.

THE JOY OF WELCOME.

PRELUDE.   i. *As soon as the voice of Thy salutation sounded in mine ears: the babe leaped in my womb for joy. Alleluia.*—S. Luke i. 44.

ii. Elizabeth, representing human nature as bearing the burden of penitence : Mary, the Church having the grace of Christ.

POINT I. *Consider the Penitent listening for the tokens of Christ.*

     a. The incapacity of nature, shown by Elizabeth's barrenness. We must know our incapacity before we can be penitent.

     b. The hiddenness of penitent life, represented by the child in the womb.   Penitence grows secretly in the soul.

     c. The eagerness of the babe at hearing the voice of the Blessed Virgin Mother. Penitence learns to welcome Jesus with holy joy in the means of grace.

POINT II. *Consider the greeting wherewith Divine Providence approaches mankind.*

     a. The Providence of God approaches the soul with the sanctifying power of the Incarnate Word. It is the Virtue of His Presence which speaks home to every heart.

     b. It is the presence of the child within her womb which is the cause of joy in this salutation. The message of love from God avails not without the Presence of God.

     c. The Word of God speaks with power through the outward agencies wherewith He is pleased to clothe Himself. The Sacraments give forth real power, because they contain Christ.

POINT III. *Consider the recognition of a Saviour's Presence by faithful hearts.*

     a. Penitence recognizes the voice of the Incarnate Word in outward means, whereby He draws near, although they seem to be merely of earth, and akin to our own nature.

     b. Penitence must be found in lofty hope, praising God, if it is to welcome Jesus. Dulness cannot recognize God's voice. Elizabeth dwelt in the hill country of Juda, *i.e.* Praise.

     c. Penitence exults at the first sound of the Saviour's grace, longing to hear His Voice in the Resurrection hereafter.

AFFECTIONS. Expectation. Faith. Consciousness of Supernatural Presence. Thankfulness for Divine condescension.

PRAYER.

O Lord Jesu, Who dost wonderfully draw near to us, grant that I may so meditate upon Thy Holy Incarnation, that I may experience the virtue of the Holy Spirit, whereby Thou approachest, illuminating me to the apprehension of Thy Love ; Who livest and reignest with the Father in the Unity of the same Spirit, One God, world without end.   Amen.

THE MANIFESTATION TO ALL.

PRELUDE. i. *Every valley shall be exalted, and every mountain and hill shall be made low : and all flesh shall see the salvation of God.*—Isa. xl. 4. S. Luke iii. 6.

ii. The coming forth of the Divine Presence as a flood bursting out from the depth of Creation, and levelling all the world in one great ruin.

POINT I. *Consider the overthrow of all worldly distinction.*

a. The order of Creation has no support, save the Divine Word, which is as a law of force hidden within it. When that ceases to act, all earthly distinctions vanish.

b. Earthly distinctions hide the working of God, so that it cannot be manifested until they are destroyed. Then the nothingness of the creature is made evident.

c. The pride of the natural heart must be abased in penitence now, if the soul is to find safety in that day of terror.

POINT II. *Consider the manifestation of God's saving work.*

a. God will be manifested in the salvation of His people when He is manifested in the destruction of all worldly things.

b. The salvation of God cannot now be realized, because we cannot appreciate what it shall be to be entirely delivered from the present evil world.

c. Hereafter all flesh shall see the glory of God's people, and all will know then that God Who sent His Only Son has loved them as He has loved Him.—S. John xvii. 23.

POINT III. *Consider the effect of the manifestation of Christ.*

a. The joy of those whose hearts are detached from the world. The overthrow of the world is the loosing of the bonds by which they were held.

b. The agony of the children of the world. All on which they set their hopes perishes before the terror of that salvation which they despised.

c. The manifestation of Christ is final. Other manifestations of God led up to this; but men heeded them not, would not despise the world, would not rest in the Love of God.

AFFECTIONS. Fear of God. Contempt of the world. Anxiety for the things of Heaven. Hope of the salvation about to be revealed.

PRAYER.

O Lord God, by Whose Word all things were made at the first, and are now kept in store waiting for the Judgment of the Great Day ; grant me such detachment from the world, that when Thy dear Son shall appear, I may find in Thee my security in Whom I shall have learnt to find my satisfaction; through the same Thy Son Jesus Christ, our Lord. Amen.

THE CRY OF PREPARATION.

PRELUDE. i. I *am the voice of one crying in the wilderness,
Make straight the way of the* Lord : *as said the prophet Esaias.*—
S. John i. 23.

ii. A voice from Jordan, swelling through all nations, and announcing the speedy approach of Christ.

POINT I. *Consider the necessity of Preparation.*

     a. Man's nature was originally formed to be perfected by the
Incarnation. It therefore has a fitness to receive the Divine
Presence, if it be true to itself.

     b. Man's nature was fallen away by sin, and therefore was
essentially unfit by reason of its corruption.

     c. Man's nature required an interior impulse of penitence,
by which to cast off its sin when grace should be given,
otherwise man could not rise to newness of life.

POINT II. *Consider the Prophetic announcement of Preparation.*

     a. Prophecy gave a Divine sanction to the Voice in the wilderness. When God speaks to us solemnly, He gives us
indications by which our attention may be directed to His
utterance.

     b. Prophecy by putting its mark upon the Voice, used it as a
means of certifying the truth of Christ, Who should come
afterwards.

POINT III. *Consider the Divine character of Preparation.*

     a. The Divine Call. God speaks in many ways to various
hearts. We must listen.

     b. The Divine Warning. God warns mankind of His great
dispensations, that surprise may not render His grace
destructive to us.

     c. The Divine Promise. God would have the way made
straight for Christ as an act of loving faith. As of old, so
now, we need to be looking to Him, if we are to find His
second coming to be really for our salvation.—Heb. ix. 28.

AFFECTIONS. Assurance of God's Truth. Resolution to
prepare for Christ. Hope of Christ's appearing.

PRAYER.

*O Lord Jesu Christ, grant that as Thy Messenger prepared men's
hearts to receive Thee, so the various ministries of Thy love may
help me to get my heart in readiness, and when Thou appearest in
Thy final triumph over sin, I may be partaker of Thy salvation
Who livest and reignest, One God, world without end.* Amen.

REPENTANCE.

PRELUDE. i. *The Lord saith, Repent ye, for the Kingdom of Heaven is at hand. Alleluia.*—S. Matt. iii. 2.

ii. S. John calling to Repentance : the people standing round.

POINT I. *Consider the necessity of Repentance.*

a. Self-examination. Christ is a Light in Whose Presence all will see their sins. Let Him be our Light in grace, that we may judge ourselves now. Each manifestation of Christ is a Light preparing for a further manifestation.

b. Confession. As the indulgences of sin have been individual, so the acknowledgment of sin ought to be. We must speak to the Incarnate Word of God, uttering our sinfulness; otherwise we shall not hear Him uttering the Divine holiness.

c. Contrition. The Son of God makes manifest the Father's hatred of sin. We cannot rise to the Life of His Divine Sonship without a proportionate hatred of sin.

POINT II. *Consider the reality of Repentance.*

a. As real as the sin which has been done. The pleasures of sin have been more than imaginations. Our vengeance on sin ought to equal the pleasure we have found therein.

b. As real as the Heaven for which we look. Repentance cannot restore the hope of Heaven, unless it be moved in reality by the powers of the Heaven we are called to regain.

c. As real as the Incarnation of God. He came to redeem us; and our acceptance of His work will vary in its reality as we hated the sin from which He delivers us.

POINT III. *Consider the immediateness of Repentance.*

a. Delay is an insult to the Incarnate Saviour. We are setting aside His Love while we delay.

b. Delay is a peril to ourselves as creatures of time. We know not that we shall have another day to repent.

c. Delay makes us less fit to meet Christ whenever He may come. We become daily more corrupt by negligence.

AFFECTIONS. Abhorrence of sin. Eagerness in turning to God. Desire of the glory which we have forfeited. Definite purpose to seek a cure for our besetting sin.

PRAYER.

O Lord *Jesu Christ, Who requirest us to hate sin with that hatred which Thou hast manifested, in that Thou didst die upon the Cross, grant us so to avenge upon ourselves the sin which we have done, that we may praise Thee for the Redemption which Thou hast effected, and evermore walk in the power of Thy renewing Spirit to the glory of God the Father.* Amen.

PRAYER.

PRELUDE. i. *Awake, awake : put on strength, O arm of the Lord.*—Isa. li. 9.

ii. The nations in their bondage crying out to God to hasten the advent of their deliverance.

POINT I. *Consider the necessity of Prayer.*
  a. To move God. It is a law of the relationship in which He has placed Himself to His creatures, that He should regard their will when they desire that which is good.
  b. On our own account. We recognize the Personality of Christ's love, by speaking with Him.
  c. By our prayer Jesus comes to us. His Advent externally would be nothing to us unless there were a movement of His Spirit speaking within our hearts, opening our faculties to communion with Him. That work of the Spirit is prayer.

POINT II. *Consider the dignity of Prayer.*
  a. It is an anticipation of the gifts for which we cry. When we pray, we recognize our rich portion in God's Love.
  b. It terrifies the powers of darkness. They can no longer keep their hold upon us, while they tremble at the Name of their Conqueror, to which we call.
  c. It is an evidence of Divine Life. The Spirit of God fills us with the Love of God, while we speak to God Who is Love.

POINT III. *Consider the infinite consequences of Prayer.*
  a. Far beyond our request. God answers not as we ask, but as He sees us to require.
  b. Far beyond our imagination. God has unrevealed gifts which He will give, if we will ask as He has taught us.
  c. Far beyond earthly possibility. Prayer, as it brings us to God, transforms earth into Heaven, and communicates to us the power of God.

AFFECTIONS. Diligence of heart. Filial love to God. Desire of gifts which surpass our present conception.

PRAYER.

O Lord Jesu, Who art the Word of God making manifest to us the Love of the Father, speak Thou within me by the power of Thy Holy Spirit, that as my desires are enlarged towards the infinity of that Love, my joy may be perfected in the satisfaction which that Love contains, according to the fulness of Thy merit, Who livest and reignest with the Father in the unity of the Spirit of Love, One God, world without end. Amen.

PRAISE.

PRELUDE. i. *Let them give glory unto the* Lord, *and declare His Praise in the islands : for behold, He cometh and will not tarry.* —Isa. xlii. 12.

ii. The glory of God as a mighty Orb of Light, which the nations dwelling is darkness welcome as it rises upon them.

POINT I. *Consider the glorious expectation of the faithful.*

    a. Glorious through ages. It has cheered successive genera-tions in their deepest sorrows.

    b. Nourished by prophecy. The original hope has been developed in the details of earthly circumstance and the infinity of heavenly issue.

    c. Conscious that the time appointed is at hand. God Who has promised, will not fail to fulfil.

POINT II. *Consider the glorious confidence of the faithful.*

    a. In the truth of God's Word. However great the promises may be, God will do what He has said.

    b. In the Power of Christ's Kingdom. It may be weak in its beginnings, but it is indestructible.

    c. In the immediateness of His Manifestation. How little did they know what that Manifestation should be !

POINT III. *Consider the glorious utterance of the faithful.*

    a. Addressed in worship to God. The heart of man acquires dignity as it pours forth to God its own longing for God.

    b. Announcing His Truth to the heathen. The Covenant of Christ shall surpass the limits of Israel. God shall send His Apostles to call all nations to the obedience of faith.

    c. Expressing the joy of their hearts. The nearer the heart finds Christ, so much the greater does it find its joy. Its joy is indeed fulfilled by the coming of the Son of God.

AFFECTIONS. Gratitude for the gift of Christ. Zeal for the Propagation of the Kingdom of Christ. Trust in God for the future development of Christ's Kingdom.

PRAYER.

O Lord *Jesu* Christ, *we praise Thee for Thy Holy Incarna-tion, for therein Thou hast humbled Thyself to our low estate that Thou mayest raise us up to Thy Divine glory. Open Thou our understandings to know, our hearts to love, our lips to praise Thy glorious Name ; and make us so to worship Thee with loving hearts, that others may learn from our lips to praise Thee for Thy redeeming Love.* **Amen.**

COMFORT.

PRELUDE. i. *Comfort ye, comfort ye, My people: saith your God.*—Isa. xl. 2.

ii. The people of God borne upon a stormy sea, and Jesus, as He draws near, making the waters to be still.

POINT I. *Consider the sorrow which needs comfort.*

a. The manifold troubles of earthly life. There is no power on earth to heal the sorrows of earth with any lasting consolation.

b. The bondage of sin. Sin is a trouble within, greater than all troubles that can afflict from without.

c. Separation from God. Man's nature is ever craving for God, and yet he finds himself in his natural condition shut out from his Father's Presence.

POINT II. *Consider the people who are comforted.*

a. They are God's people. God recognizes them as such, by hasting to make known to them this comfort.

b. They are suffering affliction as such. Their union with God involves suffering at the hands of the world. Therefore God is eager to bring them health.

c. They are looking to Him for comfort. In their suffering they committed the keeping of their souls to Him, knowing that He was mighty to save.

POINT III. *Consider the Giver of the comfort.*

a. He is the Covenant God. He is Eternal Truth, and cannot deny Himself.

b. He longs to give comfort to His people, for He loves them with a changeless Love.

c. He gives them comfort worthy of Himself, for He gives Himself to be their comfort.

AFFECTIONS. Joy in the privilege of the Divine Covenant. Patience amidst the afflictions of the people of God. Homage to the Divine Wisdom which rules all.

PRAYER.

O Lord Jesu, Who after Thou hadst ascended into Heaven didst send Thy Holy Spirit to comfort Thy people on the earth; grant that as our tribulations abound in the world, so we may experience increasingly the abundance of Thy comfort, according to the mighty working of the same most blessed Spirit; Who with Thee and with the Father liveth and reigneth One God, world without end. Amen.

UNEXPECTEDNESS.

PRELUDE. i. *The day of the Lord cometh as a thief in the night; be ye therefore also ready: for at such an hour as ye think not, the Son of Man cometh.*—1 Thess. v. 2 ; S. Matt. xxiv. 44.

ii. A flame suddenly bursting out and consuming the whole earth.

POINT I. *Consider what the day of the Lord is.*

   a. The Creator manifested amidst His creatures. It is the Advent of a Power altogether distinct from the world, and superior to it.

   b. The victory over the evil of the creature. The plagues are brought upon Death.—Hos. xiii. 14.—Death and Hell are cast into the lake of fire.—Rev. xx. 14.

   c. The New Creation of Righteousness and Light springing up in the midst of the darkness of the Old Creation. The Presence of God is darkness to the ungodly, but Light to the righteous.

POINT II. *Consider why that day is so unexpected.*

   a. Not for want of warning. God has given many signs by which the approach of that day may be recognized.

   b. Man's heedlessness is the reason. Immersed in the darkness of the creature, he does not recognize the dawn.

   c. The night is the darkness of man's sin. The children of the Light, welcome Christ's Advent as the fulness of a day which has already begun to shine in their hearts.

POINT III. *Consider what that day comes to do.*

   a. To take away, as a thief, all that the children of the world account their own. Blessed they who have nothing to lose!

   b. To destroy for ever the tyranny of the Prince of darkness.

   c. To gladden those that are found ready with the gift of salvation for which they have been waiting.

AFFECTIONS. Detachment, and contempt of the world. Expectation of the Day of the Lord.

PRAYER.

O Lord Jesu Christ, before Whose Face the earth shall flee away; grant me now to behold Thee by faith, and to rejoice in Thy sustaining power, that when Thou art manifested, I may rejoice in the fulness of Thy Love, for which I have waited in Thy sanctuary. **Amen.**

PRELUDE. **i.** *When Mary the Mother of Jesus was espoused to Joseph, before they came together she was found with Child: for that which was conceived in her was of the Holy Ghost. Alleluia.* S. Matt. i. 18, 20.

ii. The Blessed Virgin meditating upon the Saviour about to be born.

POINT I. *Consider her consciousness of the Divine origin of her Child.*

    a. The communication by the angel, announcing the work of the Holy Ghost, and awakening her expectation.

    b. The Inspiration of the Holy Ghost overshadowing her, and opening her faculties to apprehend the Mystery.

    c. The wondrous love wherewith the Incarnate Wisdom makes known to her His mysterious Presence in her womb.

POINT III. *Consider her consciousness that the Son of God has really taken a body of her substance:*

    a. The mystery of a supernatural order of Being springing from her human nature.

    b. The passive simplicity of heart, wherewith she yields herself to the operation of God.

    c. The adoration wherewith she regards Christ's Presence. His Body is God's Temple, and her body the enclosed garden of the Temple while she bears this Body within her.

POINT III. *Consider her consciousness of the change effected in that substance by becoming His Body.*

    a. In her it was the inheritor of sin, separated from God since Eve's transgression. In Him it is purified from all sin, glorious with the Divine Presence, inheriting all the energies of the Divine Wisdom by the Eternal Sonship.

    b. In her it was a thing of death, needing support from without. In Him it is a Thing of Life, living by the power of God, not needing support, but rather giving support to that whereby it is nourished and augmented.

    c. In her it needed salvation. In Him it is the very instrument whereby salvation is given.

AFFECTIONS. Adoration of the Incarnate God. Welcome to Him as He comes to dwell among us. Confession of our own incapacity.

PRAYER.

O Lord Jesu Christ, Who didst vouchsafe to come upon the earth, choosing our humanity as the instrument of Thy sanctifying power; grant that I, welcoming Thy Presence with holy worship, may abide in the sanctification whereby Thou seekest to perfect all of Thy members, Who with the Father and the Holy Ghost livest and reignest, One God, world without end. **Amen.**

PRELUDE. i. *Glory to God in the highest, and on earth peace; goodwill towards men. Alleluia, Alleluia.*—S. Luke ii. 14.

ii. The Angels filling Heaven with their songs.

POINT I. *Consider the exultation of the Angel hosts at the birth of Christ.*

    a. The ancient command which they have looked forward to fulfil now claims accomplishment: "Worship Him, all ye gods."—Ps. xcvii. 7.

    b. God, Whom they have hitherto worshipped unseen, is manifest to them in the flesh. Creation feels the thrill of His Incarnation.

    c. The Word of God, thus manifested in the perfection of humanity, begins to make known that manifold wisdom which shall be completely revealed when His Body is glorified in the perfection of His Church.—Eph. iv. 10.

POINT II. *Consider their joy at peace being inaugurated upon earth.*

    a. This peace is the close of their war through ages against the spirits that fell. Now the Lord is present to rebuke them.—Jude 9.

    b. Jesus brings not earthly peace. Rather He comes to save us from the false peace of friendship with the world.

    c. It is Divine Peace which is given to man: Peace *with* God, Peace *in* God, Peace by God's indwelling.

POINT III. *Consider their congratulation with mankind in God's goodwill.*

    a. God's predestination of man has been eternal. Satan envied it. The Holy Angels rejoice therein.

    b. The lovingkindness of God towards man, now at length manifested by the Incarnation, transcends all expectation.

    c. All holy beings find their joy in that which is the pleasure of God. They rejoice for their own sakes; they rejoice for man's sake; but chiefly they rejoice because God rejoices.

AFFECTIONS. Fellowship in joy with the host of Heaven. Gratitude for the gift of a Saviour. Resolution to live worthy of our calling in Christ. Surrender of all things to the glory of God.

PRAYER.

O Almighty God, Who hast given us Thine Only-begotten Son to be born as Man among men, grant that I, ever living in remembrance of this inestimable benefit, may put aside the deeds of the old man, and dedicate myself wholly to Thy glory, through the same Jesus Christ our Lord. Amen.

PRELUDE. i. *The wicked thrust sore at him to give him over unto death, but he endured the stones : rejoicing that he was counted worthy to receive the crown of glory. Alleluia.—* Ps. cxviii. 13, 18.

ii. S. Stephen in death sees Heaven opened, and Jesus standing at the Right Hand of God.

POINT I. *Consider the stedfastness of S. Stephen.*

    a. In rebuking the Jews for their habitual hardness of heart from one generation to another.

    b. In meeting those manifold troubles which came upon him, counting nothing dear if only he might make Jesus known.

POINT II. *Consider the hatred which the confession of Jesus' Name involves.*

    a. The world knows Him as its Conqueror, and cannot tolerate any who look to Him truly for Life.

    b. The world knows that if we acknowledge Him, we must surrender all things to Him. To contemplate Him in His Ascension involves dying to the world He left.

    c. The world may patronize the moral character of Jesus, but cannot bear to be censured for not accepting His supremacy.

POINT III. *Consider the strength which Jesus gives to those who are in peril for His Name's sake.*

    a. His face shone like the face of an Angel ; for the glory of Jesus, which filled His heart, overpowered all the feebleness of nature.

    b. His understanding was enlightened by the blessed Vision of Jesus glorified. The Light of Heaven opened made him see the nothingness of earthly opposition.

    c. His will was strengthened to lay hold upon that which He contemplated. He rejoiced to give himself to Jesus : Lord Jesus, receive my spirit.

AFFECTIONS. Boldness on behalf of Jesus. Confidence in Jesus as ready to be our strength. Elevation of heart to Jesus glorified.

PRAYER.

O Almighty God, Who hast exalted Thy Son Jesus to the Right Hand of Thy glory, grant me, by the power of Thy Holy Spirit, so to contemplate that glory while I am upon the earth, that all my earthly actions may be wrought to the glory of Thy Holy Name ; through the same Jesus Christ our Lord. Amen.

PRELUDE. i. *This is that John who leant upon Jesus' Bosom at the Last Supper: blessed is the Apostle to whom were made known the secrets of Heaven.*—S. John xiii. 23; Rev. i. 1.

ii. S. John reclining on our Lord's Bosom at the Last Supper.

POINT I. *Consider the love wherewith John followed Jesus.*

> *a.* This love was but the consciousness of being loved. We love Him because He first loved us. In proportion as we know the love of Jesus, so must we love Him.
>
> *b.* This love was eager to do all things for the Beloved, even to call down fire from Heaven.
>
> *c.* This love would not suffer natural eagerness to rebel against supernatural obedience.

POINT II. *Consider the fellowship of suffering in which that love involved Him.*

> *a.* His close communion with our Lord's suffering Heart as He lay on His Bosom.
>
> *b.* His nearness to our Lord in the humiliation of His Passion.
>
> c. His old age of sorrow, as He beheld the Church falling away from the purity of the first Love.

POINT III. *Consider the revelation of glory for which that love prepared Him.*

> *a.* His heart was enlightened to contemplate mysteries of Divine Love in all the outward acts of Jesus.
>
> *b.* His faith was strengthened to apprehend the reality of Divine Life communicated to us while we abide in Jesus.
>
> c. His eyes were opened to behold the final purposes of that Love in the glory which shall be hereafter.

AFFECTIONS.—Delight to acknowledge the Love of Jesus. Desire to be transformed by that Love. Satisfaction in the glory of that Love.

PRAYER.

O God, Who hast declared the fulness of Thy Love by sending Thine Only-begotten Son that we might live through Him, grant me so to behold the Love whereby Thou callest me to abide in His Life, that in suffering I may be strengthened to show forth Thy Love, and by suffering may be purified for the perfect Vision of Thy Love; through the same Jesus Christ our Lord. **Amen.**

PRELUDE.   i. *Be of good comfort, O my children, and cry unto God: for ye shall be remembered of Him.*—Baruch iv. 27.

ii. One of the mothers of Bethlehem weeping over her child.

POINT I.   *Consider the sense of tyranny which this massacre awakened.*

    a. Herod's cruelty was known before: now it was experienced. None can value freedom under the King of Righteousness, unless they have felt the misery of sin's bondage.

    b. There was no possibility of relief. This tyrant's power was backed up by the Roman Emperor. We must learn the hopelessness of our bondage when the world and Satan are allied against us.

POINT II.   *Consider the hope of the Messiah's deliverance which this massacre should have awakened.*

    a. The usurpation of Herod was itself an evidence that the Lord was come, had they had eyes to see the truth. The sceptre was departed from Judah. Shiloh must be come.

    b. Other children had natural hopes attending their birth. These infants had supernatural hopes anticipating their death. The voice of the prophet bids the mother cease from weeping.

    c. Messiah's deliverance shall be not from this world's sorrow, but from the power of sin; since He shall bring these children back from the land of the enemy, which is Death.—Jer. xxxi. 16.

POINT III.   *Consider the participation of Messiah's suffering, which must prepare us to share His glorious return.*

    a. In the time of suffering, Jesus is very near to us. We forget too often that the world hates not us but Him.

    b. Those who shall partake of the deliverance of Jesus suffer for His sake with the simplicity of children. Better is the child that dies, than the pride that escapes death.

    c. Those who suffer with Jesus shall reign with Him hereafter. The world's opposition only tends to guarantee our share in Jesus' Love.

AFFECTIONS.—Childlike simplicity and meekness in the midst of the world. Confidence in the better Life with Jesus hereafter. Faith in Jesus when earthly things give no hope.

PRAYER.

O Almighty God, give me a childlike heart, that I may die unto the world, and fear no evil, rejoicing in fulness of hope, to welcome Thine Only-begotten Son, Whom Thou hast given to us to bear our sorrows, and to raise up in life eternal those who share His Life of pain. Grant this for Thy mercy's sake; through the same Jesus Christ our Lord. Amen.

THE CHANGELESS WORD.

PRELUDE. i. *While all things were in quiet silence, and night was in the midst of her swift course, Thine Almighty Word, O Lord, leaped down from heaven, out of Thy royal Throne.*—Wisd. xviii. 14, 15.

ii. The Eternal Voice of God, heard by the ear of faith.

POINT I. *Consider the Word of God existing eternally with the Father.*

> a. The Word of God expresses not a transitory thought passing through the mind as the word of a man, but the Eternal Consciousness of God, which cannot change.
>
> b. The Word of God is the eternal utterance of the Divine nature whereby the Father exults to know Himself.

POINT II. *Consider the Word of God sustaining the fixed operations of nature.*

> a. The Word of God abiding in the unchangeableness of the Divine eternity, creates nevertheless the things of time. Creation is a relation between the finite and the infinite, and therefore inconceivable by us who know the finite only.
>
> b. The Word of God is changeless, and works in time by changeless laws. The changelessness of the laws of nature results from the changelessness of the Word of God.

POINT III. *Consider the Word of God coming forth into the realm of the lower nature, but remaining unchanged.*

> a. The Word of God becoming Incarnate takes created nature into union with Himself, but He does not become changed by doing so. The two natures remain distinct.
>
> b. The elevation of human nature by the hypostatic union with the Divine nature in Christ is only the perfect development of that law of progress under which all things were created. Without this the law of progress must have been arrested, and God's work for ever incomplete. We are complete in Christ.—Col. ii. 20.
>
> c. The Word of God works in us individually by the same law of progress, perfecting us by the fuller manifestation of Himself in us, having taken us sacramentally into union with Himself. Outside of His Flesh, there can be no true progress—no progress but by His Spirit.

AFFECTIONS.—Conformity to the law of Divine Life in Christ. Thankfulness for being called to the Divine Life by this communication of Himself. Adoring love towards the mysteries of grace as perfecting the work of the Divine Word in nature.

PRAYER.

O God, Who hast created all things for the glory of Thy dear Son, grant that I may so listen to His voice ever speaking in my heart, that I may always fulfil His bidding, abide in His Love, and be perfected in the Vision of His glory, Who with Thee and the Holy Ghost liveth and reigneth for ever and ever. Amen.

D

THE ALMIGHTY WORD.

PRELUDE. i. *As before.*—Wisdom xviii. 14, 15.

ii. All created intelligences that have Life and Truth acknowledging Christ as Lord by the power of the Holy Spirit.

POINT I. *Consider the Word as being Almighty.*

    a. All things were made by Him. All existing powers in
creation spring from the Word of God.

    b. Nothing was made nor can be made without His knowledge.

    c. All things consist by Him (Col. i. 16), so that whatever
has not His Power to sustain it, perishes in nothingness.

POINT II. *Consider the Word as being One Almighty with
the Father.*

    a. He is of one Substance with the Father; and this substance
is the pure act of Divine Life, free from all restrictions of
body, space or time. The eternal act of God is an act of
utterance. His Word in coming forth is not separated
from Him. The fulness of His Power lives in His Word.

    b. He is of one Power with the Father. He would be no
true Image of the Father if not equal in Power, but cannot
be equal if not one with Him. What things the Father
doeth, these doeth the Son likewise.—John v. 19.

    c. He is of one Eternity with the Father. God is Almighty,
because self-existing. The Word is not merely God's Instrument in creation, but He is the Eternal utterance,
whereby He the Almighty exists in Himself.

POINT III. *Consider the Word as being One Almighty with
the Holy Ghost.*

    a. The Will of God and His Wisdom are identical in action.
The Holy Ghost acts Almightily as that Wisdom dictates.

    b. The Holy Ghost never acts without the Son of God. An
act which goes beyond the Wisdom of God is nought.

    c. The Flesh of the Incarnate Word conceived by the Holy
Ghost is the Sword of the Spirit (Eph. vi. 17), for
He acts therein to accomplish the Will of the Eternal
Wisdom. God and man are one in the One Person of the
Word of God: the Holy Ghost, eternally Proceeding from
the Word, fills that Humanity with the omnipotence of
the Divine nature. Without the Spirit the Flesh, if it
could be separated, would profit nothing.—John vi. 63.

AFFECTIONS.—Reliance, Contentedness, Hope.

PRAYER.

*O God, teach me by Thy Holy Spirit so to abide in unity of
action with Thy Divine Wisdom, that I may always live to Thy
glory as befits my vocation in the Body of Thy dear Son, and may
attain to behold Thy glory by the illumination of the same Spirit,
through the same Jesus Christ our Lord. Amen.*

THE WORD MADE MANIFEST.

PRELUDE. i. *As before.*—Wisd. xviii. 14, 15.

ii. The Body of Christ shining with the glory of God.

POINT I. *Consider that the Word of God is not manifested by conversion of the Godhead into flesh.*

   a. The Spiritual Nature of the Son of God cannot change. The act of Divine Life is complete in itself eternally.

   b. The Divine glory cannot be lowered, although a Divine Person descend into a lower sphere of being. The Person of the Son leaped down, but His glory was not forfeited.

   c. The Divine glory cannot be communicated to a nature that is finite. He took upon Himself man's nature in its emptiness, that He might fill it with Divine glory.—Phil. ii. 7.

POINT II. *Consider that the Word of God is manifested by taking of the Manhood into God.*

   a. From the first moment of the Incarnation, our human nature assumed by Christ lived in God, and God lived therein. The germ of our manhood is taken into God to be developed according to the Truth of the Divine purpose.

   b. At His Birth the completeness of man's individuality was glorified by the indwelling of the Holy Ghost, so as to act in all things by that Divine Life. Angels worshipped God manifest in the flesh.—1 Tim. iii. 16.

   c. His Manhood perfected in the fulness of holy obedience, manifests in its reward the glory of the Divine Righteousness, and shines as the object of worship to all creation.

POINT III. *Consider that the Word of God is manifested not by confusion of substance, but by unity of Person.*

   a. The nature of the emptiness assumed, and the glory of the Godhead which fills it remain for evermore distinct.

   b. The Manhood of Christ is worshipped, not in itself, although transcending all perfection we can conceive, but by reference to the glory of God, with which it is united.

   c. God the Son exists in both Natures conjointly, not deriving any additional perfection from Manhood, but manifesting His eternal perfection in the Manhood assumed.

AFFECTIONS. Thankfulness to God for the knowledge of His Son. Desire to show forth in our own nature the glory of Jesus.

PRAYER.

O God, *Who hast exalted our Manhood that it should manifest the glory of Thine Eternal Word, grant that I, ever living in the grace of this Holy Incarnation, may acknowledge the Person of Thine Only-begotten as the Head whereto I must belong, and may experience the power of His glorious Godhead perfecting me in eternal Life according to His infinite merit, Who ever liveth and reigneth with Thee and with the Holy Ghost, One God, for ever and ever.* **Amen.**

THE ONE SAVIOUR.

PRELUDE. i. *A wonderful Mystery is made known. Now is nature to do a new thing. God is made Man: That which was, still abideth, and that which was not, that He taketh into Himself without confusion or division.*

ii. All creation as with one voice uttering the Name of Jesus with holy worship.

POINT I. *Consider that Jesus is One.*

    a. Without this unity of Person the gift of Divine Life could not be poured into us. Even in Jesus, there would otherwise be a gulf between man and God, shutting up the faculties of our manhood in natural incapacity.

    b. All the faculties of our nature being assumed by His glorious Person are made efficacious to convey the saving grace of His Divinity to all His members.

    c. The Divine Sonship to which the Humanity is assumed, is the Rock which cannot be shaken.—S. Matt. xvi. 18.— Whereas all that is not God is shaken and removed.—Heb. xii. 27.

POINT II. *Consider that God is our Saviour.*

    a. We learn to value the gift of salvation, because it is the gift of God.

    b. We learn to love God, because He has come to us that we might have this gift.

    c. We learn to rest in Him with the obedience of faith, that His work in us may be accomplished according to His Will.

POINT III. *Consider that He saves us by taking us into the Unity of His Eternal Life.*

    a. God cannot save in an imperfect manner. He must therefore perfect us in union with Himself.

    b. God cannot take us into union with Himself save by working in us with all the power of the Holy Ghost.

    c. God cannot work in us, save by the union of our will with His Will, to do all He commands. Otherwise He would be acting for, but not in, us, and we should remain in the deadness of nature.

AFFECTIONS. Self-dedication to do the work of Jesus. Determination to live in the power of the New Life which He gives. Self-mistrust in the consciousness of our own natural weakness.

PRAYER.

O Almighty God, Who hast created me anew unto all good works by Thy Word revealed within me; grant that I may so live in the power of this renewal, that Thy dear Son may be manifested in me in all holiness; and when He shall appear without sin unto salvation, I may live with Him in that glory wherein He liveth and reigneth, with Thee and with the Holy Ghost, One God, for ever and ever. Amen.

THE ROYAL WORD.

PRELUDE. i. *A wonderful Mystery*, etc.—Vide last page.

ii. The Word of God on the White Horse, going forth conquering and to conquer, manifested as King of kings and Lord of lords.

POINT I. *Consider that the Word of God reigneth eternally.*

   a. He is the Wisdom whereby the Father reigns. Without the eternal Word, the Father would be dumb. By this Word He reigns, with a spontaneous sovereign energy.

   b. He is not the mere instrumental Wisdom of the Father. He is the Wisdom of the Father, shining forth as the express Image of His Person in unity of the Divine Life.

   c. He is not the mere lifeless or superficial Image of the Father's Wisdom. God has no parts. The act of the Father's Wisdom cannot be imaged, save by a correlative Person abiding with God—S. John i. 1—acting in the same Wisdom, in perfect personal Sovereignty of Being.

POINT II. *Consider that the Word of God reigneth over creation.*

   a. All things were made by Him. He rules them still.

   b. All things were made for Him. The Father's creative power does not die out in the blank unlove of a selfish majesty. The Father delights in the Love whereby the Son rejoices to be the Heir of all things.—Heb. i. 2.

   c. All things exist in Him. Whatever is not regulated by Him must decay, for it exists apart from God's Wisdom.

POINT III. *Consider that the Word of God reigneth by the Incarnation.*

   a. His human nature manifests His invisible Sovereignty.

   b. As man He goes forth conquering and to conquer, asserting His Sovereignty not only by necessity over brutes, but by supremacy of Will over created wills, and by the loving appeal of His Sacred Passion.

   c. As man He waits at the Right Hand of God.—Ps. cx. 1.

   d. As man He dispenses gifts of grace, that we may be so united with Him here as to share His Kingdom hereafter.

AFFECTIONS. Homage to Jesus as our King. Thanks for the revelation of His Kingdom. Boldness in self-dedication to live as befits that Kingdom.

PRAYER.

O Jesu, King of kings and Lord of lords, reveal within me the power of Thy grace, that I may ever act as Thy true subject, and in the accomplishment of Thy Sovereign Will may attain to that holy purpose which Thou hast prepared for me in Thyself, even that I may reign along with Thee in Thy glory, where, with the Father and the Holy Ghost, Thou livest and reignest One God and One Lord, world without end. Amen.

THE SON WHICH IS THE WORD OF THE FATHER.

PRELUDE. i. *A wonderful Mystery*, etc.—Vide p. 36.
ii. The glory of God shining out with a brightness from its inmost depth, full of transcendent wisdom and love.

POINT I. *Consider the Word as the Eternal Son.*

  a. Generated eternally in the Divine Mind. The Divine Wisdom is not unfruitful. That which is generated therefrom is worthy of itself.

  b. Not separated from the Divine Mind. The offspring of a creature is separated from the parent, for no creature has life within itself, no power to give life in itself to any other. God has life in Himself, and gives this Life to His Son.

  c. Not a mere empty thought, but full of power, with all the energy of Godhead. The thoughts in man's mind are empty conceits, for man's mind is empty. The Mind of God, perfectly fruitful within itself, retains its Offspring within its own fulness of Being, as partner of all its actions.

POINT II. *Consider the Love of the Father to the Son.*

  a. The Father rejoices in His Son as the Brightness of His own Most excellent glory.

  b. As the Son is co-equal with the Father, there is nothing that the Father has to desire which is not in Him. The Word and Wisdom of the Father is His complete delight. In Him the Father is well pleased and satisfied.

  c. The Father loves the Son, by the communication of the Holy Ghost, the Bond of Eternal Life.

POINT III. *Consider the Love of the Son to the Father.*

  a. The Son loves the Father with an equal Love. The only difference is that, in the Father this Love is gratuitous ; in the Son it is a debt of Love. In this interchange of Love the Righteousness of God eternally consists.

  b. The Son loves the Father with a correlative Love. As the Son has received, so He returns Love.

  c. The Son loves the Father with a consubstantial Love. The Holy Ghost proceeding from Both in one eternal act, is the undivided mutual Love of Father and Son.

AFFECTIONS. Glory to Jesus. Union with the Father in the love of His Only-begotten Son by the power of the Holy Ghost. Union with the Son, in love to the Father by the same power.

PRAYER.

O Lord Jesu, Who art the Only-begotten of the Father, grant that I, being adopted into the unity of Thy glorious Sonship, may ever live as befits Thee, the Son of God, my Head, and may attain to hear the Blessed Voice of the Eternal Wisdom, and may live with Thee in the perfect love of the Father by the power of the Holy Ghost. Amen.

THE WORD IN SILENCE.

PRELUDE. i. *Shepherds, what saw ye? tell us. We came with haste and found Mary and Joseph and the Babe lying in the manger, wrapped in swaddling-clothes.*

ii. The Shepherds coming to the Manger.

POINT I. *Consider the Child lying in the Manger.*

a. His Divine Personality. He is the Eternal Son of God. This Infant is the centre of all men.

b. His Perfection of Power. He though so weak, yet needs no power from any, can receive power from none. All power is His. He gives all power to all others.

c. His Perfection of Wisdom. He is not ignorant as other children. He is the Incarnate Wisdom of God. Life shall only develop in Him that wisdom and knowledge which is inherent. He knows *thee.*

POINT II. *Consider His Self-restraint.*

a. His consciousness of power. Life is to Him no experiment. He knows all the capacities which are treasured up in Himself, and in things around.

b. His knowledge of all needs. He knows all sorrows, as no one else ever did. He suffers with them in not helping them.

c. His intense love for all those who needed His help.

POINT III. *Consider the cause of that Self-restraint.*

a. He is come to do the will of God. His life is to be meritorious by what He does not do as much as by what He does. Obedience, not visible result, is the principle of His actions.

b. He can do nothing but God's will. This is no imperfection, but the height of perfectness. The Son can do nothing, save what He seeth the Father do, for they are one Almighty. As man, He can do nothing but God's will, for He is perfectly united to His Almighty power, and acts thereby.

c. He finds His perfect joy in doing the will of God. In outward suffering, He is "glad of God's word, as one that findeth great spoils."—Ps. cxix. 162.—He hears, He is, He does, God's Word in the perfect joy of the Holy Ghost.

AFFECTIONS. Contentedness and restfulness in God. Waiting upon God while sympathizing with man. Consciousness of a Divine Mission, and rejection of all else that can solicit us.

PRAYER.

O Almighty God, Who didst send Thy Son in our nature to accomplish upon the earth Thy Holy will for the deliverance of mankind, grant that I may so abide in the law of Thy Holy Word, that I, following the steps of His Incarnate Life, and resting in the sustaining power of His all-sufficient grace, may accomplish all that Thou wouldst have me to do, and contemplate with obedient heart the manifold purposes of Thy ceaseless Love, through the same **Jesus Christ our Lord. Amen.**

THE WORD IN UTTERANCE.

PRELUDE. i. *Shepherds, what saw ye? tell us. We came with haste and found Mary, and Joseph, and the Babe lying in a manger, wrapped in swaddling-clothes.*—S. Luke ii. 16, 17.

ii. The shepherds round the manger where Jesus lies.

POINT I. *Consider the silent utterance of the Incarnate Word.*

    a. His appeal to natural love. The weakness of infancy is the most powerful of appeals. A Divine Authority seems to fit it by nature for the manifestation of God Himself.

    b. His appeal to faith. The Shepherds know Him, proclaimed by Angels as possessing a mysterious-predestination, coming to be a Saviour.

    c. His appeal to hope. They know He will accomplish some great blessing, although they know not how.

POINT II. *Consider this utterance appealing to different degrees of intelligence.*

    a. Some look for the overthrow of an oppressive external tyranny. But the power of the Word of God manifested in judgment does not subdue those who behold it.

    b. Some look merely for deliverance from the punishment of sin and the misery of the world. But the mere promises of the Word of God would not transform the life, even though they might remove the fear.

    c. We must look to Jesus as saving us from ourselves ; sanctifying with the regenerating Spirit all those who come to Him. It is the fellowship of the Word made flesh dwelling amongst us and calling us to dwell in Himself, which lifts us up so as to be one with God.

POINT III. *Consider this utterance appealing to different conditions of heart.*

    a. Some exult in Christ as with Jewish expectation, merely as a national hero. Nearness to Christ makes us proud, unless we know Him in the Truth wherein He is naturally separated from us. He the infinitely Holy God, we sinners.

    b. Some rest in the all-sufficiency of the Divine Wisdom. Yet the sense of God's power paralyzes rather than helps us, unless it be felt as the stay of our weakness.

    c. We must know the individual Love of God to each individual man whom He calls into union with Himself. This is the Word which satisfies the soul.

AFFECTIONS. Faith. Hope. Love. Earnest desire for the Kingdom of Christ.

PRAYER.

O Lord *Jesu, Who claimest the love of each according to the degree in which Thou makest Thyself known, call me near unto the Father with ever-increasing experience of Thy goodness, that I may in the end be perfected in the glorious apprehension of Thy Truth, Who art with the Father and the Holy Ghost, One everlasting God.* Amen.

THE UNIFYING MYSTERY OF THE DIVINE MANIFESTATION.

. PRELUDE. i. *To-day is the Church joined to her heavenly Bridegroom: in Jordan is Christ baptized; the wise men bring gifts to the Royal Marriage; and by water made wine are guests rejoiced.*—S. Matt. iii. 13; ii. 11; S. John ii. 9.

ii. Christ hallowing matrimony by His first miracle to be a symbol of the union betwixt Godhead and manhood.

POINT I. *Consider the Hypostatic union which is manifested.*
   a. The Child of Bethlehem manifested by a sign from heaven. He comes in poverty, yet ceases not to be the Lord of all. Heaven ministers to Him though earth be blind.
   b. The Eternal Son manifested by a herald on earth. The human heart cannot judge of the Divine Presence. The sure word of prophecy enables man to recognize God.
   c. Christ uses daily life to show His inalienable glory.

POINT II. *Consider the Sacramental union manifested.*
   a. The sanctification of water to the mystical washing away of sin. The touch of Christ leaves a virtue in every outer form with which it is associated.
   b. The voice of adoption, whereby we are owned as God's children. The Father proclaiming Christ as His Son, adopts into the Eternal Love all Christ's members.
   c. The abiding Spirit, whereby we are born again. The Spirit resting upon Christ sanctifies His members. If we have not the Spirit of Christ we are none of His.

POINT III. *Consider the Mystical union which is manifested.*
   a. The mystical union begun in Poverty. The marriage of the poor who had no wine symbolizes the poverty of creation in which Jesus assumes our human nature.
   b. The mystical union perfected in glory. The change of water into wine symbolizes the glorification of created faculties with the virtue of the Divine Presence which it is made to enshrine.
   c. The mystical union accepted by faith. We must become the disciples of Jesus by the power of the Holy Ghost making us one with Him. All manifestations of Jesus to us are unavailing, unless there be the manifestation of Jesus within us.

AFFECTIONS. Desire of transformation. Acceptance of Divine Promises in all the fulness of Truth. Union with God in Christ.

PRAYER.

O Jesu, very God and very Man, as Thou hast taken me into Thyself, so also be pleased to manifest in my soul the brightness and power of Thy glory, that amidst all the circumstances of the outer life I may acknowledge the greatness of Thy Divine gift and live to the glory of Thy Holy Name. Amen.

THE DIVINE GLORY OF THE MANIFESTATION.

PRELUDE.   i. *The Star in the East shone like a flame, and showed where God the King of kings was. The wise men saw it and brought gifts to Christ the King.*

ii. The wise men watching the Star.

POINT I.   *Consider the miraculous power attendant upon this manifestation.*

     a. The manifestation of God in the flesh demands some preternatural phenomena. Nature becomes changed, by entering into a new relation to God through the Incarnation.

     b. God hides His Presence from the evil spirits, but makes known to the blessed angels as well as to men that He is come. Some sign is therefore only consistent with the dignity of His advent. Nothing actually found in nature would suit the occasion.

     c. Only by some miraculous sign could this advent possibly be made known. A sign was chosen for the wise men in that department of nature where they specially recognized the fixity of Nature's laws. This phenomenon would be to them more striking than any other.

POINT II.   *Consider the heavenly brightness of this manifestation.*

     a. Jesus is the Sun of Righteousness, and it is fitting that Heaven should welcome His appearance by some new form of brightness.

     b. All who watch for the manifestation of Jesus must find a heavenly brightness guiding them. This may indeed be withdrawn from them at times, but the joy of preventing grace will cheer them according to God's will.

POINT III.   *Consider the prophetic dignity of this manifestation.*

     a. The wise men have been long expecting that Christ would come. Now they recognize in this Star the fulfilment of prophecy.

     b. They come with loving hearts to Christ as soon as His coming is known. No dangers or difficulties retard them.

     c. We must watch for all the indications of prophecy if we would rise up so as to read God's purpose in the events of the day.

AFFECTIONS.   Expectation. Reliance upon Divine Promises. Diligence to follow Christ whenever He is made known.

PRAYER.

O God, Who by the leading of a Star didst call the wise men from afar to the cradle of Thy dear Son; Grant me grace evermore to give heed to the sure light of prophecy, that I may behold Thy will in all things, and rejoice in the tokens of Thy Love; through the same Jesus Christ our Lord. Amen.

THE ILLUMINATING POWER OF THE DIVINE MANIFESTATION.

PRELUDE. i. *The Star in the East*, etc.—Vide last page.

ii. The wise men recognising the Star as a prophetic token.

POINT I. *Consider the manifestation of the way to Christ.*

  a. Individual illuminations must be corroborated by authoritative teachings. If we rely upon suggestions which come to ourselves alone, we shall fall into idle dreams.

  b. Signs which are accepted as coming from God to illuminate us must be really supernatural. If we take common events as having uncommon meanings, we shall fall into many superstitions.

  c. God can indeed speak to us through natural phenomena. It is safe to recognise in events which strike our imagination a call to fulfil duties which are independently certain.

POINT II. *Consider the manifestation of Christ as the Beginning of Grace.*

  a. The way to Christ must make known to us Christ as the Way. We do not come to Christ that we may rest in His earthly manifestation, but that He may lead us onward in Heavenly life.

  b. Prophecy, miracles, nature, lead to Christ—but Christ is the beginning of grace. We come to Him, but we could not take one step unless He first came to strengthen us.

  c. The Light of Grace opens to the soul a revelation of the higher world, which otherwise would be to us all darkness.

POINT III. *Consider the manifestation of Christ, as the consummation of glory.*

  a. The Endless End. The Eternal, Infinite, Glory of God. Jesus leads the soul to search out this glory in manifold experiences.

  b. The Living End. Our life shall not cease by any development of Christ. Rather we live the more truly as He leads us onward in more perfect experiences of Divine Truth.

  c. In all the glory of God that we behold we can only see Christ Himself, for He is the illuminating Mediator in Whom the Father is seen, and He is One God with the Father.

AFFECTIONS. Delight in watching for God to speak to Thyself individually. Submission to external authority.

PRAYER.

O Lord Jesu, Light of Light, Who hast called us to Thyself by the Light of many outward tokens that in Thyself Thou mayest guide us to the Father by many inward experiences of Thy goodness, teach me so to contemplate Thee, and to walk as Thou guidest, that I may rejoice hereafter to follow Thee in that way of glorious Life wherein Thou callest me eternally to abide in the exhoustless communication of Thy glorious love. Amen.

THE HEAVENLY WONDER OF THE MANIFESTATION.

PRELUDE. i. *The Star in the East shone like a flame, and showed where God the King of kings was. The wise men saw it, and brought gifts to Christ the King.*

ii. The star shining over the house.

POINT I. *Consider the star of prophecy.*

    a. It makes good the claims which otherwise would have been beyond belief. Heaven attests the truth of man's expectation.

    b. It shines forth to be the guide of those who patiently carry out God's will. It may be obscured for a time, but God will make it plain when there is necessity.

    c. The star shines, but there is no voice. When God has spoken, He would have us recognize the symbols which He promises as being sufficient assurance of His work.

POINT II. *Consider the house over which it rested.*

    a. It was the home of human poverty. No wealth of man would have sufficed to make man's poverty worthy of God's greatness.

    b. It was the home of Divine royalty. Jesus is the heir of David's throne not only by transitory occupation, but by eternal and indissoluble covenant.

    c. It was the home of heavenly worship. The star is the symbol of the adoration wherewith Heaven would acknowledge the Universal King.

POINT III. *Consider the fitness of the portent.*

    a. Though Jesus be born in earthly poverty, yet is it fitting that the universe should testify to the Incarnation of the Son of God. O my soul, let His coming wake forth in thee fresh forms of heavenly light!

    b. Earth cannot put forth any offering which can symbolize the Heavenly Visitor. Alas! the earthly nature is too dull even to recognize His glory.

    c. As He comes from Heaven, so the Star from Heaven indicates the Heavenly Origin of Him that is born. From above the Heavens He comes. Though He comes to earth, the Heavens wait upon Him.

AFFECTIONS. Homage to Jesus. Brightness in the thought of His coming. Expectation during times of darkness.

PRAYER.

Grant, O Lord, that as by the star of old the wise men were guided to the house of Thine infancy, so by the brightness of Thy covenanted Truth I may seek Thy Presence in the earthly ordinances of grace; and may rejoice with Angels and Archangels to draw near to the hidden Presence of Thy Majesty, Who dwellest and reignest with the Father in the unity of the Holy Ghost, One God for ever and ever. Amen.

THE JOYOUS DISCIPLINE OF THE DIVINE MANIFESTATION.

PRELUDE. i. *When the wise men saw the Star, they rejoiced with exceeding great joy: and when they were come into the house, they presented unto Him gifts, gold, frankincense and myrrh.*— S. Matt. ii. 10, 11.

ii. The joy of the wise men at the re-appearance of the star.

POINT I. *Consider the expectation fulfilled by this manifestation.*

   a. They had long watched for Christ. Their joy is proportionate to their expectation.

   b. That which they see is the long predicted sign. Their expectation is the warrant of their joy. The prophecy proves the supernatural character of the event.

   c. Theirs was a practical not a dreamy expectation. Therefore they acted at once upon the appearance of the expected token.

POINT II. *Consider the withdrawal of manifestation.*

   a. They are not dismayed at the withdrawal. In the Holy City they seek the guidance of those who ought to know, and in this they are satisfied.

   b. They do not fear to be taunted with folly for yielding to an apparition which seems to have failed them. They are sure that God Who gave the guidance will perfect it.

   c. They are content to receive instruction even from those who show no love. The loss of prophetic ardour in Jerusalem is worse than the obscuration of the star.

POINT III. *Consider the unexpected return of manifestation.*

   a. God restores gifts to those who are faithful in the time of His withdrawal.

   b. God's gifts become brighter to us in their joy when we have experienced their temporary withdrawal.

   c. When God restores His gifts, He is ready to guide us to the end, if we are ready to welcome them as they deserve.

AFFECTIONS.—Diligence in using natural means. Contentedness to be without supernatural tokens. Vigilance to recognize God's will.

PRAYER.

O Almighty God, grant me always cheerfully to accept Thy Fatherly discipline, that when Thou vouchsafest the supernatural tokens of Thy grace I may walk in Thy guidance, and when Thou withdrawest them, I may patiently seek Thy Face; through Jesus Christ our Lord. Amen.

THE ROYAL CLAIMS OF THE DIVINE MANIFESTATION.

PRELUDE. i. *When the wise men saw the Star*, etc.—Vide last page.

ii. The wise men opening their treasures.

POINT I. *Consider the love due to the manifestation of our King.*

    a. Gold the symbol of all that is valuable. Though He is not a King dependent upon this world's wealth, He is a King in whose honour all wealth must be lavished.

    b. All wealth comes from Him. In nature as truly as in grace.

    c. Nothing is true wealth unless it be used for His service. What is used for the world alone, perishes with the world. What is used for Him lives in eternal enjoyment.

POINT II. *Consider the love due to the manifestation of our God.*

    a. Incense the symbol of worship. Every earthly affection must be consumed in the fire of His Love.

    b. Outward fragrance is brought to Him. The true fragrance is the incense of His own merits which He gives to us.

    c. No worship is acceptable to God unless it be offered to Christ, and through Him, so as to be presented before the Father in the Eternal Love wherewith He loves the Father.

POINT III. *Consider the love due to the manifestation of our Redeemer.*

    a. Myrrh, the symbol of mortality. If Jesus comes to suffer and die, we must offer to Him the soothing myrrh of our gratitude and affection.

    b. As He condescends to receive in our human nature the gift whereby its pain may be soothed, so are we to look for Him to soothe us in every consolation with the bitter myrrh which exudes from the Tree of Life, even His own most sacred Cross.

    c. If we offer Him myrrh in His sufferings, we must not shrink from suffering along with Him, according to the will of the Father. He will soothe us if we serve Him.

    d. Death by nature is foul and corrupt. Mortification by grace is embalmed in imperishable sweetness.

AFFECTIONS. Self-oblation. Welcome to Christ. Worship. Penitence.

PRAYER.

O Lord Jesu, Who didst accept the offerings which the wise men brought to Thee in Thy Childhood, mercifully accept my unworthy oblation; and grant that I, abiding in the kingdom of Thy grace, may behold the hidden glory of Thy Godhead, and may be preserved from the corruption of the death of sin, according to the efficacy of Thine own Redeeming Love. Amen.

THE TRANSCENDENT TRUTH OF THE DIVINE MANIFESTATION.

PRELUDE. i. *Lo, a Voice from Heaven, saying, This is My Beloved Son, in Whom I am well pleased.*—S. Matt. iii. 17.
ii. The Baptism of Christ.

POINT I. *Consider the Eternal Relationships manifested.*

a. The Father is manifested in the utterance of the Eternal Word acknowledging Jesus as the Only-begotten in the glory of the Holy Ghost.

b. The Eternal Son is manifested receiving in His Humanity the bright outpouring of the Holy Ghost, Who proceedeth from the Father.

c. The Holy Ghost is manifested as the Bond of Divine Delight between the Father Who speaks the Word, and the Only-begotten Son in Whose Love He finds His satisfaction.

POINT II. *Consider the Eternal Activity manifested.*

a. These Relationships are manifested upon this occasion, but they are Eternal. *We* receive gifts of grace in Holy Baptism. Jesus contained all grace within Himself before He was baptized, by reason of His Divine Sonship.

b. Creation springs from the Eternal Joy which the Triune God has in Himself.

c. By the Incarnation, the creature is taken into the active fellowship of the Divine love.

d. If the two natures of Christ were not joined together in One Person, we could not be taken up into the life of God by regeneration; and now, by reason of this hypostatic union, we cannot be joined to Christ without participating in the fulness of the Divine Love.

POINT III. *Consider the Eternal Unity manifested hereby.*

a. The Holy Ghost does not descend from the outer Heavens, but He proceeds from the Person of the Father.

b. The Holy Ghost does not rest externally upon the Body of Christ, but inwardly abides with Him as His Eternal Life.

c. The unity of the Spirit of Love proceeding from Both, is that identity of Godhead wherein the Father beholds the Son as His own true, perfect, consubstantial, Eternal Image.

AFFECTIONS. Adoration. Love. Ecstacy.

PRAYER.

O God, Who hast caused me to be born again into the life of Thy Divine Covenant, delivering me from the bondage of my natural life wherein I was born into the world, grant that I may contemplate the glory of Thine Eternal Love, and, abiding in the unity of Thy Holy Spirit, may be known of Thee according to the grace of Thy dear Son, and may love Thee according to the glory of Thy truth; through the same Jesus Christ our Lord. Amen.

THE ABIDING RESULTS OF THE DIVINE MANIFESTATION.

PRELUDE. i. *The wise men, being warned by God in a dream, departed into their own country another way.*

ii. The cavalcade starts from Bethlehem, and turns its back upon the Old Jerusalem.

POINT I. *Consider the manifestation of Divine Communion.*

a. God accepted their watching, and revealed to them the Truth by the Star, knowing that they would accept it as a sign.

b. God welcomed them, accepting their gifts in the form of a Child.

c. God sanctifies their sleep to make known His will. If we are with Christ waking, He will be with us sleeping.

POINT II. *Consider the manifestation of the better country.*

a. Their old home was not enough for them. They desired to enter into the Presence of God. They left all. . They sought a better country.

b. Jerusalem does not satisfy. They went there for guidance, not for rest.

c. They go back to their homes, and yet not as they came out. They return with eyes open to behold God. Their true home is to be in His keeping. All things are changed. They have now a better country than their old country.

POINT III. *Consider the manifestation of the New Way.*

a. The way of Prophecy. The way shone for them as a light in a dark place, and by its light they came near.

b. The way of Suffering. If we have come to Bethlehem, we must go away as the disciples of the Persecuted, turning our back upon the world, and its power and glory.

c. The way of Grace. The Child of Bethlehem will bring us to our proper country if we cling to Him. He is the true way to our true Home. The Law brings us to Christ, but it is by Christ alone that we can advance from Bethlehem to the Jerusalem which is above.

AFFECTIONS. Hope in God. Repudiation of the world. Attention to Divine warning. Indifference to the earthly way in which God calls us.

PRAYER.

O God, teach me so to watch for the manifestation of Thy will, that I may be ready at all times to obey Thy call, and so to look upward to Thyself in the accomplishment thereof, that by Thy constant guidance I may be delivered from the dangers of the evil world, rejoicing in the way that leadeth to eternal life; through Jesus Christ our Lord. Amen.

THE ACTIVE MANIFESTATION OF DIVINE SONSHIP.

PRELUDE. i. *Son, why hast Thou thus dealt with us? behold, Thy Father and I have sought Thee sorrowing. And He said unto them, How is it that ye sought Me? Wist ye not that I must be about My Father's business?*—S. Luke ii. 48, 49.

ii. The finding in the Temple.

POINT I. *Consider the detachment which God's work requires.*

    a. Joseph and Mary represent humanity. They return home. Jesus abides in Jerusalem. This is the home of the regenerate humanity, which it cannot leave.

    b. Natural ties drew Jesus after them. The Incarnate Son must surrender the affections of earth. (See Ps. xlv. 11.)

    c. Jesus does not break away from natural ties for any mere fancy, but in obedience to the call of His Father.

POINT II. *Consider the sorrows of the supernatural life.*

    a. The demands of God involve some sacrifice of the natural heart. If we have God's call, others will suffer as well as ourselves whilst we withdraw from their natural claims.

    b. The human heart complains as if it were wronged by that which God requires. Not finding Jesus amongst kinsfolk and acquaintance, it mourns over the estrangement which a supernatural vocation seems to involve.

    c. The third day is the day of finding, *i.e.*, the discovery of the risen or supernatural life. And it must be in the Temple, in God's own House. Yet Nature is not satisfied.

POINT III. *Consider how man wonders at supernatural life.*

    a. The first word addressed to Jesus, is His mother's wonder at His withdrawal from her. Human nature is perplexed at the supernatural life, and complains of natural loss.

    b. Human nature puts forward a father's claim,—Thy father and I,—forgetful of the true personal relationship which binds the Supernatural Offspring to God as His Father.

    c. The human understanding cannot fathom the Divine relationship. The call of God is recognized by those whom the Holy Ghost has raised above nature. Natural righteousness and natural piety cannot see into Divine mysteries.

AFFECTIONS. Readiness to hear God's call, or to recognize it in others. Patience amidst the misunderstandings of those whom we love and respect.

PRAYER.

O *Blessed Son of God, Who having taken upon Thyself our nature wast ever occupied about Thy Father's work, grant unto me, that as Thou hast called me into the fellowship of this Divine Life by the power of the Holy Ghost, so by the same power I may ever live detached from every earthly consideration, content to act in all things as the Divine Word requires, according to the power of Thy grace, Who with the Father and the Holy Ghost livest and reignest One God, world without end.* Amen.

THE DELIVERANCE FROM OUTWARD NECESSITY.

PRELUDE. i. *There was a marriage in Cana of Galilee, and the Mother of Jesus was there. And Jesus also was called.*—S. John ii. 1, 2.

ii. The House of Poverty, and Jesus among the friends.

POINT I. *Consider the Marriage as symbolizing—*

a. The union of Godhead with manhood in the Person of Christ. The Ascension was the day on which this marriage was solemnly consummated in glory. Our nature was a widowed nature married to a new Husband, even Christ. Jewish widows were married on Thursdays.

b. The union of Christ with His Church. The Church is wedded to Christ in the Resurrection on the Great " Third Day," which is also the First Day of the new life.

c. The union of Christ with the individual soul. This union is celebrated in Cana of Galilee. Not the corporate body of the earlier national covenant, but the individual soul from the Gentile world attains to this.

POINT II. *Consider the Mother of Jesus as the representative of the Church.*

a. In the poverty of the fallen humanity, " the low estate of God's Handmaiden."

b. In the zeal of devotion. Cana symbolizes zeal. The soul whereof Jesus shall be born must be given to God in holy zeal. Or if Cana signifies "reed," it may be that in the place where was only the reed shaken with the wind there is the manifestation of the glory of God.

c. In the blessedness of election. If there is to be any espousal of humanity to God, there must be an election of grace. The Elect, of whom Christ is born, are the occasion of His manifestation in the world.

POINT III. *Consider Jesus being called.*

a. The Presence of Jesus and His disciples may have occasioned the need. Yet the need which springs from liberality to Jesus will be rewarded by the manifestation of His power.

b. Jesus requires to be invited by the soul, although He is ever willing to come.

c. We must show our simple trust in Jesus. Our poverty is no hindrance to our inviting Him, no hindrance to His coming. Rather it is the very reason why we must ask Him.

AFFECTIONS. Desire to associate Jesus with all the acts of life. Acceptance of poverty. Joy in the riches of grace.

PRAYER.

O Lord Jesu, Who didst hallow the estate of poverty by the manifestation of Thy Glory, grant that we may so welcome Thy Presence to share our poverty that the riches of Thy grace may be manifested amongst us, to the glory of Thy Holy Name. Amen.

DELIVERANCE FROM HUMAN INFIRMITY.

PRELUDE. i. *When He was come down from the mountain, great multitudes followed Him. And, behold, there came a leper and worshipped Him, saying, Lord, if Thou wilt, Thou canst make me clean. And Jesus put forth His hand and touched him, saying, I will; be thou clean.*—S. Matt. viii. 1-3.

ii. Jesus—the multitude—the leper.

POINT I. *Consider the leper's acknowledgment.*

  a. Its publicity. A multitude were following. The leper had a need too great to be held back by their presence.

  b. Its boldness. He had not yet known of any whom Jesus had healed, but he was convinced that the power of Jesus sufficed to meet his own case.

  c. Its submission. He threw himself upon the will of Jesus. He did not put forward any claim.

POINT II. *Consider the leper's miserable estate.*

  a. An outcast from society. He had to warn them away, crying out, Unclean, unclean.

  b. An outcast from the Temple. As the atoning sacrifice was burnt without the camp, bearing the curse, so the leper had to be without the camp.—Lev. xiii. 46.

  c. There was no other hope for him but in Jesus only. The Law could not restore Him. Jesus, the Atoning Sacrifice, Who should bear our curse dying without the camp as an accursed one, could restore.

POINT III. *Consider the touch of Jesus.*

  a. He Who came to be "stricken of God" as a leper (Isa. liii. 4) took away our curse by His touch; but in His interior purity received no pollution from that touch.

  b. His touch heals, as being the instrument of His Personal Will. It does not act as a charm, but with a moral purpose.

  c. The cleansing is individual. Not merely universal cleansing by Christ's redemption, but a special cleansing, to be manifested in sacramental communication to individual souls. So does Jesus touch and cleanse us one by one.

AFFECTIONS. Personal desire for Jesus. Boldness in confessing Him. Expectation in looking to Him. Diligence in coming to Him.

PRAYER.

O Lord Jesu, though I am unclean, yet do Thou regard the greatness of my need, and as Thou comest to share the exile of my sin, grant that I may be gathered by Thy touch into the fellowship of the Divine Sanctuary, and live henceforth to the glory of the Father in the power of the Spirit of Thy Grace. Amen.

E 2

DELIVERANCE FROM OUTWARD PERIL.

PRELUDE. i. *And when He was entered into a ship, His disciples followed Him. And, behold, there arose a great tempest in the sea, insomuch that the ship was covered with the waves; but He was asleep. And His disciples came to Him and awoke Him saying, Lord, save us: we perish.*—S. Matt. viii. 23-25.

ii. The vessel in the storm with Jesus sleeping.

POINT I. *Consider the tranquillity of Jesus.*
- *a.* The joy of resting in God. No outward storm can destroy the abiding calmness of the soul which is really stayed upon God.
- *b.* The security amidst earthly vicissitudes which this rest engenders. Jesus sleeps not with the sleep of indolence and incapacity as Jonah, but with the sleep of perfect confidence and love.
- *c.* The outward manifestation of the inward peace. The outward bearing towards trouble shows what is really the inward state of the heart. Troubles prove us.

POINT II. *Consider the outburst of the tempest.*
- *a.* Its suddenness. We must not be surprised when sorrows overtake us. Satan will stir them up all the more if he knows that Jesus is with us.
- *b.* Its violence. The ship may be covered with the waves, and yet not sink; the Church lost to sight, but not lost. Jesus asleep, yet present.
- *c.* Its hopelessness. No human aid can avail; but we must not on that account doubt the sufficiency of Jesus.

POINT III. *Consider the earnest cry of the disciples.*
- *a.* Jesus apparently neglectful. Jesus sleeps in order to teach us confidence. Alas! that we should be so occupied with the anxiety that we cannot learn the lesson. We neglected Him. Had we held active converse with Him during the calm, He had not gone to sleep.
- *b.* Destruction apparently imminent. Jesus suffers danger to increase, in order to awake our simple faith in Him.
- *c.* The arousing of Jesus. The storm which shows our negligence and timidity will show the power of Jesus if we cry to Him.

AFFECTIONS. Peace in the assurance of Jesus' presence. Expectation of storms. Joy in meeting them.

PRAYER.

O God of Peace, grant that I, always rejoicing to hold communion with Jesus Christ Thine only Son, may never suffer His Presence to be neglected in seasons of tranquillity; and whensoever dangers threaten, hear Thou my cry, and grant me deliverance through the same, Thy Son Jesus Christ our Lord. Amen.

DELIVERANCE FROM FALSE RELIGION.

PRELUDE.. i. *Sir, didst not Thou sow good seed in the field? from whence then hath it tares? He said unto them, An enemy hath done this."*—S. Matt. xiii. 27, 28.

ii. The servants complain to the Householder.

POINT I. *Consider the craft of the enemy.*

   a. He sows the germs of evil imperceptibly. What he has done makes no appearance until it begins to grow.

   b. He sows what is very like the good grain. Even as they grow together, the good and the bad are liable to be mistaken one for the other.

   c. When he has done his work, he retires from view. We do not recognize the personal agency of Satan in the errors which affect the Church, but he is their author.

POINT II. *Consider the perplexity of the servants.*

   a. At the fact. They are annoyed to find anything in the field but what the Householder had sown.

   b. As to the manner of dealing with it. A growing evil seems intolerable, and yet immediate handling is dangerous, for good and evil cannot be accurately separated.

   c. As to hope of getting the better of it. They are anxious to do something at once, and fear lest by and by it may be too much for them. Too much it is for them at any time, but the Householder will deal with it hereafter.

POINT III. *Consider the patience of the Householder.*

   a. With the servants. All comes from their negligence. While men slept, the spurious seed was sown.

   b. With the fact. The Master remains unmoved, though he hears of the evil seed. He knew beforehand that there would be this overgrowth of evil. Yet in the end He will purge it out. The field may have an evil crop, but none shall find its way into the barn, yet shall the barn be full.

   c. With the Enemy. He takes all as a matter of course. When the evil crop is destroyed, then shall the enemy be punished also. God delays His punishments until the end.

AFFECTIONS. Firmness of faith, unshaken by the corruptions of the Church. Patience with those who are deceived. Confidence as to the future victory of Truth.

PRAYER.

O Lord Jesu Christ, Who hast filled Thy Church with gifts of grace and truth, grant that we may diligently cultivate the grace which Thou hast given, and abide in the Truth which Thou hast revealed, so that while we grow with the perfection which Thou requirest, the seed of the Evil One may find no place in our hearts, and our lives may be sanctified to the manifestation of Thy Glory, Who with the Father and the Holy Ghost livest and reignest God for ever and ever. Amen.

THE OBSCURATION OF THE LAST DAYS.

PRELUDE. i. *Immediately after the tribulation of those days shall the sun be darkened, and the moon shall not give her light, and the stars shall fall from heaven, and the powers of the heavens shall be shaken.*—S. Matt. xxiv. 29.

ii. The course of Nature wholly overturned.

POINT I. *Consider the sun darkened.*

a. At the beginning was the Epiphany, at the end shall be the Obscuration of Christ the Sun of Righteousness.

b. This is indeed a night, when none can work any longer. God will first make complete the number of His elect.

c. Periods of darkness anticipate that final darkness. If Christ is hidden, it is because none seek Him truly. If our Gospel be hid, it is hid to them that are lost.

POINT II. *Consider the moon not giving her light.*

a. The moon is the Church, which shines during the night of this world's existence, with a light reflected from Him Who is the Lord of the true day. The gates of hell cannot darken the light of the moon. The failure of the Church to give light is because Jesus withdraws His Light. If she shines no more on earth, it is because she is not needed.

b. There may be various occasions on which the moon shines pale. Her light is not in herself. Nevertheless her light shall not be withdrawn until the end of the world.

c. The Church shines brightly as she reveals Christ most fully. The Church cannot sustain the Truth apart from Christ, but His grace sustains her in the Truth.

POINT III. *Consider the stars falling from Heaven.*

a. "Yet once more shall I shake not the earth only but also Heaven."—Heb. xii. 26. In the great catastrophe of the last days, the stars, the ruling powers of the Church, shall fall. Those that are shaken shall be removed.

b. There is no pledge of perpetuity. There is a prophecy of overthrow. But there is also a promise that this collapse shall not happen until after the tribulation of Antichrist. If we see weakness in the Church we need not wonder, but we need not fear. The powers of Heaven will not be shaken and removed until their work is done.

AFFECTIONS. Faith. Stedfastness. Humiliation for man's sin. Security amidst Christ's promises.

PRAYER.

O God, Who hast warned us of the troubles that shall come upon the earth, grant that we may not be moved by any distresses incident to our own day, but may walk in the Light, and serve Thee with unshaken faith, waiting for the final manifestation of Thy Son Jesus Christ, that we may be found abiding in the kingdom which cannot be shaken, through His merits, Who liveth and reigneth with Thee and the Holy Ghost, One God, world without end. Amen.

THE CALL OF GOD.

PRELUDE. i. *The Kingdom of Heaven is like unto a man that is an householder, which went out early in the morning to hire labourers into his vineyard.*—S. Matt. xx. 1.

ii. The Parable.

POINT I. *Consider the early morning.*

    a. The morning of youth. God has called thee from the first. How hast thou corresponded with the call? He called thee to labour, not merely to look on. He had a work for thee which would require the whole day of thy life.

    b. The morning of opportunity. God calls us to work for Him on various occasions; He never calls too late. The fault is with man if the work is not done.

    c. The morning of grace. Jesus cometh forth early in the morning from the sepulchre. The grace of His resurrection brings man to the work of the day, but before that resurrection, man was in the darkness of night, and could not work.

POINT II. *Consider the Householder.*

    a. The Personal Government of God. He does not rule the world merely by abstract laws. He comes forth to visit His people. The moral dealing of God with mankind does not admit of mechanical fixity like the material universe. Moral life varies as the vineyard's growth, and needs individual treatment though according to fixed laws.

    b. The Personal appeal of the Incarnation. God the Son comes into the world to see who will work for Him. He chooses His labourers, but He does so by making trial of their fitness.

    c. The Personal appeal of Grace. God does not merely permit us to come to Him. By His Holy Spirit He comes to draw us to His work, and fits us for it.

POINT III. *Consider the hiring.*

    a. God might claim our work as a due, but He offers us hire if we will do it. He hires us not because He needs, but because He loves us.

    b. He hires us for the work of Love. We must love as He loves.

    c. The love of God is the only hire which He offers. He would have us claim as payment what His own pure bounty offers.

AFFECTIONS. Promptness in working for God. Confidence in the reward of any work. Gratitude for having a call to it.

PRAYER.

O God, Who hast called me to serve Thee according to the power of Thy Love, grant that I may praise Thee for this call by diligence in fulfilling all Thy commandments, and pardon Thou the negligence of my past years, which by the grace of Thy renewed vocation I would fain repair, through Jesus Christ our Lord. Amen.

THE HIRE OF THE LABOURERS.

PRELUDE. i. *Call the labourers, and give them their hire,*
saith the Lord.—S. Matt. xx.

ii. The labourers coming to the steward.

POINT I. *Consider the labourers.*

    a. Variously called. We are not to think that we are better
than others by any specialty of call. All in the vineyard
have been equally called by the Householder in Person.

    b. All called to work. None receive pay who have not
worked. Our labour shall not be in vain. Those who will
not work need not come. The Lord knows who are working.

    c. All working on till evening. God calls us earlier or later;
but unless we persevere unto the end we cannot receive
our hire. If any left off too soon they would get nothing.

POINT II. *Consider the hire.*

    a. A penny a day, *i.e.*, sufficient for their day's support.
"Day by day our daily bread." This penny is the gift of
grace.

    b. The same to all. God has special gifts for those who seek
them properly. His sustaining grace, the Body and
Blood of Christ feeding the soul, the Presence of the Holy
Ghost quickening it, are the same to all. Daily sufficiency
of grace is the hire according to the Covenant. More
grace than enough is neither promised nor given to any.
The amount of daily Manna is the same for all.

    c. Whether called early or late, all would want their hire for
subsistence during the work of the morrow. God does not
give us grace for the past, but for the future. We are not
to think what we did yesterday, but what shall we do to-
morrow.

POINT III. *Consider the steward.*

    a. God dispenses His grace by His ministers. *He* calls the
labourers into the vineyard. T*hey* have the oversight
and care of them when there.

    b. All need the Sacraments alike, and all find in them the
same gifts.

    c. The Lord of the vineyard is the Lord of Creation, of
Nature, and of Grace. When He speaks, He makes things
to be what He saith they are. The value of the Sacraments
is by reason of His Word.

AFFECTIONS. Gratitude for the call. Faith in the sufficiency of God's promise. Resolution to continue in God's
service.

PRAYER.

O Lord *Jesu Christ, Who hast mercifully called me into Thy*
vineyard, grant that I may thankfully receive Thine inestimable
benefit, and serve Thee evermore with gladness of heart. Amen.

THE DISMISSAL OF THE DISCONTENTED LABOURER.

PRELUDE. i. *But the Lord of the vineyard answered one of them and said, Friend, I do thee no wrong; didst not thou agree with me for a penny? Take that thine is, and go thy way.*—S. Matt. **xx.** 13, 14.

ii. As before. The Lord also standing by,

POINT I. *Consider the agreement.*

a. Enough for the day. God does not promise us more grace than our need requires. To desire more is to rob Him. Superfluities are better in God's hand than in ours.

b. Sustenance for labour. Daily bread is given not that we may excel others, but that we may serve God. If we serve God truly, we must rejoice in the well-being of others.

c. Itself undeserved. God makes this covenant with us, but we had no claim to it. To claim it is to separate it from God's Love; and the gift of God separated from His Love loses its life.

POINT II. *Consider the debt.*

a. Dead works can only claim dead rewards. That is ' thine' which thou hast agreed for. It cannot give life nor sustain life. The penny needs the love of the Creator to give it living value. If we will not let others receive of the Creator's unlimited Love, we cannot receive it ourselves.

b. What the labourer claims as his own by right is his, and no longer is in the Householder's power. What is ours must be held in union with God's Love, otherwise it cannot live. Nothing lives which we call our own. What lives belongs to God. It is dead without the Creator's partnership.

c. What is ours we can take. It is of less value than ourselves. What belongs to God takes us up into God. We are apprehended of God when we receive His living gift.

POINT III. *Consider the dismissal of the labourer.*

a. What is ours? Either the Cross of Christ, which "take and follow Me," or earthly reward, which " take and go thy way."

b. Perseverance is an unlimited gift of love. To take our own is to go away. Christ would say to us, Thou art ever with Me, and all that I have is thine. If we take what comes to us, we must go into a far country with it and find its worthlessness.

c. The steward pays. The Lord dismisses. How careful we must be so to receive sacramental grace, that we may abide in Him whose Love is the Life of the Sacraments.

AFFECTIONS. Protestation of never leaving Christ. Contentedness without spiritual solace.

PRAYER.

O Lord Jesu Christ, teach me so to abide in Thy Love, that I may ever rejoice in Thy bounty toward all; and in conformity to Thy likeness may be perfected in Thine eternal Life. Amen.

THE EQUALITY OF THE GIFT.

PRELUDE. i. *I will give unto this last, even as unto thee.—*
S. Matt. xx. 14.

ii. As before.

POINT I. *Consider the universality of the gift.*

a. The gift is not assigned by arbitrary election. All who
were found were called, and all were to receive according
to the law of justice. Justice is universal and equal.

b. " Unto this last as unto thee." Love is superior to justice,
but not antagonistic. Love gave to the last not only the
penny, but its own infinite self besides. Love is ready to
give the same to the first if he will receive it. Works of
nature cannot merit grace. Perseverance is a reward to
those who have used the grace of the Covenant rightly.

POINT II. *Consider the bountifulness of the gift.*

a. Irrespective of length of service. One hour is with the
Eternal as a whole day. Immediate obedience is all.

b. Immeasurably beyond all value of work. Man's work
is earthly. God's payment is Divine Love, Eternal Life.

c. Pressingly offered even to the unthankful. God is still
willing to give even to the discontented one, if he will lay
aside his discontent. If he will give himself to God, God
will not send him away. It is his own fault if he goes
away asserting his own rights and rejecting God's love.

POINT III. *Consider the substance of the gift.*

a. It is the same to all, Eternal Love. But Love cannot be
without Truth. It is a gift of righteousness—" whatsoever
is just ye shall receive"—and to have it we must live in it.
We must be made righteous by the Love of God.

b. Eternal Love is the welcome of those who accept God's
call, even though that call do not come to them until the
eleventh hour. None can claim it, who have neglected it.

c. Eternal Love drives the discontented away as surely as it
quickens the faithful with the gift of life. It were no love
to sustain man with an unchanged heart of envy. If we
are to have God's Love, it must enable us to love as God
loves. The same gift is reward to one and punishment to
another.

AFFECTIONS. Praise to God for His bounty. Admiration
at the Love of God in rendering to us so much beyond our own
merit.

PRAYER.

*O God, Who in infinite mercy hast called me near that I may
partake of Thy Love, grant that I may so rejoice in Thine infinite
goodness, that I may evermore experience its power; and being
transformed into the glory of Thy Heavenly Life, may receive
Thine Eternal reward, through Jesus Christ our Lord. Amen.*

THE FREE GIFT.

PRELUDE. i. *Is it not lawful for Me to do what I will with Mine own?*—S. Matt. xx. 15.

ii. As before.

POINT I. *Consider the Divine Almightiness.*

    a. All things are His by Creation. None of His creatures can have anything unless He first creates it, that He may give it to them : He need not create, He need not give.

    b. All persons are His by creation, created for Himself, so that He has a right to use them as He will, and sustained by Himself, so that none can claim any existence but what God gives. No act merits reward, for all act by God's power.

    c. In giving various persons various things, God acts according to sovereign rights. " It is the Lord: let Him do what seemeth Him good."—1 Sam. iii. 18. Words of complaint against God's Will show their falseness by their feebleness.

POINT II. *Consider the Divine Freedom.*

    a. As He has creative power, so likewise He has legislative power.

    b. There is no one who has a right to gainsay His Will. His Power is not a mere collection of possibilities combined by chance, but a Personal Power of individual Will. Without the energy of individual Will, He would not be Himself.

    c. He is a law to Himself, for there is no one who can demand of Him an account. All must yield to His Will. There is no judge of His own actions external to Himself.

POINT III. *Consider the Divine Wisdom.*

    a. He is a law to Himself, and rejoices in His own Righteousness. The Freedom of God is a perfect basis of creative well-being; for His infinite Wisdom rejoices in the universal good. If His Freedom were void of infinite Wisdom, His infinite Power would be the terror of His creatures.

    b. His Wisdom cannot act without co-equal Love, for Wisdom consists in the knowledge of that wherein Love delights.

    c. If any have to " go their way," forfeiting their reward in God, it is because they " take their own" wisdom instead of God's Wisdom. His Wisdom did not fail to provide. Their folly rejected what He had provided.

AFFECTIONS. Self-surrender. Humiliation. Confidence. Joy in God.

PRAYER.

O Almighty God, Who in Thy wonderful goodness hast been pleased to call me to salvation in Thy Church, grant that I may always praise Thee for Thy glorious Sovereignty, wherein alone is my security, and accept the free gift of Thy Love, wherein alone I can attain to the predestination of Thine infinite Wisdom, through Jesus Christ Thy Son our Lord. Amen.

THE CONTEST BETWEEN GOOD AND EVIL.

PRELUDE. i. *Is thine eye evil, because I am good?*—S. Matt. xx. 15.

ii. As before.

POINT I. *Consider the goodness of God.*

  a. God is good. It is the simple goodness of God which provides for the well-being of His creatures, not according to their deserts, but according to His own desire.

  b. God is good in that He calls mankind everywhere to repent. If man could retain his evil, even when coming to God, then the Divine Being would be but a consummating evil, not a final good.

  c. God is good, in that He requires man to partake of His goodness ere he can partake of what His goodness provides. Dead gifts are not God's real gifts to man. We cannot know God's living goodness but by acting in His Love.

POINT II. *Consider the estimate of that goodness.*

  a. The goodness of God is but falsely seen from without. No one who is not abiding in God can know the mind of God. Even the features of goodness which can be recognized outside of Him rather bewilder than edify.

  b. The goodness of God must be estimated from within. Only with the mind of God can any one know the purpose of God.

  c. None can have this interior knowledge of the Divine goodness which the mind of God conveys, unless there be identity of loving action. We cannot appreciate God's actions unless we act in accordance with His goodness, and in the power of His Love.

POINT III. *Consider the evil of man as evidenced by His estimate of that goodness.*

  a. Man complains of God's goodness because he does not act along with it. We cannot complain of God's bounty to others, if we love them as God loves them.

  b. Man cannot complain of God as doing a wrong to any one, but his complaint manifests the evil regard with which he surveys the Divine Love in its glorious operations.

  c. The Divine goodness is the very test of man's evil, because it shows how incapable man is of rising up in a corresponding large-heartedness to desire simply the universal good.

AFFECTIONS. Self-mistrust. Praise of God. Desire of God's Truth. Detestation of man's littleness.

PRAYER.

O God, Whose goodness surpasseth all that I can desire, I entreat of Thee to perfect me in the holy energies whereby Thou wouldest have me to be conformed to Thyself, that loving others with the Love which Thou inspirest, I may know the Love wherein these inspirations shall find their reward; through J. C. our Lord. Amen.

THE FEWNESS OF THE ELECT.

PRELUDE. i. *So the last shall be first, and the first last: for many are called, but few chosen.*—S. Matt. xx. 16.

ii. As before.

POINT I. *Consider the largeness of God's call.*

a. The Householder goes forth into the market-place. The offer of salvation is not made in any private way. All that are without work, *i.e.* all who have found that the work of this world is not man's true work, are called in.

b. He goes forth again and again. Possibly those called before sunrise are the old Israel. A penny is promised. The law had temporal promises. Those at the third hour may be the Christians at Pentecost. "What is right, I will give you." Eternal life is a free gift. The Righteousness of God is given. The sixth and ninth hours imply special ages of missionary revival. Christ heads every mission. No man can effect anything unless Christ call the idlers in. The eleventh hour indicates a missionary age just before the judgment.

POINT II. *Consider the fewness of the Elect.*

a. Few come out of the market-place. How many are enslaved in the world's work and cannot come! Why are ye standing idle? Wilful idlers are not brought in.

b. There is no hint of any receiving the call more than once. If we slight God's Love, it will be hid from our eyes.

c. All who receive the call do not persevere. Have they endured the heat? Not enough. Love as Christ loves. Do Christ's work. So shalt thou persevere.

d. Few persevere; few love. Men grudge others the same grace as themselves. They think themselves wronged, unless God give something special. They labour not in the love of God, nor rejoice in the love of their neighbour.

POINT III. *Consider the results.*

a. The first become last; for the more we have known of God's gifts, the greater is our fall unless we abide in His grace.

b. The last become first. God's primary purpose for His elect does not fail. The last-called do not suffer because called last. God is as truly to be served by us now, as by any in any age before us; and His reward will be as complete now as it was to the first Martyrs of the Church.

AFFECTIONS. Diligence in serving God. Joy that others are blest by Him. Desire to bring others to Him.

PRAYER.

O Lord Jesu, grant that I may have such lively thankfulness for the Love wherewith Thou hast called me, that I may always rejoice to behold others partakers of the same ; so that whatever be the work in which by Thy grace I serve Thee, I may find my joy in the glory of Thy mystical Body, according to the power of the H. Ghost. Amen.

THE REGENERATIVE POWER OF GOD.

PRELUDE. i. *When much people were gathered together unto Jesus, and were come to Him out of every city, He spake by a parable, A sower went out to sow his seed.*—S. Luke viii. 4, 5.
ii. The Parable.

POINT I. *Consider the barrenness of the world.*
  a. Life is of God. The vegetable world sprang forth by the Word of God. No lifeless elements can generate a growing thing. So nature cannot generate the fruits of grace.
  b. Neither does the world desire it. The grades of life need what is inferior to themselves, but what is higher than themselves they perceive not. The plant does not conceive of the animal existence, nor the brutes of the rational. What is above is foolishness to that which is below.
  c. Without Life the world is profitless. What is of the world falls back naturally into the world. No creature rises above itself. Life which God gives raises the creature up towards Him. Divine Life lifts us out of ourselves to God.

POINT II. *Consider the coming forth of the Sower.*
  a. The Sower. He is the only Sower, for none can sow unless He first give the seed. All germs of life are His.
  b. He comes from the Father—from the existence which is true Life—into this life of ours, which is only death, having in Himself true Life that we may be regenerated.
  c. He comes forth into all the nations of the world. He Himself sows the seed. If He come not with His ministers, the seed could have no life. He comes repeatedly.

POINT III. *Consider the seed which He sows.*
  a. It is the seed of Life. Not an element of earthly origin alone, but a force superior to earth. The Divine Nature operates through Christ's Humanity with resistless power.
  b. It is Himself. He is the Word Incarnate. The Word which created all things at the beginning, becomes in the mystery of the Incarnation a seminal principle of life.
  c. It is full of power to grow up in all who receive it. It shows its power by gathering into itself our earthly nature, so that we are to become the Righteousness of God in Him, bringing forth supernatural fruit to the glory of His Name.

AFFECTIONS. Desire of holiness. Praise to God for the gifts of supernatural power. Simple self-surrender to the Divine Life. Diligence in using the means of grace.

PRAYER.

O Lord Jesu Christ, Who hast come forth into this world of ours from the glory wherein Thou art ever abiding with the Father, grant that we may so accept Thee in the means of Grace which Thou hast ordained, that we may bring forth the fruits of righteousness according to Thine eternal purpose, and may attain to dwell with Thee in that Glory by the power of the Holy Ghost. Amen.

THE SEED SOWN.

PRELUDE. i. *The seed is the Word of God: but the Sower is Christ.*—S. Luke viii. 11.

ii. As in the Parable.

POINT I. *Consider the seed of Intellectual Truth.*

  a. Man's mind has a craving for higher truth than it can reach by nature. No knowledge naturally acquired can give the mind rest. We desire to know more. The wisdom of God is that wherein the mind can repose.

  b. All knowledge naturally acquired is superficial only, not real, essential knowledge. That can only be obtained by union with the mind of the Creator.

  c. The Wisdom of God is the supernatural Truth wherein the mind of man finds perfection. This we can only get by having Christ as our Life, and knowing truth not by external experience, but by interior germinating consciousness.

POINT II. *Consider the seed of Moral Truth.*

  a. The moral nature of man is moulded by external discipline, and habits are formed. But after all these may be lost or changed. We are conscious of their being hollow. Man's nature lost its substantial morality by the Fall.

  b. The nature of Christ fills up this hollowness with a living principle operating from within, and forms the life externally by its germinating power. The supernatural virtues are thus infused into us.

POINT III. *Consider the seed of Spiritual Truth.*

  a. The fallen nature has no natural capacity of spiritual Truth remaining. It is dead. S. Jude says of those who separate themselves from the Body of Christ, " They are sensual :" *i.e.*, capable only of the life of the lower soul; "having not the spirit." The spiritual nature is dead within them. In the hour of man's sin he died. This spiritual life was lost.

  b. The humanity of Christ having the Divine Nature indissolubly present within itself by reason of the hypostatic union, is a renewing principle of Spiritual Life, by which those who receive Him have power to become the sons of God, becoming identified with the Only-begotten Son.

AFFECTIONS. Desire of growth according to this new life. Care in cherishing the supernatural faculties thus given. Love of Christ, Who thus transforms and raises us.

PRAYER.

O God, Who hast given Thine only Son to be within us the seed of a new creation, whereby we may become faithful unto Thee, grant us so to abide in union with Him Who is Thy Word, that we may attain to Thy Truth, and so to act in His power, that we may be perfected in Thy likeness; through the same Jesus Christ our Lord. Amen.

THE ETERNAL LIFE OF THE SEED.

PRELUDE.   i. *He that heareth Him, abideth for ever.*—
S. Luke viii. 11.

    ii. As in the Parable.

POINT I.   *Consider the Eternal Life of the Seed.*

    a. The seed of earth has a life which can be destroyed. The
Body of the Incarnate Word has a Life that cannot be destroyed. Natural life has no existence save as quickening
the seed. Eternal Life exists in itself without any body,
and by reason of the hypostatic union it cannot be lost by
the Body of Christ. His living Person yields not to death.

    b. The Life of the Seed is a force which takes things external
into union with itself. The seed grows. The life is one.
The Eternal Life of Christ's Body takes us into Christ.
The Church grows as a Body having one imperishable Life.

POINT II.   *Consider the hearing of Eternal Life.*

    a. Faith cometh by hearing, and hearing by the Word of
God. Human words avail not. The Word *is* God.

    b. First there is the external hearing. The gift of preventing
grace draws us to Christ, but this is not enough.

    c. Next, internal hearing. Christ, the Word, is the Seed of
Divine Life given to our whole nature by the Sacraments,
first of all in Holy Baptism.

POINT III.   *Consider the results of Eternal Life in the hearers.*

    a. The results of this interior hearing vary according to the
disposition of the heart.

    b. The individual thus incorporated into Christ partakes of
Eternal Life. The Life is Eternal in itself and in the
whole Church, but is not inherent in the individual.

    c. Unless the "hearing" be complete, there is no assurance
of grace being indefectible. Advanced Christians may fall
away. The Life, however, is still eternal, for it does not
belong to the individual. As long as we hear we abide.
Not he that hath heard, but he that does hear, abides.

    d. The Life is not augmented by the growth of the seed.
The Church is the fulness of Him that filleth all in all;
but the Divine Life is not increased by the multitude of the
faithful. This One Life makes the Church one in spite of
external differences.

AFFECTIONS.   Adoration of the Mystery of regenerate Life.
Care in watching for its preservation.

PRAYER.

O *God and Heavenly Father, Who hast given Thy Son to bring
us out of our natural deadness to the participation of Thy glorious
Life, grant that I may so abide in Him with constant faith and
love, that the power of His indwelling may be manifest within me,
and I may have my portion with Thy whole Church, in Thine
everlasting kingdom, through the same J. C. our Lord. Amen.*

THE GOOD GROUND.

PRELUDE. i. *But that on the good ground are they, which in an honest and good heart, having heard the word, keep it, and bring forth fruit with patience.*—S. Luke viii. 15.

ii. As in the Parable.

POINT I. *Consider the necessity of cleansing the soil.*

    a. It must be free from stones. The heart must be cleared of all hardness of pride or unbelief, which prevents the good seed of grace from striking its fibres into it.

    b. It must be cleared from weeds. The heart must not be choked with the cares of this world, which exhaust all its energies, so that they can no longer nourish what is good.

    c. It must be soft, so as to receive the moisture which falls upon it from heaven. The heart must not be crusted over by worldly maxims, habits of routine, and the like.

POINT II. *Consider the necessity of richness in the soil.*

    a. There must be the properties necessary for the growth of the plants. The heart must have proper dispositions. It must be honest or honourable by its nature.

    b. The excellence of the soil consists in the decay of the former vegetation which clothed it. The excellence of the heart consists in mortified dispositions. Primary excellence belongs not to the fallen heart of man, but richness resulting from decay. That which grows by nature must die so as to make soil fit for the growth of grace.

    c. There must be depth. The heart must be dug deep with penitence, otherwise it will not be good. Mortifications without penitence are like a heap of leaves that have not been dug into the soil.

POINT III. *Consider the receptive power of the good soil.*

    a. It lays hold upon the seed, drawing out its fibres. The mortified penitent heart lays hold on Christ.

    b. More truly, the seed lays hold upon the ground. The grace of Christ lays hold upon the heart that has proper dispositions.

    c. The ground can germinate in fruitfulness only through the seed. Its own natural growth, however strong, is unfruitful. The heart germinates only by becoming one with Christ, and as a member of Christ. It receives Christ into itself. It grows up through the organic power of Christ's Body.

AFFECTIONS. Patience. Deadness to the world. Welcome to grace.

PRAYER.

O God, Who hast sent Thy Son to form us anew with living power unto all good works, grant that I may so die to every thought of this world, that I may be truly incorporated into Him, and bring forth fruit with the energy of Eternal Life, through Him Who liveth and reigneth with Thee One God, world without end. Amen.

PATIENT FAITHFULNESS.

PRELUDE. i. *But that on the good ground are they which, in an honest and good heart, having heard the word, keep it, and bring forth fruit with patience.*—S. Luke viii. 15.
ii. As in the Parable.

POINT I. *Consider the necessity of apprehension.*
   a. The soil must lay hold of the seed, neither losing it by carelessness nor leaving it unappropriated by dryness. The soul must keep and appropriate the seed of grace by the softening energy of the Holy Ghost.
   b. It must become identified with the seed. The soul must be taken into the living organism of the Body of Christ.
   c. It brings forth fruit by the virtue of the power which incorporates it. The soul brings forth fruit unto Christ, and that fruit is the substantial reproduction of Christ communicating a supernatural form and power to the earthly elements of our nature, which He incorporates.

POINT II. *Consider the necessity of endurance.*
   a. The plant will have to bear parching suns and violent storms. The life of grace can never be exempt from difficulties. These show what nourishment the ground is giving to the seed.
   b. It may be checked by frosts, but it is not killed by them. The outward manifestation of divine growth may be hindered, but the inner life must ever work. There can be no intermission of spiritual life if there is to be fruitfulness in the end.
   c. These struggles of the plant with the exterior difficulty tend to its final strengthening and greater fruitfulness. We must so meet every difficulty that we may have our union with Christ strengthened thereby.

POINT III. *Consider the necessity of perseverance.*
   a. The plant must live through its complete period ere it can bear fruit. There is no short way of attaining to sanctification in Christ.
   b. Each plant while developing has its appointed measure of maturity. There is a predestination of grace which God has for each faithful soul, and we must keep the hope of it in remembrance.

AFFECTIONS. Patience. Interior watchfulness. Conformity to Christ. Stedfastness.

PRAYER.

Grant, O Lord God, that I may so yield myself up to the transforming power which is in Thy dear Son, that I may bear fruit to the glory of Thy Name which shall be accepted of Thee in the day of His appearing, Who liveth and reigneth with Thee in the unity of the Holy Ghost, God for ever and ever. Amen.

THE DANGER OF WITHERING.

PRELUDE. i. *If ye would be My disciples, have root in your-selves, lest in time of temptation ye fall away.*—S. Luke viii. 13. ii. As in the Parable.

POINT I. *Consider the will to be Christ's disciples.*

 a. Many wish to be saved by Christ from punishment, never having learned of Him. If we would be His disciples we must be saved from sin, being taught in the way of holiness by the Holy Ghost.

 b. Many are convinced of the Truth of Christ, and yet cannot be His disciples for want of a good will. There must be the love of the Truth if we would be saved.

 c. If we would know the Truth, we must have Jesus for our Master. In vain we know the abstract truth of Christianity. We must know Christ as the Personal Truth Incarnate.

POINT II. *Consider what it is to have root.*

 a. The root has life in itself, not from the soil. The Life of Christ in the soul is His, not ours. The best soil makes no root, and the best natural disposition makes no Christian.

 b. The root absorbs the juices of the soil, transforming them into itself. We must have all the true elements of our nature taken up into Christ and transformed by this absorption. Henceforth they can be given to nothing but Him.

 c. The root spreads through the soil. The Life of Christ takes more and more possession of the character. It must go on growing until it have absorbed our whole nature.

POINT III. *Consider the falling away.*

 a. Temptation is certain. The gift of Christ cannot be secure to us unless it be tested. It is worth nothing unless it bear the test.

 b. To be Christ's disciples we must appropriate His Life. In proportion to our consciousness must be our appropriation. We appropriate Christ by giving ourselves up to Him.

 c. If the Life of Christ wither within us, it is because we are wanting to it, not it to us. The best seed grows not in bad soil. The seed is Eternal Life, but we fall away.

AFFECTIONS. Love of Christ. Absorbing surrender to Him. Endeavour to grow in His likeness. Desire of perseverance.

PRAYER.

O God, Who hast made me partaker of Eternal Life by the gift of Thy Son, grant that I may be so absorbed in His Love, that I may be conformed to His Truth and strengthened to abide in my hour of trial, through the same Jesus Christ our Lord. Amen.

F 2

THE HINDRANCES TO PERFECTION.

PRELUDE. i. *If ye would bring fruit to perfection, be not choked with cares and riches and pleasures of this life.*—S. Luke viii. 14.

ii. As in the Parable.

POINT I. *Consider the necessity of perfection.*

    a. Our life must be to God's glory. No imperfect work can truly glorify Him.

    b. Our life must be our own joy. The fuller our knowledge of God may be, the greater will be our shame if we are not perfect, and our sorrow because we do not glorify God.

    c. Our perfection must consist in fruitfulness. The righteousness of the law is to be accomplished in us who are made the righteousness of God in Christ. There is no being righteous save by doing righteousness.—1 S. John iii. 7.

POINT II. *Consider how the good seed is choked.*

    a. The Divine Life within us is a principle of perfect life, however much it may be hindered by our sinfulness. There is no such thing as imperfect life.

    b. Its natural consequence is to produce all the blessed fruits of the Spirit, according to the new Creation of God (Gal. v. 22). This supernatural fruitfulness is its very nature.

    c. It requires to be carefully cleansed from all surroundings of natural evil. The work of the flesh growing up in the heart prevents the development of the good seed.

POINT III. *Consider the choking upgrowth of natural evil.*

    a. Cares. The good fruit ripens for another world. If we are anxious about results in this life, however good, they choke the good seed. Our fruit becomes matured, not by our living long, but by our dying well.

    b. Riches. It matters not how much we have done, but how divinely we have done it. The power of this world chokes our spiritual life. It is hard to think of the things of this world, whether as matters of desire or of possession, without being drawn back from the simple joy of Divine power.

    c. Pleasures. Pleasure in this life is only abortive fruit. The righteousness which is of God yields its fruit in another world. The works of God's people still follow them. Here we deceive ourselves, forgetting our sin. We mistake present pleasure for Divine fruit.

AFFECTIONS. Detachment. Shrinking from this world. Watchfulness over the conscience. Hope of eternal reward.

PRAYER.

O Lord Jesus Christ, Who hast sent me forth into the world that my life may be to the glory of the Father by the power of Thy grace, grant that I may keep both my mind and my affections so free from the pollution of earthly desires, that I may be found fruitful unto Thee in all which of Thy mercy Thou wouldst effect. Amen.

GOING UP TO JERUSALEM.

PRELUDE. i. *Behold, we go up to Jerusalem, and all things that are written concerning the Son of Man shall be accomplished. For He shall be delivered unto the Gentiles, and shall be mocked and spitted on: and they shall scourge Him, and put Him to death: and the third day He shall rise again.* S. Luke xviii. 31–33.

ii. The Apostles wondering and sorrowing at the words of Jesus.

POINT I. *Consider the City Jerusalem to which ascent is made.*
- *a.* The earthly Jerusalem. The City which prophecy seemed to mark out so gloriously for Messiah. This glory was to be, but could not be yet. Jesus goes up to suffer.
- *b.* The heavenly Jerusalem, the mystical City of God. Wonderful things are spoken of this city. Nevertheless this also, *i.e.* that part of it which is upon the earth, must fall into harlotry, rebellion against God. Here too Jesus suffers.
- c. The glorious Jerusalem, adorned for the Marriage Feast. Hither the company of Jesus ascend. Sweet Vision of Peace at the great Easter! Gladly we go up. Predicted sorrows are but a token of the truth of promises to follow.

POINT II. *Consider their expectation of suffering.*
- *a.* They used to overlook the prophecies of sorrow. Jesus bids them open their eyes to these. Difficulties which encompass the Jerusalem that now is, must not blind us.
- *b.* Suffering is not to stop short of death. How He can reign upon David's Throne if He die, they could not tell. We must not despair of the Church, however fallen; God can give her deliverance just when He pleases, but on His own conditions. Foretold sorrows must be accomplished in the mystical as in the earthly Jerusalem for our discipline The resurrection and its glory shall follow.

POINT III. *Consider the moral ascent to Jerusalem.*
- *a.* The way lies through the Valley of the Shadow of Death. The glory of the end warrants no exemptions by the way.
- *b.* Jesus still suffers in His people. He is morally delivered to the Gentiles when the way of the world is set in place of His law.
- *c.* We must not deliver Jesus to the Gentiles in our hearts by worldly maxims. We must go up to Jerusalem with Jesus, and abide with Him there. Troubles are round about, but our hearts abide in the Vision of Peace.

AFFECTIONS. Desire of Heaven. Acceptance of temptation. Stedfast faith.

PRAYER.

O Blessed Jesu, as Thou callest me to go up with Thee to the Heavenly Feast, suffer me not to fall away, but even though the unfaithful prevail within Thy Holy City, grant that I may endure with Thee unto the end in all temptations, and at length may attain through Thy merits to the Vision of Eternal Peace. Amen.

THE PENITENT'S CRY FOR MERCY.

PRELUDE. i. *Jesus, Thou Son of David, have mercy on me.*
—S. Luke xviii. 38.

ii. As in the narrative of the miracle.

POINT I. *Consider the title of Jesus.*

    a. If we would go up to Jerusalem as penitents, we must cry unto Jesus. He is going up. We cannot follow unless He opens our eyes. So shall He save us.

    b. The blind man called Him by that name, as he might have called any one else. Yet, did not the Name of Saviour have a meaning to his heart as he spake it? We must be blind indeed, if we do not perceive its meaning for ourselves.

    c. The multitude said that Jesus passed by, yet they knew not the meaning. Are we Christians, because those around us own Jesus as the Christ? Unless we know Him in some better way than they do, we shall get little good.

POINT II. *Consider the appeal to Him as Son of David.*

    a. The appeal is not to human sympathy alone, but to Divine Love. The gift of Messiah was originated in God's purpose, not in man's request. "God so loved the world that He sent His Son." David was the Beloved.

    b. Also to Divine Truth. God had promised. The sure mercies of David could not fail.

    c. Also to Divine Power. Messiah must be powerful to restore not only a nation, but the individual members thereof. No difficulty could be too great for him.

POINT III. *Consider the individuality of the need.*

    a. Suffering is individual. The general progress of society helps the individual but little. Messiah must help individually. Do I know Jesus as helping *me?*

    b. Men feel their individual pain; not always their individual sin. Sin must be felt as an individual burden, otherwise Jesus cannot be known truly.

    c. Individually we must come before Jesus. It is not enough to let Him single us out for help if He will. We must single ourselves out before Him, crying out to Him with the particular burden of our own sin. The multitude must not stop us.

AFFECTIONS. Confidence. Expectation. Forgetfulness of the world. Absorbing sense of need.

PRAYER.

O Blessed Jesu, bring me to the Vision of Thy Peace, and purge away the darkness of sin from mine eyes, I beseech Thee; so that following Thee in grace I may be with Thee in the glory to which Thou callest me, Who ever livest with the Father in the unity of the Holy Ghost, God for ever and ever. Amen.

THE PENITENT BEFORE JESUS.

PRELUDE. i. Lord, *that I may receive my sight.*—S. Luke xviii. 41.

ii. The man standing in the midst of the crowd before Jesus.

POINT I. *Consider his sense of need.*

a. He knew not whither he was going. In sin we know not whither our actions tend. There is an Enemy who is ever turning the blind out of the way. Yet he heard Jesus call.

b. He knew not who might be near him. In our blindness we see not God, nor the holy Angels, nor the cloud of witnesses, nor the multitude of devils that are ever near us.

c. He despaired not as He stood before Jesus. He could not see Jesus; Jesus saw him. We in prayer see not. By faith we must see Jesus while we pray to Him. He sees us.

POINT II. *Consider the necessity of the gift.*

a. Jesus did not mock him when He called him. The man trusted Jesus. Do we trust Jesus, as meaning what He says when He offers to answer our prayer?

b. He looked for a real gift from Jesus. He dropped his cloak, though he could never hope to find it again. The gift of Jesus was worth more. Do we so look to Jesus as to be without anxiety whatever we may lose in coming to Him?

c. He expected to experience a change in himself by the gift of Jesus. The truest gifts of Jesus are His gifts within, whereby He changes our very selves.

POINT III. *Consider the power implied by the word, Lord.*

a. The conventional titles of respect must rise to the full demands of faith as we address Jesus. Every title by which we know Him must enshrine the consciousness of Divine glory. It were vain to know Jesus merely as a fellow-man upon the earth.

b. Titles of human respect have no truth when addressed to any but Jesus. All human relationships serve only to symbolize the Truth wherein we are bound to Him.

c. He to Whom we cry for help is the Lord, Who rules all. There is no necessity in which He cannot help, for there is no place in which He is not Lord.

d. If we would know Him as Lord to supply all our need, we must honour Him everywhere as the Lord to Whom our homage is due. The blind man was not ashamed of Jesus before the multitude. I must not be ashamed of Him.

AFFECTIONS. Joy in the presence of Jesus, though unseen. Attachment to Jesus unseen more than to the world of sense.

PRAYER.

O Blessed Jesu, enable me so to realize Thy continual Presence wherein I have to live, that I may alway rely upon Thine assistance, act in Thy grace, obey Thy commands, honour Thee in the presence of all men, and fear nothing save to lose Thy Love. **Amen.**

THE PENITENT ACCEPTED.

PRELUDE. i. *Receive thy sight: thy faith hath saved thee.*
—S. Luke xviii. 42.

ii. As before.

POINT I. *Consider the dignity of the Speaker.*

   a. The simplicity of power. Jesus speaks without effort, without hesitation, without display.

   b. The readiness of the reply. It is the simple acceptance of the petition. Great as is the gift, yet it is given without any conditions or inquiries.

   c. The certainty of the result. The sight comes to the man immediately. His former blindness passes away. Jesus, the Eternal Light, will give light to all who ask Him.

POINT II. *Consider the transformation effected.*

   a. The surprise of the man waking to see the world. What new sensations rushed into his mind. What does faith reveal to my soul? Do I see things invisible to the natural heart?

   b. The changed relationship between him and the multitude, of whom he had begged in his blindness. Formerly pitied or despised, as having God's chastisement; now honoured and almost feared, as the special object of God's power.

   c. His gratitude and his consciousness of the power of Jesus. His very nature testified to that power. What has God done for me? Do I in the consciousness of deliverance from the yoke of sin feel God's power in myself?

POINT III. *Consider the triumph of faith.*

   a. The approbation of Jesus was of even more value than the gift of sight. It is not the glory of Heaven which the penitent seeks. He triumphs in a Saviour's Love. The approval of Jesus is the sufficient reward of His faith. To seek anything more would be an injury to faith.

   b. With what confidence would one approach Jesus who had heard such words from Him. Jesus is not displeased at us because we seek much. Rather he bids us ask more.

   c. How much better blindness with faith than eyesight as that of the multitude who had not faith. They gained no blessing, as Jesus past away from them to go to Jerusalem. Jesus came into the world to save sinners. They who would profit by His coming must feel their need of it.

AFFECTIONS. Trust. Prayerfulness. Perseverance in prayer. Gratitude. Humiliation.

PRAYER.

O Lord Jesus, I come to Thee in the blindness of my sinful nature, beseeching Thee to open mine eyes to Thy Glory. Perfect Thou my faith, and lead me onward with increasing desire to the attainment of Thine increasing revelations here below, that I may at length receive the fulness of sight in the unity of perfect Love, according to the fulness of Thine own unchangeable Truth. Amen.

GOD GLORIFIED IN PENITENCE.

PRELUDE. i. *All the people, when they saw it, gave praise unto God.*—S. Luke xviii. 43.

ii. The multitude shouting on all sides in wonder and praise.

POINT I. *Consider the sympathy of the bystanders.*

    a. Their wonder. The multitude applaud marvels, but praise not God for His ordinary gifts of nature or of grace.

    b. Their want of love to God. God's wonders excite imagination, but do not stir love. The blind man loved before the miracle more than the multitude did after seeing it. The sight of God's power does not awaken love.

    c. Their curiosity as to the man himself. They think of what Jesus had done for him, rather than feel their need that Jesus should do something for themselves.

POINT II. *Consider the world's estimate of the penitent.*

    a. Worldly advantages of reformation. The multitude can appreciate the benefit of eyesight, but the approval with which it was given has no response in their hearts.

    b. Hear many complaining that Jesus should help the beggar, whereas He leaves them in their trouble, though much more deserving. " Why does He do so much for that man, and not set my trouble right?" Because they ask not.

POINT III. *Consider the glory of God as the true end of penitence.*

    a. We must not shrink from letting God's gifts be seen. Better the approval. of Jesus than the gift of eyesight. Better to praise Jesus than to see the world. We must give all glory to Jesus if we would be acknowledged by Him.

    b. We must remember to use them for His glory. Wonderful to see the world! O much more wonderful to see Jesus the Saviour of the world! If our eyes are opened, how can we look at anything save Jesus!

    c. We must seek to bring others to partake of the same Almighty Love. If we know what it is to have been blind, we must gaze upon the world with the intense sympathy which its blindness demands. To be blind to it, matters little. To be blind to Jesus, is to be dead indeed. Our life must show His praise who gives us sight.

AFFECTIONS. Desire for Jesus to be known. Endeavour to bring others to make their needs known to Him.

PRAYER.

O Jesu, Lord of Light and Power, grant that I may have my understanding filled with the Light of Thy Truth, and my heart purified with the Light of Thy Love, so that I may behold Thy Glory as the glory of my inmost soul, and show forth Thy Glory in the radiance of Thy grace, whereby others may be drawn to Thee, and all may be established in the perfection of Thine Eternal Light, to the glory of God the Father. Amen.

THE DUTY OF FASTING.

PRELUDE. i. *When ye fast, be not as the hypocrites, of a sad countenance.*—S. Matt. vi. 16.

ii. Our Lord taking us with Himself into the wilderness.

POINT I. *Consider our Lord setting us the example.*

a. " I have given you an example, that ye should follow My steps." Wherever our Lord goes we must follow Him in this world. So shall we, whithersoever He goeth in the next.

b. Fasting were a burdensome task in the loneliness of our own sense of sin. We must fast with Him Who fasted for us.

c. We must not expect the sensible consolation of His Presence whilst fasting. His fasting was a hiding of His Godhead as a penitent. We must have Him hidden with us in penitence, to be afterwards manifested to us in pardon.

POINT II. *Consider the reasons of our Lord's Fast.*

a. For our sins. He humbled Himself to bear the necessary pains of our sinful estate, and so also to voluntary penitential suffering for our sins.

b. For the subdual of the Flesh. Although His Flesh was pure and spotless, yet it was necessary to develop therein the energy of the Holy Spirit, by the sacrifice of its natural desires, although they were sinless.

c. For the overthrow of Satan. Satan had overthrown Eve by leading her to eat what was forbidden. Jesus would overthrow Satan by abstaining from that which was naturally lawful, waiting upon the sustenance which the Father gives.

POINT III. *Consider the duty of following Him.*

a. We cannot else show our gratitude. It were a poor recompense for us to seek nothing save bodily gratification when He endured such pains of fasting for our sake.

b. We cannot else carry out His work undertaken for our sanctification. If fasting was needful in the purity of His nature, much more must it be in the sinfulness of ours.

c. We cannot else fight against Satan. Our Lord says of some evil spirits, that they go not out save by prayer and fasting. We must not deny this. We may suffer in being beaten by Satan, otherwise we must suffer in beating Satan down. Our flesh is His stronghold.

AFFECTION. Contrition. Desire of humiliation. Gratitude to Jesus. Self-surrender.

PRAYER.

O Lord Jesu, Who didst fast forty days and forty nights on my account, grant that I, beholding Thy humiliation, which Thou didst willingly undergo for my sins and for the whole world, may humble myself, so that being sanctified in the fellowship of Thy triumph, I may be perfected in holiness with all Thy Saints to the glory of God the Father. Amen.

THE REALITY OF FASTING.

PRELUDE. i. *When ye fast, be not as the hypocrites, of a sad countenance.*—S. Matt. vi. 16.

ii. Our Lord's example.

POINT I. *Consider His forty days in the Wilderness.*

   a. Its voluntary character. The Holy Ghost led Him thither, but His own will accepted the discipline. He would not work a miracle to alleviate His own pain, although in a few days' time He was going to work a miracle to enhance the simple joys of others.

   b. Its bodily suffering. He suffered from hunger as truly as we do. We must not think that His inherent Life made Him indifferent to natural sustenance.

   c. Its exposure to the assaults of Satan. Satan is sure to be aroused against any effort of spiritual life. This mysterious Fast demonstrated the truth of the words which he had heard spoken at Jordan. The Beloved Son is the object of his special hatred.

POINT II. *Consider the reality of the penalty due for sin.*

   a. The reality of Christ's satisfaction. He took our nature in its truth, and paid our debt in the truth of our nature.

   b. The reality of our participation. We must participate in what He has done, by using the power which He gives us to carry on the same law of action which He began.

   c. The reality of the change to be effected. Sin is a reality. Contrition a reality. Grace a reality. The transformation of a pardoned life a reality. The change cannot be attained unless the reality of grace be shown by real works of contrition.

POINT III. *Consider the reality of the enemies whom by fasting we assail.*

   a. The body needs real discipline to overthrow its evil passions, which cannot be mortified without real pain.

   b. Satan does not find us really aggressive unless we rise up to struggle against him in his own spiritual life. While we remain under the dominion of bodily gratification, we fail of grappling with him.

   c. The world is attacked by fasting. We must be separated for a time, and live in witness against the world.

AFFECTIONS. Antagonism against our three enemies. Reliance upon the grace of Christ. Resolution to join with Him in His struggle.

PRAYER.

O Lord Jesu, help me to use Thy grace in mortifying the natural desires of my sinful flesh, that I may rise superior to its dominion, and in the freedom which Thou givest may be able both to triumph over the assaults of evil spirits and to exult in the fruition of Thy Divine Love, Who with the Father and the Holy Ghost livest and reignest God for ever and ever. **Amen.**

THE EXTERIOR PEACEFULNESS OF FASTING.

PRELUDE.   i. *When ye fast, be not as the hypocrites, of a sad countenance.*—S. Matt. vi. 16.

ii. The calmness of Christ.

POINT I.   *Consider the devotional self-surrender of penitence.*

    a. The sense of duty owing to Almighty God Whose goodness has been outraged. We fast in vain, if we do it not as an act which God requires. The thought of God must hush all else in hearts that love Him.

    b. The sense of our utmost efforts being nothingness in comparison with that which Christ has done. The stimulus of human example gives earnestness and tranquillity. Much more the example of the Incarnate God.

    c. The sense of the Holy Spirit's guidance. Penitence is the work of the Holy Ghost in the heart. This cannot be along with any hypocritical assumption. It rather seeks to hide itself than to be known.

POINT II.   *Consider the patient acceptance of suffering.*

    a. The penitent soul is thankful to suffer. It dies to the world which has led it into sin. Mortification no more permits of display than exhaustion does. The soul learns the greatness of Almighty God and the reverence due to Him.

    b. Without the Holy Ghost, our fast will be no mortification. If the Holy Ghost is with us, we cannot boast of His Presence. He withdraws from the proud.

POINT III.   *Consider the tranquil expectation of Divine Love.*

    a. The Hope of Divine Love soon to manifest itself fills the heart with satisfaction. That loving fellowship will not allow of any feigned or exaggerated pretence.

    b. We must seek to be worthy of the Love which we desire. We can only attain to God's love by abiding in His Truth.

    c. The world is incapable of entering into the joy of this Love. Therefore the heart cannot seek its sympathy; for it knows that its penitence is folly to the world, and cannot be explained to it.

AFFECTIONS.   Restfulness.   Love of retirement.   Secret contemplation of God.

PRAYER.

O Lord Jesu, grant that I may abide in the calmness of Thy Holy Life hidden from the world, so that by secret mortification in the power of Thy Holy Spirit, I may attain to the manifestation of Thy glory, which the world seeth not, and may be accepted of the Father through Thy merits, Who art our only Mediator and Advocate. Amen.

THE INTERIOR JOY OF FASTING.

PRELUDE. i. *When ye fast, be not as the hypocrites, of a sad countenance.*—S. Matt. vi. 16.

ii. Thyself alone with Jesus, Who encourages thee to suffer by manifestation of His own glory while He speaks with Thee.

POINT I. *Consider the joy which Jesus gives.*

    a. The joy of sympathy. He has felt thy hunger. The sympathy of God manifest in the flesh sums up all joy. It equals all sorrow, outshines it, disperses it.

    b. The joy of spiritual strength. Jesus is an energetic principle of power. The creative Word speaks through our nature as the recreative Word. We live by the Word which cometh forth from the mouth of God.

    c. The joy of revealed glory. Jesus bids us think of the glory into which He entered after His suffering. That glory He sets before us as our own reward in penitence.

POINT II. *Consider the joy of uniting our will to God's Will.*

    a. The joy of Fatherly approval. The Father delights in us as members of His Son, if we are true in our flesh to the Life which that Eternal Son exhibited below.

    b. The joy of spiritual consciousness. The Holy Ghost is the Spirit of joy, the oil of gladness. In the emptiness of what would naturally satisfy we begin to experience the sweetness of His blessed energy by Whom alone God's will can be done.

    c. The joy of renewal in grace. By fasting in a devout sense of union with Christ and with the power of the Holy Ghost, we partake of Divine gifts which are ever increasing.

POINT III. *Consider the joy which holiness brings.*

    a. Ours is a victorious war with the great enemy. However great the struggle against Satan may be, nevertheless the joy of resisting him is proportionately great. Fasting brings grievous temptations along with it, yet is there great joy in enduring until the hold of Satan over us be loosed.

    b. We experience the blessedness of God's original Predestination. In setting earthly joy aside, our hope revives.

    c. We gather encouragement by which to carry out holy resolutions for the time to come. The successive struggles of holiness do not leave us as they found us.

AFFECTION. Spiritual boldness. Joy in the Holy Ghost. Union of heart with Jesus. Consciousness of God seeing us.

PRAYER.

O Lord Jesu, grant that I may so abide in union with Thee in every act of penitential self-discipline, that I may bring my body under control to Thy Holy Spirit by fasting, and may, by the unction of Thy Holy Spirit, experience the joy of the Father's Love which is shed forth on us abundantly in Thee, and through Thee, while we remain stedfast in the acts of that life of penitence which Thou callest us to share with Thee in this sinful world. Amen.

THE REALITY OF TEMPTATION.

PRELUDE. i. *Then was Jesus led up of the Spirit into the wilderness to be tempted of the devil. And when He had fasted forty days and forty nights, He was afterward an hungred.*—S. Matt. iv. 1, 2.

ii. Jesus weak and worn with hunger. Satan standing over Him in great display of power.

POINT I. *Consider the weakness of Christ's Humanity.*

a. Reàlized in personal consciousness by suffering.

b. Contrasted with the power of him who is the Prince of this world.

c. Sustained by the indwelling Spirit of God, by reason of the indissoluble union wherein that humanity is hypostatically joined with the Eternal Godhead of the Onlybegotten Son.

POINT II. *Consider the weakness of Christ's Church, His Mystical Body.*

a. Brought out from age to age in various modes of experience, while the faithful in the world seem to be left, as— 1. The scorn of men. 2. Forsaken of God in appearance. 3. A prey to the Evil One.

b. Contrasted with the political organization, power, dignity of the world.

c. Sustained by the promised gift of the Spirit received at Pentecost. (1) abiding, although hidden; (2) personally ministering, so as to avert the triumph of the powers of death; (3) binding in covenanted fellowship of life with the Incarnate Saviour.

POINT III. *Consider the weakness of the individual Christian.*

a. Suffering from temptations which seem to crush us.

b. Experiencing temptation all the more whilst we seek in exercises of devotion to resist Satan.

c. Sustained by gifts of grace, which we must lay hold of continually, as pledged to us in that we are members of Christ.

AFFECTIONS. Confidence. Endurance. Acceptance of difficulty. Gratitude towards the Holy Ghost.

PRAYER

O Almighty God, let me flee to Thee in every season of temptation; and the greater may be the assaults of the Enemy, so let me find the power of Thy grace increasingly manifested for my support, through Jesus Christ, Thy Son our Lord. Amen.

THE ENCOURAGEMENT OF THE FAITHFUL.

PRELUDE. i. *Come, ye blessed of My Father, inherit the Kingdom prepared for you from the foundation of the world.*—S. Matt. xxv. 34.

ii Christ upon His Throne. The faithful gathered out from amongst the multitude of mankind to the welcome of His glory.

POINT I. *Consider the separatedness of the faithful from the world.*

    a. *Now,* by obedience to the Rule of Christ under the law of His Kingdom. This is a law of power which separates us by the gift of a nature distinct from the unregenerate world.

    b. *Then,* by the welcome of the Voice of Christ in the revelation of His Kingdom. This welcome is no mere external call, but a manifestation of indwelling, glorifying lustre, whereby the members of Christ are like to Him in His Majesty.

POINT II. *Consider the reward of the Faithful.*

    a. Prepared from all Eternity according to the fulness of God's predestinating Love.

    b. Inherited in time by the communication of Christ's unmerited grace.

    c. Secured in probation by obedience to His commands. All the acts of life which have been wrought in the power of Divine grace, live on in the brightness of this Eternal welcome.

POINT III. *Consider the call of the Faithful.*

    a. *Now,* from the Cross, to follow Christ in the endurance of the world's hatred. Blessed are the ears which hear this call of Christ. The love of the Crucified more than compensates for all evil which the world can do.

    b. *Then,* from the manifested Throne of Glory to enter into the fulness of His Joy.

    c. Appealing to our will *now,* that we may come out from the world, though we see the Cross close.

    d. Filling us with rapture *then,* that the will which has chosen Christ may have its delight in Christ by the perfect contemplation of His Glory whereinto it enters.

AFFECTIONS. Separation from the world. Joy in taking up the Cross. Imitation of Christ.

PRAYER.

O God, Who hast sent Thy Son to call us near unto Thyself, grant that I may so follow Him in holy obedience, that the gifts of grace whereby He has conformed me to His likeness here below, may ever live on as an inheritance of glory, perfecting me in the contemplation of Thy Love, through the same Jesus Christ our Lord. Amen.

THE NECESSITY OF SEPARATION FROM THE WORLD.

PRELUDE. i. *And Jesus went into the Temple, and began to cast out them that sold and bought in the Temple, and overthrew the tables of the money-changers, and the seats of them that sold doves.*—S. Mark xi. 15.

ii. Christ purging the Temple.

POINT I. *Consider the evil which pollutes the Sanctuary—the Church.*

    a. Borne with through many ages by the Divine patience, but not for ever.

    b. Hindering the manifestation of Jesus, as it blinds the eyes of the Covenanted people, so that they cannot see Him.

    c. Driven out by the Divine Justice, at the appearance of Jesus, with unerring certainty.

POINT II. *Consider the evil which pollutes the Sanctuary of my heart.*

    a. Worldly aims—those that buy and sell. Evil spirits seem to be bargaining one with another for the souls of men ; some tyrannizing over them in one way, others in another ; so that even the very things of God are polluted by their abominable interference.

    b. Worldly means of action—the tables of the money-changers. Religion, instead of being a life of immediate communion with God, is changed into earthly acts according to human convenience.

    c. Worldly maxims, by which the simplicity of God's Truth is reduced to the price of human expediency. The seats of them that sold doves.

POINT III. *Consider the necessity of welcoming the Presence of Christ.*

    a. By having nothing to do with that which He hates. We must eschew the world, because it hides Christ from our sight. We cannot live in the low ways of popular worldly religion and see Christ.

    b. By inviting Him to reveal Himself increasingly.

    c. By co-operating with Him in the use of His grace, lest His final visitation of judgment find us still uncleansed.

AFFECTIONS. Abhorrence of the world. Self-dedication to God. Desire of purity. Self-abasement for sin.

PRAYER.

O my God, grant that I may always recognize Thy Holy Covenant whereby I am separated from this evil world, so that here I may worship Thee with a holy worship, and hereafter I may behold the glory of Thy Holiness, through Jesus Christ our Lord. Amen.

THE BLINDNESS OF THE WORLD.

PRELUDE. i. *An evil and adulterous generation seeketh after a sign; and there shall no sign be given to it, but the sign of the prophet Jonas.*—S. Matt. xii. 39.

ii. The Jews mocking at the suggestion of Christ's Resurrection.

POINT I. *Consider the blindness of the worldly heart.*

a. As to duty, not content to obey without a sign. The pure heart can recognize God's will; and God will lead the pure and simple continually to know of His Will more and more.

b. As to self, fancying its desire for a sign to be a token of sincerity. It scorns the instructions which the Holy Ghost gives, as if they were delusions, for it does not know how to distinguish between spiritual and natural certainty.

c. As to God, not seeing God's power in the warnings of prophecy and revelation. It closes its eyes to the natural means through which God has made Himself sure to human reason, and consequently it cannot see the spiritual glory which God makes to shine upon the inner conscience.

POINT II. *Consider the terror of this state.*

a. By reason of its incapacity for seeing the things of God. It is beyond the reach of illumination. Blinded men cannot see what God gives.

b. By reason of the nearness of God's supernatural visitations, as exemplified in Jonas, brought from the whale's belly to warn. It is within the reach of Almighty investigation. That which man rejects is the power of God.

POINT III. *Consider the danger of falling into this state.*

a. The Ninevites who repented were outside of the covenant of God, and found mercy. Their previous darkness did not hinder their seeing their danger when God spoke to them.

b. The Jews who repented not, were the children of the Covenant. Yet they rejected mercy. Am I relying upon my position in Christ's Church?

c. The falling into such a state is not known until it is tested. Am I relying upon any gifts which may have been forfeited, even though once possessed? If I turn aside from the fulfilment of plain duties there is great danger of my being led away in my blindness, by doubts and fancy and self-will, being deceived by false signs, which are from Satan.

AFFECTIONS. Distrust of self. Seeking for perseverance. Preparation for God's teaching.

PRAYER.

O Lord, grant me purity of heart, that I may see the way wherein Thou wouldest have me to walk. And in the use of Thy grace and the fulfilment of Thy Holy Commandments, may at length attain to behold Thy glory surpassing all that the natural heart can know or even desire, in the kingdom prepared for Thine elect, through Jesus Christ our Lord. Amen.

G

Second Thursday in Lent.

THE CONTINUOUS GROWTH OF THE FAITHFUL.

PRELUDE. i. *If ye continue in My Word then are ye My disciples indeed; and ye shall know the truth, and the truth shall make you free.*—S. John viii. 31, 32.

ii. The Blessed Virgin and S. John at the foot of the Cross with the others.

POINT I. *Consider the necessity of perseverance.*

a. By faith, abiding in Christ's word. To hear the Word of Christ, and to leave Him, would be only the anticipation of their lot who shall hear His Word, saying Depart from Me.

b. By hope, braving difficulties according to the ordering of His Providence. Hope which is not tested by hard struggle is not worthy of the name.

c. By love, rejoicing in His Presence though not perceptible to sense. The word of Christ is indeed sweet beyond all description in the ear which truly listens to it and obeys.

POINT II. *Consider the illumination of those who persevere.*

a. By experience, realizing the power of Christ.

b. By grace, receiving increased capacities of Divine knowledge in the fellowship of the Holy Ghost.

c. By Providential interferences, guided by God in the ways of fuller teaching.

POINT III. *Consider the freedom of those who are thus illuminated.*

a. From natural weakness, since they find the grace on which they rely. The greater their sense of natural weakness, the more are they forced to live, not in themselves, but in Him.

b. From sin, since they recognise the intrinsic evil of what might ensnare them.

c. From error, since they acquire intuitions of Divine Truth.

d. From danger, since by death they are established in the life of Him whose Death was their safety whilst they lived.

AFFECTIONS. Deadness to the world. Joy in God. Readiness to forego mere outward signs. Appreciation of spiritual training as God may be pleased to bestow it.

PRAYER.

O Blessed Jesu, Who art the Eternal Word, uttering the Eternal Joy of the Father, wherein Thou ever livest with Him in the unity of the Eternal Spirit, grant that as Thou hast made Thy Word to sound in mine ear, it may be for evermore the Joy of my life, and that I, abiding therein, may grow in holy experience of Thy Truth, until I am prepared according to Thy Will for the fulness of Thy Manifestation, Who ever livest with the Father and the Holy Ghost, one God, Blessed for ever. Amen.

THE HEALING OF THE FAITHFUL.

PRELUDE. i. *An Angel went down at a certain season into the pool, and troubled the water; whosoever then first after the troubling of the water stepped in was made whole.*—S. John v. 4.

ii. One stepping in quickly and healed : many trying.

POINT I. *Consider the necessity of devotion and promptness.*

a. Waiting near at hand, so as to find God's gifts. It must be the object of our lives to wait upon God. Blessed are those outward necessities which force us to do so.

b. Continuing instant in prayer, even though we seem to have missed God's gifts. Over and over again must we pray. God sees us. He will not cast out our prayer if He sees that we really trust in Him to accomplish it.

c. Corresponding with grace without delay, whenever it be vouchsafed. Let us not complain of the alacrity of others, but let us learn to be more diligent ourselves.

POINT II. *Consider the individuality of effort.*

a. Assured of God's power, as ready to assert itself on our behalf, whether our individual need be in a great matter or a small.

b. Accepting the offer of grace with a complete thankfulness, as if it were for ourselves alone.

c. Acknowledging our entire inability to gain health without it, whether in a matter great or small.

POINT III. *Consider the Passion of Jesus, the true Bethesda of sin-stricken souls.*

a. Needing no Angel, but ever full of power by the ever-active Divine Love which resides within it. The Passion of Jesus is ever operative by the power of His perpetual Intercession.

b. Full of grace, for all who can step in, to heal all.

c. Profitable to none, unless they step in. It is in vain looking to Christ, unless we come to Him in the ordinances of His grace.

d. Having alongside of it the gift of a ministerial Priesthood representative of Christ, by which we may be bathed in its virtue. Christ has provided a man to put us in.

AFFECTIONS. Desire of Sanctity. Earnestness of Penitence. Love of the Passion. Gratitude for Absolution.

PRAYER.

O Jesu, look upon me as I lie in the helplessness of my sinful estate, and grant that as I yield myself to the guidance of those whom Thou hast sent for my assistance, I may find in Thy Sacred Passion the healing virtue whereby I may be enabled to walk henceforth in the way of Thy holy Commandments, and live to the praise of Thy glorious Name. Amen.

G 2

THE REWARD OF THE FAITHFUL.

PRELUDE. i. *Jesus taketh Peter, and James, and John his brother, and bringeth them up into an high mountain apart, and was Transfigured before them.*—S. Matt. xvii. 1, 2.

ii. The Transfiguration.

POINT I. *Consider that Christ leads to behold His glory—*

   a. Those who have come to Him in His humiliation. The vision was one which they had not expected. There needed a long training before they were fit to see it.

   b. Those who gave up all for Him. If the world fills our hearts we cannot see Jesus. What am I giving up?

   c. Those who cling to Him : with faith, S. Peter; with hope, S. James ; with love, S. John. Do I really cling to Him?

POINT II. *Consider that Christ's revelation is in special separation.*

   a. Apart, even from the rest of the Apostles, for no man can know the revelation of God except as it is vouchsafed to his own soul.

   b. Upon a high mountain—above the world—for the world understandeth not the things of the Spirit of God.

   c. In the night season, for Divine Joys are most truly made known in earthly sorrow. Joyous night if Jesus is seen!

POINT III. *Consider burial with Christ, the true taking of us apart.*

   a. In Baptism. By Baptism the early Christians were taken out of the world. It was to them a real burial. It was a real taking into fellowship hidden by darkness from the world, although it was an ascent to the Holy Mountain of God. Do we realize this separation from the world, either the ascent, or the darkness? If not, our Baptism is void.

   b. In obscurity, poverty, reproach, and the various separations of Divine Providence.

   c. In Lent, observance of Rules of devotion, deadness to the world. Am I coming with Christ this Lent into the wilderness with a sure hope that He will make me to behold His glory, if I abide with Him?

AFFECTIONS. Adherence to Christ. Willingness to be separated from all else. Love of the hidden life. Repose in the Holy Ghost.

PRAYER.

O Lord Jesu, grant me grace to come apart with Thee, not seeking signs from Thee in the midst of the glory of the world, but rather content to abide with Thee in this world's darkness, waiting until Thou show me Thy glory in the fellowship of all Thy Saints, in the presence of the Father, in the unity of the Holy Ghost. Amen.

THE OUTCAST SOUL.

PRELUDE. i. *Jesus went thence, and departed into the coasts of Tyre and Sidon. And behold, a woman of Canaan came out of the same coasts, and cried unto Him, saying, Have mercy on me, O Lord, Thou Son of David.*—S. Matt. xv. 21.

ii. The Canaanitish woman coming to Christ.

POINT I. *Consider her outcast condition.*

a. Dwelling in Tyre and Sidon, *i.e.*, the world as a place of merchandise, covetousness, and sin.

b. Dwelling where our Lord came, *i.e.*, by the Incarnation.

c. Cut off for ever from the Jewish Temple. For the race of man could not be reconciled to God by things of earth.

d. Suffering individually by the power of Satan exerted upon her daughter. " O ! my nature, how evil thou art, held in bondage by Satan ! O ! Jesu, Thou art my only hope !"

POINT II. *Consider her cry.*

a. For mercy. " O ! my God, I have forfeited the good gifts of Thy justice, but Thy mercy is as great as Thy justice."

b. To Christ. " O ! my Saviour, why hast Thou come amongst us, but that I may cry unto Thee ?"

c. Recognizing Him as Lord. " Thou art the Lord of all that live : let not Thy servant be in bondage to any other."

d. With confession of her individual need of Him. "Surely as Thou camest here, Thou carest for my need. How shall I doubt or distrust Thine individual goodness ?"

POINT III. *Consider her reliance upon the promises of revelation, calling to Jesus as the Son of David.*

a. The casting out of the Canaanites for ever, implies the greatness of the Israelitish blessings. So discipline implies covenanted gifts, guarded because valuable. The warning of eternal damnation implies the truth of Eternal Life.

b. I can praise Thee that my nation was outcast from the Temple, since the Temple was to prepare the way for Thee.

c. The security of Divine Promises. "As Thou art sent of God to fulfil the promises made unto the fathers, Thou canst not come short of the Almighty Love which sends Thee. If first to Israel, yet not less to all mankind."

AFFECTIONS. Humility. Penitence. Impotence. Confidence. Faith.

PRAYER.

O Lord Jesu, as Thou hast found me when I was outcast, grant that I may be delivered from the tyranny of Satan, and may praise Thee with Thy redeemed for ever. **Amen.**

THE UNCHANGEABLE WORD.

PRELUDE. i. I *am the Same that I said unto you from the beginning.*—S. John viii. 25.

ii. Jesus meeting all around in perfect Love.

POINT I. *Consider Jesus as the Eternal Word, in Whom the Divine Love shines forth.*

    a. In Eternity: breathing forth the co-equal Spirit Who proceedeth from the Father.

    b. In Time: creating the Heavens and the earth and all things that are therein, by the co-operation of the same Spirit.

    c. In Providence: regulating all things that are created by Him, for the accomplishment of the purposes of Divine Love.

    d. In the Incarnation: elevating created things to the perfect fellowship of the Divine Love.

POINT II. *Consider the earthly teaching of Jesus, as the manifestation of the same Divine Love.*

    a. In His prophets: making known beforehand that which He would do.

    b. In His own acts: acting by no transitory impulse, but so as to fulfil the ancient predictions.

    c. By His own lips: declaring the unchangeable Truth with the unchangeableness of enduring Love.

POINT III. *Consider Jesus teaching us now in His Church.*

    a. By the gift of the illuminating Spirit of Pentecost to abide with the Church for ever.

    b. By the deposit of the unchangeable Faith.

    c. By the voice of the Spirit in the hearts of His faithful ones, yet always speaking in accordance with that which was handed down from the beginning.

AFFECTIONS. Worship. Constancy. Endurance.

PRAYER.

O Lord *Jesu, Who ever abidest the same in holiness, in love, and in power, grant that I may always listen to Thy Truth; exercise Thy grace, accomplish Thy Will, and experience Thy sweetness, to the glory of Thy Holy Name.* Amen.

THE HEAVENLY MASTER.

PRELUDE. i. *One is your Master Which is in heaven.—*
S. Matt. xxiii. 8, 9.

ii. Jesus upon the Throne of God claiming our service.

POINT I. *Consider the only True Master.*

  a. Himself unchangeable. We so changing, and therefore
  ready to fall away to others, and so becoming again and
  again as outcasts.

  b. Himself supreme. All others as false, unless leading us to
  Him, as representing Him.

  c. Himself the source of unity to all, so that not to obey
  Him is to be outcast and lonely, but to live in submission
  to Him is to be gathered into the fellowship of all saints.

POINT II. *Consider the reality of His sovereignty.*

  a. Not an unthinking fate, but a personal sovereignty
  exercised according to His own all-holy Will.

  b. Not a necessity, but a sovereignty, requiring the submission of our wills to accept it.

  c. Superior to our criticism ; so that His arrangements will
  often seem to be at variance with our judgments, otherwise
  there would be no real obedience.

  d. Regulating all and each, so as to govern for the good of all
  and each.

POINT III. *Consider the Heavenly character of His reign.*

  a. Seated in Heaven, and to be revealed in Heaven.

  b. Bringing earthly things to Heavenly subjection and
  Heavenly purposes.

  c. Requiring from us a Heavenly consciousness, while we are
  to act in the power of the Holy Ghost, outcasts by nature,
  but strengthened to serve Him by Heavenly gifts.

AFFECTIONS. Stedfastness. Detachment. Love. Worship. Spirituality.

PRAYER.

*O Lord Jesu, grant me so to recognize Thy Heavenly glory that
I may never be moved by outward threatenings, but may serve Thee
with a perfect love, and when earthly things have passed away may
be partaker of Thine Eternal Kingdom, for Thy mercy's sake.*
Amen.

REDEMPTION.

PRELUDE. i. *Behold, we go up to Jerusalem, and the Son of Man shall be betrayed to be crucified.*—S. Matt. xx. 18, 19.

ii. Jesus going up to the Last Passover.

POINT I. *Consider the predestined Sacrifice.*

  a. According to the prophecies of the unchangeable Word.

  b. In obedience to the will of His Heavenly Father.

  c. Though so close at hand, yet not realized by His disciples.

  d. Having effects of which those who surrounded Him, friend and foe, knew nothing.

POINT II. *Consider the universality of the Redemption.*

  a. The Son of Man dies not for a part of mankind, but for all.

  b. All the human race were looking forward to the Son of Man, although they knew it not; all sacrifices pointed to Him.

  c. He, the Son of Man, to Whom all men look, is the Lord of Glory, whom all must obey.

  d. Not to recognize Him, the Son of Man, as the Saviour, is to be outcast not only from God in Heaven, but from the true hopes of the human race.

POINT III. *Consider the chosen City.*

  a. Jerusalem, *i.e.*, the Vision of Peace, knows not the obedience in which alone peace can be found.

  b. The City of David, in rejecting the Son of Man, becomes outcast; whereas the Canaanitish woman, by recognising the Son of David, is accepted.

  c. We must own Him as our Redeemer, crucified in the Old Jerusalem if we would go up with Him and see Him enthroned in the New Jerusalem, our Master in Heaven.

AFFECTIONS. Trust in God's Word. Obedience. Self-surrender. Acceptance of humiliation.

PRAYER.

O Lord God, Who hast provided for us a glorious redemption, grant that as I have been redeemed from the perishing condition of earthly life by the death of Thy dear Son, I also dying to the things of earth and pressing onward to the Vision of Peace in the Life which never perisheth, may have my portion with Thine Elect, through the same Jesus Christ our Lord. **Amen.**

THE CALL TO SALVATION.

PRELUDE. i. I *receive not testimony of men : but these things do I say, that ye might be saved.*—S. John v. 34.

ii. Jesus pleading with man.

POINT I. *Consider the insufficiency of human testimony to Jesus.*

    a. The greatest of men, even John the Baptist, cannot testify of God.

    b. The merciful provision ot the prophecies uttered through 4000 years, to prepare us to receive Christ.

    c. The blindness of the human heart, hesitating to accept the testimony which God gives of His Son.

    d. The insufficiency of the human heart, ever to realize, by its own highest experiences, the blessedness of the gift of Christ.

POINT II. *Consider the Voice of Jesus making Himself known.*

    a. Appealing to human testimony, in order to win man's love.

    b. Speaking to us on our own level, that we may accept Him.

POINT III. *Consider His desire to recall the outcast.*

In order to save us, the Unchangeable Word—

    a. Came down from Heaven and became flesh.

    b. Condescended to our infirmities in reasoning with us.

    c. Sealed His testimony with His Death.

POINT IV. *Consider the necessity of this salvation.*

    a. Jerusalem knew it not, and was rejected.

    b. The outcast Canaanite knew it, and found mercy.

AFFECTIONS. Desire of illumination. Gratitude to Jesus for His condescending Love. Attention to His Call. Mistrust of present position.

PRAYER.

O Blessed Jesu, although no words of mine can make Thee known to any, nor express the Truth which Thou art, grant that the power of Thy Holy Spirit proceeding from the Father may speak in my heart, giving heavenly efficacy to the Message of Thy Love, and may so enable me to accept Thy Truth in all its saving virtue that I may ever have the witness in myself, and abide in the security of Thy Covenant, to the glory of God the Father. **Amen.**

THE CASTING OFF OF THE UNBELIEVING.

PRELUDE. i. *He will miserably destroy those wicked men, and will let out His vineyard unto other husbandmen, which shall render Him the fruits in their seasons.*—S. Matt. xxi. 41.

ii. The overthrow of Jerusalem.

POINT I. *Consider the time of probation and the call of grace.*

  a. These serve to make manifest the wickedness of those who reject them.

  b. Are the gifts of God's condescending Love. We cannot conceive of God as failing to show those tokens of His undeserved love which He has given, but nevertheless they are the gift of His free bounty, neither should we have conceived them to be possible had He not shown them.

  c. Cannot be slighted for ever; else there would be no probation or grace, but salvation would come by necessity.

  d. When slighted, cannot be recalled; else the moral nature of obedience would be destroyed. We must choose God for the sake of His own excellence, not merely as a necessity for our own deliverance from evil.

POINT II. *Consider the rejection of the wicked men.*

  a. Its certainty. (i.) The Jews; (ii.) The unfaithful Christians.

  b. Its justice.

  c. Its misery.

POINT III. *Consider the recall of the outcast.*

  a. An act of bounty.

  b. Vouchsafed upon conditions. The necessity of attending to the conditions is proportionate to the mercy which gives the call. If they who were first called were cast off, much more shall we be if we heed not when God recalls us in Christ.

  c. Irreversible to them that welcome it truly.

AFFECTIONS. Diligence. Fear. Gratitude.

PRAYER.

O Lord God, Who in these last days hast spoken unto us by Thy Son, grant that I may not neglect Thy great salvation, but may be constant in obedience to Thy holy revelation, so that adoring the Truth of Thy warnings and abiding in the Truth of Thy Commandments, I may attain to the fruition of Thy Truth in Thine eternal manifestation, through Jesus Christ our Lord. Amen.

THE RETURN OF THE PRODIGAL.

PRELUDE. i. I *will arise, and go to my Father, and will say unto Him, Father, I have sinned against heaven, and before Thee, and am no more worthy to be called Thy son; make me as one of Thy hired servants.*—S. Luke xv. 18, 19.

ii. The Prodigal Son.

POINT I. *Consider his arising to return in the consciousness—*

a. Of his utter wretchedness. The outcast soul may have sought for happiness in the world, but finds none since it has lost God.

b. Of the persuasion of his Father's welcome. Our nature feels itself drawn to return by the instinct of love whereby it remembers God. Yet it is only by the promises of Holy Scripture that this welcome is made sure to us.

c. Of the relationship which, though so marred, is not destroyed. The nature which was formed in the Divine Image retains a dignity which asserts itself as long as God abstains from a final sentence of reprobation.

POINT II. *Consider his confession of unworthiness.*

a. In the remembrance of past ingratitude.

b. In the contemplation of present degradation.

c. In the knowledge of future incapacity.

POINT III. *Consider the offer of service.*

a. As the necessity of his life. O blessed necessity which draws us to Christ.

b. Without the expectation of honour. The honour of being accepted as one of God's penitent children is greater after all than any honour which the world has to give.

c. With acceptance of shame before others as being in this lower position.

d. With a satisfaction in his heart in knowing this, that his Father will not altogether reject him.

AFFECTIONS. Contrition. Self-abasement. Trust in God's Love. Surrender to his Father's goodness.

PRAYER.

O Lord *Jesu Christ, I come to Thee, the Father of the world to come, entreating Thee to welcome me, although I be unworthy, and though I have forfeited my heavenly inheritance by my sin. Let my life on earth be a life of obedience, having Thy living power for its acknowledged support, Who with the Father and the Holy Ghost, livest and reignest, God for ever and ever.* **Amen.**

DELIVERANCE FROM SATANIC DUMBNESS.

PRELUDE. i. *Jesus was casting out a devil, and it was dumb. And it came to pass, when the devil was gone out, the dumb spake ; and the people wondered.*—S. Luke xi. 14.

ii. The dumb man speaking, and the people wondering.

POINT I. *Consider that Satan makes the soul dumb.*

    a. The true voice of the soul is in the utterance of love; for it is the Voice of God, Who speaks in the soul of man ; and God is Love.

    b. All utterance that is not of God is after all but dumbness, for it is :—(i) A dead and not a living voice ; (ii) It reaches not to the ear of Truth and Life ; God does not acknowledge it ; (iii) It reveals not the true purposes of the soul.

    c. Love is the life of the soul ; Truth its living utterance. Jesus restores utterance as He restores Life.

POINT II. *Consider the delivered soul speaking.*

    a. To God in prayer, thanksgiving, and praise.

    b. To man, in praise of God.

    c. By declaration of His love, received as a speaking power. Being set free by love it strives to exercise the love it has experienced.

POINT III. *Consider how all who hear the voice of the soul wonder at its deliverance.*

    a. Angels ; and they praise God.

    b. Devils ; and they go away the more enraged.

    c. Men. Saints ; and they welcome the lost ones into the fellowship of their joy. Evil men ; and they are the more condemned by the manifestation of the power to which they could not yield.

    d. The soul itself ; and it worships God, dwelling within itself and listens for the Voice of God, that it may speak the Words of God.

AFFECTIONS. Contemplation of God. Perseverance amidst spiritual dryness. Confidence in God's power to set us free from Satan.

PRAYER.

O Lord God, open Thou my lips, which have been closed by the palsy of sin, and grant, that I may be so freed from the possession of Satan's tyranny, that I may exult in the inspiration of Thy living power, through Jesus Christ our Lord. Amen.

NATURAL INAPTITUDE FOR THE DIVINE MESSAGE.

PRELUDE. i. *Verily I say unto you, No prophet is accepted in his own country.*—S. Luke iv. 24.

ii. Prophets raised up by God from amongst His people but put to death by them.

POINT I. *Consider that the sinner can know nothing of God.*

  a. A prophet must come not from earth, but from Heaven. "We speak that we do know, and testify that we have seen."

  b. A prophet must speak with the voice not of earth, but of Heaven; for earthly tongues cannot teach the mysteries of God.

  c. A prophet must not be of this country, but Heaven must be the home of his affections, otherwise he cannot speak worthily thereof; for we must speak with the voice of Heavenly Love.

POINT II. *Consider that the sinner cannot trust his fellow in the things of God.*

  a. We may accept from one another the teachings of earthly reason, or philosophy, but not Supernatural Truth.

  b. We cannot feel confidence in individual claims to Divine authority. No excellence that we can see in man, can raise him to be more than man.

POINT III. *Consider that the prophet must be accredited as an ambassador from that other country.*

  a. Hence the necessity of a Divine revelation, bearing no mere internal evidence of its truth. Miracles are not enough alone, but prophecy requires a growing inheritance of external evidence from previous prophecy proportionate to the growing majesty of its declarations. "By the Prophets who went before Me My Father beareth witness of Me."

  b. The limits of a Prophet's trustworthiness are ascertained by the terms of his Divine appointment.

  c. The prophet must be accepted within these terms, as the adequate exponent of the Divine Will.

AFFECTIONS. Praise for the gift of revelation.

PRAYER.

O God, My heart is incapable of beholding Thee, but it is not incapable of desiring Thee. Grant unto me the gift of supernatural faith, that I may receive Thy message, not with the dreariness of natural vacancy, but with the joy of loving certitude, which Thou alone canst give; through Jesus Christ our Lord. Amen.

THE RESTORED POWER OF SPEAKING TO GOD.

PRELUDE. i. *If two of you shall agree on earth as touching anything that they shall ask, it shall be done for them of My Father which is in heaven.*—S. Matt. xviii. 19.

ii. The Church at Jerusalem praying for S. Peter in prison.

POINT I. *Consider the supernatural voice of prayer. It belongs to the Body of Christ.*

   a. In its collective action. Christ the Head is not adequately represented by any one of His members. There should be union. Prayer requires organized union for its integrity.

   b. In its united affection. There must be the agreement of mutual Love. God must see the work of Love, where He is to recognize the voice of Love.

   c. In its covenanted adoption. The Church living in Christ is to put forth the claim of Christ. It is Christ's voice which the Father hears when His Church prays.

POINT II. *Consider the security of prayer. "Whatsoever ye shall ask."*

   a. All things belong to God, and are ruled by His Love.

   b. What is not good for us to have, is rather a nothingness, a hindrance, a source of decay, than a real object of desire, a blessing, a strength. Therefore it is no imperfection in the answer to our prayer that God withholds evil.

   c. If God withholds from us the form of our request, which may through our ignorance be evil, yet He will grant the substance of it; the good thing which underlies the form.

POINT III. *Consider the reach of prayer.*

   a. It reaches beyond the outer world, to the Ear of our Father Who is in Heaven; for it is not the mere expression of natural desire, but an inspired utterance of the Holy Ghost, peculiar to the Body of Christ.

   b. It moves the Will of God, for what He thus hears becomes a principle of action to which He can and must yield by reason of the character of Love, which is His essence.

   c. Agreement in prayer is Love amongst brethren. Utterance of prayer is Love towards God. Answer to prayer is Love from God.

AFFECTIONS. Brotherly Love. Oneness with Christ. Rejoicing in the Covenant of Adoption.

PRAYER.

O Almighty God, by Whose Word all things were made, grant me by the Spirit of Thy dear Son so to speak in the unity of His Mystical Body, that the feeble words of my prayer may rise to Thee in the perfect energy of Thy Word which ruleth all things; through Jesus Christ our Lord. Amen.

THE RESTORED POWER OF HEARING WHAT GOD SAYS.

PRELUDE. i. *Hear, and understand.*—S. Matt. xv. 10.

ii. The Apostles gathered round Christ as their Teacher.

POINT I. *Consider the mystery of Revelation, spoken by the very Incarnate Word of God.*

    a. The words of the Man Christ Jesus are no inadequate expression of the Truth, for they contain within themselves the fulness of the Divine Life.

    b. They must be heard with the outward ear.

    c. They are not duly apprehended until they are heard, as they are spoken, in the power of the Holy Ghost; so "He that hath an ear, let him hear," with the inner hearing also.

POINT II. *Consider the gift of spiritual understanding.*

    a. The natural understanding cannot accept the Truth of God.

    b. The Holy Ghost enables us first to receive the elements of Divine Truth by spiritual hearing, and then to reflect upon its substance by spiritual understanding.

    c. This gift is vouchsafed collectively to the Church in its integrity: to each individual subordinately. Hence the divisions of outward Christendom mar the apprehension of truth derivately by each individual; for it were impossible that any should profit by the revelation of Truth, unless his own understanding were raised to its apprehension.

POINT III. *Consider the necessity of its exercise.*

    a. Divine Truth is of no more value than any other truth, unless it become the Life of the soul. But life is energy; therefore the powers of the soul must be put in exercise if they are to profit by the gift of Divine Truth. Divine Truth cannot be received, as mere dead knowledge can, at the lips of another. It must be received into the living understanding of each individual. This is the work of the Holy Ghost dwelling in the Body of Christ, and in every member of that Body.

    b. The natural powers of the soul do not suffice. It is by the exercise of the Holy Ghost that we can alone have to do with the things of God.

AFFECTIONS. The love of contemplation. Joy in the Holy Ghost.

PRAYER.

Grant me, O Lord, I pray Thee, so to abide with childlike faith in the unity of Thy Church, that the eyes of my understanding may be enlightened by the Holy Spirit to behold the truth as it has been delivered unto Thy Saints; through Jesus Christ our Lord. Amen.

THE SPIRITUAL FOOD.

PRELUDE. i. *Labour not for the meat which perisheth: but for that meat which endureth unto everlasting life.*—S. John vi. 27.

ii. Jesus feeding thee with Himself.

POINT I. *Consider the labour given for the perishing food of earth.*
- *a.* The folly of toiling thus.
- *b.* The misery which accompanies the toil of the world.
- c. The result : nothing but loss.

POINT II. *Consider the necessity of labouring for the heavenly food.*
- *a.* As diligently as for that of earth.
- *b.* The blessedness of all such labour even during its continuance. The joy of serving God surpasses all earthly reward.
- *c.* The example of Christ. In Divine obedience He found support.
- *d.* His sympathy and fellowship in the labour.
- *e.* His strength for it : grace given according to our need.
- *f.* The result : everlasting life with Christ.

POINT III. *Consider the bread of heaven.*
- *a.* Communicated to us in our earthly state: to bring us thither.
- *b.* Under earthly forms : suited to our present condition.
- *c.* Abiding eternally. Earthly food abideth not; perishes with earth. Eucharists become the resurrection power of the body of the faithful. Do I think while I communicate, that I am taking that which shall raise my body up in the glory of Christ at the last day? Do I labour so as to receive devoutly the Body of the Eternal?

AFFECTIONS. Reverence to the Blessed Sacrament. Hope of Resurrection—Cherishing Christ's Presence after Communicating.

PRAYER.

O my God, as Thou hast brought me near unto Thyself, to hear Thee and speak with Thee, grant that I may be ever nourished by Thy Word in the mysteries of grace, until I come to feed upon Thee in the manifest joy of Thine Eternal glory; through Jesus Christ our Lord. Amen.

HEAVENLY WORSHIP.

PRELUDE. i. *Sir, I perceive that Thou art a prophet. Our fathers worshipped in this mountain.*—S. John iv. 19, 20.

ii. The multitude around the Lamb upon Mount Zion.

POINT I. *Consider the Mountain of Expectation (the earthly Zion).*

a. Chosen of God. There can be no true expectation of God's Love save by the call of God's Love.

b. Hallowed by long discipline. God has made it a place of training by sacrifice and by prophets.

c. The centre of covenanted blessings.

d. Yet finally rejected, although furnishing the remnant who pass onward to the Election of Grace.

POINT II. *Consider the Mountain of Folly (Samaria).*

a. Chosen of men. The wisdom of man is foolishness with God.

b. Powerful through self-will. The centre of a great earthly system. Making ancient gifts of God minister only to its pride.

c. Continually insulting the chosen City. Satisfied with its own religious traditions, and despising the covenant of God, because there was so little manifestation of present power.

d. Passing utterly away.

POINT III. *Consider the Mountain of Revelation (the Heavenly Zion).*

a. Predestined of God, Who will bring His purpose to a triumphant issue.

b. Perfected by the discipline of earth. The inhabitants have come out of the valley of the shadow of death.

c. Strong with the fulness of spiritual glory.

d. Treasuring up within itself all the inheritance of sacred experiences within the Divine Covenant.

e. Rich with the abundance of the merits of Christ her Lord, and gladdened by His voice of constant Benediction.

AFFECTIONS. Trust in God's Covenant. Hope of its final and speedy Triumph.

PRAYER.

O Lord God, bring me to Thy Holy Hill, that I may have my portion in the Heavenly Altar, where Thine Only-begotten Son gathers the faithful together in the unity of His own most perfect oblation, to worship Thee in Spirit and in Truth; and grant that the discipline of earth may perfect me for the obtaining of Thy glorious inheritance, through the same Jesus Christ our Lord. Amen.

H

SELF-CONDEMNATION OF THOSE WHO SHALL BE EXALTED.

PRELUDE. i. *Jesus stooped down and wrote on the ground, He that is without sin among you, let him first cast a stone at her.* —S. John viii. 6, 7.

ii. Jesus writing on the ground.

POINT I. *Consider how He writes upon the ground of our nature.*

    a. Stooping down to us in the humility of the Incarnation. Every act of His Life is written on man's nature as an example. Alas! We are slow to read!

    b. Waiting silently in the midst of us, yet by His Presence stirring our conscience.

    c. Looking up to each individual that will really speak to Him and seek His counsel.

POINT II. *Consider why He does not condemn us.*

    a. As yet is not the time for Him to pass sentence. By-and-by He will do that.

    b. Rather this is the time of discipline, that we may escape the sentence hereafter.

    c. And it is the time of testing, and we cannot be judged by His Voice until we have been tested by the opportunities of His grace.

POINT III. *Consider how He wants us to condemn ourselves.*

    a. As the first step towards forgiveness and newness of life. Let us not go out from His Presence because we are convicted of our own conscience, but rather come to Him now for pardon, lest we be driven from His Presence hereafter in punishment.

    b. As the means of forestalling His judgment upon ourselves, that our hearts may be one with Him in holiness.

    c. As the means of exercising charity towards others, that we may be one with Him in forgiveness, and may receive that which we have practised.

AFFECTIONS. Charity. Forbearance. Remembrance of our own sin. Expectation of Divine Judgment. Hope of mercy.

PRAYER.

O Almighty God, as Thou callest me to worship Thee, teach me to abase myself in the remembrance of my sin; that as by sin I have forfeited communion with Thee, so by penitence and humble confession of my sin I may be restored; through Jesus Christ our Lord. Amen.

JESUS WITH MANKIND.

PRELUDE. i. *Jesus went over the sea of Galilee, which is the sea of Tiberias. And a great multitude followed Him, because they saw His miracles which He did on them that were diseased.* —S. John vi. 1, 2.

ii. The multitude following Jesus across the sea.

POINT I. *Consider Jesus crossing the sea.*

> *a.* The departure, because the Jews did not recognize Him as the Son of God. He leaves them. Those who would know His power must follow Him.
>
> *b.* Across the sea, typifying the waters of Baptism. Those who would know Him in His Divine character, must be partakers of His grace.
>
> *c.* The sea of Galilee: the nations of the world. The gift of grace is to all mankind, that they may know Jesus.

POINT II. *Consider the multitude following Him.*

> *a.* They were coming up to the Passover, a great feast of the Jews. So does the Jewish law draw them near to Jesus.
>
> *b.* They cross the sea with Jesus. A greater exodus than crossing the Red Sea with Moses.
>
> *c.* A great multitude, whom no man can number, are to follow. Am I one of them?

POINT III. *Consider their reason : they saw His miracles.*

> *a.* Jesus must be followed as the Lord of Power.
>
> *b.* The diseased that He heals, are mankind in their sin. No power can avail but the power of Jesus, for He is the only Healer.
>
> *c.* What He has done for others, He can do for me. Have I health? Not that which I need, unless it be His gift to me. The health which Jesus gives is the only true health.
>
> *d.* Great is the joy of having the Son of God come to us. Yet no joy except to those who see His wonders, leave the world, cross the sea, so as to live in grace, and follow Him so as to know Him better.

AFFECTIONS. Rejoicing in Christ. Confidence in Him. Hoping for greater manifestations.

PRAYER.

O Jesu, how can I praise Thee for the goodness whereby Thou healest our infirmities! Teach me to abide in the experience of Thy Love, that leaving what the world loves, I may love Thee in Truth. Amen.

JESUS IN THE TEMPLE.

PRELUDE. i. *Take these things hence ; make not My Father's House an house of merchandise.*—S. John ii. 16.

ii. The Dignity of Christ in asserting His Divine Sonship.

POINT I. *Consider the Temple as the House of God.*

a. The Father of Jesus Christ. Only as the Father of Jesus Christ can we approach Him in the Sanctuary.

b. Forming for Himself an habitation amongst men. He had formed man's nature to be His dwelling-place. The Temple is the beginning of a new manifestation whereby He would carry out His ancient and unchangeable purpose.

c. That His Son may enter it, to offer propitiation for the world. It was separated from the world that the Son of God might cleanse it with sacrifice. They defiled it by bringing the world into it.

POINT II. *Consider the merchandise going on therein.*

a. Under the pretence of religion.

b. Making the worship of God serve the covetous desires of men.

c. Setting an earthly price upon Divine things.

d. Earthly gains taking possession of the heart.

POINT III. *Consider the command to purge the Temple.*

a. Earthly habits must be done away, to make room for Heavenly.

b. God, as the Father of Jesus Christ must be approached, not with earth-bought sacrifices, but with the true and priceless Lamb.

c. The purging of the heart, that God may be worshipped, while we acknowledge His Only-begotten Son as our true Lord.

AFFECTIONS. Purity of aim in Divine Worship. Acknowledgment and Love of Jesus as the Lamb of God given to us by the Father.

PRAYER.

O Jesu, Who hast formed my heart to be a dwelling-place consecrated by Thy mediation to the glory of the Father, grant that I may always acknowledge Him to Whom I belong, and remember the price which Thou hast paid for my redemption, so that I may never rest upon earthly convenience, but may rise to Thee with spiritual devotion and love, that Thou mayest be glorified. Amen.

JESUS REVEALING THE FATHER.

PRELUDE. i. *Ye seek to kill Me, a Man that hath told you the truth.*—S. John viii. 40.

i. Jesus rebuking the Jews.

POINT I. *Consider His Message.*

    a. The Declaration of the Eternal Truth.   He comes to make known to us the Person of the Father and the glory of the Divine Nature, which is Eternal Love.

    b. The Revelation of the claims of the Truth.   God cannot be known in Truth unless His supremacy be acknowledged, for to refuse His claim would be inconsistent with the very nature of Godhead.

    c. The Manifestation of the beneficence of the Truth.

POINT II. *Consider His Person.*

    a. Speaking with the lips of man.

    b. With a manhood assumed for the very purpose of effecting this revelation.

    c. Yet exposing Him to that outward humiliation, which, but for this work of love, could not have happened to Him.

POINT III. *Consider the hatred against Him.*

    a. The ingratitude which could reject so loving a Teacher. All the excellence of His character was unable to overpower the hatred which the Divine claims of Truth provoked.

    b. The blindness which could thus oppose God.   They clung to a God of their own hearts, and so they saw not the Truth in its glory.

    c. The hatred of the Truth, which made them seek to destroy the instrument of its revelation.

AFFECTIONS. Loving worship of the Truth. Acknowledgment of the Voice of God in Jesus Christ. Lamentation over the dulness of our natural heart, which rejects that Voice continually.

PRAYER.

O my God, let my whole heart be surrendered to Thy Love, that I may receive the revelation which Thou givest us by Thine Only-begotten Son, and sacrificing every natural desire to the glory of Thy Holy Name, may live by the transforming power of Thy Holy Truth; through the same Thy Son Jesus Christ our Lord. Amen.

JESUS MANIFESTING THE WORKS OF GOD.

PRELUDE. i. *Master, who did sin : this man, or his parents, that he was born blind ? Jesus answered, Neither hath this man sinned, nor his parents : but that the works of God should be made manifest in Him.*—S. John ix. 2, 3.

ii. The blind man in the Presence of Jesus with the Jews inquiring.

POINT I. *Consider the blind man's need.*

> *a.* How great, how undeserved are those gifts, which, because well-nigh universal, or at least very common, we take as matters of course.
>
> *b.* How necessary the gifts of grace, in order that we may use aright the gifts of nature.

POINT II. *Consider the inquiry as to the cause of the man's defect.*

> *a.* Readiness to blame God, on the part of those who only knew a part of His purposes.
>
> *b.* Willingness to blame man with self-righteous contempt.
>
> *c.* Blindness as to the great purposes of God in Creation, which can only be recognized in another world.
>
> *d.* The gradual progress of God's work, making manifest its Divine character. What is given, is given not of necessity but of bounty. What is withheld, is withheld not in niggardliness but with a view to greater future good.

POINT III. *Consider the manifestation of God's works, for they are all wrought through Jesus Christ His Only Son.*

> *a.* He Who is the Lord of Grace is the Lord of Nature too.
>
> *b.* He comes to perfect in grace that which is by nature imperfect.
>
> *c.* His works are measured forth in gradual development of power now, that they may be manifested in the fulness of Infinite Love hereafter.

AFFECTIONS. Praise to God for His Power. Trust in Jesus as bearing the power of the Father. Submission to present privations in the confidence of future blessing.

PRAYER.

O God, teach me, in all the troubles which I see around, to behold the blessed operation of Thy Love, that by the discipline of Thy Providence I may be trained to receive the revelation of Thy grace, through Jesus Christ our Lord. Amen.

JESUS IN THE PRESENCE OF THE FATHER.

PRELUDE. i. *The Father loveth the Son, and showeth Him all things that Himself doeth.*—S. John v. 20.

ii. The human consciousness of the Incarnate Son delighting in the contemplation of God's glorious purposes.

POINT I. *Consider the eternal love of the Father to the Son.* The Father's delight in His consciousness of Being is not a selfish, dead, idle, fruitless delight, but self-communicating, living, active, productive.

    a. The whole love of the Father passes on to the Son, so that there is nothing which the Father holds back.

    b. The Father can hold nothing back, for if He did, it would be a violation of that perfect undivided Love, which is His very essence. The Godhead is indivisible.

    c. This Love is without beginning and without end and without change. The Godhead cannot change.

POINT II. *Consider the mind of the Son contemplating the eternal purposes of the Father.*

    a. Jesus delights to receive into His Human consciousness and will, the full knowledge of the Divine Mysteries.

    b. He knows all the works of God, not by gradual revelation, but by virtue of that Divine Love wherein He dwells eternally One God with the Father.

    c. Only by the same power, and as members of the Son of God, can we know the things of God.

POINT III. *Consider the co-operation of the Incarnate Son with the Almighty workings of the Godhead.*

    a. The Father is eternally known to the Son, not by mere external contemplation, but by unity of action. The Son sees the works of the Father by doing the same.

    b. He does the same by dwelling in the energy of the Divine Love in the unity of the Holy Ghost.

    c. We can only know the works of God by working along with God, rising out of ourselves into the blessedness of His Divine Love.

AFFECTIONS. Praise to God for the revelation of Himself in Jesus Christ. Thankfulness for the exaltation of our humanity in Jesus Christ. Also for the gift of the Body and Blood of Christ to be our own Food, that we may act in His strength and behold the Mysteries of the Godhead.

PRAYER.

O Jesu, as Thou beholdest all that the Father doeth, grant that I may abide in Thee and praise Thee for that which Thou revealest; and by the fellowship of Thy grace may so participate in the energy of Thy inspiration, that I may have the fruition of Thy perfect knowledge in the glory of the Father everlastingly. **Amen.**

JESUS IN THE PRESENCE OF DEATH.

PRELUDE. i. *Our friend Lazarus sleepeth; but I go, that I may awake him out of sleep.*—S. John xi. 11.

ii. Jesus standing by the grave of Lazarus.

POINT I. *Consider death.*

    a. As a sleep. Not non-existence, but a hushing of consciousness to the outer world.

    b. As a separation from present life. Those who are locally nearest are entirely cut off from the dead form.

    c. As a punishment for sin, which has forfeited the Presence of God, Who is the true Life of the Soul.

    d. As a state of expectation; waiting for the call of Jesus.

POINT II. *Consider the Love of Christ.*

    a. Death does not separate from it. "*Our friend* Lazarus."

    b. He cares for the departed as for those on earth. "For all live unto Him."

    c. He purposes to effect a great good for those who have died in His Love. Jesus is "the Resurrection," and whithersoever He goes, He goes in order to arouse those who receive Him to a consciousness of life unknown before.

POINT III. *Consider Christ coming to the dead, to awaken them out of sleep.*

    a. By the Incarnation, to dead humanity.

    b. By Personal Ministry, to those whom the law could not save.

    c. By His own death, to those who had died before Him. "Thy dead men shall live. Together with My dead Body shall they arise."

    d. By His Grace and Holy Spirit, to those whom He calls from the death of sin.

    e. By His final Advent, to all the dead, that they may be brought to Judgment.

AFFECTIONS.—Praise to Jesus as Deliverer from death. Love for the departed. Hope of the resurrection.

PRAYER.

O Blessed Jesu, Who art the Life of all to whom Thou comest, grant that I may rise up in obedience to Thy call, even though I be bound by the grave-clothes of this miserable world, so that I may rise with joy at the sound of Thy Voice, when Thou shalt call forth Thine elect to come out of their graves in the brightness and freedom of Thine own immortality. Amen.

JESUS THE LIGHT OF THE WORLD.

PRELUDE. i. *Then spake Jesus*, I am *the Light of the world:* *he that followeth Me shall not walk in darkness, but shall have the Light of life.*—S. John viii. 12.

ii. The Pillar of fire guiding the Israelites.

POINT I. *Consider the darkness of the world.*—Is. ix. 1.

    a. Darkness of Galilee. (Vide Sunday.)

    b. Darkness of worldly business and sin. (Monday.)

    c. Darkness of ignorant opposition to truth. (Tuesday.)

    d. Darkness of imperfection and expectancy. (Wednesday.)

    e. Darkness of estrangement from the Son of God. (Thursday.)

    f. Darkness of the sleep of death. (Friday.)

POINT II. *Consider Jesus, the Light, revealing the Father.*

    a. To the nations that follow Him—Galilee. (Sunday.)

    b. In the sanctity of His covenanted worship. (Monday.)

    c. In antagonism to the corrupt heart which hateth the Truth. (Tuesday.)

    d. To those who have by nature no capacity of seeing. (Wednesday.)

    e. According to the fulness of His own Divine Knowledge. (Thursday.)

    f. Raising those who hear His Voice to a new life by this revelation. (Friday.)

POINT III. *Consider the necessity of following Him.*

    a. From the darkness of the worldly heart, acknowledging His miracles. (Sunday.)

    b. From the formality of mere Jewish worship, reverencing His Sanctuary. (Monday.)

    c. With docility, confessing our ignorance. (Tuesday.)

    d. Looking for His Grace, to the praise of His Glory. (Wednesday.)

    e. In the power of the Holy Ghost, worshipping Him in the Truth of His Godhead. (Thursday.)

    f. Rising to newness of life, as the fruits of His Resurrection. (Friday.)

AFFECTIONS. Praise to Jesus as the refreshment of our souls. Newness of heart and desire of union with Him.

PRAYER.

O Thou Light of Light, grant that I, being delivered by Thy grace from the kingdom of darkness, may attain to behold Thee in the Light which is to our natural faculties unapproachable, where, with the Father and the Holy Ghost, Thou livest and reignest God for ever and ever. **Amen.**

THE PURITY OF THE REJECTED SAVIOUR.

PRELUDE. i. *Jesus saith, Which of you convinceth Me of sin? and if I say the truth, why do ye not believe Me? He that is of God heareth God's words; ye therefore hear them not, because ye are not of God.*—S. John viii. 46, 47.

ii. Jesus claiming to be judged.

POINT I. *Consider the purity of Jesus tested by Satan.*

   a. In the wilderness.

   b. In His Passion. " The Prince of this world cometh, and hath nothing in me."

   c. By the terrors of those that were possessed whensoever He came near them. " What have I to do with Thee, Thou Son of God?"

POINT II. *Consider the purity of Jesus tested by the world.*

   a. They strove how they might entangle Him in His talk.

   b. Our Lord spake without ceasing in the Temple. " Ask them that hear Me."

   c. Never man spake like this man. His words were the utterance of His Life.

   d. I find in Him no fault at all. This man hath done nothing amiss.

POINT III. *Consider Jesus rejected, not because of any sin in Him, but because of His purity.*

   a. Only God's people can welcome God's message; for it is suited to the truth of God's nature who speaks, not to the corruptness of our nature who hear.

   b. Only the mind which is illuminated by the Spirit of God, can receive the Word of God.

   c. The mind that wills to do the will of God will receive the illumination of God.

   d. We must act as the creatures of God, if we are to recognise the Prophet of God.

AFFECTIONS. Desire to be conformed to God. Love to Jesus because of His Purity. Surrender of self to be His disciple.

PRAYER.

O Jesu, Who wast rejected of the world in spite of Thy Divine purity, whereby Thou art accepted of the Father, although Thou didst take upon Thyself the sins of the whole world, grant that I may both praise Thee for the propitiation which Thou hast effected, and follow Thee in the purity which Thou requirest of all whom Thou hast redeemed out of the world, for Thy great Name's sake. Amen.

THE INVITATION OF JESUS.

PRELUDE. i. *In the last day, that great day of the Feast, Jesus stood and cried, saying, If any man thirst, let him come unto Me and drink.*—S. John vii. 37.

ii. Jesus crying out at the Feast, " Come unto Me and drink."

POINT I. *Consider the greatness of the invitation.*

a. The great day of the Feast. All Feasts sink into smallness before the Presence of Christ. Only in the greatness of His grace can we keep the Feast in the fulness of His joy.

b. The last day of the Feast. All other Feasts lead up to the Feast of Jesus.

c. Jesus standing to give the invitation. As He standeth to help the martyr.

d. Jesus crying with the Voice of God. It is the same Voice which shall awaken the dead; when those who would not come to the waters of grace shall be driven away in the thirst of eternal damnation.

POINT II. *Consider the universality of the invitation.*

a. If *any* man thirst.

b. Why do so few come? Because they thirst not.

c. Do I thirst? If I thirst not, it is of no use for me to come.

POINT III. *Consider the necessity of the invitation.*

a. There is no one else who can satisfy man's thirst. " Come unto Me."

b. Not enough to come, unless we drink.

c. The blessedness of a thirst thus satisfied by the gifts of His Grace.

d. The terror of the thirst when the Day of Grace shall be over.

AFFECTIONS. Resolutions to profit by the offer of Christ.

PRAYER.

O Jesu, Who in Thy mercy callest me near, that I may drink of the fulness of Thy grace, grant that I may experience the blessed refreshment of Thy heavenly power sustaining me amidst the weariness of earth, and may rise in the joy of Thine eternal fruition, perfected in the possession of Thy Life-giving Spirit, to the glory of God the Father. Amen.

PROMPTNESS IN COMING TO CHRIST.

PRELUDE i. *My time is not yet come; but your time is alway ready.*—S. John vii. 6.

ii. Jesus urging us to the Feast.

POINT I. *Consider that we must not wait for signs.*

a. Jesus waits for the time appointed of the Father. He accomplished the Father's will by a law of action which we do not know, neither can we tell the times and seasons when He will work.

b. If we waited for signs, then our going would be without value. If we will do our part, we may trust to God to do His.

c. We may be content to leave Jesus for Jesus. If we go up to the Feast we shall be sure to find Him there, though we seem to be losing some other manifestation of His Presence.

d. Jesus waits to come until there are loving hearts to welcome Him.

POINT II. *Consider that we must obey God's call at once.*

a. Enough that God has commanded any duty. We must do it.

b. Obedience must be prompt not only on occasions, but at all times. "Alway ready."

c. Our time is at God's disposal. If we use it not in prompt obedience, we shall spend it to no purpose.

POINT III. *Consider the importance of a ready will.*

a. The will is too prone to follow the eye rather than the ear; to choose what it can see, not to do as it is bidden.

b. If the will and the time always went together, how much we should be able to do. We fail because we will do things at our own time, not at the time God gives them; so we labour for naught.

AFFECTIONS. Promptness. Trustfulness. Seeing special tokens with God.

PRAYER.

O my God, let me not delay in the fulfilment of Thy commands nor doubt the co-operation of Thy covenanted mercy; but draw Thou my heart in eager acceptance of Thine invitation, and strengthen me to receive the fulness of Thy gift; through Jesus Christ our Lord. Amen.

HEARING CHRIST'S VOICE.

PRELUDE. i. *My sheep hear My voice, and I know them.*—S John x. 27.

ii. Jesus, the Good Shepherd, leading His sheep.

POINT I. *Consider Christ's sheep.*

  a. Belong to Christ.

  b. Are marked by Christ.

  c. Are constantly with Christ.

  d. Know His voice.

  e. Live for His glory.

  f. Trust in His care.

POINT II. *Consider the hearing of Christ's Voice.*

  a. With the inward ear, as the voice of God.

  b. With an obedient ear.

  c. With a loving ear.

  d. With an understanding ear.

POINT III. *Consider Christ's knowledge of His sheep who hear His Voice.*

  a. He knows our capacity for hearing.

  b. He knows our capacity for following.

  c. He knows our need of help: (i) its kind; (ii) its degree.

  d. He knows our love, or the want of it.

  e. He knows: (i) what is in man by nature; (ii) what is in us by grace.

  f. He knows the purposes for which He designs us.

  g. He knows how to train us for those purposes.

AFFECTIONS. Listening for Jesus. Love to Him. Reliance upon Him.

PRAYER.

O Jesu, Thou Good Shepherd, grant that I may alway listen for Thy Voice, and follow Thee with loving obedience, rejoicing to bear Thy mark, if I may be associated with Thy glorious Passion; and resting in the security of Thy wisdom, that I may attain to hear Thy Voice as the joy of eternity, and may be known of Thee in the Great Day amongst Thy faithful and elect children, to the glory of Thy Holy Name. Amen.

THE NATURAL HEART IN ITS HATRED TO CHRIST.

PRELUDE. i. *Why trouble ye the woman, for she hath wrought a good work upon Me.*—S. Matt. xxvi. 10.

ii. Our Lord pointing to the woman whom those around were blaming.

POINT I. *Consider how the world will trouble those who do any good work for Christ.*

    a. Because it hates Christ, and does not understand any goodness in doing a thing for Him.

    b. It regards what is done for Him, as so much loss to itself.

    c. It supposes that all such acts of love are tokens of weakness in those who do them.

    d. It thinks it can assert its power over the feeble who live in the Love of Christ.

POINT II. *Consider the weakness of our present state in the world.*

    a. Yet perhaps the contempt put upon us, does not hinder our doing good works for Christ.

    b. She whom Jesus praised for her act of devotion was—

    i. A woman who had been a great sinner.

    ii. One whose touch had been defilement to any but Him.

    iii. One, the greatness of whose love was measured, not by the greatness of present power, but by the greatness of forgiven sin.

POINT III. *Consider that the work of love done for Christ is good.*

    a. Because love comes from Him.

    b. Because He perfects and sanctifies those works of love which He dictates.

    c. Because He blesses when it is done, what He has sanctified in the doing.

    d. Because what is done for Him on earth passes, through His atoning death, into the glory of His Resurrection.

AFFECTIONS, Oblation of self to Christ. Readiness to bear obloquy. Praise to Him for accepting our acts, which are so worthless in themselves.

PRAYER.

O Jesu, Who for my sake didst suffer at the hands of the world, grant that I may refuse no suffering for Thy sake, content to bear the world's hatred, if I may abide in Thy Love. Amen.

NATURAL RELIGION IN ITS HATRED TO CHRIST.

PRELUDE. i. *Now the feast of unleavened bread drew nigh, which is called the Passover, and the chief priests and scribes sought how they might kill Him; for they feared the people.*—S. Luke xxii. 1.

ii. Chief priests and scribes in conclave.

POINT I. *Consider the chief priests and scribes desiring to kill Christ.*

   a. Because His Presence is a reproof to them.

   b. Because His coming shows their insufficiency.

   c. Because they cannot continue unless they get rid of Him.

   d. Because His Life, being founded on a Heavenly basis, is antagonistic to theirs which is the growth of natural pride.

POINT II. *Consider how they feared the people.*

   a. They have popularity, but hate the truth.

   b. They can brave God's anger, though they measure human consequences.

   c. They are even kept back from sin by that fear of man, which is itself a sin.

   d. They stand the more condemned in their sin by their knowledge of the judgment which others would pass upon their act.

POINT III. *'Consider how they sought to avoid the Feast Day.*

   a. The act was theirs. The time was God's. They can only act when He lets them.

   b. They would keep up the outward seemliness of the Feast, although they were filled with the spirit of Satan.

   c. They regarded the Feast Day as valuable in a human point of view, not as a Divine Ordinance.

   d. They did not know that the death of Jesus, which they were compassing, would indeed elevate their Feast to a Heavenly character, and would shut out themselves from all participation in its real glory.

AFFECTIONS. Love of Divine Truth, rather than human praise. Acceptance of man's rebuke, when it should seem like a warning against proposed sin.

PRAYER.

O Eternal Father, Who hast given to us Thine Only Son that we may approach Thee in the merits of His Passion, purify my heart from earthly desires, that, being one with Him in the purpose of Life by the power of Thy Holy Spirit, I may be one with Him in the glory everlasting; through His merits. Amen.

THE FELLOWSHIP OF GRACE.

PRELUDE.   i. *With desire have I desired to eat this Pass-over with you, before I suffer.*—S. Luke xxii. 15.

ii. Our Lord and His Apostles.

POINT I.   *Consider Christ's desire to communicate His grace.*

a. In accordance with the eternal predestination of the Father's will, He desired to feed them with Himself.

b. In the fulness of His Incarnate Love.

c. In spite of knowing how we shall misuse His gift.

d. As a means of helping us to eventual restoration.

POINT II.   *Consider our ignorance of the grace to which He calls us.*

a. He knows the greatness of what He desires. We know not.

b. We should learn to estimate it by the measure of His desire to communicate it.

c. That desire cost Him His Life, and therefore that gift cannot be valued at a less value. He desired to give Himself.

POINT III.   *Consider His sufferings which follow.*

a. The gift of grace is to prepare us for trials, not to set us free from them.

b. In the fellowship of Christ's grace, we must be supported for the contemplation of His weakness, manifested now in His Mystical, as then in His natural, Body.

c. In the grace of Christ we are pledged to a life which the world hates, and seeks to destroy.

d. As Christ rose from His sufferings, so will He raise us up, if we suffer and die along with Him. But we must go through the law of suffering and death if we would find the Eternal Truth of the grace given.

AFFECTIONS.   Thankfulness. Worship. Deadness to the natural estimate of things. Reliance upon Christ in time of weakness.

PRAYER.

O Blessed Jesu, Who hast called me out of a state of nature into Thy kingdom of grace, grant that I, being nourished by Thy Body as the true Paschal Lamb, may learn to suffer with Thee now, and hereafter may partake of Thy Glory which Thy Passion has procured. Amen.

THE DIVINE AMBASSADOR.

PRELUDE. i. *And the multitude that went before, and that followed, cried, saying, Hosanna to the Son of David: Blessed is He that cometh in the Name of the Lord: Hosanna in the highest.* —S. Matt. xxi. 9.

ii. The multitude crying Hosanna.

POINT I. *Consider that Jesus is the Son of David.*

   a. The word "Jesus" means God our Saviour. The word " Hosanna" means save us—" Be our Jesus."

   b. The multitude went before Him in hope, the Patriarchs: Christians follow Him now with praise.

   c. He is Blessed, the true David ; for David means "The Beloved," and blessing is the onflow of the Love of God ; and He is the fount of blessing, for from Him the Love of God flows forth, and the fulness of Blessing ; since in the contemplation of Him, the Father is blessed in the consciousness of His own Eternal Love.

POINT II. *Consider that He cometh in the Name of the Lord.*

   a. As the Son of God.

   b. As the Messenger of God.

   c. As the Anointed Prophet, Priest, and King.

   d. As the accepted Victim.

   e. As the Mediator of the Eternal Covenant.

POINT III. *Consider that His Incarnation, Passion, Death, are the glory of the highest Heavens.*

   a. By manifestation in created form of God the Invisible.

   b. By exhibition of the perfect energy of the Divine Love.

   c. By the overthrow of the rebel powers of Satan.

   d. By the communication of Divine Life and Grace, not only to man on earth, but to the host of Heaven.

   e. By revelation of the mysterious purposes of God, which in ages past even the blessed Angels had not understood.

AFFECTIONS. Welcome to Christ's sufferings. Following Him with trustful dependence and praise.

PRAYER.

O Blessed Jesu, save us from our enemies, and bring us to that manifestation of Thy love which awaits Thine elect in the Heavenly Sanctuary. Amen.

THE DIVINE ENDURANCE.

PRELUDE. i. *Thou couldest have no power at all against me, except it were given thee from above.*— S. John xix. 11.

ii. Christ before Pilate.

POINT I. *Consider the security of Christ in the keeping of the Divine Power.*

    a. The weakness of the flesh does not destroy the Almightiness of Him Who is Incarnate. His character is the same.

    b. The inner Divine Life remains unimpaired by the weakness of mortal nature. His being is ever self-sustaining.

    c. Living and Almighty, He manifests the glory of His Inner Being, by the greatness of the suffering through which He can pass unharmed. Suffering shows His inherent glory, as temptation tests His grace in ourselves.

POINT II. *Consider the dispensation of this present time, by which the authority of God is communicated to man.*

    a. Outward power is God's gift, for all power is His alone.

    b. It is a trust to man, and however it be misused God's authority must be recognised therein.

    c. The purposes for which God thus communicates His Power, often to the evil, are to us unknown.

POINT III. *Consider the security of the issue of events, since the authority thus given to man is given by the Love of God.*

    a. Whatever appearances may be, there can be no power against the Truth, but for the Truth. Evil, however great, shall be discomfited. Truth shall triumph all the more.

    b. God's love is far-sighted. To doubt God's loving wisdom is to doubt His Truth.

    c. To resist authority, on pretence of zeal, is want of faith. We must commit the keeping of our souls to God in well-doing, as to a faithful Creator in Whose promise we can rely, and rely not upon our own plans.

    d. Joyousness in suffering on behalf of Truth. Patience in looking for the sure manifestation of God's love.

AFFECTIONS. Submission to authority. Reliance upon Divine authority.

PRAYER.

O Blessed Jesus, as Thou didst bear witness to the Truth before Pilate's judgment seat, grant that I may in like manner give myself up with an entire confidence to Thee amidst every outward difficulty. Amen.

THE DIVINE OBLATION.

PRELUDE. i. *No man taketh from Me My life ; but I lay it down of Myself.*—S. John x. 18.

ii. Christ offering up His Spirit with a great cry to the Father.

POINT I. *Consider the impossibility for all the multitude around to take away His Life.*

a. They received their life only from Him, and by His good pleasure They retain it. He has life in Himself.

b. Life is to others a result of certain combinations ; but no dissolution of the outer framework of being can affect Him who is the Life of All.

c. His life, even though manifested in a fleshly form, is the very Life of God, which no man can touch. The Divine Life sustains the human.

POINT II. *Consider the impossibility for all the Hosts of darkness to drag Him into sin, so that he might forfeit it.*

a. Death is really but the outward expression of sin. We live unto God under all circumstances while we are what God means us to be.

b. The prince of this world had no part in Christ. Although His Body was within Satan's reach, yet Satan could not touch His soul, which ever rested in God.

c. The attempts of Satan to overpower Him did but make His inherent glory the more manifest.

POINT III. *Consider the stedfastness with which He clung to God, and thus gave Himself up in the act of Death.*

a. He was not only one with God by Divine generation ; but His human will ever clung to God in perfect Love.

b. His human will, whatever might be His natural desires of present good, always chose the Divine purpose as its true aim and its only good.

c. In death He gave up everything in the world, choosing God as the true portion of His inheritance. In giving Himself up to God, He claimed God. God is ours only as we die.

AFFECTIONS. The offering to God of all that one is or has Gift of ourself to Christ to be presented to the Father by Him Joy of loving all with the new love which is found in Him.

PRAYER.

O Blessed Jesu, grant that I may offer myself to the Father in union with Thee ; and as Thou didst offer Thyself upon the Cross, grant that He may accept Thee in me, and may bring me to that inheritance of His Love, which by Thy death Thou hast obtained for all Thy faithful ones. **Amen.**

I 2

THE DIVINE LONELINESS.

PRELUDE. i. *Peter, what, could ye not watch with Me one hour?*—S. Matth. xxvi. 40.

ii. Christ finding His Disciples asleep.

POINT I. *Consider the loneliness of the place and hour in the garden by night.*

    a. The multitude of the city were gone to rest. So little does the world know of the great events which are at hand for Christ and His Church.

    b. The lonely place was chosen as suitable for prayer. Times and places of prayer are apt to be times of loneliness in which Satan will assail us.

    c. The enemies of Jesus were near at hand, thinking that here He would have none to help Him for they see not the nearness of God to Him as His ever present help.

POINT II. *Consider the loneliness of the Heart of Jesus reaching out into the abyss of Godhead, where no human affection could follow Him.*

    a. No other human heart could rise up to God in love as the heart of Jesus did. In the intensity of the Love of God, He felt all the more how separate He was from man.

    b. The Love of God required the surrender of every human love. He could retain no human love, being wholly given to God. The love which He had for man was a love which God whom He loved, gave, as it were, back to the humanity as a command. His very Love to the dearest objects of earthly affection was no matter of human impulse but of obedience to God.

    c. He knew every created object, as being by nature unworthy of His Love, until He had sanctified it by Divine reward.

POINT III. *Consider the loneliness of a Redeemer in the consciousness of His work.* "*Of the people there was none with Me.*"

    a. None could take part in His work.

    b. None could appreciate the purpose of Divine Love for which this work was undertaken.

    c. None could know the intensity of struggle which this work required.

AFFECTIONS. Separation of heart from every worldly object in worshipping God. Expectation of assaults in loneliness. Joy in the all-satisfying Presence.

PRAYER.

O Blessed Jesu, Who didst endure to be alone upon the earth that Thou mightest bring Thine elect to be along with Thee in the fellowship of the Father's glory, grant that I may so acknowledge Thy Presence with me in every time of loneliness, that I may hereafter have my portion with Thee when the multitude of Thy redeemed shall be made manifest in Thine eternal kingdom. Amen.

THE DIVINE PRISONER.

PRELUDE. i. *Now he that betrayed Him, gave them a sign, saying, Whomsoever I shall kiss, that Same is He : hold Him fast.* —S. Matth. xxvi. 48.

ii. The kiss of Judas, and the apprehension by the soldiers.

POINT I. *Consider Jesus undistinguishable from others, except by the teaching which disclosed Him.*

> *a.* Jesus imprisoned by our senses. We cannot estimate His divine glory. Yet let us hold him fast, however feebly appreciated. He will lay hold upon us and make us free. Jesus delights to be made prisoner by loving faith.
>
> *b.* Jesus imprisoned in sacramental manifestation. The spiritual grace of the Divine Word cannot be bound by our want of intuition. His power is there ready to act.
>
> c. Jesus is undistinguishable when we lay hold on Him; but He manifests Himself when we have made Him our own.

POINT II. *Consider the Eternal Truth imprisoned by the machinations of falsehood.*

> *a.* The falsehood of human incapacity prevents our knowing the Truth of Jesus.
>
> *b.* The falsehood of human perverseness makes us cling to our partial conception, instead of rising up to worship His mysterious fulness.
>
> *c.* The falsehood of party spirit makes us desire to be masters of the Truth, instead of giving ourselves up to Him to be His servants.

POINT III. *Consider Him Who is the Strength of the world held fast by the world's weakness.*

> *a.* Too often we hold down God's power by our weakness, because we would use it for the weak purposes of our own will.
>
> *b.* We hold down God's power, and turn it to our own destruction, when we regard it as being adverse to us.
>
> *c.* We should hold fast God's Power by holy Love. Then would He perfect our weakness in His strength.

AFFECTIONS. Worship of Jesus hidden in sacramental mysteries. Surrender of self to their transforming power.

PRAYER.

O Blessed Jesu, Thou art our only strength. Help me so to lay hold upon Thee in the power of Thy Divine Love, while I approach Thee with the weakness of my outward faculties, that I may attain to know Thee more and more, and worship Thee not with the unworthy kiss of outward reception alone, but with the perfect Love of unwearied contemplation in the glory of Thine eternal Spirit. Amen.

THE DIVINE KING.

PRELUDE. i. *And they set up over His Head, His accusation: written,* THIS IS JESUS THE KING OF THE JEWS. —S. Matth. xxvii. 37.

ii. The accusation affixed to the Cross.

POINT I. *Consider the Promised King.*

a. The Second Adam, the Head of the human race, King over all by birthright and inherent dignity.

b. The object of all the prophecies, to Whom Patriarchs looked forward as their deliverer from the bondage of death ; King of the chosen race by special covenant.

c. The Heir of all things ; for Whom all things were made; Himself truly King over all, as He is the Creator of all.

POINT II. *Consider the Rejected King.*

a. Rejected through ignorance, because men would not look at the mystery of Truth.

b. Rejected because of the very victory which He achieved, because men did not want to be delivered from the world to which He died.

c. Rejected in spite of warnings. Men would not believe their danger, and so they could not recognize their Deliverer.

POINT III. *Consider the King of the newly chosen people whose praise is not of man, but God.*

a. Head over all things to the Church. Blessed are they who have eyes to see Him as their King.

b. A King demanding separation from the world that we may acknowledge His sovereignty, taking up our Cross and following Him.

c. A King ready to reward all His faithful followers when He shall come in His Kingdom, and to punish all who would not have Him to reign over them.

AFFECTIONS. Worship of Jesus. Love of the Cross. Deadness to the world.

PRAYER.

O Blessed Jesu, as Thou art come to save me by Thy death from Him that had the power of death, grant that I may die unto the world, and have my portion through Thy grace in the heavenly Kingdom where Thy redeeming Love shall be truly known. Amen.

THE DIVINE DEATH.

PRELUDE. i. *And there was Mary Magdalene, and the other Mary, sitting over against the sepulchre.*—S. Matt. xxvii. 61.

ii. Christ in the midst of the trembling spirits of Hell.

POINT I. *Consider how their Creator remains unharmed by Death.*

    a. The Body and Soul of Jesus are separated, but Satan has no power over either of them. Death cannot taint them nor hold them.

    b. Jesus in hell shows the perfect spotlessness of His human life.

    c. Jesus shows the true glory of His Divine Life, which until His death had been hidden from Satan.

POINT II. *Consider how their Conqueror is seen triumphant in Death.*

    a. The bonds are burst by which Death had hitherto held captive the souls of God's chosen people.

    b. Satan and his evil angels are bound down in terror at the sight of the Conqueror.

    c. The prisoners of hope worship Him with holy joy as they find the Light of His Presence filling the dark region in which they had been held.

POINT III. *Consider how their Judge spoils them of their prey by dying.*

    a. He makes known to the intelligences of the faithful departed the truth and glory of those promises for which they hoped.

    b. He sets them free from Death; for Death being paralyzed in struggle with Him, has no longer power to hold any in his grasp.

    c. He calls them round Himself by the communication of His holy Spirit, that they may rise along with Him in the perfected Life of body, soul, and spirit, which death cannot assail.

AFFECTIONS. Expectation and joy in watching the blessedness of the faithful departed. Confidence and desire to depart and to be with Christ.

PRAYER.

O Blessed Jesu, Who hast destroyed the power of Death, and cheerest the grave with the sweet Light of Paradise by Thy countenance, grant that no thought of earth may hold me down, so that Satan should again claim me for his captive; but keep Thou me ever with Thyself in the grace of Thy Sepulchre, that I may be Thine in the glory of Thy resurrection. Amen.

THE WELCOME OF THE NEW LIFE.

PRELUDE. i. *And very early in the morning, the first day of the week, they came unto the sepulchre at the rising of the sun.*— S. Mark xvi. 2.

ii. The women coming to the sepulchre with their offering.

POINT I. *Consider the darkness passing away.*

   a. Darkness of sin. We are justified by participation in the resurrection of Christ. Who shall roll away the heavy stone of our reproach? We must have the body of the sins of the flesh put away by the Circumcision of Christ.

   b. Darkness of sorrow. The death of Christ deepens sorrow, does not remove it. In all sorrow let us look forward. Heaviness for a night, but joy in the resurrection!

   c. Darkness of ignorance. The women did not yet know the power of Christ's resurrection. Until we do know that experimentally, we do not know anything.

POINT II. *Consider the women.*

   a. The penitent race of man. S. Mary Magdalene represents the redeemed people in penitence.

   b. The Jewish Church. Mary, the wife of Cleopas, the mother of James, who represents the ancient people, being Bishop of Jerusalem. God's ancient people as prisoners of hope learning the mystery of the resurrection.

   c. The Christian Church. Mary Salome, the mother of the Sons of Thunder, of the disciple whom Jesus loved, whose name tells of the Peace which belongs to those who rest in Christ. In what peace must we look to death!

POINT III. *Consider the rising of the sun.*

   a. The Sun of Righteousness. The resurrection manifests the righteousness of God illuminating all the world.

   b. The worker of healing. The righteousness of God heals the corrupt nature of fallen man. The Light is the Life of man, dispelling all the diseases of darkness.

   c. The brightness of God. Jesus is the brightness of the Father's glory. That glory was veiled during His mortal estate, but now shines forth transforming the nature which he had assumed, and capable of transforming us also.

AFFECTIONS. Eagerness to behold Jesus risen. Diligence in coming to the grave. Delight in the reward which is to be found there.

PRAYER.

O Jesu, Light of Light, Who shinest upon our darkness, calling us out of the grave of earthly existence to live in Thy Light and contemplate the glory of the Father, grant that in earthly weakness I may experience the Truth of Thy Heavenly Power and rejoice in that triumph over death which Thou hast accomplished, for all who look to Thee with Love. Amen.

THE RESURRECTION INVOLVING THE NATURAL HEART IN SADNESS.

PRELUDE. i. *What manner of communications are these that ye have one to another as ye walk and are sad ?*—S. **Luke xxiv. 17.**

ii. The three walking together as in the Gospel narrative.

POINT I. *Consider the vacancy of earth with Jesus gone.*

   a. We walk upon earth and are sad. There is no escape from this sadness unless we know the risen Saviour, and the power of His resurrection, and walk along with Him.

   b. We communicate our thoughts one to another, and increase our sadness by so doing, if we know not the truth of His power.

   c. Words of sadness pass from one to another. The word of joy ever rests in the glory of God and is satisfied.

POINT II. *Consider how the glorified life seems but a stranger to those who are satisfied with the unrisen life.*

   a. Jesus seemed to be a stranger in Jerusalem, yet it was His Presence which entitled the City of God to bear that name. The gifts of the church are infinitely beyond our thought in our present estate.

   b. "Hast Thou not known the things?" It seems as if a soul rejoicing in the risen Life of faith must be unaware of the troubles of the outer life.

   c. The natural heart wonders at the risen life—in the world and not of it—indifferent not through ignorance, but by reason of higher, truer knowledge.

POINT III. *Consider the incompetency of the natural heart to conceive the issues of its own belief.*

   a. The natural heart knows Jesus as a Prophet, but does not know that He comes from God and must go to God.

   b. Knows Jesus as mighty in deed. Yet it stops short of that without which all mightiness indeed would be valueless, the triumph over death by the Life of Resurrection.

   c. Knows Him as mighty in Word. Yet it dwarfs His Words to earthly expectations, and doubts their truth unless it finds them fulfilled upon the earth.

AFFECTIONS. Disregard of earthly expectation. Confidence in the Truth to be manifested in another world. Elevation of the soul to rest with Jesus there, while having outwardly to be here.

PRAYER.

O God, Who hast exalted Thine only begotten Son beyond the dominion of death, to reign triumphantly, in Life with Thyself, grant that we who abide for awhile in this mortal state may cast away all solicitude as to earthly accident, and experience the joy of faith according to the true Word of heavenly hope, in the security of Thy changeless Love, through the same Jesus Christ our Lord. Amen.

THE RESURRECTION BRINGING PEACE TO THE FAITHFUL.

PRELUDE. i. *Jesus Himself stood in the midst of them and said unto them, Peace be unto you.*—S. Luke xxiv. 36.

ii. The disciples seated all round the chamber upon the floor, Jesus appearing in the midst.

POINT I. *Consider Jesus standing.*

  a. He is there without motion. His apparent Form draws near to the outward sense (xxiv. 15). His real Presence is with His people whether seen or not.

  b. He stands erect, tranquil, self-sustained, elevating their hearts to a Life no longer needing earthly rest.

  c. In the midst of them. However seen He is the same. What though His back were turned to some : yet His Heart was open to them all. All felt the power of His Love.

POINT II. *Consider their fear.*

  a. They thought they were contemplating a spirit. Truly He was a spirit, but it was in the world of material Life that He was manifest.

  b. They feared to see Him, thinking Him to be a spirit, and yet it is only by seeing Him that we can see the spiritual world and live.

  c. We seldom fear to be elevated by nature to things beyond ourselves. Yet such elevation is always dangerous. We fear when God, Who is a spirit, comes to us, and yet unless He does come to us we must perish.

POINT III. *Consider Jesus speaking the word of peace.*

  a. Before their fear is shown, His Love is uttered. In His very appearing He says Peace, for He Who appears is the Word Who is Himself our Peace.

  b. Blessed are the peacemakers, for they shall be called the Sons of God, and He speaks the Word of Peace who has power to make us the sons of God.

  c. Peace be to you. Peace belongs not to the world, but to those who see the Risen Saviour. In Jerusalem the vision of Peace is really given by the resurrection of Jesus Christ.

AFFECTIONS. Reverence to Jesus unseen. Regard for Him as the Central principle of Life-giving unity to us all. Love to Him through Whom we have Peace with God.

PRAYER.

O Lord God, grant that the Presence of Thy dear Son may be manifest in the midst of us, awaking us to the solemn consciousness of Heavenly rectitude, so that we may evermore live as those who are delivered from death, and may abide in the Peace which Thou hast wrought for us, through the same, Thy Son Jesus Christ, our Lord. Amen.

THE RESURRECTION GIVING POWER TO OUR ACTS.

PRELUDE. i. *Cast the net on the right side of the ship, and ye shall find.*—S. John xxi. 6.

ii. Picture to yourself the scene as set forth in the Gospel.

POINT I. *Consider the provision.*

a. In the sea. It is a type of the multitude to be gathered into the Covenant of God, by Baptism. The sea exhibits the power of God, for it is quite beyond the control of man. The prosperity of work done in Christ's Name is wholly due to Him.

b. Its hiddenness. When we do work for Christ, we cannot anticipate the success. Yet is it foreordained by Him.

c. Its excellence. The provision of nature is good and bad. That which is sanctified by Christ is altogether perfect and efficient for its proposed end.

POINT II. *Consider the act of throwing the net.*

a. An act of obedience. If we will obey Christ, we may trust that His word will not return unto Him void. Our acts often fail because they are done rather as of our own wisdom than out of obedience.

b. Of faith. How much of the anxiety of life would be removed if we expected our acts to prosper because of Christ's bidding, instead of letting our minds dwell upon the apparent prospects of success.

c. Of promptness. Christ is not obeyed if we hesitate. His promise is not sure beyond the moment of His command.

POINT III. *Consider the finding.*

a. The words of the Apostles. The purposes of Christ are always greater than our thoughts. Let wonder at what He has done increase our expectations for the future.

b. Their surrender to Christ. The more Christ does by us the more we must be bound to Him, and consequently the more detached from our work. Let us not idly look upon the fishes, but open the eyes of our hearts to see the Lord.

c. Their gratitude. As we recognize the Lord we must also acknowledge ourselves as His servants, and give Him thanks for all His acts of Love.

AFFECTIONS. Trustfulness in Jesus to supply every need. Alacrity. Consciousness of the risen Life as beyond Nature.

PRAYER.

O Lord God, enable me by Thy grace always so to act in the Name of Thine Only-begotten Son, that I may accomplish the purposes of Thy Holy Word, and so to receive all things as Thy gift, that I may give myself to Thee in entire detachment from all save Thyself, through Jesus Christ our Lord. Amen.

THE RESURRECTION GIVING FELLOWSHIP WITH ANGELS.

PRELUDE. i. *Mary stood without at the Sepulchre weeping; and seeth two Angels in white sitting, the one at the Head, the other at the Feet, where the Body of Jesus had lain.*—John xx. 11.
ii. As in the Gospel narrative.

POINT I. *Consider the penitent standing without.*

a. Penitence weeps at the resurrection, for it feels itself powerless to follow Jesus. During the Passion He seems to be near, but in the glory of the resurrection to be gone.

b. Penitence stands outside of the sepulchre; for until it receive the illumination of faith, it does not realize how it can truly find Jesus by dying to the world.

c. Penitence stands still; transfixed in sorrow, coming to the knowledge of its own helplessness.

POINT II. *Consider the empty sepulchre.*

a. It is the last place whither the penitent has been able to follow Jesus with loving honour.

b. The penitent seems to be out of the reach of Jesus, because Jesus is out of his own reach.

c. The penitent must learn the vacancy of death until the resurrection be known; the grave remains merely to tell of helplessness.

POINT III. *Consider the Angels appearing there.*

a. There are two Angels, for the vision of Angels is an imperfect knowledge of the higher Life, and the number two implies incompleteness. They wait upon a Third. In Jesus is perfection.

b. "One at the Head, the other at the Feet." The earthly manifestation had its limitations. By the resurrection Jesus is past into the Infinite glory.

c. Penitence beholds the power of Heaven waiting upon all that Jesus has touched, and yet it needs the knowledge of the resurrection to rise into the Heavenly fellowship, and appreciate Jesus as the Lord of power.

AFFECTIONS. Sense of unworthiness. Patience in waiting. Gratitude to the risen Saviour. Longing to be with Him.

PRAYER.

O Lord God, grant that I may watch beside Thy grave whilst Thou art waiting to do Thy wonderful works. Yea, let men and angels wait for the manifestation of Thy glory, that they may find therein the fulness of their joy, through Thee our Lord. Amen.

THE RESURRECTION CALLING US APART TO WORSHIP CHRIST.

PRELUDE. i. *Then the eleven disciples went into Galilee, and when they saw Him they worshipped Him.*—S. Matt. xxviii. 16.
ii. As in the Gospel narrative.

POINT I. *Consider the eleven going away from Jerusalem to Galilee.*

a. Their wonder as they act upon their risen Lord's command, in the consciousness that He acts by a Law of Presence unknown before.

b. Their consciousness of a new development of mystery, in being summoned away from the ancient home of their religious hopes for this solemn interview.

c. Their detachment, in acknowledging that all the world is the same to Him.

POINT II. *Consider our Lord appearing to them.*

a. It was according to His Promise. Jesus requires us to rise superior to all natural anticipation, in obedience to His appointment, and then He will meet us in truth.

b. There seem to have been more than five hundred present to witness His appearing. In that mountain where a multitude would have made Him King, He shows Himself to the multitude in a royalty which transcends human will.

c. As He shows Himself here by mysterious Presence, so He requires His Presence henceforward to be recognized whether visible to the naked eye or no.

POINT III. *Consider the worship which they gave to Him.*

a. They saw Him with the heart as well as with the eye, and were satisfied. Therefore they worshipped.

b. Some were of those who would go to Galilee, as He had bidden; nevertheless, could not go onward to acknowledge the mystery of His risen life. They could go *where* He pleased, but He must show Himself *as* they pleased. Therefore they doubted.

c. To see Jesus risen is to worship Him. If we see Him not so, we do not see Him truly.

AFFECTIONS. Detachment. Mystery. Supernatural joy in Christ. Truthful obedience to His appointment.

PRAYER.

O Jesu, grant that I may always in outward acts accomplish Thy bidding, and with the heart welcome the blessed Truth of Thy promises, so that I may be prepared to worship Thee with an entire devotion in whatever way Thou art pleased to make Thyself manifest, Who with the Father and the Holy Ghost livest and reignest God for ever and ever. Amen.

THE RESURRECTION QUICKENING LOVE WITH EAGERNESS.

PRELUDE. i. *So they ran both together; and the other disciple did outrun Peter, and came first to the sepulchre.*—S. John xx. 4.

ii. As in the Gospel narrative.

POINT I. *Consider the eagerness of the two disciples.*

a. Peter and John represent the active and the contemplative life, or the Judaic and the heavenly characters of discipleship. Both forms of service have Christ for their end.

b. In whatever way we would seek the risen Saviour we must run after Him with eagerness, otherwise we shall not reach to Him. " Draw me ; we will run after Thee."

c. If we would come to Christ we must run together in love. However different we may be we must not disparage one another.

POINT II. *Consider whither they are going.*

a. To the sepulchre. The place where we last saw Jesus is the place for us to look for Him still.

b. In both lives we must learn deadness to the world before we can know the power of Christ's resurrection. Come to the sepulchre.

c. Soldiers had watched the sepulchre. Apostles had left it. The Jews strove to prevent the resurrection which they feared. They who should have placed their hopes in it, were negligent and missed their share in it.

POINT III. *Consider the disciple whom Jesus loved.*

a. If we know how Jesus loves us we shall not be held back, but shall outrun all others.

b. Peter comes afterwards. The Apostle of the Circumcision represents the people of the elder Covenant, slowly apprehending the death of earthly hope, through which we must pass to the living hope of Heaven.

c. The eyes of love must look through the empty grave and see the life beyond, which faith accepts.

AFFECTIONS. Persevering hope in Christ. Diligence in seeking Him though there be no earthly hope.

PRAYER.

O Lord Jesu, as I hasten to Thy sepulchre, grant unto me the blessing which I desire, even to see Thee with the eye of faith in the knowledge of that love which death cannot destroy, and in the cessation of all natural relationship teach me the power of Thy Resurrection and the glory of Thine eternal Life. Amen.

THE RESURRECTION-LIFE A SECLUSION.

PRELUDE. i. *Then the same day at evening, being the first day of the week, when the doors were shut where the disciples were assembled for fear of the Jews, came Jesus, and stood in the midst, and saith unto them, Peace be unto you.*—John xx. 19.

ii. As in the Gospel narrative.

POINT I. *Consider the disciples assembled.*

    a. The discipleship of Jesus is a bond of union. To have been taught by Him is a prerogative which separates from all others.

    b. The sufferings of Jesus are a bond of union. If we know that He suffered for our sins, the common interest in Him which such a consciousness involves makes all the redeemed a special chosen race.

    c. The love of Jesus is a bond of union. Our love to Him is not impaired by His death. He lives on as no one else can live on in the hearts of His faithful people, making them one.

POINT II. *Consider the closed doors.*

    a. The chosen people of Jesus are not only a separate people. They are shut in from the world. The world cannot understand them.

    b. We may be shut in by sickness, poverty, coldness of others, religious opposition, continuous labour, rule of life.

    c. We must be assembled together, otherwise the world's being shut out will do us no good. We may be assembled together either by outward companionship or by common agreement, or by love or largeness of heart. Even solitude must not degenerate into isolation.

POINT III. *Consider the appearance of Jesus.*

    a. He has promised to come when two or three are gathered together in His Name. The more we shut the world out, the more ready He is to come in.

    b. Jesus may appear to us in different forms; by His Word, in His Sacraments, by the power of His Spirit.

    c. Jesus speaks Peace wherever He appears. We can only have Peace in proportion as we see His risen glory.

AFFECTIONS. Love to Jesus. Detachment from the world. Love of seclusion. Interior contemplation.

PRAYER.

O *Blessed Jesu, grant that I may live so hidden from the world in the acceptance of Thy Heavenly Covenant, that I may realize my position in the Communion of Saints, and partake of the revelation of Peace, wherewith Thou hast enriched them in Thyself, who livest and reignest with the Father, in the Unity of the Holy Ghost, one God, world without end. Amen.*

THE INDIVIDUALITY OF RESURRECTION-LIFE.

PRELUDE. i. *Thomas, because thou hast seen Me thou hast believed: blessed are they that have not seen and yet have believed.* — S. John xx. 29.

ii. As in the Gospel narrative.

POINT I. *Consider our Lord calling St. Thomas by his name.*

a. Jesus speaks to us individually, although in union one with another. He knows our individual sins and our individual needs.

b. The voice of Jesus shall call us out of our graves hereafter. If we hear the voice now, it will call us out of our sins, and nothing else can.

c. When Jesus calls us by name, and we respond to the call, then we are reconciled to God, for in the Word of individual Love whereby He knows us our Eternal Life consists

POINT II. *Consider what it is to see Jesus.*

a. There is a sight of Jesus which hinders the true knowledge of Him, a sight of the outward natural form alone, which precludes the sight of the inward and spiritual power of His Presence. The Jews believed not, because they saw.

b. There is a sight of Jesus which the natural reason is apt to demand, requiring Jesus to conform to ourselves instead of rising up to the law of Divine Love. So was it with Thomas.

c. There is a sight of Jesus in the form of Divine Love which transforms us into His own likeness. This is the illumination of the Spirit. This sight is the reward of faith.

POINT III. *Consider the fellowship of the risen.*

a. Jesus speaks to us individually; that we may hear with the interior energy of the spiritual life what His Spirit saith unto the Churches, and may understand the Message.

b. Jesus shows Himself to us that we may contemplate His glory, and our soul, as we gaze, becomes the living mirror of His perfection, and we become one with Him.

c. Jesus bids us handle Himself, for with the spiritual grasp of His glorified Being He takes us, and with the spiritual touch whereby our nature is transformed He requires us to take Him and to partake of Him.

AFFECTIONS. Consciousness of our need. Reliance upon the discipline of Jesus. Desire of transformation into His likeness.

PRAYER.

O Blessed Jesu, since I cannot see Thee now with that vision which alone gives blessing, grant that I may so give myself to Thee in my blindness that Thou mayest give Thyself to me as the true Light of my soul, wherein I may see the Eternal Light of Thy Love, and may be satisfied in Thy contemplation for ever. Amen.

THE SIGNS OF JESUS UNWRITTEN.

PRELUDE. i. *And many other signs truly did Jesus in the presence of His disciples, which are not written in this book.*—S. John xx. 30.

ii. The apostle S. John contemplating the glory of Jesus.

POINT I. *Consider that they are not written by reason of their number.*

    a. Every moment of our Lord's life on earth was a sign both in the deep out of which He spake as man, and in the height above where He lives as God.

    b. Each act comprised within itself countless acts of glory beyond enumeration, to live on to ages yet unborn.

    c. All His acts were the infinite development of a law. To know Jesus in one act truly, is to know all His acts.

POINT II. *Consider that they are not written by reason of their greatness.*

    a. No act of Jesus can be told save in some small feature, for in itself it involves the whole relation of God towards the creature. It is an act of the Incarnate Word.

    b. Also each act of Jesus spreads in its consequences throughout all creation. These signs waken up fresh phenomena of Divine Life by the sacramental power wherewith they quicken the natural universe.

POINT III. *Consider that they are not written by reason of their Divinity.*

    a. The written word can reveal nothing more than the external operation of the Divine Word. What Jesus does, He is. His acts in Creation are the outcome of His Eternal Self-acting Godhead. To know what Jesus did we must know Him as the Word of God, the Eternal Son.

    b. The signs which Jesus works are written by the power of the Holy Ghost in the hearts of the faithful, and cannot be communicated by pen and ink from man to man.

    c. The signs which Jesus wrought can never be fully told. No evidences of the Christian faith can sustain such consequences by logic. They supply the necessary preparation. "He that believeth hath the witness in himself."

AFFECTIONS. Adoration and wonder at the glory of Christian Truth. Acknowledgment of the Divine Glory of Jesus.

PRAYER.

O Jesu, Who art the Word of God by Whom all things were made, grant me so to contemplate Thy Divine Majesty, hidden beneath the veil of Thine outward actions in the world, that I may attain to behold the glory of that Love wherewith Thou art ever acting towards Thine Elect, Who with the Father and the Holy Ghost livest and reignest One God, world without end. Amen.

K

THE WRITTEN SIGNS.

PRELUDE. i. *But these are written, that ye might believe that Jesus is the Christ, the Son of God; and that believing, ye might have life through His Name.*—S. John xx. 31.

ii. S. John in the Spirit on the Lord's Day calling us to enter with him into the contemplation of that which he has written.

POINT I. *Consider that they are written by the power of the Holy Ghost.*

    a. The Holy Ghost alone can discern. "The things of God knoweth no man, but the Spirit of God." Our senses cannot see that Divine reality which gives Life.

    b. The Holy Ghost alone can select. The acts of Jesus were symbols. The work of His Church existed in the germ of His Life.

    c. The Holy Ghost alone can describe. That which is written in His power is preserved by Him from all falsehood, and all its details are true to His living purpose.

POINT II. *Consider that they are adequate to the purpose for which they are written.*

    a. Finite words cannot sustain the infinite by logic, but these signs require the Divine glory of Jesus to explain them, as the human frame requires the intelligent soul.

    b. They cover the whole surface of sacramental truth, so that the whole system of grace is involved in their interpretation,—all things necessary to salvation.

    c. They have living power, a value beyond mere logical result. A speaker's manner gives meaning to his words. The Holy Ghost operates livingly in these words.

POINT III. *Consider that they must be read in the Spirit in which they are written.*

    a. Love is quick to catch the meaning of mere hints. The Holy Ghost enables us to see truths beyond human words.

    b. There must be an experience of the things of God by the power of the Holy Ghost, if we would understand what God says of Himself. Holy Scripture is given for "the man of God to be perfect unto all good works."

    c. We must desire to grow in grace as God desires to give it. We must be transformed into what we read.

AFFECTIONS. Love of Eternal Truth in contemplating mysteries.

PRAYER.

O Blessed Jesu, Who by the Holy Ghost didst take our nature upon Thyself, do Thou by the same Spirit take possession of my intelligence, so that however I be compassed with infirmity, yet I may grow in the knowledge of Thy Truth, until I attain to the perfect conformity of Thy glorious Life, Who livest with the Father in the unity of the same Spirit, God for ever and ever. Amen.

THE OBJECT OF FAITH.

PRELUDE. *i. These are written, that ye might believe that Jesus is the Christ, the Son of God; and that believing ye might have life through His Name.*—S. John xx. 31.

ii. Jesus gazing upon us with holy Love, and making the brightness of His hidden glory to shine increasingly upon our souls as we worship Him.

POINT I. *Consider Jesus.*

a. The Heir of the promises. The faith of Christ is no new invention. Without Jesus the expectation awakened throughout preceding ages would be frustrated.

b. The rejected of the world. Messiah was to be rejected of men. This rejection is but a proof of the truth of Jesus. It must go on in every age of the world.

c. The Saviour of mankind. He saves us, not for the world that we should live to it, but from the world that we may die to it and live in the glory of the resurrection.

POINT II. *Consider that Jesus is the Christ.*

a. Foreordained of God. As the Gospel shows the signs of Jesus worthy of God, so the history of the world speaks with the voice of Divine Predestination to mark Him out.

b. Anointed with the Holy Ghost. "God was with Him." The Holy Ghost abode upon Him unchangeably.

c. Bearing a threefold commission as Prophet, Priest, and King. We must always regard Him as abiding to us in this threefold character, and remember that it involves a threefold habit of conduct towards Him on our part.

POINT III. *Consider the Divine Sonship.*

a. Consubstantial with the Father. The Son of God lives with the Father's Eternal Life. Otherwise He could not communicate it to us.

b. Begotten of the Father. The Father puts forth in Him all the energy of His own Eternal Being. He is not merely received into this Life as we are, but He comes forth from the inherent power thereof and acts therewith.

c. Representative of the Father. He is come not as a servant, but as a Son over His own House. We must not merely believe what He says, but know Him as He is.

AFFECTIONS. Confidence in Jesus as communicating to us the Divine Life. Simplicity in coming to Him as our only Hope.

PRAYER.

O Jesu, as Thou hast been pleased to show Thyself to me, so give me grace to acknowledge in Thee that Divine glory which Thou hadst with the Father from the beginning, that by the ordinances of Thy grace I may be perfectly established in that Life wherein Thou wouldst have Thy people to live with Thyself and behold Thy glory everlastingly. Amen.

THE LIFE OF FAITH.

PRELUDE. i. *These are written that ye might believe that Jesus is the Christ, the Son of God ; and that believing ye might have life through His Name.*—S. John xx. 31.

ii. Jesus Christ breathing upon His Apostles and quickening them with the gift of the Holy Ghost, that we may receive the same through them.

POINT I. *Consider the faith which is required.*

a. Faith must accept Christ. If we know Christ as what He is we must welcome Him as bringing to us an authoritative message from God.

b. Faith must bring us to Christ. We must come unto Him that we may have Life. To know the truth of Christ at a distance is not enough.

c. Faith must lead us to seek to be one with Christ. No external nearness will suffice. To know Him as God we must be His living members.

POINT II. *Consider the Name whereby this Life is given.*

a. The Name of the Eternal Trinity is involved in the Name of God the Son, for He and the Father dwell together in the Unity of the Holy Ghost, and their Name is One.

b. It is not His action for us in our nature, neither His teaching nor His death, which gives us Life ; but His assumption of ourselves into union with His own living Person, both as God and man.

c. His Mediatorial Name is the foundation of all the Sacraments of grace by which we are brought under the operation of His Divine Nature by the Holy Ghost Which proceedeth from Him.

POINT III. *Consider the Life which is communicated.*

a. The Life which He gives by grace is that very Life which He receives of the Father by eternal generation in the Unity of the Holy Ghost.

b. This Life is given to us by incorporation into Him so as to have His Name, and it can be retained only by remaining in Him.

c. This Life must be active in us as in Him, making us like to Him in thought, word, and deed, bringing forth in us the manifold fruits of the Spirit.

AFFECTIONS. Desire of heavenly things with Christ in God. Sense of deadness pervading all the world around us.

PRAYER.

O Jesu, Who ever dwellest in the eternal joy, grant that I may so accept in faith the means of grace whereby Thou wouldest unite me to Thyself, that I may attain to behold Thee even as Thou ever livest in the knowledge of the Father, with Whom Thou livest and reignest in the Unity of the Holy Ghost, one God for ever and ever. Amen.

THE JOY OF THE RESURRECTION.

PRELUDE. i. *The Lord is risen from the Tomb, Who died to save us from our doom.*

ii. Jesus appearing to Mary Magdalene.

POINT I. *Consider the past darkness of death.*

 a. We are corpses in the world by reason of sin.—Rom. vi. 11. Man has died. The world was made for man to live in. Sin has made him incapable of having true enjoyment here. All dies around us.

 b. There was no hope of change. Each generation is born to inherit the doom of decay, disappointment, and dread.

 c. The dead body of Christ lay in the tomb. He subjected Himself to that surrender of all things which death involves.

POINT II. *Consider the living freshness of Resurrection-Life.*

 a. Jesus passes through the grave into a new life, and death hath now no more dominion over Him.

 b. By baptism He brings us into union with Himself that we may live in the power of the Holy Ghost, free from the world over which death reigns.

 c. The Life thus given to us is renewed continually by fresh gifts of grace perfecting us for the fulness of joy which is set before us.

POINT III. *Consider the consciousness of salvation.*

 a. The glory of our Lord's risen Body exhibits to us the reality of that Life into which we are called.

 b. The personal action of our Lord towards His disciples shows us the continuing fellowship wherein we are to live with Him. " Then were the disciples glad when they saw the Lord."

 c. The heavenly life must be to us a reality of joyous sympathy as we contemplate the Communion of Saints.

AFFECTIONS. Sense of freedom. Contempt of the world. Hope of glory.

PRAYER.

O Jesu, illuminate my understanding with the joy of Thy contemplation, that here I may act in the power, and hereafter may rejoice in the glory, of that Eternal Life which Thou givest to us in Thyself by the power of the Holy Ghost, Who by the same Spirit hast conquered death, and raised our nature to the glory of the **Father. Amen.**

THE GOOD SHEPHERD.

PRELUDE. i. I *am the Good Shepherd: the Good Shepherd giveth His Life for the sheep.*—S. John x. 11.

ii. Israel in the Wilderness with the pillar of fire to guide them.

POINT I. *Consider how the Good Shepherd loves the sheep.*

a. He created them to be the object of His care. He has "formed them for Himself," and gives them all His Love, that they may love Him in return.

b. He leads them through the Wilderness, and feeds them there. The desolation around only shows His tenderness, as He supplies them day by day, and carries them in His arms when weary.

c. He is bringing them to the pasturage of a higher life than that which they now have. From wandering here they are to attain to rest in the perfect manifestation of His love.

POINT II. *Consider the glory of the Good Shepherd.*

a. The Good Shepherd is the Lord of all Creation. Whatever dangers be round about, yet He leads His flock safely if they trust in Him.

b. He is the Author of all Life. He feeds with earthly things, but these give sustenance only by reason of His power.

c. He reveals His glory more and more as He leads His flock onward to partake of it. Each stage of progress is really an advance in the experience of the Life of God.

POINT III. *Consider the joy of belonging to the Good Shepherd.*

a. Security amidst seeming danger. The threatenings of earth have no reality, but serve to prove the Almightiness of His Love.

b. Hope amidst the weariness of earth. The toil of the journey develops a capacity of joy. The fulness of the end would have had no pleasure without the hunger preceding it.

c. Consciousness of a love sustaining us which counts no cost too great if we will only let Him lead us onward to the full experience of His glorious power.

AFFECTIONS. Joy in the leading of Providence. Acceptance of sorrow. Personal communion with God.

PRAYER.

O Jesu, Thou Good Shepherd, as Thou leadest us in Thy Love, open mine eyes to behold Thee. So shall I never fear the dangers which seem to be round about; yea, they shall be welcome to me, as bringing ever to my remembrance that on Thee alone can I rely. Nothing is sweet unless it be Thy gift, nothing strong, nothing durable. Teach me to find sweetness in the loss of everything, that I may find myself plunged in the fathomless glory of Thine all-sustaining Love. Amen.

THE GOOD SHEPHERD GIVING HIS LIFE.

PRELUDE. i. *Jesus said, I am the Good Shepherd: the Good Shepherd giveth His life for the sheep.*—S. John x. 11.

ii. The Blood of the Shepherd as it flows, rising up in a wall of fire to encircle the sheep, whereby the wolf is destroyed.

POINT I. *Consider how He destroys the wolf by giving His Life for the sheep.*

    a. "By death, He destroyed him that had the power of death." The loss of the outer life shows the truth of the inner life and the falsehood of the Enemy.

    b. By passing into the simple life of God, He rose superior to Satan's dominion, and bruised the Serpent's head.

    c. By the entire gift of Himself in sacrifice to God, He received triumphantly of God the keys of hell and of death to bind Satan.

POINT II. *Consider how He rescues the sheep thereby.*

    a. By destroying Satan, He frees those who had been in bondage all their lives through fear of death, and led captivity captive—the Patriarchs who died in faith.

    b. He reveals the security of the hidden life. His sheep cannot now fear outward death. His people shall not die.

    c. He gathers His sheep when they die into that Eternal Life which, although given here in Sacraments, cannot be truly known. Death frees them from sin, and the power of the enemy hurts them no more.

POINT III. *Consider how He glorifies the sheep by the Life which He gives.*

    a. He makes the way into the holiest open by shedding His Blood. They who have this Blood sprinkled upon their consciences with regenerating power come to God as His children.

    b. His Blood shed in death cleanseth from all sin those who are washed therein by faithful use of the Sacraments of grace.

    c. The Blood wherein the new Life of Divine Sonship is thus communicated fills the soul, which it regenerates with energies and desires proper to itself, that they may rejoice before God in Faith, Hope, and Love.

AFFECTIONS. Joy in the pardon of Christ. Longing for Jesus to come. Desire of heavenly things.

PRAYER.

O Jesu, Who by shedding Thy most precious Blood hast destroyed the tyranny of Death, grant that I may always rejoice in the new Life which Thy Blood conveys, and having a cleansed conscience, may serve God with the living and acceptable service for which it strengthens us, to the glory of Thy Holy Name. Amen.

THE LIFE OF DIVINE KNOWLEDGE.

PRELUDE. i. *As the Father knoweth Me, even so know I the Father: and I lay down My Life for the sheep.*—S. John x. 15.

ii. Holy Baptism as a Well of Life placed in the Sepulchre of Christ, so that those who bathe therein find its waters shining with the brightness of the Revelation of the Eternal Trinity.

POINT I. *Consider how this Life makes the life of human experience indifferent.*

> *a.* Life is consciousness, and the consciousness of God's glory makes all earthly objects insignificant.
>
> *b.* The consciousness of God's power makes all instrumentalities indifferent, since He can effect His purpose through any.
>
> c. The consciousness of God's Love makes present things indifferent, because we know that He will use all alike for the accomplishment of some special good towards us.

POINT II. *Consider this Life as resulting from the Father's Will.*

> *a.* God sent His Son to lay down His Life, that we might have Eternal Life thereby, as His children.
>
> *b.* God sent His Wisdom, the Word of Truth, by His Incarnation to make manifest the folly of all created intelligence apart from Him, and the falsehood of the Prince of this World.
>
> *c.* God sent His Son, that by participation of His Spirit we might know Divine Truth in the mystery of resurrection-life.

POINT III. *Consider this Life as perfected in the Father's Revelation.*

> *a.* By this Life the Word of Christ dwells in us, and instructs us to praise God truly.
>
> *b.* As outer things pass away, this Life is developed in the faithful with ever-increasing experience of the all-surpassing excellency of God.
>
> *c.* Hereafter we shall know as we are known, living in the perfect fellowship of the Divine consciousness, even as God the Son knoweth the Father eternally.

AFFECTIONS. Delight in the Articles of the Faith. Acceptance of Divine Truth as the foundation of all living power.

PRAYER.

O Jesu, Who art the Only-begotten Son, the Word, abiding eternally in the knowledge of the Father, Whom Thou declarest, grant us to be made partakers of Thy Death, and by the power of Thy Resurrection so to live now through Thy Grace in the exercise of faith, that hereafter our Life may be perfected in the Vision of that Glory which Thou hast with the Father in the unity of the Holy Ghost. Amen.

THE HIRELING.

PRELUDE. i. *But he that is an hireling, and not the Shepherd, whose own the sheep are not, seeth the wolf coming, and leaveth the sheep and fleeth; and the wolf catcheth them, and scattereth the sheep.*—S. John x. 12.

POINT I. *Consider that the hireling has only a temporary care of the sheep.*

    a. The Jewish Covenant had the wages of temporal reward, whilst looking after the sheep. The gifts of Christ are not of this world. The sheep shall be with Him where He is (S. John xvii. 24), and where the wolf cannot follow.

    b. The sheep were kept within the fence of the Law to protect them until Christ came; but the Law could not give Life.

    c. The Life of Divine knowledge (Heb. viii. 11) belongs to the New Covenant established upon better promises than the first, which waxed old; and instituted not by means of an hireling, but by the Son Himself. (Heb. iii. 5, 6.)

POINT II. *Consider how he fleeth.*

    a. The Jews feared the approaching doom saying, The Romans will come and take away both our place and nation.

    b. They left the sheep. They said, This people knoweth not the Law. They themselves really knew not Him Who is the fulfilling of the Law in whom Life is found.

    c. They fled from God's Covenant, when they said, His Blood be on us. No power could have hurt them else.

POINT III. *Consider how the sheep are scattered by the wolf.*

    a. The wolf, the symbol of Roman Empire, represents the power of this world. The parable has reference to the loss of Eternal Life not by *any* sin, but by worldly-heartedness.

    b. The world-power caught the sheep of the Old Covenant. Their rulers kept them not in spiritual life, whereas God's promises availed only for those who were kept for this hope. The siege of Jerusalem and the dispersion followed.

    c. This wolf feeds now on men's hearts. Rome swallowed up the Church. Love of the world secularized the things of God. The sheep were scattered. What the wolf seized was after all not the sheep. The Good Shepherd will yet gather His dispersed flock into His Own new Life.

AFFECTIONS. Desire of heavenly reward. Distrust of earthly gifts. Confidence in Jesus as the One Good Shepherd.

PRAYER.

O Blessed Jesu, Who wouldest not that Thy people should have any abiding city in this world, grant that our affections may be so fixed on heavenly things that we may watch for Thy coming, and rejoice to hear Thy Voice when Thou shalt call Thy dispersed sheep together, that we may be free from the tyranny of the world. Amen.

THE SHEEP THAT ARE BROUGHT.

PRELUDE. i. *And other sheep I have, which are not of this fold: them also I must bring, and they shall hear My Voice; and there shall be one fold and One Shepherd.*—S. John x. 16.

ii. The scattered sheep upon the mountains hearing the Shepherd's call and awakening to a supernatural life at His bidding.

POINT I. *Consider the scattered sheep of the Gentile world.*

 a. The Covenanted people were gathered into the fold; but the Good Shepherd was not less careful of those that had not been brought near.

 b. His Covenanted people are not His sheep because of being in the fold, but they are in the fold because they are His sheep. He will not leave His sheep outside when He has found them.

 c. However scattered, yet we are known to Him. He seeks out them that know Him not. Much more will He bring home those that have a true love towards Him, however far away.

POINT II. *Consider how they hear the Good Shepherd's Voice.*

 a. The Voice of Jesus fills them with joy, whereas the voices of other lords who had had dominion, were never able to win their hearts.

 b. It is not enough to be His sheep by right of ownership. We must be in the fold of His Covenant, so as to be the people of His pasture, and the Sheep of His Hand.

 c. They hear His Voice and come to Him that He may bring them into a new Fold, the Covenant of His Church. There can be no stragglers recognized by Him.

POINT III. *Consider the unity of life into which they are brought.*

 a. The Old Covenant was but an external fold. The New Covenant is a new Life, Eternal Life. They are one flock. None other is like them.

 b. There is One Flock and One Shepherd. One Lord, and His Life-giving Name One. The Shepherd gives His own Life to the Flock.

 c. We cannot be His sheep save in this One Life, as His Voice calls us. So have we fellowship one with another. Both Jew and Gentile are made One New Living Flock, in the Church of Christ.

AFFECTIONS. Gratitude for being brought near. Separation of heart from the world. Love to the Brethren.

PRAYER.

O Jesu, as Thou hast been pleased to bring me into Thy flock, grant that I may always follow Thee in newness of Life, and evermore look up to Thee as the Shepherd by whom I hope to be guided unto the glory of the Father. Amen.

THE SHEPHERD'S VOICE.

PRELUDE. i. *And other sheep I have which are not of this fold : them also I must bring, and they shall hear My voice; and there shall be one fold and One Shepherd.*—S. John x. 16.

ii. The multitude of sheep upon the mountain side. The true sheep leaving their pasture and coming near at the Shepherd's call.

POINT I. *Consider how the Good Shepherd speaks in the conscience.*

    a. They that are of the truth hear His Voice. Man was originally formed in God's Image, and has a natural aptitude for recognizing God's Voice in so far as he is true to his own nature.

    b. The Word is the Light which lighteneth every man. All utterances of truth in the soul are His Voice. The conscience speaks not of itself, but as His Voice fills it.

    c. He calls again and again, but we will not hear. They who give themselves to evil hear the voice of the thief, and are deceived. None who seek the Truth sincerely shall fail of hearing the Voice of the Truth.

POINT II. *Consider how the Good Shepherd speaks by His messengers.*

    a. The messengers whom He sent before Himself were His servants, and spoke of Him. He was with them. He spake by them.

    b. His Voice is with His messengers now in His Church. If speaking to worldly hearts with worldly results, they are but thieves. The true sheep hear when the Voice of the Good Shepherd speaks in them, but the world loves his own.

POINT III. *Consider how the Good Shepherd speaks by His Spirit.*

    a. He speaks in the heart by preventing grace. His regenerating voice gives a supernatural ear to the soul.

    b. He makes Divine power accompany the earthly voice of His messengers in all ministrations, teaching, exhortation, remission of sins, building up in holiness.

    c. He guides His Church collectively into all truth. The sheep, the new, the beautiful flock, hear what His Spirit saith unto the Churches.

AFFECTIONS. Joy in listening to the Voice. Trust in Jesus as a Teacher. Ready obedience.

PRAYER.

O *Blessed Jesu, speak in my heart and give me grace to hear that which Thou sayest, and, as I hear, to do. O seek Thy servant, for I do not forget Thy commandments, but let Thy word dwell in me richly, that in my weakness Thy praise may be perfected. Amen.*

THE UNITY OF THE FOLD.

PRELUDE. i. *And other sheep I have which are not of this fold: them also I must bring, and they shall hear My Voice and there shall be one fold [flock] and One Shepherd.*—S. John x. 16.

ii. The sheep gazing up as the Shepherd calls.

POINT I. *Consider the supernatural unity of Life, which makes the flock to be one.*

    a. The flock lives with the same Life as the Shepherd. His Voice gives them Life, and that Life His own.

    b. The supernatural ear is that higher living consciousness in which all share. By this they are one, and hear His Voice.

    c. No outward division destroys this identity of life, for it is a unity beyond the reach of natural perception.

POINT II. *Consider the love to Himself wherein they are one.*

    a. Supernatural life cannot be without Divine love. "Every one that loveth is born of God, and knoweth God." We cannot be of His flock unless we abide in His Love. ·

    b. This love is given to Him as One Who personally cares for us. The act of life which binds the flock together is their love to Jesus ever near.

    c. This love is a power by which the sheep follow Him whithersoever He goeth. His likeness rests upon them all. Their actions are those, not of nature, but of grace.

POINT III. *Consider the means by which the unity of the flock is maintained.*

    a. Of old, the Jews were fenced in by a fold which was to be destroyed. Now, the sheep are separated from the world by life-giving ordinances, the ministration of the Spirit.

    b. The Divine utterance is just as truly fixed by sacramental appointment for the maintenance of the flock as it is by natural laws for the natural life of man.

    c. Any voice which sets aside the laws of the Good Shepherd must be treated as the voice of the thief who comes to destroy. The working of the Good Shepherd is the same yesterday, and to-day, and for ever. Nothing can be added to His command: nothing taken away from it.

AFFECTIONS. Joy in the Heavenly Life. Love to Jesus. Careful use of Sacraments of Graces.

PRAYER.

O Jesu, Who of Thy great mercy has called me into Thy Church, grant that I may rejoice to belong to Thee in that new life which Thou hast given, and ever keeping the unity of the Spirit in the bond of peace may grow up in the perfect knowledge of the glory to which Thou callest me, Who with the Father and the Holy Ghost livest and reignest God for ever and ever. Amen.

THE VISITATIONS OF JESUS.

PRELUDE. i. *Jesus said to His disciples, A little while and ye shall not see Me, and again a little while and ye shall see Me; because I go to the Father.*—S. John xvi. 16.

ii. Jesus visiting the soul, and hastening onward, unless we detain Him by great entreaty.

POINT I. *Consider the discipleship of Jesus.*

a. Jesus is training the soul. He desires that we should learn by His visitations and by His absences, so as to follow His guidance, and be with Him in the glory of the Father.

b. Jesus warns us of coming difficulty. He does not lead us to expect continual manifest guidance from Himself. In time of perplexity when He is not seen to be near, yet we are to wait and trust.

c. Jesus points us onward to the end. We must be content to have Jesus go, otherwise we could not go after Him. He goes to the Father. His going to the Father is better for us than His staying with us in our exile.

POINT II. *Consider how Jesus hides Himself.*

a. For a little while Jesus leaves us, but He will return in greater power than He left. During the time of His absence He would have us profit by the gifts of His Presence. If we turn these not to account, we are not fit for more.

b. The defect is on our side, not on His. When He leaves us He does not lose care of us, nor power. We see not Him. Even though not seeing, we must seek to hold Him.

c. He is triumphant on our behalf where He is gone. Whether He go for a little while down below, or ascend to reign at God's Right Hand for ever, it is for our sakes.

POINT III. *Consider how Jesus shows Himself.*

a. Occasionally. We must not expect to have Jesus with us always. By leaving us, He would have us learn to value His Presence, to seek to detain Him, to invite His return.

b. As belonging to another world. Each manifestation of Jesus will demand some fresh effort on our part, ever new, although the same, yesterday and to-day and for ever.

c. With purpose of leading us to the Father. Each new manifestation calls forth a fresh energy of faith. So also it transforms us into a higher fellowship of Divine Love.

AFFECTIONS. Rest in the Love of Jesus. Earnest expectation of closer intercourse.

PRAYER.

O Jesu, do Thou of Thy great goodness abide with me and lead me onward to the contemplation of the glory of the Father. Let Thy Presence be my strength; and when I see Thee not, let me cling to Thee, that by Thy absence I may learn to hold Thee, until I never lose Thee any more at all. Amen.

THE SORROWS OF THE CHURCH.

PRELUDE. i. *Verily, verily, I say unto you, that ye shall lament, but the world shall rejoice : and ye shall be sorrowful, but your sorrow shall be turned into joy.*—S. John xvi. 20.

ii. The faithful waiting in darkness without shelter until the morning :—the world making merry in a building which is ready to fall and crush those that are therein.

POINT I. *Consider the Church sorrowing by reason of the world's persecution.*

    a. The outer nature suffers by the violence of the world. Her own habits of peace do not shelter her. Her enemies only make themselves the more ready for battle.

    b. The Church is feeble and unequal to resist. The world is strong. Her strength belongs to another world. She is the less able to guard herself because she has to secure that other world at all costs.

    c. The Church does not look for triumphs on this side of the grave, rather distrusts them. She looks forward to death as the only end for her of the sorrows of life.

POINT II. *Consider the Church sorrowing by reason of the sin which is around.*

    a. The Church sorrows more in seeing the world's evil than in bearing her own. All her own external suffering is but the result of the evil which she deplores in the world.

    b. The Church bewails the evil around her as being her own reproach, because she is so mingled with the evil world.

    c. The Church sorrows in thinking of the end which awaits the world, which she so earnestly longs to rescue and cannot.

POINT III. *Consider the Church sorrowing by reason of her desire for God.*

    a. The Church deplores her loss of God's Presence. This spiritual void is a greater anguish than any temporal one. It must be deeply felt, for until its depth be realized it cannot be removed.

    b. The manifestation of the Love of Jesus only makes it the more terrible to have forfeited His Presence ever so slightly.

    c. The days of life are weary, while we are waiting for God; but thereby patience and faith are perfected.

AFFECTIONS. Patience. Longsuffering. Hope.

PRAYER.

O Jesu, Who hast pronounced those to be blessed who sorrow and weep, grant that I may so deplore my sins and the sins of the whole race, that in due time I may have my portion in the joy of Thy Redeemed, Who livest and reignest with the Father and the Holy Ghost now and for ever. Amen.

THE REJOICING OF THE WORLD.

PRELUDE. i. *Verily, verily I say unto you, that ye shall weep and lament, but the world shall rejoice: and ye shall be sorrowful, but your sorrow shall be turned into joy.*—S. John xvi. 20.

ii. A crackling fire blazing on earth, while the morning sun rises calmly upon the darkness around.

POINT I. *Consider the world exulting over the Church.*

 a. We are not to repine at the world's joy, although we must grieve that it does not know the value of our sorrow.

 b. The world exults in consciousness of present strength, but does not know that that strength is only for a moment.

 c. The world is the Ishmael who ever mocks at Isaac: but its joy must be repudiated; the world cast out at any cost.

POINT II. *Consider the world having a transient delight.*

 a. The world rejoices because God made man to rejoice, and gave him the means of rejoicing: but the rejoicing of the world is evil, because it knows not the evil of that wherein it rejoices, nor its own incapacity of joy in the loss of God.

 b. The things of the world give immediate joy to those who know not how to use them aright; but they are used aright only when they are so used that they abide.

 c. The joy of the world only testifies to the greater joy which remains for the people of God when the evil of the world is done away. Let us learn to rejoice in our eternal joy, while we see the world rejoicing in that which perisheth.

POINT III. *Consider the world using joy as a means of forgetting God.*

 a. Joy is from God, and should bring us to God, but the joy of the world takes the place of God. The world is satisfied therewith. It hurries the world off to the things of God's creation, and away from Himself.

 b. Joy is for God, and should be offered to God. The faithful offer it to God by every act both of penance and of thanksgiving. The world wants God to minister to its joy; does not wish by its joy to glorify God.

 c. Joy is in God. Only in looking to God can we know the Eternal. False joy is changeable, and makes us avoid the Eternal. The changeless is wearisome when no living and true joy is yet found.

AFFECTIONS. Contempt of the world's pleasure, and sorrow for the world's ignorance. Joy in Christian hope.

PRAYER.

O Jesu, Who didst come forth from the Eternal Joy to share the sorrows of our transitory life on earth, grant that I may never be deceived by that which perisheth, but may consecrate every earthly thought to obtain that joy which shall be revealed when the deceitful pleasures of time have passed away. Amen.

SORROW AT THE LOSS OF JESUS.

PRELUDE. i. *Ye now therefore have sorrow; but your sorrow shall be turned into joy.*—S. John xvi. 22.

ii. The soul wrestling in darkness and loneliness.

POINT I. *Consider the soul feeling itself left alone by Jesus.*

   a. The soul of man is formed for companionship. Jesus is the only true Companion. When the soul feels that He is gone, then all else is worthless.

   b. The soul which has known the blessedness of Jesus, knows what it is to have lost Him. The sorrow is proportioned to the experience of joy.

   c. The soul feels itself unable to recall Jesus, but Jesus wants the soul to cry out after Him. Blessed is that pain wherein we learn to lay hold on Jesus, by crying after Him.

POINT II. *Consider the soul toiling unfruitfully while Jesus is away.*

   a. The soul can do nothing when Jesus is gone. All labour is fruitless without Him. Nothing comes to us save by His bidding.

   b. The energies of the soul are paralyzed unless Jesus strengthen us by His Holy Spirit. We need to be left alone sometimes, in order that we may know how helpless we are.

   c. That which we do gives no joy, unless Jesus give it. Earthly results only make us feel the misery of our own earthliness.

POINT III. *Consider sorrow as the heritage of the Cross.*

   a. Jesus bore the Cross. We must bear it with Him. Otherwise we cannot know what He has suffered for us.

   b. Each suffering developes in us some fresh sense of gratitude. Suffering would cease to be if Jesus were always manifest. His presence would suffice to cheer any sorrow.

   c. We cannot share the benefits of the Cross without being partakers of the Crucified Life. The gifts of power are proportioned to the participation of its anguish.

AFFECTIONS. Love of the Cross. Acknowledgment of God's will as effecting our final happiness by present discipline.

PRAYER.

O Jesu, Who didst endure so much pain in body and soul for the redemption of mankind, grant that we may never refuse Thy discipline, but may be enabled hereafter to claim the rewards of Thy Cross, having been nailed along with Thee in the mystery of grace. **Amen.**

THE SIGHT OF JESUS RESTORED.

PRELUDE. i. I *will see you again, and your heart shall rejoice, and your joy no man taketh from you.*—S. John xvi. 22.

ii. Jesus appearing to the disciples on their way to Emmaus.

POINT I. *Consider the outward sight of the risen Saviour.*

a. Its mystery. Although He appeared before their outward senses, yet He no longer belonged to the world of sensible objects. He appeared in their midst when the doors were closed.

b. Its certainty. He could make His Body manifest in its solidity as before. They might touch His wounds.

c. Its encouragement. As we behold Him passed into a state of higher life than of old, so we feel His power to bring us after Himself.

POINT II. *Consider the mystical sight of the risen Saviour.*

a. In the acts of His Providence. We feel the power of His resurrection as a bright mystery to uphold us in danger. We see Him guiding us.

b. In the persons of His people. We act towards them with a remembrance of His Life dignifying them with the claims of gratitude. This is He that died for us.

c. With the claims of honour. This is He that is alive for evermore.

POINT III. *Consider the sublime sight of the risen Saviour.*

a. The eye of faith contemplates Him according to the truth of the Church's dogma in His Personal glory.

b. By acts of dogmatic faith in the power of the Holy Ghost, the heart learns to experience the transforming energy of His resurrection.

c. By varied acts of devotion, according to the several articles of the faith respecting Him, the soul learns to develope the beneficence of Him who loves us still.

AFFECTIONS. Confidence. Intimacy, and habitual continuance along with Jesus.

PRAYER.

O Blessed Jesu, though Thou art past away from our state of humiliation, yet Thou dost condescend to walk with us who remain therein. Grant us, therefore, we beseech Thee, grace so to contemplate the mysterious power of Thy Presence, that we may be transformed according to the fellowship of Thy Love, Who livest and reignest with the Father and the Holy Ghost for ever and ever. Amen.

L

SORROW CHANGED TO JOY.

PRELUDE. i. *Verily, verily, I say unto you, that ye shall weep and lament, but the world shall rejoice, and ye shall be sorrowful, but your sorrow shall be turned into joy.*—S. John xvi. 20.

ii. Jesus making a heavenly Light to shine around us in the darkness while we walk with Him.

POINT I. *Consider how every element of former sorrow remains in the joy which succeeds.* .

a. The whole Body of Christ is raised with all the marks of His Passion.

b. Each act of His former suffering has its own true reward in the glory which follows.

c. Each act of sorrow wherein we have felt His Passion becomes a chamber of delight within the soul, where we may welcome the joy of His risen glory. ·

POINT II. *Consider the transforming power of the Holy Ghost.*

a. By the Holy Ghost He raised Himself from the grave.

b. By the Holy Ghost He opens our eyes to behold Himself.

c. By the Holy Ghost He elevates our hearts to delight in the things of God, if we wait upon Him.

POINT III. *Consider the personal sense of joy whereby we abide with Him.*

a. However transformed He is the same Saviour; we are the same redeemed ones whom He has saved from sin.

b. The rewards of Jesus, as we contemplate His glory, are felt by the loving soul as if they were its very own: yea, more truly than any thing it could have of itself.

c. The soul exulting in this joy is conscious of being itself the object wherein Jesus the glorified Saviour delights. He rejoices to be glorified in His Saints.

AFFECTIONS. Acceptance of sorrow. Joy in suffering. . Patience and Hope.

PRAYER.

O Jesu, Who didst suffer as Man ere Thou didst enter into Thy glory, grant that I may accept all the sufferings of this present time as the instruments whereby the power of Thy glory may be revealed to me for Thy mercy's sake. Amen.

THE ETERNITY OF THE RESTORED JOY.

PRELUDE. i. *I will see you again, and your heart shall rejoice, and your joy no man taketh from you.*—S. John xvi. 22.

ii. Jesus calling us to walk with Him, because the night is far spent, and the Eternal Day is already beginning to shine.

POINT I. *Consider the security of this joy.*

a. It is beyond the assaults of any enemy. It is triumphant over death.

b. It has a Life abiding in the power of God. It is the very joy of God communicated to the Creature in the Person of the Incarnate.

c. It makes us secure from any despondency which other circumstances of our probation might occasion. Difficulties do but enhance it instead of destroying it.

POINT II. *Consider the development of this joy.*

a. The more we know of Jesus, the more we learn to rejoice in His companionship. We can only come to this knowledge by a growing experience.

b. The growing sense of His Godhead makes us to be more and more absorbed in His Personal Love.

c. The circumstances of life, as they effect a change in us, teach us how this joy is inexhaustible and unchangeable.

POINT III. *Consider the completeness of this joy.*

a. We are complete in Christ, filled with His joy according to the measure of our capacity.

b. We are enlarged by union with Him to that dignity of joy which befits His Divine Person.

c. The joy of each of His members is a true individual joy; but it does not exclude, rather it appropriates with an intense consciousness of identity, the joy of all the members wherewith it is associated in His Body.

AFFECTIONS. Humility in accepting God's discipline. Desire to learn His Truth. Joy in the fellowship of the risen Lord.

PRAYER.

O Jesu, open Thou mine eyes to behold the brightness of that Heavenly Joy wherein Thou wouldst have me walk with Thyself amidst the children of the Eternal Light; and grant that in the consciousness of this Eternity I may put away from me the deceitful pleasures of the lower world, to live simply in the satisfaction of Thine own all-sufficing Truth and Love. Amen.

L 2

THE OBJECT OF THE DEPARTURE.

PRELUDE. i. *Jesus said unto His disciples, Now I go My way to Him that sent Me, and none of you asketh Me, Whither goest Thou? But because I have said these things unto you, sorrow hath filled your heart.*—S. John xvi. 5, 6.

ii. Jesus speaking these words to the Eleven.

POINT I. *Consider the announcement.*

  a. Leaving the world was no afterthought, disappointment, scorn. It was the purpose for which He came into it, that He might return when His mission was done.

  b. He tells the disciples where He is going, for that knowledge ought to overcome the sorrow at His being gone.

  c. He seemed to be going to death, but only as into a dark valley, thence to climb the heights beyond. He was not going to death, but rather from death. This world is under death, and He was leaving it. Life Eternal is found in God.

POINT II. *Consider the uninquiring ignorance of the Apostles.*

  a. The human heart limits God's universe to its own experience. Yet we should think of Life as it is with God, and learn to desire it. Even the Apostles did not now think of that higher Life.

  b. Jesus speaks to us of the future because He wants us to have a living interest in the future. Therefore He reproaches them with their dulness. The thought of the Father ought to waken our eager inquiring Love.

  c. It were in vain to speculate as to another world. Jesus must tell us about it, otherwise we cannot know it.

POINT III. *Consider the sadness of that ignorance.*

  a. The Apostles' hearts were heavy through their ignorance, and their earthliness prevented their seeking that higher knowledge which could heal their sadness.

  b. The thought of losing Jesus made them sad, because they did not yet know that Jesus is better known by being gone, than by being here.

  c. If we are to gain joy from Jesus' going, we must know the glory of the Divine Life. He goes thither, for He came thence. He, Who is God eternally, must take into God's glory the created nature which He assumes.

AFFECTIONS. Wonder at God's Love, and man's destiny.

PRAYER.

O Jesu, assist me with Thy grace to contemplate the glory of Thine Ascension, that in the fulness of Thy Love I may attain to the gifts which Thou hast promised; and living here in holy hope, may hereafter abide with Thee in the joy of Thine eternal kingdom at the Right Hand of God, by the power of the Holy Ghost. Amen.

THE COMFORTER REPROVING THE WORLD OF SIN.

PRELUDE. i. *When the Comforter is come, He will reprove the world of sin and of righteousness and of judgment.*— S. John xvi. 8.

ii. Jesus speaking these words.

POINT I. *Consider the world.*

    a. The world rejects Christ in His own Person, and offices, and in His Church, His ministers, His Sacraments, His Word, His doctrine.

    b. The world prides itself upon its own security, wealth, reason, power. Like the giant defying Israel.

    c. The Holy Ghost comes to reprove the world, and to guide the faithful. God's enemies though left for a little while shall come to shame in the end.

POINT II. *Consider the sinfulness of the world.*

    a. The world is sinful of itself, and as such is condemned already. The Prince of this world first, then Adam, involved the whole course of nature round about us in sin and death.

    b. The world will not believe its own sinfulness, scorns the idea of a fall, and regards itself as irresponsible.

    c. The world is sinful because it is not now what God made it. It is fallen under death. Darkness has been upon the face of the deep ever since Satan's rebellion.

POINT III. *Consider the manifestation of that sinfulness by the coming of the Holy Ghost.*

    a. The Light shineth in darkness. There is a separation between the two. The darkness comprehendeth not the Light. The Light shows the evil of the darkness.

    b. The Holy Ghost shows God's purpose, justifies God (Ps. li. 4.), and makes the world bear the whole burden of its sin.

    c. The Holy Ghost shows by His coming that the world cannot raise itself out of sin, that sin is terrible because it is tyrannical, that there is no escape save by coming to Christ in the Covenant of faith.

AFFECTIONS. Praise for the gift of the Holy Ghost. Earnest love of the Sacraments, as the channels of Divine Power for our deliverance. Patience amidst the taunts of the world.

PRAYER.

O Blessed Jesu, in Whom alone we can find Life and Freedom, grant me now coming to seek Thy grace in the hidden operation of the Holy Ghost, so to profit by Thy Sacraments as the instruments of Thy Covenant of Life, that I may not find Thy Holy Spirit witnessing to my condemnation, when Thou shalt be glorified in Thy Saints in the great day of the manifestation of Thy power. Amen.

THE COMFORTER REPROVING THE WORLD OF RIGHTEOUSNESS.

PRELUDE. i. *When the Comforter is come, He will reprove the world of sin and of righteousness and of judgment.*—S. John xvi. 8. ii. Jesus speaking these words.

POINT I. *Consider the righteousness of God.*

a. God is righteous, and Righteousness is the Life of God. It is not merely a state of innocence, but of power.

b. We know sin only by knowing righteousness. Through want of this knowledge man estimates sin but feebly, with reference to himself alone and not to God.

c. We know Righteousness only by being admitted to the Life of God. The Righteousness of God is revealed in the Gospel because mankind are brought into a new Life, as partakers of the Divine Nature.

POINT II. *Consider the Holy Ghost making this manifest.*

a. The Holy Ghost does not speak to our intellect from without but in our heart, and through our intellect, thus enabling us to know the things of God.

b. The Holy Ghost reveals Christ, the Image of God, within the soul, that by union with His Incarnate Life we may be conformed to the demands of His Eternal Life, wherein He ever abides with the Father.

c. The Holy Ghost reproves the world which will not 're- cognize its own true state of death and of condemnation, by revealing this Righteousness in the faithful here and glorifying them accordingly with the Life of God in the Great Day, to the confusion of the unbelieving world.

POINT III. *Consider the Ascension of Christ as the necessary preliminary to this manifestation.*

a. The living, active Righteousness of God could not be given save by the Holy Ghost coming forth in union with the Man- hood of Christ as the Head of the living Body, the Church.

b. This gift could not be until Christ was glorified in the glory of the Father. He must go to the Father before He could send the Comforter from the Father.

c. The Humanity must be lost to sight in the glory of God, else it could not transmit the Divine glory. This Righteous- ness dazzles the whole nature more than any brightness can the outward eye. When this Righteousness is seen by the world it will destroy the world.

AFFECTIONS. Exultation in the Righteousness of Christ. Self-surrender to Him in its power.

PRAYER.

O Jesu, in Whom the Righteousness of God shineth forth as the Life of all Thy members, grant that my eyes may be opened to con- template Thee in the glory of the Father by the power of the Holy Ghost, and my heart transformed, so as evermore to be true to Thy Heavenly guidance. Amen.

THE COMFORTER REPROVING THE WORLD OF JUDGMENT.

PRELUDE. i. *When the Comforter is come, He will reprove the world of sin and of righteousness and of judgment.*—S. John xvi. 8. ii. Jesus speaking these words.

POINT I. *Consider the judgment of the Prince of this world.*
- *a.* Satan for a long time had exercised his sovereignty over the world. The fire was prepared for him and his angels, but their sin could not be punished without a judgment.
- *b.* The Son of Man was to exercise the judgment upon him; and by His glorification in Righteousness as the Elect of God, the Prince of this world was cast out.
- *c.* Already is he judged, but he is left for a while, and the world which clings to him is deceived by him.

POINT II. *Consider the Holy Ghost making this manifest.*
- *a.* In the triumph of Christ. The Holy Ghost shows thus to faithful souls the judgment whereby Satan is bound; but the world does not believe in it.
- *b.* In the glorification of the Saints. The Holy Ghost shows the weakness of Satan by enabling the people of Christ to triumph over him from age to age. The supernatural Life of Christ and His Church is as a voice of judgment, declaring Satan's power to be at an end.
- *c.* In the overthrow of every earthly power. The nations who are willing to be deceived by him will behold his overthrow when Christ being glorified in His Saints, the Prince of this world shall be cast into the lake of fire.

POINT III. *Consider the consequences of this judgment to the world at large.*
- *a.* The world does not believe in his having been judged, because the world loves his work, his rule, and his reward.
- *b.* The Holy Ghost will make manifest to the world the Righteousness of God in judging Satan and delivering His Saints. Mankind rebel now at God's sovereignty. Then shall He be justified before them.—Ps. li. 4.
- *c.* The Holy Ghost pleads with men now to leave the way of Satan. Jesus, who would have saved them from Satan by the power of the Holy Ghost, will cast them into the pit with Satan whom they chose, judging them in the power of the Holy Ghost.

AFFECTIONS. Renunciation of the Devil and his works. Praise to the Spirit of Truth. Contempt of the perishing world.

PRAYER.

O Jesu, grant that we, abiding in the remembrance of Thy victory over Satan, may be kept free from his deceits now, and may be preserved from his punishment hereafter, so that when Thou appearest in judgment we may rejoice in Thy salvation, and praise Thee for Thy goodness. Amen.

THE NEED OF PREPARATION FOR TRUTH.

PRELUDE. i. *I have yet many things to say unto you, but ye cannot bear them now.*—S. John xvi. 12.

ii. The Blessed Virgin as the representative of humanity waits for the Holy Ghost to take of her substance a body for the Word of God.

POINT I. *Consider God's purpose of making truth known.*

    a. The mind of man was formed in God's image to receive Divine Truth. No other intelligence was like it. Man was God's living image as long as he abode in the Truth.

    b. The Word was made flesh. The Truth was brought to man's mind, by reason of the hypostatic union, as a living faculty within himself. The God-man was the Truth.

    c. God purposed to shed forth the Spirit of His Son into the hearts of those who should receive Him, in order that they, as His Sons, might have Eternal Life and know Him truly.

POINT II. *Consider man's natural incapacity of receiving Truth.*

    a. By the Fall man died, and his mind, though formed after God's image, being dead, lost the fellowship of Truth.

    b. By repeated acts of sin man fell more and more away from God. His nature passed on to further corruption.

    c. No "overshadowing" power of the Holy Ghost could undo the Fall or restore the Life of Truth to the dead. Life must be within. It was necessary for God to make man's flesh His own in order to make the mind which dwelt therein capable of supernatural apprehension.

POINT III. *Consider the work of the Holy Ghost in preparing man.*

    a. By the discipline of ages He prepared them to expect a deliverer, and by ceremonial acts to acquire some knowledge of what His work should be.

    b. At the Incarnation He took of the flesh of Mary a body which He sanctified to be the Body of the Eternal Wisdom. The mind could not be raised to God without the body. The body being raised necessarily raised the mind.

    c. By the Sacraments the Holy Ghost makes us members of Christ's Body. So mind receives through body the power of supernatural Faith. Until the Body of Christ was glorified no human mind could accept mysteries which must be spiritually discerned.

AFFECTIONS. Love of bodily discipline in the power of the H. G. Desire to contemplate Divine Truth. Joy in Divine Life.

PRAYER.

O Lord Jesu, Who by Thy Holy Spirit has taken me into union with Thyself, grant that by the power of the same Spirit I may be guided in holiness of Life, so that I may rejoice in the fellowship of the mysteries which Thou hast revealed, Who livest and reignest with the Father and the Holy Ghost one God world without end. Amen.

THE COMFORTER GUIDING THE CHURCH INTO ALL TRUTH.

PRELUDE. i. *When He, the Spirit of Truth, is come, He will guide you into all Truth, and He will show you things to come.*—S. John xvi. 13.

ii. Jesus looking upon His Apostles as He speaks with the fulness of Divine knowledge and love.

POINT I. *Consider the Spirit of Truth.*

  a. He is the Spirit in Whom the Eternal Word ever dwells with the Father. In the energy of His Procession the Eternal Word is one with the Father.

  b. He is the Spirit by Whom the Eternal Father acts, so that His Procession is the Law of Eternal Life. He quickens all things in accordance with the mind of God.

  c. He takes of the things of Christ, and reveals His Divine power and glory according to the measure of the intelligences wherein He comes to dwell.

POINT II. *Consider the Church as led by Him.*

  a. The Church is led collectively by Him. One Life, one Mind, fills the Church, and we cannot violate this collective action without serious loss.

  b. We are led by Him, each individually, but only so long as we seek to keep the unity of the Spirit in the bond of peace. If we trust in our own wisdom, we forfeit His guidance.

  c. He guides by " showing the Way," which is Christ, revealing Christ within the soul. [This is the literal meaning of the word in this place.] He does not force us hither or thither.

POINT III. *Consider the things to come.*

  a. He shows things to come, not the future of earth, but the glory of Christ. Christ is " He that cometh."

  b. He shows them by enabling us to experience their power as existing in God. Thus Christ's Kingdom comes to our minds.

  c. He shows them by His power quickening the ear of the soul to hear the supernatural utterances of God. Thus Christ's Kingdom comes in us with power.

AFFECTIONS. Desire for spiritual illumination. Confidence in Divine teaching.

PRAYER.

O Lord *Jesu, grant me by the attraction of Thy Spirit so to long for the full knowledge of Thy Truth, that I may joyfully yield myself to the holy teaching of Thy Blessed Spirit, and may be perfected for the Vision of Thy glory in the ages of Eternity.* Amen.

THE COMFORTER GLORIFYING JESUS.

PRELUDE. i. *He shall glorify Me, for He shall receive of Mine, and shall show it unto you.*—S. John xvi. 14.

ii. Jesus looking upon His Apostles as He speaks with the fulness of Divine knowledge and love.

POINT I. *Consider the great purpose of His coming.*

a. He glorifies Christ, by exhibiting the glory of Christ. Christ can receive no glory from without, but His glory is shown by the operation of the Holy Ghost.

b. The sending of the Holy Ghost is itself the great glory of Christ, for if Christ were not God and Man in One Person, He could not send the Holy Ghost, a Divine Person, to dwell with His people.

c. The work of Christ's Incarnation would have been incomplete, unless the Holy Ghost did bring a chosen people into the fellowship of the Incarnate Life.

POINT II. *Consider the Holy Ghost receiving of Christ.*

a. The Holy Ghost abides in the glory of Christ by the consubstantial unity of Godhead. He does not receive by outward gift, as if He were external to the Godhead.

b. The Holy Ghost receives of that glory which belongs to Christ, because in the Godhead He proceeds from Christ. He receives not economically but essentially.

c. He receives of Christ the Godhead wherein the Father and the Son dwell consubstantially, not any remunerative glory to which Christ has attained in Creation, but the glory wherein He and the Father are One.

POINT III. *Consider the Holy Ghost showing the things of Christ to the Apostles.*

a. He shows the things of Christ by giving Divine eyesight, to the souls of the faithful. Man must be raised to a fellowship of the Divine Nature—born again—before he can see the things of God.

b. He shows abidingly. We can only see the things of God by abiding in the Presence of God. In the darkness of nature we can see nothing.

c. He shows increasingly. As He leads us on in holiness so He shows man of the things of Christ, until we come to know Him in the fulness of Divine Life.

AFFECTIONS. Joy in the thought of Christ's glory. Praise to Christ for His promises. Surrender to the guidance of the Holy Ghost.

PRAYER.

O Lord Jesu, grant that I may so abide in the power of Thy Holy Spirit that I may attain increasingly to contemplate Thy glory with holy joy, and to find my only joy in Thy contemplation, Who livest and reignest with the Father in the unity of the same Spirit, God for ever and ever. Amen.

THE NAME OF CHRIST.

PRELUDE. i. *Hitherto have ye asked nothing in My Name : ask and ye shall receive.*—S. John xvi. 24.

ii. Christ giving to us a signet-ring, that we may exercise His authority in all our prayers.

POINT I. *Consider the inadequacy of prayer before Christ came.*

    a. Man was outcast from God. When God admitted man to speak with Himself, it was an act of special favour, overriding the edict of universal banishment, which was still unrepealed.

    b. Even in the covenanted worship of the Sanctuary, there was the veil of separation, teaching man to remember his outcast condition. The Jewish covenant did not set aside the penalty incurred by the Fall.

    c. All the constituted means of access to God were only typical of that which was to be afterwards. Therefore they had no permanence. The sure mercies of David waited for their living energy until the Covenant of Christ.

POINT II. *Consider what it is to ask in Christ's Name.*

    a. It is to claim His authority. His people speak with God as members of His Body. He speaks in them.

    b It is to speak with His Power. As the Human Nature is indissolubly joined to the Divine Nature in His Person, the members of His Human Body speak with the power of His Holy Spirit.

    c. It is to plead His merits. The Baptized must therefore speak to God with all the claim which His Divine self-sacrifice has effected.

POINT III. *Consider the certainty of receiving.*

    a. The promise is unlimited. If our prayer be consistent with the oblation of Christ, there is nothing God holds back. " All things are yours, and ye are Christ's."—1 Cor. iii. 22.

    b. The power is all-sufficient. All authority is given to Christ in heaven and earth. Prayer in Christ's Name is as the word of a king.

    c. The truth is never-failing. The Kingdom of Christ has no end. All the promises of God in Christ are Yea and Amen.

AFFECTIONS. Filial confidence. Delight in prayer. Large-heartedness towards God.

PRAYER.

O Lord Jesu, as Thou hast obtained for us access in Thy Name unto the Father, grant us by Thy Holy Spirit to plead Thy merits with unfailing confidence, dying unto the world by the power of Thy Grace, that we may obtain the glorious gifts of that New Life whereunto Thou hast called us, Who livest and reignest with the Father and the Holy Ghost, one God, world without end. Amen.

THE ASSURANCE OF ANSWER TO PRAYER.

PRELUDE. i. *Ask and it shall be given you: seek and ye shall find: knock and it shall be opened unto you.*—S. Matt. vii. 7.

ii. Christ giving to us a signet-ring that we may exercise His authority in all our prayers.

POINT I. *Consider the necessity of asking.*

a. God will ordinarily give in proportion as we ask. Things which we know not, He will give of Himself.

b. God has fixed this law of prayer, as the means of developing our desire and our effort. Were his gifts purely spontaneous, our moral being would be depressed rather than elevated by them. We learn to love by desiring.

c. Asking implies the concurrence of the whole nature in seeking to obtain. All prayers must be accompanied by work, and all work must be done as an expression of prayer.

POINT II. *Consider the importunity which is implied.*

a. Prayer in Christ's Name must have the energy of Christ. His Name avails not without His Life. A dead name is not Christ's Name.

b. Prayer which is not importunate misses one character of life. If our prayers die out, they were not worthy to have the answer of the Living God. Life has no stops.

c. Prayer that grows weary lacks faith, and if we speak without consciousness of the authority of Christ, we are not really speaking to God. If we begin in Him, we rise to God.

POINT III. *Consider the authority in praying.*

a. We must pray because Christ commands us. The more we ask for, the more do we fulfil His command.

b. We must pray because Christ inspires us. If we do not utter our desires to God, we cannot be living in the fellowship of His Life, for Christ is ever speaking to God.

c. We must pray because Christ encourages us. The more we pray, the more we shall desire to pray, for we shall experience the power of prayer. Success gives confidence.

AFFECTIONS. Desire to pray. Faith in God's loving power. Praise to Christ for His grace.

PRAYER.

O *Blessed Jesu, help me so to draw near unto the Father in the power of Thy grace, that I may acknowledge all good things as His gifts when I receive them, and may rely upon His goodness to give me everything that is good when I shall ask Him, for the glory of Thy holy Name. Amen.*

CHRIST EFFECTING THE ANSWER TO PRAYER.

PRELUDE. i. *If ye shall ask anything in My Name, I will do it.*—S. John xiv. 14.

ii. Joseph acting in Pharaoh's name, a type of Christ.

POINT I. *Consider Jesus receiving our prayer upon the throne of His glory.*

    a. His joy when He sees that we believe in His Power. He rejoices to receive our prayer more than we do to receive the answer.

    b. His interest in watching the desires of our hearts for His glory. Our prayers show the measure of our spiritual life, both in the things which we desire and in our way of desiring them.

    c. His co-operation, as He assists us to make our desires known to Himself. He enlightens us that we may see what is really good, and seek for it in the way that is fitting.

POINT II. *Consider Jesus communicating all that the Father gives Him.*

    a. The Father hath given all things into His hands. He has received all, as Man, not for Himself, but for His brethren.

    b. He delights to apportion His gifts, so that they may not only be the stay of our outward nature in the world, but may also sustain us unto Life everlasting.

    c. He holds back His gifts when He sees that giving immediately will prevent our possessing eternally.

POINT III. *Consider Jesus working unceasingly by the power of the Holy Ghost.*

    a. Jesus acts in the power of the Holy Ghost, being one God with the Father. The Holy Trinity is ceaseless action.

    b. The Father cannot give anything to man save through the merits of Christ's Manhood receiving representatively, and through the co-operation of His Divine Person as the Eternal Word, accomplishing instrumentally whatever we ask for.

    c. Jesus desires that our prayer should rise up to the worthiness of His Kingdom in glory.

AFFECTIONS. Dignity in prayer. Glory to Jesus. Joy in contemplation of the Eternal Trinity.

PRAYER.

O Blessed Jesu, teach me so to acknowledge all things as Thine, that I may ask all things from Thee, use all things for Thee, and rely upon Thee for all things in the power of the Holy Ghost, to the glory of God the Father. Amen.

CHRIST'S GLORY THE OBJECT OF PRAYER.

PRELUDE. i. *Now, O Father, glorify Thou me with Thine own Self, with the Glory which I had with Thee before the world was.*—S. John xvii. 5.

ii. The glory of God, wherein the Body of Jesus waits to receive into Itself all the multitude of the faithful.

POINT I. *Consider how Christ is glorified as Mediator.*

 a. In our manhood. The manhood is henceforth to be the instrument of all Divine actions, being seated on the Right Hand of Power.

 b. By manifestation of His Eternal Godhead. The invisible glory shines forth through the manhood of Christ, as an instrument worthy to make it known.

 c. Through the communication of that glory to the members of His Body. This manifestation is no empty declaration, but a real gift of Divine Life, enabling the intelligence to apprehend it.

POINT II. *Consider how Christ is glorified in His people.*

 a. As the Conqueror Who has carried them Home in triumph. They show His power, by the very marks of bondage wherein Satan held them. He has rescued them from the power of sin. He changes sufferings into glories.

 b. As the Head of the Body. He and they are one. Every hurt which they can suffer, is a real loss of lustre to Himself. He will not allow such hurt to abide.

 c. As the Power of each individual member. Whatever glory they have, is but the forth-streaming of His indwelling Life, Who is their Righteousness, Sanctification, and Redemption.

POINT III. *Consider how Christ is glorified through our prayers.*

 a. Jesus was heard in that He feared. He attained His glory not by mere obedience as a slave, but by prayerful self-sacrifice as a Son.

 b. Jesus prays through us. The glory of the Life of the Incarnate Word speaks through us in proportion as we pray. Thus He glorifies us by bringing us to God.

 c. Jesus obtains the full manifestation of His glory through our prayers. What He has received in Himself requires to be developed in each one of His Members by the discipline of prayer, ere His Body can attain its final glory.

AFFECTIONS. Desire for Christ's glory. Acceptance of our Lord's Ascension as a principle of power.

PRAYER.

O Lord Jesu, hasten the manifestation of Thy kingdom, and so replenish our hearts with the desire for Thine appearing, that in us Thou mayest be glorified everlastingly, Who livest and reignest with the Father, in the Unity of the Holy Ghost, One God, world without end. Amen.

THE MYSTERY OF THE ASCENSION.

PRELUDE. i. *I ascend unto My Father and your Father, and to My God and your God.*—S. John xx. 17.

ii. The narrative as in S. Luke's Gospel.

POINT I. *Consider our Lord as He ascends from the midst of His Apostles.*

a. He leads them out to Bethany, the House of humiliation, and then He ascends. We must know His humiliation if we would know His glory.

b. As He blessed them, He was parted from them. His Ascension is in Blessing, and it is the very foundation of all Blessing. If He were below, He could give no Blessing.

c. A cloud received Him out of their sight. He was separated from their sight, not they from His. They were only the more immediately under His Power.

POINT II. *Consider the Divine Father to whom He goes.*

a. He goes to the Father with Whom He ever dwelt, One God. He does not come as from a distance, but He elevates His Humanity to a closeness of intercourse with the Father befitting His Divine Person.

b. In the Ascension He experiences the fulness of Filial joy; the oil of gladness penetrating every faculty of the created nature which He has assumed.

c. His Humanity being thus taken up to God receives God's Presence as an energy, so that it necessarily also gives forth the glory which It receives. It is no dead glory.

POINT III. *Consider our participation in the glory of the Divine Sonship.*

a. The Father of J. C. is our Father as His members. By His Ascension man lives in God's Sonship for ever.

b. The Father is also the God of our Lord Jesus Christ, because Jesus lives in the Eternal Life of Godhead derived from the Father. He is our God, because we partake of this Life in Christ.

c. We share individually in this relation to the God and Father of our Lord J. C., for we are one with Jesus in the Bond of the Spirit of Life.

AFFECTIONS. Consciousness of interior union with Christ in His Heavenly Glory. Praise to Him for the powers which His Manhood exhibits by the Ascension.

PRAYER.

O Lord Jesu, Who dost ascend to the Right Hand of the Father, in order to glorify our manhood with the fulness of the Divine Majesty, grant that I may so look up to Thee and long for Thee, that I may be detached from every earthly thought, and transformed into the glory whereon I delight to gaze, by the power of the Holy Ghost. Amen.

THE PROCLAMATION OF THE KING.

PRELUDE.   i. *Go ye into the world and preach the Gospel to every creature. He that believeth and is baptized shall be saved; but he that believeth not shall be damned.*—S. Mark xvi. 15, 16.

ii. Jesus giving the command to His Apostles.

POINT I.   *Consider the desire of Jesus for the promulgation of His Truth.*

- *a.* The desire of Jesus is co-extensive with the will of God, who will have all men to be saved, and to come to the knowledge of the truth.
- *b.* Jesus, by whom the worlds were made, claims a universal acknowledgment as the Redeemer of all. Yet must the proclamation of His work as Man amongst men, be announced by man to men. God treats the race of man as a whole. We are made to be dependent one upon another.
- *c.* The acceptance of the faith thus preached, is part of the mystery of godliness (1 Tim. iii. 16), for it is only by supernatural power that when preached it can be accepted. The few believe; the world rejects.

POINT II.   *Consider the need which all men have of this Truth.*

- *a.* It is a Truth from heaven, which the human heart could not devise for its own self.
- *b.* Man is by nature in a state of universal condemnation. The miseries of the world and the words of the Gospel attest it. All nations feel the need of some deliverance.
- *c.* Without Christ's kingdom man must have been left for ever in his woe. No covenant that had not the power of an Ascended Lord for its foundation, could raise man above his natural state.

POINT III.   *Consider the consequences of its reception.*

- *a.* Man being united to the Ascended Saviour acquires Eternal Life as the Son of God.
- *b.* Man is saved from the deadness and the doom of his natural state if he continues in the living service of God, to which the baptismal covenant admits him.
- *c.* Man is required to lay hold upon Christ as the object of living faith, with continual devotion in the power of the Holy Ghost, in order that he may be made partaker of the kingdom wherein Christ is received up and glorified.

AFFECTIONS.   Devotion to the kingdom of Christ. Separation from the world. Union with God.

PRAYER.

O Lord Jesu, King of Eternal glory, to whom all the nations of the world must bow, grant me so to live in the constant acknowledgment of the Truth of Thy grace, that I may hereafter behold with joy the glory of Thy triumphant manifestation, Who livest and reignest with the Father and the Holy Ghost, God for ever and ever. Amen.

THE OBTAINING OF THE COMFORTER.

· **PRELUDE.** i. *If I go not away, the Comforter will not come unto you; but if I depart, I will send Him unto you.*—S. John xvi. 7.

ii. Jesus speaking these words.

POINT I. *Consider the impossibility of the Comforter coming to man by nature.*

    a. His coming is an Act of Divine Power. If He came to man, His co-operation would destroy man's power of action, as long as man remained in his feebleness.

    b. His coming is a manifestation of Divine Love. The fallen nature of man is abhorrent to God by reason of sin.

    c. His coming could only be an external coming, for otherwise the infinity of God would be limited by the lower nature into which God came.

POINT II. *Consider the manhood being taken up in Christ's Person into God.*

    a. By reason of the hypostatic union it is made worthy of God. The human will being perfected, chooses alway the will of God.

    b. By its true perfection, this manhood is the chief object of Divine Love.

    c. By the glorification which it undergoes at the Ascension it becomes, in some sort, in energy, although not in itself identified with the Divine Infinity.

POINT III. *Consider the glorified Saviour sending forth the Comforter.*

    a. By His Ascension He completes that taking of the manhood into God, which commenced with the Incarnation.

    b. This gift on behalf of man is an infinite energy of Life, which He receives from the Father by a ceaseless Act of glorification, perpetually coming up into His manhood from the abyss of Godhead, wherein He personally dwells, eternally of one substantial activity with the Father.

    c. As the reception of this glorifying gift is perpetual, so there is a perpetual giving forth thereof. His manhood would not be glorified in this Act of Divine Life, unless that Act were operative through It as well as upon It.

AFFECTIONS. Elevation of heart to the glorified Mediator. Exultation in the consciousness of the Holy Ghost, who comes to us in Him. Glory to God the Father.

PRAYER.

O Blessed Jesu, Who art ascended into the Heavens, that Thou mayest give unto us the glory of the Indwelling Spirit, grant that I may always contemplate Thee in Thy glory with devout Love, and may also show forth Thy glory, by living in the power of the Spirit Whom Thou hast given, for Thy Name's sake. Amen.

M

THE TESTIMONY OF THE COMFORTER.

PRELUDE. i. *When the Comforter is come, Whom I will send unto you from the Father, even the Spirit of Truth, which*

POINT I. *Consider that Jesus sends the Comforter.*

a. As the Comforter comes from Jesus, He must testify of Jesus. Else He would be leaving Him. But They cannot be separated. We cannot know One without the Other.

b. As He proceeds from the Father, He cannot act otherwise than by revealing the Son, the Word of the Father, in those to whom He comes.

c. As He is the Spirit of Truth. He must make known the Truth. But Jesus is the Truth Incarnate.

POINT II. *Consider the witness which the Comforter bears.*

a. It is a Personal act. It is not merely a power influencing us to action, but acting upon us by His own Personal Will.

b. It is a true witness. He is the Spirit of Truth. He makes truly known that which by nature we could not know. We can have no knowledge of Truth, save by the teaching of the Spirit of Truth.

c. It is a living witness. He does not give a witness which shall presently die out. From age to age he gives this witness. No words of inspiration could avail, without the Presence and power of Him who inspired them.

POINT III. *Consider the testimony concerning Christ.*

a. He testifies to the efficacy of Christ's propitiation. But for this propitiation He had not been able to come to us.

b. He testifies to the glory of Christ, co-equal with the Father. He comes as the glorifying principle of Christ's Humanity. It is Christ's glory to send Him.

c. He testifies to the Eternal Sonship of Christ. He Who proceeds from the Father could not come at the sending of the Son, if He did not proceed eternally from the Son. The relation in time expresses the relationship of eternity. There is no Divine act without due Personal subordination.

AFFECTIONS. Desire to know the glory of Christ. Attention to the voice of the Spirit.

PRAYER.

O Blessed Jesu, Who dost make Thyself known to Thy people by the Spirit bearing witness in our hearts, grant that I may so listen to the Voice of Thy Holy Spirit, as to be perfected in Thy likeness by His transforming power, for Thy Mercy's sake. Amen.

THE APOSTOLIC MISSION.

PRELUDE. i. *And they went forth, and preached everywhere; the Lord working with them, and confirming the word with signs following.*—S. Mark xvi. 20.

ii. The Apostles speaking in the c⸺⸺⸺ testimony.

POINT I. *Consider the Apostles g⸺*

a. They went forth, without regar⸺ Their message was to all the wor⸺ ⸺ey were only concerned to deliver it truly. They knew God sent them.

b. They bore a living message for the ends of the earth. It did not derive life from them, but gave them life, having life in itself. It travelled on as light travels, and could not die out. They uttered in the Spirit the Word of God.

c. It was a message which brought Life. As many as received it were empowered to become the sons of God.

POINT II. *Consider the Holy Ghost working with them.*

a. He by Whom the Word of God became flesh was the Power by Whom the words of the Apostles became living words. Without His co-operation this message had been a dead one. One Spirit filled them all with One Word.

b. He prepared the heart of many to receive these words. No argument would have convinced any one without His preventing grace. He moved on the dark depth of man's heart.

c. He sealed the words to any who accepted them, by giving regenerating grace in the Sacrament of Holy Baptism, that they might henceforth be truly God's children, and walk in newness of life.

POINT III. *Consider the signs following.*

a. The Lord wrought the signs according to His Will. It is to be feared that we often hinder Him from doing so by wishing to work them ourselves, and determining of what kind they shall be. Our work is humbling; His is Divine.

b. The signs must be worthy of the worker. The signs of the Holy Ghost will be worthy of the Kingdom of Heaven, not such signs as a sinful and adulterous generation seeks for.

c. The signs are for those who can see, not for the blind world, which hates. Tongues are a sign to unbelievers. Prophesying is a sign of Divine power to the faithful while the world lasts. The one is occasional; the other constant.

AFFECTIONS. Reliance upon the Holy Ghost. Joy in an Apostolic ministry. Expectation of the Spirit's power.

PRAYER.

O Jesu, by Whose Spirit alone the truth of Thy glory can be made known to us, grant us so to accept that Spirit's teaching, that we may experience in ourselves the signs of Divine Love which belong to Thy faithful ones, for the glory of Thy great Name. Amen.

THE INTERCESSION OF CHRIST.

PRELUDE. i. *I will pray the Father, and He shall give you another Comforter.*—S. John xiv. 16.

ii. Jesus promising to intercede.

POINT I. *Consider the authority of Christ's prayer.*

a. He asks as an equal. The word translated "pray" is never used for our prayer to God, nor is the word which is applied to our asking ever used of Christ's intercession.

b. He asks as a Son. He is the Co-equal, the Only-begotten Son. None else can ask upon this claim of inheritance.

c. He asks as the constituted High Priest for Whom all the worlds were made, whose duty it is to inquire of God for the people, and obtain gifts from the Divine Treasury. He asks for what He knows the Father delights to give.

POINT II. *Consider the manner of Christ's prayer.*

a. Not by accidental and successive utterances, or human words, but in the indissoluble completeness of the longing of that created nature wherein He appears before the Father. His Human nature utters His Divine Love.

b. In the robe of perfect righteousness, the obedience of Calvary, ever remaining as the object of the Father's delight. His Human nature is not only in glory but is glorious.

c. In the power of the Holy Ghost, whereby He is the Eternal Word, so that what He asks as Man is identical with the Word of Predestination, the fulness of God's gift. The Incarnate Word of Wisdom speaks ever in the Holy Ghost.

POINT III. *Consider the Comforter sent in His place.*

a. He proceeds in all completeness from the Father. The Son has no separate substance, so that He can add anything to the Spirit of the Father. The whole Divine substance, wherein Father and Son are One, passes on to Him. He proceeds from Each, as Each is by Himself very God, and from Both, as being not two Gods, but one God.

b. He comes to man through the glorified Humanity of the Son, for He cannot be separated from God. Christ's Body is the One Temple taken up into God for Him to dwell in.

c. He is Co-equal with the Son. Otherwise He would not supply His place. The Three Persons are co-equal.

AFFECTIONS. Praise to Christ for the gift of the Holy Ghost. Looking up to Christ's Manhood as the Instrument of Divine Life.

PRAYER.

O Jesu, grant that as by Thine Ascension Thou hast obtained for us the gift of the Comforter, so by the power of the Comforter we may ever live to the glory of Thy Name. Amen.

THE IMPULSE OF THE APOSTOLIC MISSION.

PRELUDE. i. *And they went forth, and preached everywhere, the Lord working with them, and confirming the Word with signs following.*—S. Mark xvi. 20.

ii. The Spirit of Christ breathed down from His throne of glory, guiding the Apostles to their several works.

POINT I. *Consider the mightiness of the impulse.*
- *a.* Christ gave Apostles to the Church (Eph. iv. 11), by giving His Holy Spirit to the Apostles. They were to minister henceforth in the Spirit of power.
- *b.* The Spirit co-equal with Himself, acting through the Twelve, made their combined ministry co-equal with His own Mediatorial Sovereignty.
- *c.* The Spirit coming to them to effect the purposes of Divine Love for the world, could not be thwarted by any created opposition to that Love.

POINT II. *Consider the unity of the impulse.*
- *a.* The Holy Ghost does not give gifts to each individually, which each may use separately, but comes to be Himself the One Personal Agent operating through all.
- *b.* The Holy Ghost comes to effect a purpose predetermined by the Wisdom of God, and therefore all the parts of His work are entirely at one with the Divine Wisdom.
- *c.* The Holy Ghost gathers all into the one and indivisible Life of God, so that all are as truly One in this Life as the Three Persons of the Blessed Trinity, Who give it, are One.

POINT III. *Consider the efficacy of the impulse.*
- *a.* The Voice of the Redeemer is identical in utterance with the Word of the Creator, and therefore reaches throughout Creation.
- *b.* It comes forth from the Father, and therefore it is Co-equal with the Infinity of God.
- *c.* It acts upon all things according to God's will, and in the fulness of Divine Power, to bring back to God all that will receive Him.

AFFECTIONS. Love for the Church, and for the Apostolical Ministry, as coming from Christ in Heaven in the power of the Holy Ghost.

PRAYER.

O Blessed Jesu, as Thou hast sent forth a ministry of righteousness in the power of the Holy Ghost, whereby Thou wouldest have all mankind to be reconciled unto the Father, grant me so to accept the Holy Ghost at the hands of those whom Thou sendest, that I may find acceptance with the Father in the same Spirit of power, to the praise of Thy Holy Name. Amen.

THE REALITY OF THE ASCENSION.

PRELUDE. i. *I ascend unto My Father and your Father, and to My God and your God.*—S. John xx. 17.

ii. The narrative as in the Acts.

POINT I. *Consider the reality of the humiliation from which Christ ascended.*

    a. He had emptied Himself so as to exist upon earth in the nothingness of the creature, acting in the power of the anointing Spirit.

    b. He suffered upon earth from all the pains which belong to our outcast condition, having come in the likeness of sinful flesh, although Himself without sin.

    c. His human will was tempted, being subject to a law of natural good and evil in a world separate from God, although He was incapable of sin, because He was personally one with God.

    d. His work was to end in death, and the lower world would reject Him.

POINT II. *Consider the progress of the Ascension.*

    a. The bodily uplifting—a symbol of His removal into a higher law of existence.

    b. The cloud receiving Him out of men's sight, a symbol of the Heavenly Host to whom He went.

    c. The various orders of Heavenly dignity speeding Him on His way. (Ps. xxiv. 9, 10.) Probably the nine days of the Ascent refer to the nine orders of Angels through whom He passed to reign. None could be His abiding-place.

POINT III. *Consider the reality of glory in the Ascension.*

    a. He takes possession as man of the fulness of God, and sends forth the Holy Spirit as a principle of power to all His people.

    b. He is glorified in Heaven by the energy of Godhead, so that His Human Nature on the Right Hand of God is the joyous instrument whereby all Divine works are done.

    c. He is removed from all temptation, and gives His Divine power to be the strength of those who are subject to the infirmities which, when on earth, He bore.

    d. His work triumphs in living spiritual results, raising His people out of the dominion of death, by Sacraments of grace on earth and the vision of Himself in glory.

AFFECTIONS. Sense of Christ's sympathy. Rejoicing in His glory.

PRAYER.

O Lord Jesu, Who hast exalted our manhood to the Right Hand of Power, grant that I, in my weakness, may always look up to Thee for strength, and rejoicing in Thy glory, may be lifted up above all considerations of earthly difficulty, in the fellowship of Thy Holy Spirit. Amen.

THE CHURCH THE BODY OF A LIVING HEAD.

PRELUDE. i. *When the Comforter is come Whom I will send unto you from the Father, even the Spirit of Truth which proceeds from the Father, He shall testify of Me.*—S. John xv. 26.

ii. The Holy Ghost a principle of Life, making us one with Christ.

POINT I. *Consider Christ sending the Comforter.*

    a. His Manhood has truly received into Itself this Divine glory. It is not lost in the greatness of the Divine glory, but appropriates that glory as a power of supernatural Life.

    b. His Human will rejoices to accomplish the work of Divine Predestination, having this power not as a mere external possession, but as a living inherent energy of triumph.

    c. As the Head of the Body, He makes the Presence of the Comforter to be effectual throughout all His members. They live as truly as He does in the power of the Holy Ghost as long as they abide in Him.

POINT II. *Consider the Comforter coming to us.*

    a. He does not come to be near us, but to be in us, to be our Life.

    b. He comes to us from Christ the Head, as Christ's Members. We cannot have His Presence unless we abide in Christ by holy obedience.

    c. He comes to our whole nature, even as Christ is glorified in our whole nature. Body, soul, and spirit are sanctified with His Divine Presence and Power.

POINT III. *Consider the testimony of the Comforter.*

    a. He testifies of Christ to ourselves, bearing witness with our spirit that we are the sons of God in Him.

    b. He testifies of Christ to the world, strengthening us to act in Christ's Name, having a Kingdom which is not from hence.

    c. He testifies of Christ to Satan, who is unable to harm us if we resist Him in the power of our new Birth.

    d. He testifies of Christ to the Father, making intercession within us with groanings which cannot be uttered.

AFFECTIONS. Rest in Christ. Confidence in the Life of our Head.

PRAYER.

O Lord Jesu, Who dost quicken Thy Church with Thine own Life, making us partakers of Thine Eternal Spirit, grant us always so to recognize Thee as our Head, that we may live in entire conformity to Thy will, and act in Thy power according to the fulness of Thy grace. Amen.

THE OBEDIENCE OF LOVE.

PRELUDE.   i. *If ye love Me, keep My commandments.—* S. John xiv. 15.

ii. Jesus speaking the words.

POINT I.   *Consider the love which Christ desires.*

    a. It is not the mere love of human discipleship which satisfies Him. We could only love Him by nature as a fellowman.

    b. It is the love which the Holy Ghost communicates to the heart, which alone is worthy of the name of Love. Love must be worthy of its object. Love to God must be Divine.

    c. The Love which is shed abroad in our hearts by the Holy Ghost must be exercised in our nature, otherwise it would not be our Love. As Christ exercises Divine Power by His Human Will in His glory, so must we do on earth in grace.

POINT II.   *Consider the manifestation of Love.*

    a. Love is shown by action. Love is not content to receive bounty, but desires to share all with the loved one.

    b. Love does not seek to act according to its own will, but to know the will of the loved one, and to do it.

    c. Love rejoices to act under orders; for in obedience there is a real unity of Life transmitted, not a mere coincidence of judgment approved. To lose self in unity is the joy of Love.

POINT III.   *Consider the possibility of Loving Obedience to* Christ.

    a. Our loving Him is the very evidence of His being seated on the Throne of power, for His Kingdom is Love. Love to Him is the Life of the Kingdom.

    b. The Love which He communicates is equal to His commands in His kingdom, for He gives His commands by the same Spirit, wherein we are to keep them.

    c. Love to Him demands nothing save what He gives, for the fulness of its impulse is from Him, and the fulness of its aim is towards Him. Its true riches is in having nothing but Him.

AFFECTIONS.   Resolutions to obey Christ. Abhorrence of every action which does not belong to His Love. Desire to love Him better.

PRAYER.

O *Blessed Jesu, Who hast given us Thy Holy Spirit to make Thy Love manifest within us by making us to act in its power, grant that by watchfulness in keeping Thy Commandments I may grow in the experience of Thy transforming grace, and love Thee in the perfect purity of the Spirit of Thy Holy Love. Amen.*

THE EASTER BREATH COMPLETED.

PRELUDE. i. *Receive ye the Holy Ghost: Whosesoever sins ye remit, they are remitted unto them.*—S. John xx. 22.

ii. Jesus breathing upon His Apostles.

POINT I. *Consider this Breathing as the beginning of the Pentecostal gift.*

    a. Jesus breathed into them the breath of the Risen Life, free from the dominion of Death, in the power of the H G.

    b. Whilst still on earth His exterior Life, though truly spiritual and no longer dependent upon the functions of a natural organism, was outwardly limited, and could not act fully.

    c. This Life could not but ascend to the fulness of Divine manifestation. All the power of the H. G. is given in this Resurrection to the Body of Christ both for Heaven and earth. He must exert it to the glory of the Father.

POINT II. *Consider the Humanity of Christ as the Instrument through which the Holy Ghost is given.*

    a. It was formed in indissoluble integrity by the power of the H. G. Even in the emptiness of our natural condition, It was sanctified with this unction by the Hypostatic union.

    b. It was raised in Spiritual energy by the power of the H. G., so that during the Forty Days it exhibited the glory of the Spirit by a Life superior to the conditions of earth.

    c. It was glorified in Life-giving sovereignty by the power of the H. G. His Ascension was an exercise of His new powers, and now in the fulness of Divine glory He, as Mediator, gives forth from Himself the H. G. in Co-equal Majesty of Power.

POINT III. *Consider the gift of Pentecost as the completion of the Easter Breathing.*

    a. As His Body is glorified, the H. G. comes forth in ever expanding energy. The Apostles were united to Him by the Eucharist, and by the Breathing, and His Body could not be glorified in Heaven without glorifying with power from on high these His members below. The fire of Pentecost is as the outward flash of glory, exhibiting the union.

    b. No outward intimacy could have glorified them.

    c. The true operation of the Divine Breath is found in the Life-giving power of this communication. They received truly the Life of God, because they were to communicate that Life, forgiving sins, and raising souls to life, by the power of the H. G.

AFFECTIONS. Welcome to the Holy Ghost.

PRAYER.

O Blessed Spirit, by Whom the whole Body of Christ is glorified, grant me so to walk in Thy power that the perfection of Thy glory may shine out within me, and all my vileness being purged away by the fire of Thy Holy Presence, my life on earth may be made worthy of Christ to the glory of God the Father. Amen.

THE FATHER'S LOVE CONSUMMATED.

PRELUDE. i. *God so loved the world, that He gave His Only-begotten Son, that whosoever believeth in Him should not perish but have everlasting Life.*—S. John iii. 16.

ii. The Eternal Father contemplating the race of the Redeemed.

POINT I. *Consider the Eternity of this Love.*

    a. God is Love, ever active by the power of the H. G. proceeding from Himself. The eternal counsels of His Wisdom are formed in the unity of the Spirit of Love.

    b. All His works were created in the power of this spirit. Their external beauty and order is the manifestation of His excellence. All that God makes is good.

    c. The final destiny of God's works is contained in the original germ of their being. They are formed for an end to which they must come through the sanctifying power of the H. G. God rejoices in their predestination. Individuals fall away, but the purpose of God must live on.

POINT II. *Consider the gift of the Well-beloved Son.*

    a. He is begotten eternally in the unity of the Divine Substance. The fulness of the H. G. proceeding from Him is the glory of His Life, wherein the Father delights.

    b. He is Incarnate by the Love of the Father, Who would have Creation to be perfected and stablished in His Love by assuming it thus into His Life by the power of the H. G.

    c. He was given not merely to be a propitiation by death, but to be a principle of exaltation by Resurrection and Ascension, as the H. G. manifested in His glory.

POINT III. *Consider the everlasting Life which is offered us in Christ.*

    a. God ordained the Body of His Son as the means of communicating the full gift of His Love to the world, that mankind might be incorporated with Him, and live with the H. G. whereby that Body lives.

    b. As all things came forth from God's will by the power of the H. G., so the redeemed are gathered back into God's Love by being taken up into His Life by the power of the H. G.

    c. Everlasting Life is the Love of God shed abroad in our hearts by the H. G. As the H. G. is the Bond of mutual Love between the Father and the Son eternally, so He is the Living Bond of Love between God and Creation.

AFFECTIONS. Love. Gratitude. Hope.

PRAYER.

O Holy Ghost, Who art the Eternal Bond of Divine Love, as Thou didst form the Body of the Son of God to be the Instrument of Eternal Living Union between the Creator and the creature, grant that I may always act in that Love to God which Thou dost inspire, and may attain to the glory of that Life where nothing can any longer separate me from the energy of Thy Love. Amen.

THE MINISTRY OF LIFE.

PRELUDE.   i. *Verily, verily, I say unto you, He that entereth not by the door into the sheepfold, but climbeth up some other way, the same is a thief and a robber.   But he that entereth in by the door is the Shepherd of the sheep.*—S. John x. 1, 2.

ii. The Holy Ghost as an invisible Person effecting union between Christ in Heaven and His people on earth.

POINT I.   *Consider the H. G. opening the door for Christ.*

 a. The H. G. opens the door of Providence, making plain the prophecies.   He prepares external events for Christ.

 b. The H. G. opens the door of nature, accomplishing the Incarnation whereby Christ comes in our flesh.

 c. The H. G. opens the door of grace, effecting the Sacramental communication of the Incarnate Christ through substances of earth to the individual soul.

POINT II.   *Consider the thief and the robber.*

 a. A ministry which gains power in the visible Fold, without being admitted by the H. G. the Porter, comes not to give Life, but to destroy, however seemingly beneficial.

 b. Such a ministry steals men's hearts from God and Christ, as Absalom from David, taking honour to itself by what it does, to the disparagement of the One Good Shepherd.

 c. Such a ministry destroys under pretence of saving.   A ministry which is not one with God in origin cannot lead to oneness with God.   Christ admits us to God, for He comes through the door which the H. G. opens from God. The thief gives no higher life, but destroys what he finds.

POINT III.   *Consider the Life-giving Shepherd.*

 a. He brings supernatural Life into the Fold, being Incarnate by the H. G., and having the Life of God.

 b. He lays down His natural Life and is shown to be the Son of God with power, according to the Spirit of holiness, by the resurrection from the dead.

 c. He communicates supernatural Life to the sheep by gathering them into His own risen Body by the power of the H. G., Who both opens the door of the lower world that the Shepherd may come in, and opens the door of the higher world, which is Christ Himself, that the sheep may enter in.

AFFECTIONS.   Joy in the higher Life.   Reverence.   Praise.

PRAYER.

O Spirit of Grace and Power, Who bringest the Son of God near to us that in Him we may have access to the Divine Life, teach me to reverence Thy power in all holy ordinances, and to live in the fellowship of Christ, whereunto Thou leadest me, Who with the Father and the Son art ever to be worshipped and glorified, one God, world without end.   Amen.

THE PRESENT GIFT OF LIFE.

PRELUDE. i. *Verily, verily, I say unto you, He that believeth on Me hath everlasting life.*—S. John vi. 47.

ii. Thine own heart burning with a supernatural Fire, as the Light of the H. G. fills the breast.

POINT I. *Consider what Life is.*

    a. Life is power. If we have not the powers of any estate, we have not the life belonging to it. Everlasting Life is the power of doing God's work in holy fellowship with Him.

    b. Life is action. Involuntary transmission of power is not life. Our will must be using the power of God; otherwise we cannot be said to live.

    c. Life is knowledge. This knowledge is intense in proportion to the dignity of the kind of life. To know God and live, is to love God in consciousness of His excellency.

POINT II. *Consider what believing in Christ is.*

    a. It is an illuminating Love. We are identified with Him Who is the wisdom of God, by the power of Him Who is the Bond of Divine Love.

    b. It is a substantial union. We are not taken into Christ save by real union of our substance with His. He is the Door of the higher Life. Only by union with his outer substance can we have fellowship with His higher Life.

    c. It is an active apprehension. We must not be dead appendages to the Body of Christ. As He actively holds us, so must we actively keep hold upon Him.

POINT III. *Consider what it is to have Everlasting Life.*

    a. The Life is everlasting in itself. It is the Life of God, not the mere resultant of changeful combinations, such as cause the variation of earthly life, but pure, calm, glorious, in the unity of the Eternal Spirit.

    b. The Life is immediately communicated. We do not receive merely a promise of future Life, but we are born again, and are made God's children, by the gift of the H. G.

    c. The Life is individually appropriated. It is not given separately to each individual so as to die out when individuals fall away. It is given to each one as a member of the indestructible Body, and each one must seek to be abidingly quickened in the unity of this Eternal Life of the H. G. in the Communion of Saints.

AFFECTIONS. Desire of living to God's glory. Loss of self.

PRAYER.

O Thou Eternal Spirit of Life, Who dost raise us from the world of sin and death into the holiness of the Life of God, do Thou so kindle my affections with the power of Thy heavenly Light, that I may walk safely amidst the outer darkness of this present world, and may attain to the glory wherein Thou wouldest perfect the members of Jesus Christ the Only-begotten of the Father. Amen.

THE EXTENSION OF LIFE.

PRELUDE. i. *Jesus called his twelve disciples together, and gave them power and authority over all devils, and to cure diseases: and He sent them to preach the Kingdom of God, and to heal the sick.*—S. Luke ix. 1, 2.

ii. Jesus sending forth the Twelve anticipates Pentecost.

POINT I. *Consider the Kingdom as emanating from Christ.*

   a. The Kingdom of God is the extension of the glory of Christ in Heaven, communicating His Life, raising up those who come to Him from the state of sin and death.

   b. This Life is communicated by the Holy Ghost, proceeding from Him, making the faithful one living Body which grows until the number of the Elect be made complete.

   c. The Life communicated is the very same as the Life of the Giver. The Kingdom of Christ is to the sinful world what Christ Himself would have been under the same circumstances.

POINT II. *Consider the Commission given in this Kingdom.*

   a. Christ the Head. The Apostles Branches. All claim impulse of Life, or mission from Him. All, without difference, "Receive the Holy Ghost."

   b. This Commission, like the Life itself, is given collectively and individually. Complete in each of the Apostles, but only while one with each other, and so with Christ the Head. "Go ye: Make disciples;" not to yourselves, but to Me.

   c. This Commission is perpetual: to all the world and to the end of time. The Life would cease, if the Commission for propagating it were to cease, for the Life of the Head is organically communicated through this ministry: "Lo, I am with you alway," acting through you by the Holy Ghost.

POINT III. *Consider its authoritative character.*

   a. Authority over all devils. The world is to be won from their dominion, as the supernatural Life of His kingdom extends. Devils will resist, but they are conquered.

   b. Power to cure diseases. Sickness follows upon sin; healing upon pardon. This power is not given evidentially, as men now-a-days regard miracles, but in love to the faithful.

   c. Authority to preach, and make converts. Preaching is not merely man's effort, but Christ's voice.

AFFECTIONS. Confidence in Christ's Kingdom. Obedience. Courage. Missionary zeal.

PRAYER.

O God the Holy Ghost, Who fillest with Divine power all the true children of the Kingdom, make me to act in Thy holy inspiration, and to rejoice in the promises of Thy Love, so that I may faithfully exercise the prerogatives of the Christian Covenant, and may be accepted among God's elect, when the Kingdom of Christ shall be made complete. Amen.

THE SUPERNATURAL POWER OF LIFE.

PRELUDE. i. *And it came to pass on a certain day as He was teaching, that there were Pharisees and doctors of the Law sitting by, which were come out of every town of Galilee, and Judea, and Jerusalem, and the power of the Lord was present to heal them.*—S. Luke v. 17.

ii. The scene here described, a symbol of Christ in His Church amidst the philosophers of the world.

POINT I. *Consider the Divine Word of Jesus.*

  a. The Word of Jesus was perfect in its utterance, but how scanty was its result upon the hearers! We must not value words by their effect but by their origin.

  b. His Word must be in His Church now. If He be not teaching there all human teaching will be in vain. He hides Himself, but prepared hearts receive His Word.

  c. We are to be careful to follow Christ's teaching, but we are not to expect that the world will receive it. We are not to criticize Truth and leave it, but act upon it; as far as we know, and learn to love it.

POINT II. *Consider the moral systems of the world.*

  a. The Law, although given by God, was weak through the flesh. It could not heal the diseases of mankind. Much less can any systems of human invention.

  b. The worldly heart watches the Church of Christ with suspicion, envy, scorn. Yet the teaching of the Spirit is not against that of the Law, but fills up its weakness.

  c. The scorn of the worldly moralist only serves to bring out more clearly the difference between the Law and the Spirit. Their systems authenticate the truth of Christ and His Church, because this meets their own weak points.

POINT III. *Consider the effects of the Word of Jesus.*

  a. The Divine Wisdom is there to teach the understanding, the Divine Power to heal the nature. Supernatural Life is a real healing of our fallen nature.

  b. Man needs to be healed, not changed, but restored to His true self from which he is fallen. Human teaching fails for want of the Divine Spirit. Jesus can heal and re-make man because He made him at the first.

  c. Human teachers may see Christ teaching and healing, and yet need themselves to be healed, because they need to be taught. In the Supernatural Life we must seek to be healed and taught.

AFFECTIONS. Desire of Divine knowledge and Life.

PRAYER.

O Blessed Spirit of Light and Power, make Thy glory manifest in my soul, enabling me to receive the words of Truth, that I may live thereby, and all the infirmity of my nature may be done away in the strength of Thy renewing grace. Amen.

THE UNIVERSALITY OF LIFE.

PRELUDE. i. *Now, when the sun was setting, all they that had any sick with divers diseases brought them unto Jesus; and He laid His hands on every one of them, and healed them.—S. Luke iv. 40.*

ii. The sick brought to Jesus, a symbol of the human race.

POINT I. *Consider the variety of need.*

a. Man's moral diseases are manifold as his physical ones. Every faculty being fallen needs to be healed. Sin does not merely affect a part of the nature. It taints all.

b. The whole race is fallen. All are liable to sickness, because all are tainted with sin. None can be exempt save by the restoration of the Divine Life, the sustaining partner of our humanity, which the Fall forfeited.

c. Man's Fall is an individual calamity. None come to Christ pure. Each comes to Him as a Saviour to be healed.

POINT II. *Consider the Touch of Jesus.*

a. He laid His Hands, and thus brought the power of the H. G. near. The Body of Jesus heals, because it is the Temple of the H. G. The Spirit quickeneth through that Body.

b. The Touch is individual, not a general proclamation, not a look. The healing is a substantive communication from God. He touches each.

c. The Touch is penetrating. By the power of the H. G. the virtue of this Touch acts upon whatever part may be the seat of their disease. So the Sacramental Touch of Christ affects our inmost substance. The Holy Ghost quickens.

POINT III. *Consider the characteristics of this Touch.*

a. The Touch of compassion. Jesus "bore our sicknesses," felt our burden while healing them by a corresponding virtue in the power of the H. G. A consciousness of recuperative strain as it were, awoke a sigh from Him.

b. The Touch of self-communication. He gave Himself substantially to be a renovating principle. So now His Presence is real in the Sacraments. He becomes one with us, and conveys to our whole nature the Presence of the H. G.

c. The Touch of Power. By the H. G. He makes Himself the underlying activity to set in motion all the forces of our nature. We must abide in this control of the H. G.

AFFECTIONS. Joy. Trust. Humiliation.

PRAYER.

O God the Holy Ghost, by Whom the Incarnate Son of God did not merely cast out devils, but also wrought upon our natural bodies that they might be healed, grant that I, being raised to newness of Life by Thy power, may always act according to Thy Holy Inspiration, through the same Jesus Christ our Lord. Amen.

THE DOCTRINE OF THE TRINITY.

PRELUDE. i. B*lessed be the Holy and Undivided Trinity,* *the Creator and Preserver of all things, now and ever, and to ages of ages.*

ii. The Host of Heaven praising the Triune God.

POINT I. *Consider the Eternal Life of God.*

    a. God is Life. He has Life in Himself. His Life is indissoluble. He cannot give it to any separate from Himself.

    b. The Life of God is Eternal, subject to no outward accident, having its own interior law of Being.

    c. The Life of God is active. God exists in pure activity. He has no dull body like ours. He acts simply in and of Himself, Himself the Source, Object, Substance, the Voluntary Law, the Infinite Measure, of His own activity.

POINT II. *Consider the Three Persons of the Godhead.*

    a. The Father is of none. The self-originated activity of God is productive in its own calm energy. Our mind cannot be without thought. Its very Being is to think. So it images the Divine Paternity.

    b. The Son is of the Father alone ; no mere result of Divine activity as creation is, but abiding in one indissoluble act of Life with the Father. Thought fills the mind which generates it. From our imperfect minds thoughts pass away. God the Son is the eternal Image of the Divine Wisdom abiding in the undivided energy of the Father's Life.

    c. The H. G. is of the F. and of the S. ; the Love which binds them in mutual contemplation eternally. The activity of Divine Life comes from the Father and returns to Him. The H. G. proceeds from the S. as from the F.'s Image.

POINT III. *Consider the Consubstantiality of the Three Persons.*

    a. The Godhead is one, because the activity is one. If there were any breach, the Godhead would be destroyed.

    b. The whole Being of the Father coming forth in the Son, without augmentation or change, without body, parts, or passions, proceeds in the Person of the Holy Ghost, in Whom the Father and the Son exist and act undividedly.

    c. The Procession of the Holy Ghost, being not a mere motion to external things, but an internal energy of Godhead, is the Form whereby God's activity rests self contained, circulating within itself, without transmission of parts, without succession of time, uncreated, incomprehensible, eternal.

AFFECTIONS. Homage to the Divine Mystery.

PRAYER.

O *Thou, the Eternal Life, who givest Thyself in various degrees to Thy creatures, existing unmoved in the changeless energy of Thine own Being, grant that by Thy Word of Wisdom I may act in the Power of Thy Love, and find my Life in the praise of Thy Triune Majesty, to the glory of Thy Holy Name.* **Amen.**

THE FATHER OF LIGHTS.

PRELUDE. i. *Blessed be the Holy and Undivided Trinity, the Creator and Preserver of all things, now and ever, and to ages of ages.*

ii. The Light of God's Presence filling God's Temple.

POINT I. *Consider the Light of Eternity.*

   a. The Only-begotten Son, Light of Light: the Brightness of the Father's glory, wherein the Father is well pleased.

   b. The Spirit of illumination : the Love whereby God rejoices in the Light and Glory of His own Being, shining out before Him in the Person of His Son.

   c. The Purity of the Eternal Light, wherein is no darkness at all. The whole Being of the Father comes forth without reserve in the Generation of the Son and the Procession of the Holy Ghost.

POINT II. *Consider the Light of Grace.*

   a. The Eternal Life is the only Light of men. For want of this, fallen man is in darkness, but he was formed to see this Light. The lamp of his soul is evil, his body dark.

   b. When man is born again, he does gain this sight, "the eyes within" of the Living Creatures, whereby he sees the Kingdom of God, and apprehends Divine mysteries.

   c. We are the children of Light, and must abide in the Light, if we would see it. Our whole body must be "full of light," as sons of God.

POINT III. *Consider the Light of Glory.*

   a. The soul rejoices in the perfect vision of God the Light, which shall flood our being and make us like to Himself.

   b. The Body, which is sown in the dishonour of darkness, shall be raised in the glory of the Divine Light.

   c. God is glorified in us as the Body of Christ, the Living Creatures. These are not only near the Throne, but "in it," so as to be filled with the Light of God, and "round about it," so that God is seen through them. Their Being is transparent. No earthly darkness hides the glory of the Throne, which they enshrine.

AFFECTIONS. Purity. Divine Joy. Openness of heart. Loss of self. Love.

PRAYER.

O Lord God, Who dwellest in the Light unapproachable to man, and yet callest us up that we may dwell in Thy glory by the participation of Thine Eternal Life, grant that I may always walk worthy of that Light, and attain to perfection by Thy glorious Power, through Him Who is Thine own Eternal Brightness, dwelling with Thee in the glory of the Undivided Spirit, One God, world without end. **Amen.**

N

THE IMAGE OF THE SON OF GOD.

PRELUDE. i. *Blessed be the Holy and Undivided Trinity, the Creator and Preserver of all things, now and ever, and to ages of ages.*

POINT I. *Consider the Son of God as the Father's Image.*

ii. The Son of God making His Life to project itself, as a ray of glorious Light upon the Person of the Baptized.

a. He exists in the Form of God; *i.e.*, in the Divine Substance. (Phil. ii. 6.) He is in the indivisible Substance of God, one with God. He is in the substance and fashion of man, like other men but separate.

b. He is the Image of the Invisible God, begotten before all creation. All creation exists in Him. (Col. i. 15.) He is the expression of the Person of the Father (Heb. i. 3), Who, unless He did thus utter Himself by an interior co-equal Word, would not have a conscious existence.

c. His being the Image of the Father, is the reason why He is the Life-giving Head of the Church, for we, being incorporated into Him, become partakers of the Divine Image.

POINT II. *Consider the Image stamped upon us at our Baptism.*

a. Man was formed to bear this Image, being made originally as the Image and glory of God.—1 Cor. ii. 7.

b. We are con-Formed to the Son of God, being made partakers of the Divine Nature (Rom. viii. 29), renewed after our Creator's Image, by being made partakers of His manhood.

c. A growing conformation, proportionate to our acceptance into the Form of that Glory (2 Cor. iii. 18), is effected by gazing upon it until we see God as He truly is.

POINT III. *Consider the Image perfected in us in the Resurrection.*

a. We must bear the Image of the Heavenly Adam, as truly as we have borne the image of the Adam of clay.

b. This final glory is the outcome of a living righteousness, given to us when called to be Christians in Baptism. Justification is our restitution to God's living image and glory.

c. This glory is an active glory. We are made the righteousness of God in Christ (2 Cor. v. 21), in order that we do righteousness as He does.—1 John iii. 7.

AFFECTIONS. Devotion to Christ to live as God's sons.

PRAYER.

O God, Who hast called me into the participation of Thine own glory in the Body of Thy dear Son, Grant that I may so eat in the power thereof, that I may be established in the Fellowship of the Throne of His glory, Who liveth and reigneth with Thee in the unity of the Holy Ghost for ever and ever. Amen.

THE REGENERATING SPIRIT.

PRELUDE. i. *Blessed be the Holy and Undivided Trinity, the Creator and Preserver of all things, now and ever, and to ages of ages.*

ii. The Spirit of God, as the breeze, moving upon the surface of the river.

POINT I. *Consider the eternal Love of God.*

a. God loves His Only-begotten Son with the fulness of His glory. The Love which proceeds from the Father is worthy of the Father, and therefore is equal with the Father. The whole substance of the Father comes forth in this Act of Love whereby he contemplates His Son.

b. The Son loves the Father with the same Eternal Love.

c. The Holy Ghost is the Eternal Personal expression of this mutual Love. If this Love were a mere reciprocal affection of the Godhead, the Godhead would be divided. Because it is a Personal Procession, it is a Bond of union.

POINT II. *Consider the Love which comes from God.*

a. We cannot be partakers of this Spirit, save in the Body of Christ, which is His Temple. He does not leave the Godhead, or empty Himself by His Procession, or become man. He Proceeds eternally within the Godhead, and brings the fulness of the Godhead into our nature when He comes.

b. He fills every one who is joined to this Body, and comes by such means as He Himself appoints, *i.e.* by Holy Baptism.

c. His Presence is a Personal Presence conveying Divine Life and Divine Assistance, quite independently of the receiver.

POINT III. *Consider the Love which leads to God.*

a. The Spirit by Whom Christ loves the Father must lead us, as His members, to love the Father also. The regenerate Life goeth to God as it comes from God, and the natural mind cannot know its origin or end.

b. The Holy Ghost assists us as the members of Christ, not by reason of any merely natural faculties. So He assists us to do the work of Christ, makes our work Christ's work.

c. The Holy Ghost must so reveal Christ within us, that the old man may be entirely purged away, and we may love God with the perfection of the Heavenly Life, even as Christ loves Him. "Not I, but Christ liveth in me."

AFFECTIONS. Reverence to the Holy Ghost. Joy in Him.

PRAYER.

O God, Who hast shed forth in our hearts the Spirit of Thy Son, to bind us unto Thyself in His Body, grant that I may so act in the power of this Blessed Spirit, that being delivered from the bondage of my natural infirmity, I may rejoice to yield myself to Thee in holy Love, through the same Jesus Christ our Lord. Amen.

N 2

THE RECEIVING OF CHRIST.

PRELUDE.   i. *O Sacred Banquet, in which Christ is received, the memory of His Passion renewed, the mind is filled with grace, and a pledge of future glory is given to us.*

ii. Christ giving to us His own Faculties for us to act in Him.

POINT I. *Consider the power of the gift of Christ.*

a. Christ's Body is at the Right Hand of Power, and therefore it is everywhere operative. His presence is not dull, material, passive, but full of Divine energy and Life.

b. Christ's Body can no longer be divided into parts. It is not a collection of varied forces that act separately. It is raised in a perfect integrity of Life, and touches all the parts of our nature, remaining itself indissoluble.

c. Christ's Body being of one origin with our body, has power to become identified with it, and cleanse it. The soul is specially in the Blood. Christ's Blood not falling to the ground in death, but living with the power of the Holy Ghost, has power to wash our souls.

POINT II. *Consider the effect of the gift of Christ. .*

a. The Power of God coming to us through the Human Nature of Christ in the Holy Eucharist, meets the wants of our nature, in each of our faculties with the grace required.

b. The Presence of Christ thus nourishing us, should lift us up into daily habits worthy of Himself. We should think of each of our faculties as containing Him.

c. The effect of this gift ought to be increasing as our old outer nature is worn away, and we act more habitually by the law of this inward power of the indwelling Christ.

POINT III. *Consider the joy of the gift of Christ.*

a. Though we receive the substance of Christ, yet we are not really partakers of Him, unless the operation of His Power do indeed transform us. Great must be our joy if we do yield ourselves up to His transforming Love.

b. We have also the joy of freedom from the burden of the old nature of death, which naturally holds us bound so that we cannot rise to the things of God.

c. Also the joy of sweet experience of Divine things, as we use this Power thus given to us.

AFFECTIONS. Desire to be conformed to Christ. Reverence to Christ in myself.

PRAYER.

O Lord God, Who hast given Thine Only Son to be our spiritual Food and Sustenance, grant me, I pray Thee, always to live in the remembrance of His indwelling, that, acting in the power of His renewal, I may rise out of the bondage of death, wherein I am held by nature, and may glorify Thee in Love, through the same Jesus Christ our Lord. Amen.

THE MEMORIAL OF THE PASSION.

PRELUDE. i. *O Sacred Banquet, in which Christ is received, the memory of His Passion renewed, the mind is filled with grace, and a pledge of future glory is given to us.*

ii. Christ upon the Cross, seen as it were mirrored upon the glory of the highest Heavens.

POINT I. *Consider the real impetrative Presence of Christ.*

   a. Christ being truly with us under the Form of Bread and Wine, carries on therein His work of Intercession; for this is in Him not an act which He can leave off, but it is His very Mediatorial existence. As man He lives in prayer.

   b. The weakness of the outer Elements interferes not with the merit of the Mediatorial act of Christ. His glory in Heaven does not give efficacy to His Mediation, but shows its efficacy. The Elements hide it not from God.

   c. Christ's Presence is impetrative, because He is the Incarnate Word. His Human Nature ever speaks in prayer to the Father, until the full purpose of the Father be accomplished in the perfecting of His Body.

POINT II. *Consider the mystical state of death.*

   a. Christ dieth no more, but through death He entered into that state of glory wherein He lives. Only through death could He enter. Only through dying in His death can we enter. The outer tie of Life was broken, not the inner.

   b. In death the soul, which acts through the blood, is separated from the body. In the risen Life they both live by the Spirit. They are presented separately in memory of death, but each part in this offering has the new Life.

   c. Christ thus offered is the Same Who suffered. This mystical presentation of Christ, thus as it were sundered by death, is no humiliation, but is a memorial of His undying merit.

POINT III. *Consider the glory of the Victim.*

   a. The glory of His Person. It is the Incarnate Son of God, God's Word, Who pleads for us with a Love equal to that of the F., knowing, asking, obtaining, all that the F. wills.

   b. The glory of His meritorious Life. All His sufferings endured upon the earth live on and claim their reward.

   c. The glory of His Assession. He sits glorified at the Right Hand of Power. By His mediation He does not ask for what He has not, but He gives forth what He has.

AFFECTIONS. Love of Christ. Trust in His Mediation.

PRAYER.

O Lord God, Who hast exalted Thy Son, and given all things into His hands, grant that we may so devoutly celebrate the mystery of His Death, that we may obtain by His Intercession what Thy predestinating Love hath provided for us, through the same Jesus Christ our Lord. Amen.

THE PLEDGE OF FUTURE GLORY.

PRELUDE.   i. *O Sacred Banquet, in which Christ is received, the memory of His Passion renewed, the mind is filled with grace, and a pledge of future glory is given to us.*

ii. The Body of Christ within us, as a live coal in a mass of blackness communicating its own redness.

POINT I.   *Consider the security of God's Word.*

    a. Christ, in bidding us eat of Himself that we may live, promises that He will raise us up at the last day.

    b. He who gives this promise, made us at the beginning for the attainment of Eternal Life with Himself, and He has ordered the events of past ages to prepare the way for this final covenant.

    c. The Jewish Sacrifices admitted those who partook thereof to the Temple privileges. Much more does feeding upon Christ bring us near to God.

POINT II.   *Consider the sufficiency of Christ's Power.*

    a. All creation is sustained by the Word of God.. He who gives life is the Unchangeable, and upholds each creature in that nearness to Himself whereunto He has brought it.

    b. Christ's Body being raised from the dead, dieth no more. There is no power which can oppose Him in His risen Life. His Body is eternally triumphant.

    c. Christ's Body is one with our own bodies in origin, and therefore it is capable of becoming co-extensive with our own bodies, and purging off all that defiles them.

POINT III.   *Consider the character of the future Glory.*

    a. It is the glory for which man's nature was formed. The faculties of man are given him with a view to this result. The glory promised is the glory proper to man, when united to God, a restoration of our old inheritance.

    b. It is the glory wherein Jesus is already enthroned. This glory emanates from Him, and quickens with its own likeness all that are near so as to behold it.

    c. The Life of Christ thus given to us, is held in common with all saints, needs to be received individually, operates substantially, affects the whole nature, invigorates all the faculties, purges away all infirmities, prepares the whole nature for the manifestation of the One Eternal Spirit.

AFFECTIONS.   Longing for Christ to appear. Love. Hope.

PRAYER.

O God, Who givest to us the grace of Thy dear Son in this Holy Sacrament, as a pledge of glory to be given hereafter, grant me so to live in this power, that I may have my part in that manifestation, according to the merits of Jesus Christ Thy Son our Lord. Amen.

MEDITATIONS

FOR

THE SUNDAYS AFTER TRINITY.

THE FORFEITURE OF GRACE.

PRELUDE. i. *Father Abraham, have mercy upon me, and send Lazarus, that he may dip the tip of his finger in water, and · cool my tongue ; for I am tormented in this flame.*

ii. The Persons speaking together as described in the Parable.

POINT I. *Consider the claim of Sonship.*

    a. He looks to Abraham. He had felt secure as having Abraham to his father while on earth, and now he cannot shake off the idea of that privilege, although it only turns to his disappointment.

    b. He recognizes the paternal authority of Abraham. He · had not obeyed Abraham's example while living; but now he expects Abraham to assert authority over Lazarus.

    c. He expects to receive commiseration upon the score of natural kinship. Whilst living he had died to the claims of that union, for his spirit was not Abraham's. Now he finds how death has broken his claim on Abraham.

POINT II. *Consider the continuing self-importance.*

    a. He regards Lazarus as fitted only to do a servant's work. He had known him as a poor man upon earth. He expects accidental distinctions to last, but they are ended.

    b. It seems natural that Lazarus should minister to his comfort. He had ministered proudly and thoughtlessly of his overflowing wealth to the needs of Lazarus. He expects from Lazarus humility and compassion.

    c. He speaks of his misery, but shows no tokens of contrition. He had fared sumptuously every day, He does not now regret the absence of love in his past life, but the present suffering which he has to endure.

POINT III. *Consider the impossibility of help.*

    a. On earth he had boasted of being one of God's people, but had not lived in communion with God. Now he is shut out from God and cannot speak to Him.

    b. On earth he had boasted of being one of Abraham's children. What brought him near to opportunities of grace on earth, helps not now. He asks Abraham in vain.

    c. On earth there were means of grace which he received without penitence. Now he is in " the pit wherein is no water." (Zech. ix. 11.) There is for him no power of help, no hope.

AFFECTIONS. Penitence. Determination to use grace while we have Christ. Love to our brethren. Self-denial.

PRAYER.

O God, Who hast provided for us manifold gifts of grace in Thy Church, grant me so to use them for the manifestation of Thy Divine Life here on earth, that I may be comforted with all Thy Saints in the joy of that Divine Life hereafter, through the merits of Jesus Christ Thy Son, our Lord. Amen.

THE INVITATION OF GRACE.

PRELUDE. i. *A certain man made a great supper, and bade many ; and sent his servant at supper time to say to them that were bidden, Come ; for all things are now ready.*—S. Luke xiv. 16, 17.

ii. As in the Parable.

POINT I. *Consider the greatness of the invitation.*
   a. The greatness of Christ, Who makes the supper. The guests were themselves His creatures. Everywhere He fed them. He made all mankind, even though He called not all.
   b. The greatness of the multitude who are called. He bade many. Abraham's seed were to be as the stars of heaven.
   c. The greatness of the provision. All things are ready. It is not His fault that the promise to Abraham waits. The chosen seed must accept the Blessing.

POINT II   *Consider the time of the invitation.*
   a. The time was appointed by God. He knows the fitting time. If men refuse at His time, they would have refused at any other. The difficulties were not of the supper time, but of the will. So every one lives at the time best for himself. None would be better if born elsewhere.
   b. The time was declared to man. God's invitation is not sudden. Men should know not what God will call them to, but that He will call. God gives warning when it is time.
   c. The time requires to be watched by man. The call of grace is rejected because men cling to the world. We should not follow impulses in breaking away from obligations, but keep ourselves detached, waiting for the calls.

POINT III. *Consider the sending of the servant.*
   a. The message by the servant must be accepted as the Word of the Lord. The servant is not authorized to speak of himself, but he conveys the invitation from his Master.
   b. It requires prompt obedience. If we are sure that the servant is bringing us the message, we must not hesitate or wait for any further tokens of the Master's will.
   c. It will not be repeated. We may trust in God to go on speaking until He makes His will plain, but not so as to sanction our delay.

AFFECTIONS. Promptness. Detachment. Thankfulness. Expectation.

PRAYER.

O God, Who mercifully callest us out of the world into the kingdom of Thy dear Son, grant that I may live so detached from the world that I may recognize Thy call, and act thereon without delay. Through Jesus Christ our Lord. Amen.

THE SOLICITUDE OF GRACE.

PRELUDE. i. *What man of you, having an hundred sheep, if he lose one of them, doth not leave the ninety and nine in the wilderness, and go after that which is lost, until he find it?—* S. Luke xv. 4.

ii. As in the Parable.

POINT I. *Consider the sheep lost.*
a. The owner's care. He misses it from the flock when He tells them. He must take measures individually to recover it.
b. The sheep's distress. It feels its isolation; knows not where to turn. The sheep far away sees none that can hear.
c. The answering of the cry. The shepherd listens to hear the cry, and comes himself to the relief of the lost one.

POINT II. *Consider the sheep at pasture.*
a. The watchful guidance. The shepherd leads his sheep through the wilderness, knowing where feeding places can be found, although the road be barren.
b. The security of union. They who are following Christ's guidance feel the joy of His protection as He holds them.
c. The owner's joy. He looks upon them with satisfaction until He misses one. He shows his love by leaving all to find the lost one; but the love was there beforehand; an individual love amidst the general care.

POINT III. *Consider the sheep restored.*
a. The anxious search. Jesus seeks the lost soul; for though He be everywhere, yet as He knows not sin, so the soul in sin is hidden from Him, not from His Divine Predestination, but from the guiding eye of His grace. Grace needs to discover the soul before there can be true restoration.
b. The sheep left. The pasturage suffices for daily need; but Jesus leaves His ordinary Providence, and brings back the wandering soul with an individual appropriateness.
c. The finding. The Shepherd rejoices. The sheep is restored. All are gladdened. As we are members one of another, we must all feel joy or sorrow in whatever befalls each one; and yet the joy of all is only the joy of the Shepherd shared by all. Our joy in one another is from Him.

AFFECTIONS. Anxiety for salvation of men. Encouragement to rise out of our faults. Diligence.

PRAYER.

O Lord Jesus Christ, Who dost vouchsafe to seek after Thy lost sheep according to their several needs, grant that I may always praise Thee for the Love wherewith Thou seekest me out, and abide in that Love according to the fulness of Thy sustaining power, Who with the Father and the Holy Ghost livest and reignest God for ever and ever. Amen.

o 2

THE EXAMPLE OF GRACE.

PRELUDE. i. *Be ye therefore merciful, as your Father also is merciful, saith the Lord.*—S. Luke vi. 36,
ii. Any act of Divine goodness.

POINT I. *Consider the mercy of the Father.*
  a. The deserts of sin. Sin must be measured by the glory of the Father, which is outraged. Sin, as it is against God's Love, naturally forfeits God's Love.
  b. The long-suffering of God. He winked at the times of ignorance, but he did not become indifferent. He desired man's love, and He bears with men in various phases of discipline, seeking to move Him to love.
  c. The results of mercy. The mercy of God is not a mere forgiveness, but it is a raising of the sinner out of his fallen condition.

POINT II. *Consider the manifestation of Sonship.*
  a. To be like our Father. We must have a mercy which does indeed take full account of the evil of sin, but bears patiently with the sinner, striving to win him to amendment and reconciliation.
  b. To abide in His mercy. If we are to exercise mercy towards others, we must live ourselves in the constant recognition of the mercy which we experience.
  c. To exert His power. Mercy is an attribute of power, not merely in sparing, but much more in uplifting, renewing, rehabilitating.

POINT III. *Consider the claims of brotherhood.*
  a. We are sinners, as others. We can never complain of what others do against us, because, as sinners, we do not deserve to receive good at the hands of any.
  b. Sin is not done against us, but against our Father. We deserve to suffer. God might use others as His instruments of vengeance towards us, whereas He places Himself on our side, so that injuries done to us shall be sins against Him.
  c. Our greatest joy must be to exercise our Father's love. As God is Love, we become like to Him, by loving with His Love, and we must love those whom He loves. We must love God in them, and this will give us joy.

AFFECTIONS. Compassion. Gratitude. Effort to repair the sins of others.

PRAYER.

O God, Who showest mercy to us sinners, and does accept all acts of regard as being done unto Thyself, grant that I may become worthy of the mercy for which I hope, by practising towards others that mercy which I have received, through Jesus Christ our Lord. Amen.

THE DIVINE TEACHING OF GRACE.

PRELUDE. i. *And Jesus entered into one of the ships and sat down, and taught the people out of the ship.*—S. Luke v. 3.
ii. The ship moved by the waves: Jesus teaching therein.

POINT I. *Consider Jesus upon His Throne.*
 a. Christ the Governor amongst the people. Although the Church be tossed about by the waves of popular change, we must recognise His Voice as the unchanging Teacher.
 b. His Peace filling all hearts that listen to Him. He tranquillizes the stormy sea. He will soothe the troubled heart, but we must own His power if we are to experience it.
 c. His coming into this world of accident. Jesus is not at home in the world. He inhabiteth Eternity. He came into this changeful world on purpose to declare to us the unchanging Truth.

POINT II. *Consider Jesus teaching the people.*
 a. No power of man can teach them. Unless we can still the waves, we cannot teach the people. The storms of accident are not so great as those of passion and prejudice.
 b. The power of the Voice of Jesus. His voice reaches every heart in that multitude. He adapts Himself to each.
 c. The will of the Father, which He makes known, is the same for all, varying in outer signs, but changeless as to inward purpose.

POINT III. *Consider the Church as the place of His Teaching.*
 a. The dangers of the Church are the evidence of His authority. The Church is often tempest tost. Jesus can command the silence of all powers at any moment. Listen to Him, and thou wilt hear naught else.
 b. The Personal Voice of Jesus speaks through the Church. He speaks as one separated from the people by His position, but offering His gifts to all.
 c. The Holy Ghost is the power of that Voice. The words of Jesus Himself would be valueless without the Divine power. The Holy Ghost penetrates every heart, and teaches all things.

AFFECTIONS. Attention. Stedfastness. Self-surrender.

PRAYER.

O God, Who didst send Thy Son to speak to us with Divine power the words of Eternal Truth, that we might rely upon Thy promises in the midst of this changeful world, grant me so to accept Thy law that I may be established in Thy Covenant, and so to rest upon Thy Truth that I may not be moved by outward vicissitude, but may ever rejoice and glorify Thy Name, through Jesus Christ our Lord. Amen.

THE SPIRITUAL PERFECTION OF GRACE.

PRELUDE. i. *Ye have heard that it was said by them of old time, Thou shalt not kill; and whosoever shall kill shall be in danger of the judgment.*—S. Matt. v. 21.

ii. Jesus calling us to Eternal Life with Himself.

POINT I. *The Gospel full of promise rather than of threatening.*

a. The superiority of promises. They tell of growth rather than of decay. They purify instead of paralyzing. They help us to live in the future rather than in the present.

b. The positive character of hope. The one great evil which the loving soul knows is the absence of good. We are strengthened to strive after the good by its revelation.

c. The personal character of love. God is Love, personally manifesting Himself. The fear of losing ourselves in nothing is not so great as the fear of losing God and finding our own nothingness.

POINT II. *The present Love.*

a. Love to God. Faith, as the substance of things hoped for, teaches us to rejoice in Personal Being. God as our stay.

b. Love to God's creatures. Love to God requires us to love everything which He has made for the purposes for which He made. Not to love, or to love with any other love than His, would be rebellion.

c. Love, in spite of injuries. Since we love for God's sake, we cannot take account of anything we suffer, but can only be anxious for Him to be glorified in everything.

POINT III. *The Eternal reward.*

a. Likeness to God becoming perfect. Grace does not hold us down under the bondage of law, but leads us onward in the fellowship of Divine Love.

b. The understanding opened. Fear of punishment closes our eyes, in ignorance of what God will do. The Promises of God open our hearts to rejoice in the glory which we know to be attendant upon all which we do for His Love.

c. The joy of attainment. Grace leads us onward to a perfect participation of the joy of God, according to the measure in which that will of God has wrought in us.

AFFECTIONS. Generosity in God's service. Thankfulness for His vocation. Longing for the eternal fruition.

PRAYER.

O Almighty God, Who callest me to live in Thy Love by the greatness of Thy promises, grant me by Thy grace so to accomplish Thy will in all things, that I may be perfected in the Truth of eternal Life, through Thy Son, Jesus Christ our Lord. Amen.

THE COMPASSIONATENESS OF GRACE.

PRELUDE. i. I *have compassion on the multitude, because they have now been with Me three days and have nothing to eat ; and if I send them away fasting to their houses, they will faint by the way.*—S. Mark viii. 2.

ii. Our Lord speaking to His Apostles.

POINT I. *Consider the objects of Christ's compassion.*

a. The need of continuing with Him. Christ desires to test our love of Himself before making manifest to us the power of that Love. We must show our love to Him by suffering something for Him.

b. The three days. The third day is ever the day of God's power. Christ manifests His compassion at the appointed time.

c. The sense of want. We need to feel it. Otherwise we cannot know the power of His Love in supplying it.

POINT II. *Consider the manner of His compassion.*

a. The engrafting of love. The power of loving Him is the greatest of His gifts. It involves the correlative gift of being loved by Him.

b. The increase of true religion. Love must be shown by a growing practice of the duties of religion. We must be more and more bound to God in strictness of holy life.

c. The nourishment of Divine goodness. Christ nourishes us with His goodness that we may continue to follow Him.

POINT III. *Consider the results of His compassion.*

a. The manifestation of His power. If we show our love, and persevere in our observance, we may trust in Him not to let His compassion be an idle one. He will nourish us with new Life.

b. To be with Jesus on the way. Though we feel our waiting, we must not doubt His Presence. He hungered, being one with man. We must hunger if we would be one with God. God feeds with Himself those who hunger for Him.

c. To be with Jesus in His Home. His compassion does not provide us merely with the perishing food of earth. He feeds us with Himself that He may take us to Himself.

AFFECTIONS. Desire for God. Endurance. Confidence. Satisfaction in God.

PRAYER.

O *God, draw me unto Thyself, that amidst the necessities of earth I may look to Thee for the supply of all; and may be strengthened by Thy grace so to act in obedience to Thy Commandments, that I may hereafter attain to Thy perfect contemplation Through Jesus Christ our Lord.* Amen.

THE SPURIOUS IMITATION OF GRACE.

PRELUDE. i. *Beware of false prophets which come to you in sheep's clothing, but inwardly they are ravening wolves. Ye shall know them by their fruits.*—S. Matt. vii. 15.

ii. As in the Parable.

POINT I. *Consider the activity of evil,*

a. Satan's personal violence. The Prince of Death wails as he sees the people of God nourished with eternal life. He hates them as he hates God.

b. Speaking things that may do hurt. A liar and a murderer, he slays with words of falsehood, leading men from God.

c. Eager to devour. He craves after all wherein he finds the image of God, for it reminds him of his forfeited portion, and he hungers madly to destroy their joy.

POINT II. *Consider the semblance of good.*

a. Necessary for the work of evil. If there were no outward appearance of good, there would be nothing to draw the good away. Simple violence would only make them cling to God more closely.

b. Requiring spiritual discernment. Natural good deceives. Supernatural evil defies all merely natural detection. There must be illuminating grace in order to behold things in this supernatural relationship.

c. Developing a habit of caution, a firm hold of truth; an intelligent searching into truth, a loving delight therein.

POINT III. *Consider the test.*

a. The kind of fruit. Not always what teachers may personally do, but what they do as a result of their system. Good men may hide the evil of their system, and bad men may disgrace the truth they teach. But the fruit of the system is independent of such appearances.

b. The possibility of discernment. If we are watchful, we shall see that the external good and evil are affected by some alien power, and recognize the consistency in good and the conscientiousness in evil.

c. The Divine help. God works all real good, and He will not be a party to a fraud. He hides in order to produce watchfulness, not to work destruction.

AFFECTIONS. Jealous regard for Truth. Adhesion to Divine warnings in spite of human attractiveness. Trust in God.

PRAYER.

O God, Who speakest to us in the midst of this world of falsehood, grant that we may so reverently contemplate the analogy of faith, that we may triumph over all the artifices of the Evil One. Through Jesus Christ our Lord. Amen.

THE RESPONSIBILITY OF GRACE.

PRELUDE. i. *And the rich man called him, and said unto him, How is it that I hear this of thee? Give an account of thy stewardship.*—S. Luke xvi. 2.

ii. As in the Parable.

POINT I. *Consider the Master's call.*
- a. The certainty of the call. We may be left a long time, but are sure to have our case investigated by and by.
- b. The individuality thereof. God does not merely examine into the general good or evil of any age or nation, but questions each soul as to himself.
- c. The expectation. We must be getting matters in readiness for this inquiry. God warns us that we may set things in order.

POINT II. *Consider the accusation.*
- a. Satan, who tempted, accuses. Man was put into this world as God's steward, and the enemy, ever grudging us our hopes, accuses God to us of giving us less than we deserve, because we have to go through discipline before attaining the reward.
- b. God requires the accusation to be tested. Each soul must give account of itself. We must judge ourselves now by penitence, or else we must hereafter surrender ourselves as guilty for punishment.
- c. The rigour of the inquiry. We cannot make terms with the world so as to be hidden from God. All secrets will be disclosed. The evading of an accusation but increases the guilt.

POINT III. *Consider the cause of failure.*
- a. The need of Divine assistance. We fail because we do not use God's grace according to His Will. We are tempted to compromise with the world, because we have been along with the world in forgetfulness of God.
- b. The enabling power. The grace entrusted to us preserves us from the world if duly used. If we do our work now, we shall not have to dig as the world's menials hereafter.
- c. The exercise of the dependent Spirit. We must ask God for continuance of grace, and then we shall never have to beg with shame of the world, for God's grace is exhaustless to the soul which seeks Him.

AFFECTIONS. Gratitude. Zeal. Penitence.

PRAYER.

O Almighty God, Who hast bestowed upon me such manifold gifts of grace that I may glorify Thee in the world, grant that I may never seek a home in the world apart from Thee, but rather humbling myself before Thee for past sin, may so use Thy gifts which remain, that I may find my eternal Home in the Refuge of Thine exhaustless Love, through Jesus Christ our Lord. Amen.

THE VISITATION OF GRACE.

PRELUDE. i. *And when He was come near, He beheld the city, and wept over it, saying, If thou hadst known, even thou, at least in this thy day, the things which belong unto thy peace! but now they are hid from thine eyes. For the days shall come upon thee, that thine enemies shall cast a trench about thee, and compass thee round, and keep thee in on every side, and shall lay thee even with the ground, and thy children within thee; and they shall not leave in thee one stone upon another; because thou knewest not the time of thy visitation.*—S. Luke xix. 41-44.

ii. The scene as in the Gospel.

POINT I. *Consider the appeal of Jesus.*

    a. He weeps over the soul. He shows His tender compassion as possessing the same nature which we do. The Word of God speaks to each one of us with a true human Love.

    b. He warns. In many ways. He gives intimation sufficient for the watchful soul to recognize.

    c. He denounces. If the warning is unheeded, it must be followed by open judgment. The hidden Saviour declares the open judgment.

POINT II. *Consider the cause of rejection.*

    a. Want of knowledge. God gives us moral means of ascertaining His will. An adulterous generation seeks for signs to make heavenly Truth certain to the natural perception, and is rejected because it does not read the higher teaching.

    b. Want of love. This unwillingness to appreciate heavenly teaching springs from the carnal affections of the heart.

    c. Stubbornness. The stronger those affections are, binding us to some earthly conception of God's purpose, the greater will be the resistance to the Divine Message.

POINT III. *Consider the consequences.*

    a. The coming of enemies. God's vengeance comes from without, and is often such as was not looked for.

    b. Devastation. The rebellious city is made even with the ground over which it sought to rise in power. The offspring of her natural energies only adds to her sorrow as she sees them destroyed.

    c. Blindness. In her pride she would not see God's will for her, and in His last visitations she cannot recognize Him.

AFFECTIONS. Attention to God's warnings. Self mistrust.

PRAYER.

O God, Who dost never cast any away without warning them that they may turn to Thee, grant that I may always watch for Thy tokens, listen to Thy Voice, yield to Thy solicitations, and abide in outward weakness, with reliance upon Thy sure promises, so that I may find salvation through Thy Word, and partake of Thy Heavenly Triumph, through Jesus Christ our Lord. Amen.

THE JUSTIFICATION OF GRACE.

PRELUDE. i. *Two men went up into the Temple to pray; the one a Pharisee, and the other a publican; I tell you this man went down to his house justified.*—S. Luke xviii. 10, 14.

ii. As in the Parable.

POINT I. *Consider the common need.*

a. Both prayed. Prayer is the expression of our misery. We pray as sinners. Yet we often pray without penitence, and therefore pray in vain.

b. Both went up to the Temple. Prayer belongs to God's covenant. We have no right to pray by nature. We must exercise the prerogatives of grace with the humility of sinners.

c. Distinctions outside of God's covenant do not distinguish us when we are within it. Bond and free are alike. We must forget everything except the need we have of God's justifying grace.

POINT II. *Consider the sense of need.*

a. It must be real. No good that is in us naturally can mitigate the evil we have to deplore.

b. Humbling. We shall not be rejected because our sins were great, but because our knowledge of the sins has not been adequate.

c. Full of desire. Our penitence must not paralyze us with remembrance of nature, but quicken us with faithful hope in the exercise of grace.

POINT III. *Consider that they received as they asked.*

a. Nothing gets nothing. The Pharisee contemplated himself with satisfaction, and coming full of his own emptiness went away empty of God's fulness.

b. Penitence found mercy. If we feel our need of mercy we shall not be rejected for the greatness of our sin.

c. Mercy includes righteousness. God cannot show us mercy and leave us sinners. He pardons by transforming. Forgiveness is restoration to service. Justification is a power of doing righteousness and pleasing Him.

AFFECTIONS. Penitence. Open-heartedness in confession. Trust in God.

PRAYER.

O God, Who callest us, sinners, near unto Thyself in the true Temple, which is the Body of Thy dear Son, grant me grace to approach Thee with such prostration of heart that I may find Thy glorious power raising me up to serve Thee upon earth in righteousness and true holiness, so that I may attain to dwell in Thy Courts, and praise Thee for evermore; through Jesus Christ our Lord. **Amen.**

THE UNIVERSALITY OF GRACE.

PRELUDE. i. *Jesus departing from the coast of Tyre and Sidon, came unto the sea of Galilee, through the midst of the coasts of Decapolis.*—S. Mark vii. 31.
ii. As in the Gospel.

POINT I. *Consider our condition by nature.*
a. Without God in the world. How difficult it is for us to feel ourselves to be as much without God by nature as the Canaanitish nations were! Yet we cannot otherwise praise Him truly for having received us into the number of His chosen people.
b. In the shadow of death. The Light was promised to them that were in darkness. If we make too much of the light of nature, we will be liable to forfeit the Light of Grace.
c. Without claim. By nature we could have no claim, for we have marred the nature which God gave us. Our destruction is of ourselves.

POINT II. *Consider the offer of grace.*
a. Jesus comes to all in turn. He is ever passing by. He desires us to pour out all our complaints to Him. He comes seeking those who will abide with Him in their need.
b. The evil of Galilee and the evil of Jerusalem. Nature, in its degradation, is not so blind morally as are the chosen people, if they turn back to nature.
c. The welcome and the rejection. Nature, looking to Christ, catches glimpses of Heaven; but those who are with Christ, if they look to the world, turn their back on Heaven.

POINT III. *Consider the renewed visitations of God's grace.*
a. He leaves Galilee, but He returns again. Others needed Him; but those to whom He has come are not forgotten.
b. We must rejoice when Jesus manifests His power to others. If we take pleasure in what He does for others, we become fit to welcome Him when He returns.
c. Jesus does not cease to bless because He withdraws from the manifestation of Blessing. If we follow Him in brotherly love, we shall find that He is ready to give us greater gifts in due season.

AFFECTIONS. Humiliation. Gratitude. Confidence. Hope Love.

PRAYER.

O Jesu, Who in mercy dost visit us, that Thou mayest make manifest the power of Thy goodness, grant me so to welcome Thy Love, that in the fellowship of its power I may rejoice in all that Thou doest for others as for myself, and may experience the constant renewal of Thy Love, which never faileth. Amen.

THE NECESSITY OF GRACE.

PRELUDE. i. *A certain man went down from Jerusalem to Jericho and fell among thieves, which stripped him of his raiment and wounded him, leaving him half dead.*—S. Luke x. 30.
ii. As in the Parable.

POINT I. *Consider the thieves.*
    a. Satan came to plunder mankind of God's gifts in Paradise. He who was formed to live in the glory of God is goaded as it were to madness by the sight of that glory in others.
    b. He is continually sending his agents, evil spirits, and the powers of the world, to rob us of God's gifts.
    c. God does not leave us in our poverty, but the riches which God gives stimulates Satan's envy so as to make him attack us the more.

POINT II. *Consider our despoiled condition.*
    a. The robe of original righteousness was stripped off from us at the Fall. When we are born into this world, we are in a state of nakedness, and shame, and condemnation.
    b. Our former gifts of grace do not avail us when we are bereft of them. Our present state of nakedness is only the more grievous. What might I be, if I had not forfeited grace?
    c. Our first despoiling in Paradise we individually could not avoid. How often has God clothed us since then, and yet by our own fault the enemy leaves us naked by the wayside.

POINT III. *Consider that we are half dead.*
    a. Our soul is dead when we are born into the world, although our body has its own lower life. We cannot see beyond this valley of death. We cannot move without a helper.
    b. We have not energy to rise and go upon our journey unless we are renewed by the power of Divine grace. Each subsequent sin involves us in the like helpless condition.
    c. We cannot even realize the full extent of our misery, by reason of the lethargy of our wounded condition. We must not be content with our own consciousness of sin; but we must learn our misery by faith, as our Helper teaches us.

AFFECTIONS. Expectation of Divine help. Gratitude to the Good Samaritan. Hope of recovery.

PRAYER.

O Thou Who art come down from the Heavenly Dwelling-place to help our ruined race upon this sinful earth, grant that I may receive with thankfulness the ministrations of Thy grace, and commit myself with simple confidence into Thy hands; so that when Thou comest again I may be able to return with Thee, and rejoice in the Kingdom of Thy Peace, where Thy Redeemed shall ever praise Thee in the glory of the Father. Amen.

198 Fourteenth Sunday after Trinity.

THE SUPPLICATION FOR GRACE.

PRELUDE. i. *And as He entered into a certain village there met Him ten men that were lepers, which stood afar off. And they lifted up their voices and said, Jesus, Master, have mercy on us.*—S. Luke xvii. 12, 13.

ii. As in the Gospels.

POINT I. *Consider the lepers standing afar off.*

a. We must feel ourselves utterly unfit for the natural society of men if we would welcome Jesus in the Communion of Saints. We often fail to take notice of Him, because the world takes notice of us.

b. The lepers desired restoration to the earthly society of their kinsfolk. We must know the Saints of Christ as our kindred if we desire restoration to the Heavenly Jerusalem.

c. While we cry unto Jesus, we still stand afar off from Him. It is not the virtue of our sincerity, but the power of His grace which brings us near.

POINT II. *Consider their cry.*

a. They were wont to say, Unclean, as men passed by. We must be ready to acknowledge our sins before our fellow-creatures. It is a half-hearted confession which thinks to escape shame before man and fears not Christ.

b. To Jesus they call for mercy. We must recognize the power of Him to Whom we come, as truly as our own need.

c. They address Him as Master. Our unfitness to do the work of our Master does not destroy the relationship between Him and us. He created us to do His work. His mercy is shown in making us fit to do it.

POINT III. *Consider their expectation.*

a. Natural cleansing was what they looked for. Perhaps thought it but a bare chance that they might get it. If they had had higher hopes, or better grounded expectation, they would probably have shown higher thankfulness.

b. God's gifts in nature should develop our expectation of grace. Else they choke it up. We die of repletion.

c. Their expectation was of something from Him, not for Himself. What He gives must bind us to Him in the contemplation of His inexhaustible goodness. To cling to Him is Life, to leave Him Death.

AFFECTIONS. Penitence. Helplessness. Trust in Jesus.

PRAYER.

O Blessed Jesu, Who rejectest none because of their vileness, draw me unto Thyself with such a knowledge of Thy Love that I may obtain that cleansing which I need, and may be made fit to share Thy Love with all Thy Saints in the kingdom of Thy glory; where Thou livest and reignest with the Father and the Holy Ghost, One God, for ever and ever. Amen.

THE SECURITY OF GRACE.

PRELUDE. i. *Take no thought, saying, What shall we eat, or what shall we drink, or wherewithal shall we be clothed? For your heavenly Father knoweth that ye have need of all these things.—* Matt. vi. 31, 32.

ii. Our Lord assuring His disciples.

POINT I. *Consider what it is to trust in God.*

a. Our trust must be tested. Many mean to trust in God. The intention seems to be elevating. The reality seems to be discouraging, but it developes strength.

b. Trust on our part meets with love on God's part, so that a reciprocity is established between us and God.

c. Nothing is worth having save as God's gift. It is by learning the helplessness of the creature that we come to see all things as God's gift.

POINT II. *Consider the disciplinary character of the outer life.*

a. We learn our dependence upon God by being forced to look to Him alone. He never disappoints those who truly wait upon Him.

b. We learn to love God as the Giver of all good. Each experience of His willingness to help us in our need begets further confidence in His goodness.

c. We become fitted to receive His greatest benefits, by looking to Him for small ones. He provides for us as a Father, and will give us the full blessing of sons.

POINT III. *Consider the Divine knowledge of our need.*

a. God made us, and knows how our nature suffers through manifold wants.

b. God knows what is best suited to develope the moral and spiritual energies of our nature, and gives us accordingly.

c. God does not regard our need as a misfortune from which we have to be rescued, but as a condition of progress wherein we may exhibit the powers which He has given us, so that we may obtain the more.

AFFECTIONS. Joy in tribulation. Confidence. Gratitude. Hope.

PRAYER.

O *Almighty God, grant that as Thou knowest our need, so we may acknowledge Thy power; and as Thou hast ordained all things in order to lead us onward in Thy love, so we may accept all things with gratitude as a means of exhibiting Thy glory, through Jesus Christ our Lord. Amen.*

THE OPPORTUNITY OF GRACE.

PRELUDE. i. *And it came to pass the day after, that Jesus went into a city called Nain, and, behold, there was a dead man carried out, the only son of his mother.*—S. Luke vii. 11, 12.

ii. As in the Gospel.

POINT I. *Consider the meeting with Jesus.*

  a. Jesus meets us in our sorrows. Blessed are those sorrows which drive us from our home in the world, so that we may come out and meet with Jesus.

  b. Jesus helps us when the world fails us. He does not meet us with empty sympathy, but with life-giving power. .

  c. Jesus knows when He is going to meet us, and appoints our troubles in order to put us in the way of meeting Him.

POINT II. *Consider the coming out of the world.*

  a. Friends around look upon death as the end of all our hopes. We know that we cannot come out of the world truly save by dying to it.

  b. The widowed mother rejoices in having her son restored; but it is with a joy dead to the world in the marvel of a Saviour's Love and power.

  c. The dead man lives once more in the midst of earthly scenes; but death has separated him from them. He is still buried to the world. The Love of Jesus is the atmosphere which he breathes.

POINT III. *Consider the carrying out from the city.*

  a. The world sets us aside, but knows not that it is helping us to gain a knowledge of Jesus which we could not have while we were living in its fellowship.

  b. The dead are helpless in the hands of those who carry them. So must we be in the world, if we are really to show forth the power of Jesus.

  c. How many dead are carried out. Jesus meets but one. All have to learn separation from the world. We must so look to Jesus while in the world that He may show us His power when we are separated from it.

AFFECTIONS. Deadness to the world. Confidence in Jesus. Passive surrender to His discipline.

PRAYER.

Grant, O Lord, I pray Thee, that though I be dead unto Thee by reason of my sin, nevertheless by Thy grace I may be so dead unto the world that I may hear Thy Voice calling me to newness of Life in the glory of the Resurrection; through Jesus Christ Thy Son our Lord. Amen.

Seventeenth Sunday after Trinity. 201

THE ENERGY OF GRACE.

PRELUDE. i. *And Jesus spake unto the lawyers and Phari-sees, saying, Is it lawful to heal on the Sabbath day? And they held their peace. And He took him and healed him, and let him go.*—S. Luke xiv. 3, 4.

ii. As in the Gospel.

POINT I. *Consider the Sabbath of God.*
- *a.* It is a rest in energy. To rest from energy is death. The Life of God is the energy wherein He rests,—the act of joy wherewith the Father contemplates the Son, to Whom He giveth to live with Himself consubstantially in the unity of the same Spirit,—the act from whence creation begins, and wherein creation ends.
- *b.* It is a rest from external work. The development of creation is a continuous change. God is "the same."—Heb. i.—The changeable is to be perfected in the unchangeable.
- *c.* It is a rest of love. God rests not as being weary, disappointed, or neglectful, but as rejoicing to sustain a work completely organised.

POINT II. *Consider the work of healing.*
- *a.* It is the overthrow of sin, for disease is originated by decay.
- *b.* It is the restoration of the creature to its proper state of completeness, according to the Divine purpose. Man is delivered from sin, not by removal only but by renewal.
- c. It is a work of Divine power. Created agents may remove material consequences of decay God alone can renew the healthful energy of life.

POINT III. *Consider the constancy of Divine Beneficence.*
- *a.* God in this world is ever repairing the decay of sin throughout nature.
- *b.* God is ever operating as in nature so in grace, for the supply of all that is needful to sustain man in that condition of life, or nearness to Himself, wherein He has called him.
- *c.* God takes the individual man, and having renewed him lets him go, that he may exercise the grace which he has received, and live to God's glory.

AFFECTIONS. Worship. Dependence upon God. Gratitude. Activity of correspondent will.

PRAYER.

O God, Who hast renewed me in grace that I may live to Thy glory, grant that I may not yield to the decay of the material nature, so as to fall from Thee, in Whom alone my life is found, but may ever act in the fellowship of Thy Love, and attain to the glory of Thine Eternal Life, through Jesus Christ our Lord. Amen.

P

THE INTEGRITY OF GRACE.

PRELUDE. i. *Master, which is the great commandment in the Law? Jesus said unto him, Thou shalt love the Lord thy God with all thy heart, and with all thy soul, and with all thy mind.*—S. Matt. xxii. 36, 37.

ii. The lawyer reflecting upon the answer of Jesus.

POINT I. *Consider the object of our service.*

a. As the law comes from Him who loves, it can be fulfilled in no other way than by loving. The life to which God calls must be like that wherein He lives.

b. God, Who loves with an untiring love, must be equally loved in return by acts abiding and eternal, not merely occasional.

c. As God acts with an undivided energy, so He must be loved with an undivided love. The whole nature must be quickened with the life of love, in order to fulfil His law.

POINT II. *Consider the instrument of our service.*

a. The heart, the affections. The service which God needs is not a compulsory submission, but a voluntary self-surrender. Love must supply the motive of our actions.

b. The soul, the energy. This includes the bodily strength.—S. Mark xii. 30.—Love must be no dreamy sentiment, if it is to be like God or approved of God. It must exert the faculties of the whole nature for the service of the Beloved.

c. The mind, the intellectual powers. As God operates by His Consubstantial Wisdom, so man must serve God by the exercise of his understanding. An unwise service is one which does not rise it to the measure of wisdom proper to the individual, according to his place in God's creation.

POINT III. *Consider our relationship to Him Whom we serve.*

a. A changeless relationship—we the creatures, He our God. Our service must be the equivalent, not of some temporary want but of this eternal bond.

b. A dependent relationship. Whatever we are, comes from God. We owe Him gratitude for every possible joy.

c. An absolute relationship. His own absolute will is the basis on which it rests. He supplies us with all good in absolute freedom. We must serve Him with a corresponding integrity of dependent activity.

AFFECTIONS. Self-surrender. Admiration. Gratitude. Reliance.

PRAYER.

O God, Who in Love hast formed me, that by the knowledge of Thy Truth I might find joy in worshipping Thy Majesty, grant me so to abide in the acknowledgment of Thy Love, that I may love Thee according to the fulness of Thy purpose. Through Jesus Christ our Lord. Amen.

THE RESTORING POWER OF GRACE.

PRELUDE. i. *Jesus said unto the sick of the palsy, Son, be of good cheer, thy sins be forgiven thee.*—S. Matt. ix. 2.

ii. As in the Gospel.

POINT I. *Consider suffering as a token of sonship.*

   a. The suffering of the body. Whom the Lord loveth He chasteneth. Suffering does not separate us from God, but it is the means by which He seeks to recall us.

   b. The suffering of sin. Deep sorrow occasioned by sin is no sign of sonship having been forfeited. Rather it is the voice of sonship speaking within our hearts. Those who have lost their sonship, feel no anguish for their loss.

   c. The suffering of shame. Man may regard us as outcasts. God will not reject us because they do.

   d. The sweetness of hearing the Voice of Jesus saying, Son, be of good cheer.

POINT II. *Consider the receptivity of faith.*

   a. Faith embraces the promises of God in Christ. Unless we rely upon His promises, we really scorn His Mission. The substance of what we hope for, is a present possession.

   b. Faith uses God's power. This possession is not a dead treasure, but a life. By being of good cheer, we must rise to corresponding activity.

   c. Faith rejoices. The energy of the Divine Life must be a joy to us in the using.

POINT III. *Consider reconciliation to God as a new creation.*

   a. Sin the origin of disease. Sin separated man's nature from God, and even the temporary life which remained was consequently enfeebled. Natural life depends upon supernatural. Man's lower nature has no true life separate from God.

   b. Grace restores health. Our reunion with God is not a mere sentiment of friendship, but a living communication of the Divine power which we had lost. This will at length raise our bodies in the full glory of the Life of God.

   c. The removal of sin is the restoration of our nature to its original predestination. The impotence being removed, we must now go forward gladly in that strength.

AFFECTIONS. Joy in suffering. Faith. Courage.

PRAYER.

O Lord God, as Thou hast been pleased to call me to repentance by chastisement, and to obedience by the communication of grace, grant that I may rejoice to glorify Thee in that living power of holiness which Thou hast given, that I may hereafter enjoy Thy glory in the same Divine energy. Through Jesus Christ our Lord Amen.

P 2

THE PREPAREDNESS OF GRACE.

PRELUDE. i. *Tell them which are bidden, Behold, I have prepared My dinner; come unto the marriage.*—S. Matt. xxii. 4.
ii. The servants going out with the final proclamation.

POINT I. *Consider the meal itself.*

   a. The dinner, or, as we now say, breakfast. Not as in S. Luke's parable, a supper. The beginning of the Great Marriage Festivities is already set before us. There will be a greater Feast by and by.

   b. The Jews had been called by many servants to the Supper, which was the close of their dispensation. We are called to the Breakfast, the Table of the Lord, which is the first gift, enabling us to abide with Christ until the final Marriage Supper.

   c. The Holy Eucharist is always celebrated in the morning, to be our strength for the day.

POINT II. *Consider the preparation.*

   a. The offering of Sacrifice. " That every one may confess that Jesus Christ is Lord, to the glory of God the Father."

   b. The oxen and the fatlings represent the One Sacrifice of Christ, the multitude of typical offerings in the Temple. Those sacrifices had prepared the way for the One True Sacrifice. They live on in it as their true representative.

   c. All things are ready in a way which the guests could not understand; for the Son is Himself sacrificed in order to be the Food of the guests, and He gives a Life to those Sacrifices which until now were merely of death.

POINT III. *Consider those who are to come.*

   a. Those who had been called originally, now rebel. Yet they are bidden.

   b. God prepares His Feast for us, and us for It. If we have not used the preparation, we shall reject the invitation.

   c. We must prepare so as to welcome Christ in the first Feast. We shall not else be prepared so as to welcome Him in the last Feast.

AFFECTIONS. Resolution to prepare for Christ. Desire to hold communion with Him. Reverence for the great Love of God in preparing for us so great a Feast.

PRAYER.

O Lord Jesu, Son of the Father, Who callest us to be betrothed unto Thyself, grant us so to yield ourselves to the bidding of the Father, that by the power of the Holy Ghost our hearts may be drawn to Thy Love, and our lives conformed to Thy Law, while we feast upon the gifts which Thou providest, and look forward to the benediction which remaineth for them that persevere in Thy fellowship : Who livest and reignest with the Father and the Holy Ghost, One God, world without end. Amen.

THE ATTRACTIVENESS OF GRACE.

PRELUDE. i. *There was a certain nobleman whose son was sick at Capernaum. When he heard that Jesus was come out of Judæa into Galilee, he went unto Him, and besought Him that He would come down and heal his son.*—S. John iv. 46, 47.

ii. As in the Gospel.

POINT I. *Consider the sense of natural infirmity.*

a. He was a Jew; but His national prerogatives did not raise Him out of the power of sickness, and the curse of sin.

b. His position in the Court of King Herod did not raise him, nor would any greater position in the world.

c. He is helpless in the presence of Jesus, but Jesus can help him. He goes to Jesus to lay before Him his trouble. The Love of Jesus is as great as His power. All must come to Him.

POINT II. *Consider the welcome of Jesus.*

a. The nobleman showed his personal interest in the approach of Jesus. We must recognize the personal care of Jesus for ourselves.

b. He came before Jesus with a request. What is there that we desire to ask of Jesus. Let us not fear to ask too much. Rather fear to dishonour Him by having nothing to ask.

c. He came to Jesus. We must come to Him—not send words from a distance, but bring loving words. By love we draw nigh to Jesus in His glory, for Love is the gift of the Holy Ghost, seeking not merely gifts from Him, but the gift of Himself, and learning to love Him as He loves us.

POINT III. *Consider the place.*

a. Capernaum—"the village of consolation." This world is a world of sorrow, but the Presence of Jesus in His Church makes it to be a place of consolation.

b. Jesus had come down from Judæa. He ever dwells amongst "the praises" of Heaven. From thence He comes down to our home of sorrows.

c. Galilee. The district of the Gentiles had long been enveloped in spiritual darkness, but there the true Light was now to shine. Jesus identifies Himself with the circuit of our misery. And why? Because He desires to show to fallen man the Father's changeless Love.

AFFECTIONS. Love. Confidence. Intercession.

PRAYER.

O Lord Jesu, Who art come down from the glory of the Father to share with us the life of sorrow, let the Love wherewith Thou drawest near to me bring me also near to Thee, that I may make known to Thee all my need, and receive of Thee the healing of my distress. Amen.

THE ENDURANCE OF GRACE.

PRELUDE. i. *And the Lord commanded his servant to be sold, and his wife and children, and all that he had, and payment to be made. The servant, therefore, fell down and worshipped him, saying, Lord, have patience with me, and I will pay thee all.*
ii. As in the Parable. S. Matt. xviii. 25.

POINT I. *Consider the sense of justice.*
   a. God demands punishment without delay. It is not from disregard of what is due to Himself, that He defers it.
   b. God does not let punishment go by default because of our incapability of satisfying His demands. We must pay by nature as far as we can—in our persons, and those around.
   c. The physical laws of nature carry out God's judicial purposes towards mankind.

POINT II. *Consider the Ear of mercy.*
   a. God has formed us to hold communion with Himself. He is ready to hear what we have to say. He questioned our first forefathers. He is willing to hear extenuation, to welcome penitence, to receive promises.
   b. God expects us to recognize His rights and fall down and worship Him. Repentance must be an act of worship, not merely of payment; for His glory, not merely for our own clearance.

POINT III. *Consider the conditional postponement of vengeance.*
   a. Payment is to be made, and that according to the fulness of the demand. The demand is beyond our power; but God, Who postpones, gives also grace.
   b. That demand involves the fulness of the debt of love which we owe one to another. We can only pay our debt to God by acting according to His example.
   c. The endurance of grace is with a view to our growing in holiness. God will not tolerate sin, much less command anything that is sinful. When the soul is fixed upon evil, God may command certain modes of action, in order to awaken it to a sense of sin; but all His commands serve to the development of the grace which He has given. If we are not true to the law of holiness, we forfeit the gift of grace.

AFFECTIONS. Penitence. Homage. Truthfulness. Gratitude.

PRAYER.

O Lord God, Who hast proclaimed Thy just wrath against sinners, and yet callest us mercifully to amendment, grant that I may so humble myself before Thee for my sins, that when Thy vengeance shall burst forth, I may attain Thy perfect deliverance, through Jesus Christ our Lord. Amen.

THE IMPERIOUSNESS OF GRACE.

PRELUDE. i. *Master, we know that Thou art true, and teachest the way of God in truth.*—S. Matt. xxii. 16.

ii. As in the Gospel.

POINT I. *Consider grace as delivering us from the untrue.*

a. What is untrue seems to have a claim upon us which it has not really. The interests of time appear to be sovereign. He Who is true, and comes from God, sees the end of time from its beginning, and knows its emptiness.

b. What is untrue, blinds us to the demands of God. The way of God cannot run parallel with that of the world.

c. That which is untrue enfeebles us, so that we cannot accomplish God's demands. Untrue motives fail us before long, and weaken even true principles by intermixture.

POINT II. *Consider grace, as conforming us to the Eternal.*

a. Christ teaches with authority. Truth cannot be attained by cumulative argument. We must accept the sovereignty of Christ before we can be His true disciples.

b. Christ teaches by inspiration. The law which He gives is written on the heart by the power of the Holy Ghost.

c. Christ teaches by sanctification. We cannot learn from Him merely by the illumination of the intellect. The whole life must be subject to the Truth. If ye keep My words, then are ye My disciples.

POINT III. *Consider grace as accomplishing God's will.*

a. Grace strengthens us to meet the emergencies of life. It is a concurrence of Almighty God acting along with us. We must own His Presence as that of a Sovereign while He thus assists us.

b. Grace subdues our natural powers while it elevates them. We cannot work along with grace effectively unless by surrendering ourselves to it we own it as a power dominant over ourselves.

c. Grace perfects us in the unity of the Divine operation, so that we are brought to desire that which God wills, not merely by submission but by inspiration.

AFFECTIONS. Self-surrender. Welcome of God. Co-operation.

PRAYER.

O Lord God, Who callest us in Thy goodness to act in union with Thyself, grant us so to welcome Thy holy inspiration that our lives being conformed to Thy will, we may attain to the joy of Thine eternal kingdom. Through Jesus Christ our Lord. Amen.

THE LIFE OF GRACE.

PRELUDE. i. *While Jesus spake these things unto John's disciples, behold, there came a certain ruler and worshipped Him, saying, My daughter is even now dead: but come and lay Thy Hand upon her and she shall live.*—S. Matt. ix. 18.

ii. As in the Gospel.

POINT I. *Consider the Life of God,—the Author of Grace.*

    a. All life is from God and in Him. The Father has Life of and in Himself. The Son has Life in Himself, but of the Father. The Holy Ghost has Life of the Father and the Son. All created life is but one continual outcome of this Eternal Divine Life.

    b. Grace is a communication of the Life of God to the creature. It varies in proportion to the knowledge of God, which is communicated until the creature attains to glory by the perfection of Divine knowledge hereafter.

    c. God created man in His own Image for the express purpose of raising him to share this Divine Life.

POINT II. *Consider the Life of Christ, Who is the Instrument of Grace.*

    a. The Only-begotten Son lives in the unity of the Father's Life. He could not have this Life so as to be separate from the Father, for this Life cannot be divided.

    b. Christ took the manhood into perfect participation of this Life. His Eternal Person came to live in the Manhood.

    c. Death cannot touch the Manhood of Christ, for it cannot separate it from His Eternal, Everliving Person.

POINT III. *Consider the Life of the recipients of grace.*

    a. God hath given unto us Eternal Life in His Son, Whose members we become in Holy Baptism. This life is not inherent in our persons as it is in Christ's, but is conveyed to us while we abide in Christ. Therefore we may lose it.

    b. God requires us to act in the power of this Eternal Life, doing acts worthy of God by His inspiration.

    c. God enables us to appropriate this Life more and more by covenanted ordinances of grace and diligent exercises of loving obedience. So shall it at length become our own.

AFFECTIONS. Gratitude. Hope. Remember the indwelling power of God.

PRAYER.

O God, Who hast mercifully called me to this life of grace, grant me so to walk in true fellowship of the Spirit as befits the members of Thine Only-begotten Son, that I may at length be found perfect in Him, and dwell for evermore in Thy glory, through His merits Who liveth and reigneth with Thee and the Holy Ghost one God, world without end. Amen.

THE ALL-SUFFICIENCY OF GRACE.

PRELUDE. i. *When Jesus then lift up His eyes, and saw a great company come unto Him, He saith unto Philip, Whence shall we buy bread, that these may eat? And this He said to prove Him; for He Himself knew what He would do.*—S. John vi. 5.
ii. As in the Gospel.

POINT I. *Consider the multitude who receive.*
  a. The greatness of numbers. "To Thee shall all flesh come." They come gradually. All shall be gathered together at last to the Great Prophet.
  b. The greatness of want. The whole earth cannot satisfy the soul of man. It was created for God.
  c. The greatness of expectation. Their only security was in Christ's sufficiency.

POINT II. *Consider the source of supply.*
  a. Earthly means are manifestly inadequate. What there is only shows the greatness of the want.
  b. The source of supply is in Him Who created all the world at the beginning with all its possibilities. He Who sustains all His creatures by universal Providence is acting in Personal association with this multitude.
  c. He is the Only-begotten Son. That power which He receives in eternity He exerts in time. Human association occasions His action. Human limitation does not bind Him.

POINT III. *Consider the predestination of the gift.*
  a. Jesus knew what He would do. The miracle is not a weak way of getting out of a difficulty, but He had arranged the difficulty in order to display His power.
  b. This only symbolised a further gift for ages yet unborn. God's actions are not uncertain. They develope in an harmonious series, manifesting His power.
  c. He knew the individuals with whom He had to deal. The greatness of our need does not shut us out from His sympathy, but recommends the faithful to His power.

AFFECTIONS. Confidence. Gratitude. Personal Devotion to Jesus.

PRAYER.

O Lord Jesu, Who alone canst satisfy the craving of man's soul, grant that we may so follow Thee with loving faith, that in the experience of the failure of all earthly things, we may find the manifestation of Thy Love ever working with eternal purpose, for our individual good, to the glory of God the Father, with Whom Thou reignest in the unity of the Holy Ghost, One God, world without end. Amen.

MEDITATIONS

FOR

FEASTS OF THE BLESSED VIRGIN MARY.

THE PERPETUAL VIRGINITY OF THE MOTHER OF GOD.

PRELUDE.   i. *This gate shall be shut: it shall not be opened. and no man shall enter in by it; because the Lord, the God of Israel, hath entered in by it: therefore it shall be shut.*—Ezek. xliv. 2.

ii. The Virgin kneeling before the Child Jesus.

POINT I.   *Consider the Jewish wife's desire of offspring.*

a. The great desire was to transmit the life which should redeem the world and bruise the serpent's head.

b. To forget this by reason of any need, was to be like Esau. This hope was not only an ambition but a duty.

c. The glory of the coming Messiah could be but inadequately known. Yet it was to be the great hope of all who believed God's Promises.

POINT II.   *Consider the Blessed Virgin Mary rising above the thought of natural offspring.*

a. She probably felt that Messiah's glory was so far beyond earth, that His Birth could be after no earthly manner. Not in contempt of Israel's hope, but in a higher appreciation of its Divine character, she seems to have been betrothed to Joseph, for guardianship in lifelong virginity.

b. She recognised the Divine power to give her a child in some other way than that of nature. " How shall this be ?"

c. The announcement of the angel did not draw her back. She rather accepted it as a Divine approval of her self-dedication.

POINT III.   *Consider the Blessed Virgin Mary meditating upon her consecrated maternity.*

a. The intense satisfaction of her heart as a mother, contemplating the Child Jesus. No other being could share the same relationship of Love.

b. All her energies must be given to the service of the Divine Child. There must be no rival to divide her motherly toil.

c. To have this Child was like attaining to the very end of Creation. Nature could do nothing more. She only waited for the transforming gift of grace to be given from Him to herself.

AFFECTIONS.   Simple devotion to Jesus.

PRAYER.

O Blessed Jesu, as Thou art come in our nature, being born of a pure Virgin, grant that I may welcome Thy presence with a heart entirely consecrated to Thy Love, abiding in the fulness of Thy grace, satisfied with the fruition of Thy sweetness, and knowing no other glory but that of contemplating Thee, Who, with the Father and the Holy Ghost, livest and reignest God, for ever and ever, Amen.

THE VIRGIN'S OFFSPRING, THE TRUE VINE.

PRELUDE. i. *As the Vine brought I forth pleasant savour, and I am the Mother of Fair Love.*—Ecclus. xxiv. 17, 18.

ii. The Virgin owning her Child as the Author of her Life.

POINT I. *Consider the Supernatural Life of the Holy Child.*

a. As the earth, naturally barren, seems to rejoice by reason of the blossoms which clothe it when duly cultivated, so does human nature, in the person of the Blessed Virgin Mary, rejoice in the Divine Offspring of her substance.

b. The Holy Child, the Incarnate Word, in the fulness of Divine Virtue, seems to call the Blessed Virgin Mary, and all mankind along with her, to rejoice in His ineffable glory.

c. That Infant Word reveals Himself in the perfection of human nature as the Well-beloved of the Father, through Whom that Love shall be given to all who seek it.

POINT II. *Consider the pleasant savour of the Vine.*

a. It is the savour which God alone, not man, can appreciate with true delight. "In Him I am well pleased,"

b. The Fruit of the Vine transports man with an ecstacy and an energy special to itself. Thence is the wine that maketh glad the heart of man. There is a holy inebriation in the Blood of Jesus, the Heavenly Vine, whereby man is taken out of Himself into the Life of God.

c. As a field which the Lord hath blessed, so is she whom the Incarnate God owns as His Mother, from whose hallowed substance the Eternal Father, as the Husbandman, has made this glorious Branch to take earthly Form, that earth may be cheered with His Divine Merit.

POINT III. *Consider the Fair Love which this Vine produces.*

a. The Spirit of God, by Whom this Heavenly Vine is made fruitful, is as an atmosphere, breathing from it so as to bring forth the Divine Love in all who will receive it.

b. Wonderful was the joy of that mother, whose Child was thus to her the Parent of such transcendant love. "Henceforth all generations shall call me blessed."

c. Oh, the hardness of my heart, so slow to welcome the Divine Love which the Child of Blessed Mary gives. Let me take this Love which He brings, and cherish it rather than any offspring of my own.

AFFECTIONS. Adoration of the merits of Christ. Wonder at His tenderness. Carefulness respecting His gifts.

PRAYER.

O Blessed Jesu, grant me so to worship the glory of that Divine Love which Thou givest, that I may find acceptance with the Father in the Fellowship of that Love, wherein Thou callest me to dwell for evermore. Amen.

THE VIRGIN AS A TYPE OF THE CHURCH.

PRELUDE. i. I am the rose of Sharon, and the lily of the valleys.—Cant. ii. **1.**

ii. The Virgin contemplating her Child.

POINT I. Consider the Blessed Virgin Mary as the Elect of all mankind.

    a. The plain—not any garden of human enclosure—is named as the home of this heavenly Flower; for Jesus is the Christ, not of one race of men alone, nor of human culture, but of all mankind.

    b. The plain of Sharon, full of wondrous beauty, represents the Jewish nation, to which His Mother belonged, as possessing all those excellencies which by the Covenant of the Law had been vouchsafed to it.

    c. The strength of the Forest, the savour of the Fruit, the sweetness and beauty of the Flower, are all combined in the Holy Child. By His Beauty He would attract us, that by His Virtue He may feed us, and by His Strength may sustain us.

POINT II. Consider the lowliness of God's Handmaiden.

    a. We must seek his beauty in the valley of a hidden life, like Mary, if we would know Him as the Lily to cheer us.

    b. Blessed was that Humility whereby the Blessed Virgin Mary was enabled to attain this gift of the Heavenly Blossom. Oh let me ever cherish such lowliness of heart.

    c. We cannot know the loveliness of Jesus unless we delight in that retirement wherein He loves to show Himself.

POINT III. Consider the Child Jesus revealing Himself to His Blessed Mother.

    a. Other children have a life of mystery on which we may gaze and wonder; but they make no response. This Child is the Incarnate Wisdom, Who, in the eloquence of a Divine silence, makes known to us the hidden riches of God.

    b. He claims all mankind to be His kin. No little, local, natural sympathies shut up his Love. He is the Flower of the Field, the Rose of Sharon.

    c. He makes Himself known as the Lily of the Valley. We must know not only that He is found in the Valley, but seek him there with a true Humility such as befits His Love.

AFFECTIONS. Gratitude. Love. Admiration. Humility.

PRAYER.

O Lord Jesu, enable me so to praise Thee for Thy goodness, that I may rejoice in Thy comprehensive promises; and in the hiddenness of Thy condescending Love let me come unto Thee, so that I may find Thee in the fulness of Thy Truth, for Thy mercies' sake. Amen.

THE BLESSED VIRGIN GLORIFIED IN HER OFFSPRING.

PRELUDE. i. *Who is she that looketh forth as the morning, fair as the moon, clear as the sun ?*—Cant. vi. 10.

ii. The Blessed Virgin Mary as the type of Humanity glorified by the Incarnation.

POINT I. *Consider the glory of Humanity reflecting the Light of God's Presence under the Law.*

> *a.* The darkness of night. Such was the season of waiting until Christ came,—the whole world involved in sin.
>
> *b.* The moon giving light, and ruling the night. The yet unrisen Sun shining thereon, so that she is seen with a brightness not her own.
>
> *c.* The powerlessness of moonlight. The Law was weak through the flesh.

POINT II. *Consider the glory of Humanity as clothed with Divine grace.*

> *a.* The B. V. M. bore Christ in her womb. So does Humanity bear Him as a glorifying principle, though he abides hidden until the great day of travail, the final regeneration. .
>
> *b.* The brightness of Divine grace clothes the baptized with a radiant and not merely a reflected sanctity.
>
> *c.* This radiant Life is the energy of the Holy Ghost, thus making the power of the Incarnate God to be felt.

POINT III. *Consider the relation of the B. V. M. to her Child, as symbolical of the relation of Humanity to the operations of grace.*

> *a.* The Son of God takes His Human Nature of her substance. The woman, who as representing human nature is the special object of the Serpent's hatred, is personified in the Blessed Virgin.
>
> *b.* The Son of God suffers Himself to be associated indissolubly with her life for many months, so that His glory surrounds her during that time. So Humanity is seen clothed with the Sun, and waiting to be delivered (Rev. xii.) while travailing with the offspring of grace.
>
> *c.* Humanity predestined to the glory of bringing Him forth is to be afterwards taken into God by union with Him. So the B. V. M. has by regeneration a greater glory than by maternity. The one was the exaltation of nature, the other is its transformation.

AFFECTIONS. Welcome to the Incarnate God. Exultation.

PRAYER.

O God the Son, Who by the power of the Holy Ghost wast conceived in the womb of the Blessed Virgin of her substance, grant me to live in continual remembrance of that Divine glory whereby Thou hast been graciously pleased to take me into union with Thyself, that I may always show forth Thy power, and abide in Thy Light as my only Life, to the glory of God the Father. Amen.

THE BLESSED VIRGIN ENRICHED WITH GRACE.

PRELUDE. i. *Hail, thou that art highly favoured, the Lord is with thee: blessed art thou among women, and blessed is the Fruit of thy womb.*—S. Luke i. 28.

ii. The Angel appearing to the Virgin.

POINT I. *Consider the Blessedness of Preventing Grace.*

a. Jeremiah had been sanctified from his mother's womb. How had the Blessed Virgin Mary been guided, sheltered, strengthened by the same Spirit!

b. The Holy Spirit had guided her to desire that which was above nature rather than that which brought natural gratification. Yet how little had she realized the great end to which God was leading her.

c. She abode stedfastly in the faith of God's power, and was able to accept His Word when He spake by the angel.

POINT II. *Consider the Blessedness of the Overshadowing Grace.*

a. The Holy Ghost overshadowed her, separating from all taint of earthly touch that substance which was to be quickened by the Incarnate Presence of the Son of God.

b. This overshadowing grace, being external, did not give Light or Life; but as it took from her that substance which should become Christ's Body it made the material nature pure for the reception of the Divine Personality.

c. The Holy Ghost, proceeding from the Son of God, thus took hold of our material nature on His behalf, in order to take the manhood into God to be His Temple by eternal possession for evermore.

POINT III. *Consider the Christian prerogative of Illuminating Grace.*

a. How Blessed was the consciousness of ministering her own substance to that Child Who was the Incarnate Light of Light, so that the very Food she gave to Him from herself became radiant with the Life of God as He partook thereof.

b. How did she look forward with hope to the victory of her Child, and His gift of Life to others.

c. How did she long to receive from Him the higher Life in His Light as God, even as she had communicated to Him the substance of this lower life in her natural darkness.

AFFECTIONS. Following the guidance of the Holy Ghost.

PRAYER.

O Lord Jesu, as Thou hast been pleased to take me by the power of the Holy Ghost into the unity of Thine all holy Body, making me to live with Thy Life, grant that I may ever yield myself to the guidance of Thy Holy Spirit, that I may be perfected in that Eternal Light of Life wherein Thou livest for ever and ever. Amen.

Q

MEDITATIONS

FOR

FEASTS OF THE HOLY APOSTLES.

APOSTOLIC LOVE.

PRELUDE. i. *This is My commandment, that ye love one another as I have loved you.*—S. John xv. 12.

ii. The Apostle in prayer contemplating Jesus upon the Cross.

POINT I. *Consider the necessity of this Example.*

a. Without this, perfect Love would be an imaginary ideal, and in contemplating the abstract perfection we should feel that what had never been realized in act, never could be a reality.

b. Without this, imagination would fall short of that to which man is really called, or would lose the greatness of truth in some grotesque form of impossibility.

c. Without this, we should think we might love men more than God does; but herein the Love of God is manifested in that He sent His Son to be the propitiation for our sins.

POINT II. *Consider the imitation of this Love.*

a. Only in proportion as we imitate it, can we estimate it. We must know what it is to suffer through pure love before we can be really grateful for that Love.

b. If we try other forms of Love, we fail. No love really conquers but that which suffers. · We must be strengthened in suffering by seeking to be conformed to the Cross.

c. Love must approach God with sacrifice in order to obtain God's blessing. Beneficence without prayer would have no Divine efficacy.

POINT III. *Consider the power of the Spirit by which the command is given.*

a. We cannot imitate the Love of Jesus, nor the Sacrifice of Calvary save by the power of the Holy Ghost, by Whom He offered Himself for us to God. Our Love can only be the onflow of His.

b. He Who bids us imitate His Love, gives the Holy Ghost, whereby we may be strengthened to imitate it.

c. The gift of the Holy Ghost, which we receive from Him, cannot be known by us as a power, unless it makes us to be conformed to the likeness of His Redeeming Love.

AFFECTIONS. Imitation of Christ. Surrender to the Holy Ghost. Joy in suffering.

PRAYER.

O Lord *Jesu Christ, Who didst send forth Thine Apostles to be the channels of Thy Love to mankind, grant that we, having received Thy Holy Spirit, may be conformed to Thine adorable Sacrifice, and may attain to the eternal fruition of Thy glory. Amen.*

APOSTOLIC SACRIFICE.

PRELUDE. i. *Greater love hath no man than this, that a man lay down his life for his friends.*—S. John xv. 13.

ii. The Apostle in prayer contemplating Jesus upon the Cross.

POINT I. *Consider the Personal Love of Christ dying for us.*

 a. When we were enemies, Christ died for us, that He might make us His friends. He foresaw all our ingratitude.

 b. He died not for our abstract good, but for our personal benefit, as individuals, by sympathising with us in all our weakness and danger, our suffering and our need.

 c. He laid down His Life, the greatest earthly good, in order that He might bring us out of this life into the higher Life of the Divine Love, there to live with Him as His friends.

POINT II. *Consider the Personal Love which is necessary for His Apostles.*

 a. They brought this love home to the hearts of others, by loving them as Christ loved them. No general philanthropy will suffice. Human love must be individual.

 b. They rescued the perishing from the evil in which they were. We cannot raise men to a higher state by a general offer of happiness. There must be personal fellowship.

 c. They showed this love by the real sacrifice of their lives for those to whom they were sent. Our acts are the substance of our words. Unless the love of Christ be operative in our actions, our words can only tell of it as a thing that has, at least for ourselves, no real power.

POINT III. *Consider the union with Christ, whereby alone this Love can be realized.*

 a. We cannot know the Love of Jesus to ourselves unless we are taken into oneness of Life with Him; and only in the oneness of the Life of God can we know of the fulness of the Love of God.

 b. As Christ makes His Love known through His Apostles, He requires them to be one with Him, that the words which they speak may be His words, and not their own.

 c. We cannot measure this Love merely by the evil from which we are delivered: we must also know the glory into which this Love brings us. This we can only know as it is revealed in Christ.

AFFECTIONS. Gratitude. Absorbing Love for souls redeemed.

PRAYER.

O Lord Jesu, bring me of Thy goodness so to apprehend the Love wherewith Thou hast redeemed me, that I may ever seek to bring others to the experience of its sweetness, being conformed, even as Thy Holy Apostles, to the likeness of Thy Passion. Amen.

APOSTOLIC OBEDIENCE.

PRELUDE. i. *Ye are My friends, if ye do whatsoever I command you.*—S. John xv. 14.

ii. Jesus giving privately His instructions to the Twelve.

POINT I. *Consider the commands of Christ.*

a. They are what He gives unto us from the Father, for the glory of the Father. He is the Word of God, speaking to us with the lips of man.

b. They are not what our own imagination would have conceived, nor our own heart desired, nor our own reason have determined.

c. They are not what the world inculcates, approves, or loves. The world keeps not the saying of Christ, because his commands are simply for God's glory, and the world hates God.

POINT II. *Consider the integrity of obedience.*

a. Obedience must be in all things, "whatsoever I command." The Apostles had to do many things beyond the reach of their own judgment or reason. So have we.

b. Obedience is tested by acts of whose fitness we cannot judge. God does not need our assistance, but our submission.

c. Obedience defies all opposition. We must be true to His commands, regardless of all results. Difficulty makes the obedience all the better.

POINT III. *Consider the friendship which is thus vouchsafed.*

a. Obedience is the evidence of our love to Jesus. This love is itself the action of the Love which He has given us. If it were not for the gift of His Love, we could not obey.

b. It is the outward bond of Love, as the Holy Ghost is the inward Bond, for by community of action our hearts and • lives become identified with Jesus.

c. It is the beginning of a Love to be perfected eternally; for our life with Jesus in joy will be the manifestation of that hidden life which has wrought out our service to Jesus upon the earth.

AFFECTIONS. Imitation of Apostolic boldness. Joy in separation from the world along with Christ.

PRAYER.

O Jesu, grant that I may rejoice in that Love wherewith Thou callest me to obey Thee, and may so act in the fellowship of that love, that I may be found worthy of its eternal welcome, for Thy mercies' sake. Amen.

224 𝔉or the 𝔉east of an Apostle. IV.

APOSTOLIC PURITY.

PRELUDE. i. *Blessed are the pure in heart, for they shall see God.*—S. Matt. v. 8.

ii. Our Lord rejoicing as He looks round upon the Apostles to ask them, " Whom say ye that I am ?"

POINT I. *Consider the purity of heart by which they were enabled to come near to Jesus.*

    a. Some had been disciples of the Baptist. Others had recognized Christ's authority as they witnessed His public teachings.

    b. The absence of any worldly motive left their hearts clear, so as to see His supernatural glory with increasing clearness. Only one, through a mixed motive, having begun to see, became blinded and fell away.

    c. They were not drawn back from Jesus by worldly cares, for their hearts were purified from worldly desires.

POINT. II. *Consider the revelation of Jesus by the Holy Ghost.*

    a. Purity of heart is a gift of the Holy Ghost, by which we are prepared to see the glory of Jesus. We must seek His preparation that we may receive His revelation.

    b. The Holy Ghost will reveal Christ to those whom He has prepared. He gives the desire, the delight, the energy, the growth, the fulness, of this revelation.

    c. He by Whom the Son of God became Incarnate, causes His real Presence to be mysteriously given to the soul as its true Wisdom.

POINT III. *Consider the blessedness of this knowledge.*

    a. The Apostles felt so truly the blessedness of being with Christ that they shrank with fear from the thought of losing sight of Him.

    b. Much more blessed to behold Christ with the eye of faith dwelling in our own hearts, making God's light to shine through us with transforming power.

    c. Still more blessed hereafter to know as we are known, in the perfect purity of His true likeness.

AFFECTIONS. Desire for purity. Thankfulness for illuminating grace. Love of the Truth.

PRAYER.

O Lord Jesu, as Thou hast given me Thy Holy Spirit to cleanse me, grant me so to follow Thee in the Blessed Fellowship of Thy Holiness, that I may behold Thee in the glory of Divine Sovereignty, Who livest with the Father in the unity of the same Spirit, One God, world without end. Amen.

APOSTOLIC PATIENCE.

PRELUDE. i. *In your patience possess ye your souls.*—S. Luke xxi. 19.

ii. The Apostles in their scattered ministry amongst many nations, dying for the faith.

POINT I. *Consider the hope of earthly triumphs dying away.*

　　a. Nearness to Christ involves not outward peace in the world but special struggle. Nor do those who are nearest to Christ gain the most evident victories.

　　b. Abiding with Christ, the Apostles learned that their truest victory was to die with Him. We must learn this too.

　　c. The Apostles did not die in order to found Christendom as we have seen it, but Christ through them was founding the heavenly Jerusalem which we hope to see.

POINT II. *Consider the experience of Divine strength increasing.*

　　a. The greater the difficulties we have to meet along with Jesus, the greater will be the growth of grace.

　　b. As we continue with Christ in conflict we must learn to be the more patient by the remembrance of past deliverances.

　　c. The strength of Christ in his people is not manifested by shaking off the power of the enemy, but by giving light within, while all is darkness without.

POINT III. *Consider the attainment of rest with Christ in Paradise.*

　　a. Satan can shake all that belongs to the body. We must possess our souls by resting calmly in Jesus, whatever the outward shaking may be.

　　b. If we have learnt to rest in Jesus during the storms of life, we shall find rest in Him in death.

　　c. Resting from struggles were no rest if it were in vacancy. Those only rest from their labours who die in the Lord and abide in His sweet repose.

AFFECTIONS. Calmness amidst outward difficulties. Fortitude under temptations. Expectation of final victory hereafter.

PRAYER.

O Lord Jesu, grant me grace so patiently to abide with Thee in this earthly warfare, that I may find rest in Thee when the discipline of this life is ended, and may have the abundance of Thy comfort to refresh my soul in the Blessed Home of Thine elect for evermore. Amen.

APOSTOLIC TESTIMONY.

PRELUDE. i. *They will deliver you up to the councils, and they will scourge you in their synagogues, and ye shall be brought before governors and kings for My sake, for a testimony against them and the Gentiles.*—S. Matt. x. 17, 18.

ii. The Apostles before heathen and Jewish tribunals.

POINT I. *Consider the hatred of man towards them.*

    a. The world hated Christ. It could not but hate those who spoke of Christ.

    b. The hatred of the world was the very thing they had to conquer by the power of the Holy Ghost. They could not avoid it, but they breathed forth upon it the fulness of Divine Love.

    c. They came to establish the power of Christ over the power of darkness throughout the world. Each soul that was won to Christ, made Satan hate them more.

POINT II. *Consider the love which bound them to Christ.*

    a. They did not cease to love Christ by reason of their sufferings, for they knew that their sufferings were the condition of their union with Him.

    b. They were sure of His love which would outlive all that they could have against them in the world.

    c. They felt that Love to be their strength. Their love to Him was the return of His Love to them.

POINT III. *Consider the manifestation of Christ by their constancy.*

    a. They were to make Christ known as a Life to the dead world. Their sufferings showed the power of this Life in their example.

    b. No words of theirs could fully tell of Christ. No work of theirs could make Him manifest. This witness of their suffering showed that the Life of Christ in them was altogether beyond the world.

    c. The world would be without excuse for not accepting Christ when it saw how those who did accept Him were raised into a higher life even here by so doing.

AFFECTIONS. Thankfulness for opposition. Meekness. Love to our enemies. Joy in the fellowship of Christ.

PRAYER.

O Lord Jesu, Who hast called me to the knowledge of Thy Love, grant me so to abide in Thy Love that I may make known to the world which hateth Thee the Love wherein Thou callest the faithful out of the world to live with Thyself, Who art with the Father and the Holy Ghost, one God, world without end. **Amen.**

MEDITATIONS

FOR

HOLY DAYS.

ENDURING THE CROSS.

PRELUDE. i. *Who for the joy that was set before Him endured the Cross, despising the shame.* Heb. xii. 2.

ii. S. Andrew addressing his Cross as he beheld it: "Hail, precious Cross!"

POINT I. *Consider that Jesus calls thee to suffer.*

a. If thou askest Him, with S. Andrew, "Master, where dwellest Thou?" He will say to thee, "Come and see." The last Home of Jesus in this world is the Cross.

b. Jesus has not suffered in order to deliver thee from suffering in this world, but in the next. If we suffer with Him here, we shall be glorified together with Him there.

c. Thou must show in some way that thou art His disciple. How, if not by being like Him? But His example was in suffering.

POINT II. *Consider Jesus setting before thee the reward of suffering.*

a. He is a Master Who will reward His disciples according to their deserts. He will reward nothing spurious. He will not pass by any genuine act of discipleship. Thou mayest trust Him.

b. The suffering is but for a little time. The reward shall be eternal. Jesus will bring it with Himself at His second coming.

c. The reward which thou shalt receive is due to His sufferings, not to thine own. And it is worthy of Him, far surpassing all that thou couldst suffer.

POINT III. *Consider Jesus transforming suffering into joy.*

a. S. Andrew addressed His Cross as being studded with jewels by the Passion of Jesus. Thou must value the sufferings of Jesus here, if thou wouldst rejoice in them hereafter. Thou canst not value that which thou dost avoid.

b. Suffering with Christ has a gift of present grace as well as a promise of future glory. That which weakens the outer nature should be made to strengthen the inner nature.

c. A personal sense of union with Jesus in suffering must be more exhilarating than any companionship with earthly friends in the glory of the world.

AFFECTIONS. Desire to follow Christ. Love of suffering.

PRAYER.

O *Blessed Jesu, Who dost perfect our faith with the living and substantial glory of Thy Heavenly Power, give me grace so to reach out after those Divine realities which Thou hast provided for me, that I may accept with thankfulness, and use with patience and holy joy, whatever discipline Thou givest me to bear, for Thy Name's sake.* Amen.

ARCHBISHOP OF MYRA.—A.D. 342.

EARLY PIETY.

PRELUDE. i. *Well done, thou good and faithful servant; thou hast been faithful over a few things, I will make thee ruler over many things: enter thou into the joy of thy Lord.*—S. Matt. xxv. 21.

ii. The child, Nicolas, careful in fasting.

POINT I. *Consider the blessedness of holy childhood.*

a. The small acts of childhood are as important before God as anything else. Notoriety amongst men avails nothing with God; and with God the acts of a child are as public as those of a statesman, as holy as those of a Martyr.

b. A childhood kept free from sin avails to the obtaining of a special knowledge of God. Purity sees mysteries.

c. Habits of piety formed in childhood develope with later life as the manifestation of God's indwelling.

POINT II. *Consider the maintenance of a childlike spirit.*

a. God will not say to us, Well done, because of the greatness of the things accomplished. What is done with childlike love, dependence, obedience, is well done.

b. If we would be childlike we must follow God's bidding, not expect Him to follow ours.

c. We must act without fear of results. It is a great joy throughout life to know that we are simply doing our Father's bidding.

POINT III. *Consider the duty of caring for children.*

a. We ought to remember that the Image of God is seen most purely in a little child. Features which attract human admiration in later life, only hide the glory of the Divine Personal indwelling.

b. Christ accepts as done to Himself whatever is done for the least of His brethren. Nothing can be trifling that is done for a Christian child.

c. We must act towards them in the power of the Holy Ghost. Any other discipline hardens rather than helps. Children having received the Holy Ghost are specially quick to see what is from God in their training and what from ourselves.

AFFECTIONS. Childlike obedience. Purity. Care for the young.

PRAYER.

O Lord God, grant that I may always serve Thee with a childlike spirit, so that the grace which Thou gavest me in my Baptism may be perfect within me when I come to die; through Jesus Christ our Lord. Amen.

PREDESTINATION.

PRELUDE. i. *With heart and soul sing we glory to Christ on this Commemoration of His Blessed Mother.*

ii. God the Son revealing to the Heavenly Host the purpose of the Father, that He should become the Child of her that was now conceived.

POINT I. *Consider the blessedness of Predestination .*

a. God appoints His instruments for all great ends. " This is a chosen vessel unto Me."

b. God prepares His instruments. So He did Jeremiah and S. John Baptist. He does not choose because we are fitting, but He fits those whom He chooses.

c. " From the bowels of My mother hath He made mention of My Name." How did Heaven rejoice as He made mention of her with the glorious destiny of becoming His Mother ?

POINT II. *Consider the Mystery of her Sanctification.*

a. Her near relationship to the Light about to be manifested by the Incarnation, made Satan's tyranny over the children of Adam the more manifest. Yet God must die to save her.

b. God saw her subject by nature to this tyranny, and His Love for all the human race concentrated itself upon her, in whose person He also beheld all the possibilities of glory to be accomplished for His Church.

c. The Holy Ghost brooded over the dark deep before the Creation of Light. So He overshadowed this Elect Child.

POINT III. *Consider the joy of Heaven at contemplating the nearness of the Birth of Christ.*

a. One more generation and Christ shall be born. Blessed shall this Child be of Whom the Son of God shall take visible substance, so as visibly to claim our worship.

b. Of her alone the Son of God shall receive all that is needed for the perfection of human nature. The highest natural perfection was therefore gathered together in her person. It only needed the incoming of grace.

c. God gathered in her all that is necessary for the highest humanity. This includes a will to offer all to Him.

AFFECTIONS. Dedication of heart to Christ. Patience. Humility.

PRAYER.

O Lord God, Who didst prepare the Body of the Blessed Virgin, that Thine Only-begotten Son might be born amongst us of her substance, grant that I may so humble myself before Thee, that I may receive of Thee the new Life of Thy glorious kingdom ; through the same Jesus Christ our Lord. Amen.

A.D. 204.

SIMPLICITY.

PRELUDE. i. *When the Bridegroom came, they that were ready went in with Him to the Marriage.*—S. Mat. xxv. 10.

ii. S. Lucy and her mother distributing the price of her pearls to the poor.

POINT I. *Consider the worthlessness of worldly splendour.*

a. Jewels which add lustre only serve to show how much we are wanting in lustre of our own. Their brightness remains when we are in corruption, and helps us not then.

b. How worthless was the diamond when it was soot, and the sapphire when it was clay. They have gained no joy with their brilliancy.

c. That cannot waken true love which itself knows none. Worldly splendour may arouse envy, but does not help us to win love. Jewels are a dead measure of value. Human acts have a value because they are bonds of eternal consciousness between man and man.

POINT II. *Consider the joy of relieving want.*

a. Our clay like the sapphire begins to shine with the perfect hue of heaven when the fire of Divine Charity changes it into the glory of Divine beneficence by giving to the poor.

b. We may thus transform the clay of human nature according to God's purpose, bringing out of a degradation worse than our own to the very life of God, that which knew Him not.

c. What is rescued thus from the filth of sin shall indeed be a jewel of value, shining evermore to gladden those who have co-operated with the Divine Love in its transformation.

POINT III. *Consider the glory of holy charity.*

a. The eye that simply looks to God, sees God's Light, reflects God's Light, sees all other things in that same Light.

b. Jewels absorb the light but know it not. The loving soul finds its life, its energy, its joy in the Light of God, which is true Love.

c. The eye which only looks to see want upon earth that it may bring relief, shall have the Vision of God as its reward eternally.

AFFECTIONS. Liberality to the poor. Contempt of outward display. Desire of God's glory.

PRAYER.

O *Lord God, grant that I may so make Thy Light to shine before men, by the loving communication of Thy gifts of love, that I may have my portion amongst the Children of Light, to be for evermore partaker of Thy Brightness; through Jesus Christ our Lord. Amen.*

BISHOP OF ROME.—A.D. 335.

ABUNDANCE OF REWARD.

PRELUDE. i. *Well done, thou good and faithful servant; thou hast been faithful over a few things, I will make Thee ruler over many things : enter thou into the joy of thy* Lord.—S. Matt. xxv. 21.

ii. S. Silvester praising God for the victory of His Church, outwardly over heathenism, dogmatically over Arianism.

POINT I. *Consider the close of a struggle for Christ.*

a. How many Martyrs and Confessors have shed their blood in the years gone by ! Our struggles shall end in peace.

b. If we enjoy peace, we should remember the debt which we owe to those by whom God has obtained for us such benefits.

c. They are not passed away who fought of old. They are with Christ. O glorious day of the end, when all shall be together.

POINT II. *Consider the rewards of Christ.*

a. Christ gives peace and refreshment at times even in this world. Look to Him with trustfulness during the fight, and thankfulness at the end.

b. Rewards in this world soon become evils. They are still within an evil world. Our Lord prophesied that heathen persecutions would only give way to strife and heresy within the Church.—S. Matt. xxiv. 9-11.—We must not seek tranquillity founded on human power.

c. Christ's true rewards are those which He brings with Him, when He comes to be glorified in those whom He has sanctified by suffering.

POINT III. *Consider the end of the year.*

a. How many occasions have I had to do what Christ should reward at the great end? Alas for my unfaithfulness !

b. God has given me many rewards. Have I used them as means of detachment and stepping-stones to Heaven, or as means of settling down in this world to take my ease ?

c. When all the years of the world's history are summed up in the general Resurrection, what part will this year have in the joy of Christ for my sake, or in my joy with Him?

AFFECTIONS. Joy in striving for the faith of Christ. Reliance upon Christ's power. Blindness as to worldly issues. Hope. Faithfulness for the time to come.

PRAYER.

O Lord God, enable me so to yield myself up with a thankful heart, to bear whatever part thou mayest assign to me in the sufferings of Thy dear Son, that when He shall come again in His glory, I may have my portion in His Eternal Joy; through His merits Who liveth and reigneth with Thee and with the Holy Ghost, one God, world without end. **Amen.**

R

A.D. 312.

STUDY OF THE SCRIPTURES.

PRELUDE.   i. *Theirs is the Kingdom of Heaven who have despised the life of this world to gain a reward in the kingdom, and have washed their robes in the Blood of the Lamb.*—Rev. vii. 14.

ii. S. Lucian chained to the ground consecrating the holy elements upon his breast, and communicating the faithful in the prison.

POINT I. *Consider the importance of knowing the Scriptures.*
  a. Like the Jews of old, many nowadays seek to draw the words of God to their own fancies. No knowledge can compare with the knowledge of what God has truly said.
  b. We must study Holy Scripture not chiefly for controversy, but rather for edification. If we read with childlike love, God will speak to us with Fatherly compassion.
  c. God will speak to us in the Holy Scriptures proportionately to the love wherewith we study them.

POINT II. *Consider how the Scriptures enable us to despise the life of this world.*
  a. The revelation of that which is eternal makes all transitory glory and shame to be a matter of indifference. What solid nourishment have the Scriptures conveyed to faithful souls of all ages !
  b. Those who received revelations to give to us from God had not the things of this world. We who read, do not need them.
  c. The Holy Scriptures warn us not to be misled by outward appearances. Suffering in this world is a greater token of God's love than is success.

POINT III. *Consider how the Holy Scriptures teach us to value Christ.*
  a. S. Lucian valued Christ, as he and his companions fed upon Christ in the prison-house. By the study of Holy Scripture we shall come to appreciate what Christ does for us in His Holy Sacraments.
  b. The Holy Scriptures enable us to realize the dealings of Christ with us in various ways of Providence and Grace.
  c. The Scriptures set before us the Incarnate God as the central principle and final glory of all creation.

AFFECTIONS. Love of Holy Scripture. Industry in the study thereof. Prayer for illumination.

PRAYER.

O Almighty God, grant that we, following the steps of Thy Holy Servants, may have our hearts enlightened to receive Thy Truth in the study of Thy Holy Word, and our lives strengthened for the testimony of the truth which we have received; through Jesus Christ our Lord. Amen.

DOGMATIC TRUTH.

PRELUDE. i. *Well done, thou good and faithful servant; thou hast been faithful over a few things, I will make thee ruler over many things : enter thou into the joy of thy Lord.*—S. Matt. xxv. 21.

ii. A Holy Light filling the chamber when a Saint lay dead.

POINT I. *Consider the glorious Truth of Christ's Divinity.*

a. This Bishop of Poictiers went gladly into exile for the truth of Christ. He who confesses Jesus before men has a Divine Home, even in the Bosom of God, and will be indifferent to earthly place.

b. He who has the Eternal Son of God for a companion, will find His Presence all-sufficient, however removed from earthly association.

c. He who worships Jesus the Incarnate Wisdom, consubstantial with the Father, will find the Eternal Spirit of Wisdom ever ready to illuminate him with Divine Truth.

POINT II. *Consider the value of human learning.*

a. S. Hilary, as a heathen, had searched through the philosophers in vain. He found no satisfaction with them ; but his searching fitted him to estimate more truly the satisfaction which was to be found in Christ.

b. The powers of the intellect are amongst those "few things" for which we shall have to account at the last day.

c. We must use our learning to maintain God's Truth ; but we must leave it with God to make people receive our testimony, or to let them reject us.

POINT III. *Consider the benefit of a childlike heart.*

a. S. Hilary was a man of great learning ; but he teaches us the necessity of approaching Divine Truth with reverence. It is beyond our understanding, but not beyond our love.

b. There is great danger of being puffed up by knowledge ; but that knowledge alone is true which teaches us our own nothingness in God's sight.

c. If we recognize the littleness of human reason, and use it faithfully while searching into God's Truth, we shall enter into the joy of our Lord, beholding Him Whom we have loved, and rejoicing to be with Him for ever.

AFFECTIONS. Diligent investigation of Truth. Childlike acceptance of revealed Truth.

PRAYER.

O Lord God, enable me so to dedicate the powers of my mind to the contemplation of Thy Truth, that by the teaching of Thy Holy Spirit, I may become increasingly conformed to the likeness of Thine Only-begotten Son, and may hereafter be perfected in the joy of Thine Eternal Vision ; through the same Jesus Christ our Lord. Amen.

A.D. 275.

THE SUFFERING OF THE FAITHFUL.

PRELUDE. i. *When the Bridegroom came, they that were ready went in with Him to the marriage.*—S. Matt. xxv. 10.

ii. The young girl enduring martyrdom.

POINT I. *Consider the blessedness of suffering.*

    a. If our work succeeds we have reward in this world. If we suffer for the cause of Christ, then we shall have a reward in the next world. We are apt to forfeit that reward by our successes.

    b. Our great Captain was perfected through suffering. We must count it all joy to be like Him.

    c. The kind of suffering does not matter if it be really for the sake of Christ. We must be careful that our suffering is not by our fault, but for His glory.

POINT II. *Consider what it is to live before God.* ·

    a. We may be known far and wide in the world, and not known to God. Then we are dead. Those only can be said to live who are known to the Living God.

    b. If God knows us as living in Him, then it matters little whether the world knows much of us or no.

    c. We live before God in proportion as we are dead to the world. If we are dead to it, we cannot care what it may say of us.

POINT III. *Consider the Virgins who go in with Christ to the marriage.*

    a. He who calls his sheep by name and leads them out, will not forget any because the world has forgotten them.

    b. Let us be careful always to live so that God may know us. If God does not know us to be living in some way for Him, He will not call us to the marriage.

    c. Of the Antediluvian Patriarchs it is said simply, "and he died." The acts of the longest life do not add to the glory of the one fact of dying for Christ. How few people nowadays wish simply to die for Christ. We think little about the Marriage Supper of the Lamb.

AFFECTIONS. Deadness to the world. Life with God.

PRAYER.

O Lord God, enable me to listen to Thy Voice as Thou callest me through the sufferings of earth to the Marriage Supper of the Lamb. and to account every suffering abundantly rewarded in the welcome which Thou wilt then give to each of Thy faithful ones; through Jesus Christ our Lord. Amen.

BISHOP OF ROME.—A.D 250.

DIVINE ELECTION.

PRELUDE. i. *Except a corn of wheat fall into the ground and die, it abideth alone; but if it die, it bringeth forth much fruit.*—S. John xii. 24.

ii. The Dove settling upon the head of S. Fabian, which caused him, though an unknown layman, to be chosen as Bishop.

POINT I. *Consider how God overrules the accidents of life for our guidance.*

    a. Wherever we are, we must remember that God may have some great purpose for us in that place.

    b. If we are not looking up to God, we shall be unable to correspond with his sudden vocations. If we are looking to Him, then we may be sure we shall be able to accomplish His will, whatever He may call us to do.

    c. If we recognize God's action in the various accidents of life, we shall find that the most trifling events are full of inestimable blessings.

POINT II. *Consider that God calls us to die for Him.*

    a. Many a valuable life is wasted, because men are so afraid to part with it. He who will save His life shall lose it.

    b. By actions done in the world, we show the efficacy of the natural gifts which God has given; and that which is of nature alone ends in nought. Actions which spring out of deadness to the world live eternally.

    c. In so far as we live to the world, we receive nourishment from the world. In so far as we are dead to the world, our nature becomes by grace the instrument of Christ's power.

POINT III. *Consider that we may be sure that our death will be fruitful if we are the true grain of God.*

    a. No grain of the heavenly corn can be allowed of God to be fruitless. God is watchful over all His faithful ones. Right dear in the sight of the Lord is the death of His Saints.

    b. Death is the end of the world's glory, and the beginning of the Divine.

    c. Our great care must be so to live with God amidst all the accidents of life, that our death may be fruitful.

AFFECTIONS. Reliance upon God. Indifference as to the future. Joy in death.

PRAYER.

O God, by Whose Providence all the events of the world are overruled for the manifestation of Thy glory in Thy Saints, grant that I may not seek my own glory by vainly living to the world, but may rejoice, by dying unto the world, to manifest Thy glory Who callest me unto Thyself; through Jesus Christ our Lord. Amen.

A.D. 305.

PURITY.

PRELUDE. i. *Blessed Agnes standing in the midst of the flames, stretched out her hands and prayed, saying, Almighty, Tremendous, and Worshipful God, I worship Thee and glorify Thy Name for ever.*

ii. The holy girl praying in the fire until it was extinguished.

POINT I. *Consider the strength which God gives to the weakest.*

   a. The wealth and beauty of S. Agnes only enlisted the more enemies to seek her overthrow. Yet God was with her to strengthen her resolutions.
   b. We must be stedfast if we would have God's help.
   c. If we persevere in the use of grace God will give us supernatural joy in the transports of the higher life. So did S. Agnes rejoice at the very sight of instruments whereby she should be tortured.

POINT II. *Consider the Divine Protection of Purity.*

   a. The soul, if true to God, may leave events to Him. He puts out fires not to save our lives, but to show His glory.
   b. We must never expect God's help in self-sought dangers.
   c. S. Agnes prayed for the restoration of the profligate whom God had blinded by a lightning flash. So must we ever seek God's protection from our enemies, but invoke His blessing upon them.

POINT III. *Consider how much the soul must be prepared to suffer rather than forfeit the gift of purity.*

   a. We need the Divine grace to endure the natural temptations of appetite, as much as if we were called to endure martyrdom. Endure the one by thinking of the other.
   b. We must never imagine that God will leave us without sufficient strength. Unhappily the feebleness of the will too often conspires rather with the enemy than with God.
   c. Whatever may have been the faithlessness of time past, let us be sure that God will enable us to triumph if we will. But the struggle will be the harder.

AFFECTIONS. Love of Purity. Boldness in resisting what seems to be hopeless.

PRAYER.

O Almighty God, give me grace always to rely upon Thy Protection, that by Thy Grace I may henceforth be kept in purity and be acceptable in Thy sight, so that the world, the flesh, and the devil may be unable to destroy my confidence in Thy Love; through Jesus Christ our Lord. Amen.

A.D. 304.
VICTORY IN MARTYRDOM.

PRELUDE. i. *Let us humbly commemorate this day on which Vincent the unconquered Martyr of Christ, gained the palm of victory, and joyfully entered Heaven.*

ii. S. Vincent with his body already torn in many places and laid bare to the very bones, led forth to the red-hot gridiron, and going in advance of his tormentors with supernatural joy.

POINT I. *Consider the boldness which Martyrdom requires.*
   a. God calls us to glorify Him by suffering in gradual measure according as He sees us equal to bear it.
   b. He that has no desire for martyrdom is not worthy to be a Christian. We ought to humble ourselves at the sluggishness which makes us shrink from pain as we do.
   c. We are not to think that we could endure a Martyr's pains upon emergency, if we refuse little troubles.

POINT II. *Consider the supernatural joy of the Martyrs.*
   a. If we offer ourselves a living sacrifice with true faith, we may trust in God to perfect the endurance of nature with the supernatural exultation of inspired energy.
   b. The gift of faith is supernatural whereby we must offer ourselves, and so is the joy wherewith the offering is remunerated.
   c. We ought to ask and look for the help of the Holy Ghost to make us rejoice in all suffering. God loves not a grudging offering.

POINT III. *Consider the madness with which the evil hate the Martyrs.*
   a. The more the Governor saw the constancy of Vincent, the more he strove to overcome him. The witness of the faithful for Christ is a real struggle against Satan and the world.
   b. He that is in us is greater than he that is in the world. The hatred of the world is stimulated by Satan. Jesus will make us conquerors. We cannot conquer alone.
   c. The jailer was converted by the sight of Vincent in the prison. God uses a life sanctified through suffering to effect what no natural gift could do.

AFFECTIONS. Desire of suffering. Self-oblation. Humility. Cheerfulness amidst annoyances.

PRAYER.

O Almighty God, Who dost manifest the greatness of Thy power in the weakness of our flesh, making Thy faithful ones to triumph over that which were else insuperable; grant that I may never shrink from Thy call, but may rejoice to have the incapacity of my nature replenished with the sufficiency of Thy grace, so that my very weakness may turn to Thy glory; through Jesus Christ our Lord. Amen.

CHRISTIAN EVIDENCE.

PRELUDE. i. *Saul (who is also called Paul) mightily con--vinced the Jews, and that publicly, showing by the Scriptures that Jesus was Christ.*—Acts xiii. 9.; xviii. 28.

ii. Paul in the Synagogue unfolding a Roll of the Prophets.

POINT I. *Consider the evidence of Prophecy.*

> *a.* Holy men spake beforehand of Christ, as they were moved by the Holy Ghost. No other power save that of God could have given them the knowledge.
>
> *b.* They spake with meanings greater than they knew. They could not have thus used words teaching more than they knew, save by dictation of the Holy Ghost.
>
> *c.* Details of prophecy, apparently at variance, were harmonized in the Life of Christ, for One Spirit of Wisdom was speaking through all the prophets of one and the same Saviour.

POINT II. *Consider the importance of studying the prophecies.*

> *a.* We must read the mingled prophecy of joy and sorrow. Else we shall reject Christ in His Church, as the Jews rejected Him in His Person.
>
> *b.* When we learn how God foretold everything, we become less disquieted by the troubles which we experience.
>
> *c.* The mind rises up to prayerful communion with God, while looking forward to the future which is thus revealed to it.

POINT III. *Consider the end of the prophecies the manifestation of Jesus as the Christ.*

> *a.* Although Jesus surpassed all in purity, yet He requires the testimony of prophecy to guarantee his claim of coming from God.
>
> *b.* Prophecies include all nations, but only because all have to come to Christ. The only interest in the world's history is that which becomes eternal through touching upon Christ.
>
> *c.* The touches of prophecy enable us to see Divine purposes in events as belonging to Christ, when we should fail of doing so without such intimations.

AFFECTIONS. Reverence to God's Word. Love. Patience.

PRAYER.

O God, Who hast given us Thy Holy Word to be our stay, that in the promises thereof we may learn to rest securely amidst all actual dangers, grant me so to rejoice in Thine Only-begotten Son, the object of Thy Love, that giving myself wholly to Him, I may in Him obtain the fulness of grace now, and attain to the fulness of glory which Thou hast promised; through the same Jesus Christ our Lord. Amen.

CHRISTIAN DISCIPLESHIP.

PRELUDE. i. *Brother Saul, the Lord, even Jesus, that appeared unto thee in the way as thou camest, hath sent me, that thou mightest receive thy sight and be filled with the Holy Ghost.*— Acts ix. 17.

ii. Ananias standing beside the blind convert.

POINT I. *Consider the Sovereignty of Christ over His Church.*

a. He is the one Head of the whole Church, ruling in Heaven, and acting by supernatural visions or ministries of men as He pleases.

b. He in Heaven rules by the Person of the Holy Ghost proceeding from Himself, and the Holy Ghost carries out His will throughout His Body.

c. He uses men as the organs of His Body, through which the Holy Ghost works.

POINT II. *Consider the ministry of the Spirit.*

a. The Holy Ghost divides to every man severally as He will, according to the mind of Christ.

b. The Holy Ghost takes the things of Christ and shows them to us. We cannot claim any knowledge of Divine Mysteries unless He teach us. He teaches by giving new life.

c. He acts through men, as Ananias, even upon the most extraordinary occasions, for otherwise He would be ignoring the organization of the Body of Christ, which is His Temple, the sphere within which He dwells and acts.

POINT III. *Consider the illumination of the Holy Ghost.*

a. The Holy Ghost comes in all the fulness of the Light of Christ, for He is consubstantial with the Father and the Son.

b. The Holy Ghost illuminates us by uniting our several faculties with the corresponding faculties of the Humanity of Christ, making us His members, and developing within us His grace and Wisdom.

c. The Holy Ghost purges off from the human soul those clouds of sin which obscure our vision, and thus enables the faculties of Christ to work within us.

AFFECTIONS. Personal obedience to Christ. Joy in the Holy Ghost. Reverence for order.

PRAYER.

O Lord God, Who by the power of Thy Holy Spirit dost make Thy Light to shine throughout the Body of Christ, grant that we, being His members, may evermore be taught by Thy Holy Spirit; through Him Who ever liveth and reigneth with Thee in the Unity of the same Spirit, one God, world without end. Amen.

ADMISSION TO CHRIST.

PRELUDE. i. *And Ananias put his hands on him, and straightway there fell from his eyes as it had been scales, and he received sight forthwith. and was baptized. And when he had received meat, he was strengthened.*—Acts ix. 17-19.

ii. Saul recovering his sight and receiving Baptism.

POINT I. *Consider the scales falling from his eyes.*

a. The sight of Jesus blinds, unless the Holy Ghost be present to bless the vision to us.

b. The scales of prejudice must fall away from the eyes of the soul, before we can receive the Holy Ghost.

c. This preventing grace is through ministerial action ; but it does not supersede the Sacramental Gifts of the Body of Christ.

POINT II. *Consider his Baptism.*

a. His miraculous conversion did not make it less necessary for him to be baptized. He had seen Christ. He must now be joined to Him.

b. His repentance did not avail for his salvation, unless he were baptized for the remission of sins. " Be baptized and wash away thy sins."

c. God works by unforeseen operations around the Body of Christ, but by regularly appointed channels of sacramental grace within that Body, which those operations do not in any way make void.

POINT III. *Consider his returning strength.*

a. He took meat and was strengthened. Probably first of all food, the Body and the Blood of Christ.

b. He had felt his own weakness. Now He rose in the strength of Christ. The Gospel of Christ is the power of God. His very body testifies to its renewing power.

c. That strength of outward frame must be used for the glory of Him Whose Light now shone within his soul.

AFFECTIONS. Reverent use of means of grace. Expectation of supernatural results. Zeal for God's glory.

PRAYER.

O Lord God, Who didst bring Saul from being a persecutor to be a witness of Thy Truth, deliver me, I beseech Thee, from all carnal prejudice, and send out Thy Light and Thy Strength that I may serve Thee evermore in Thy Temple; through Jesus Christ our Lord. Amen.

THE TRANSFORMATION.

PRELUDE. i. *The furious persecutor fell down, and arose a faithful preacher of the Word.*

ii. The Baptized disciple looking joyously upon the face of Ananias.

POINT I. *Consider the zeal of his ignorance.*

 a. He found mercy, for he acted ignorantly in unbelief. His ignorance did not arise from idleness, nor his unbelief from sensuality or indifference.

 b. He was zealous for the Law of God, and that Law was true as far as it went. He was zealous for a true thing, but he did not know God's purpose in appointing it.

 c. He did not suffer his zeal to die with his ignorance, but retained it in the illumination of the Holy Ghost.

POINT II. *Consider the surrender of his heart.*

 a. It was a complete surrender, There was no holding back —no hesitating—no time to consider. He had found a Conqueror and a law.

 b. It was an intelligent surrender. The truth to which he yielded was beyond reason, but the circumstances which led to his conviction were, in various degrees, manifest to those around him, both the light and the sound.

 c. It was a permanent surrender. Having now come to Christ, he does not turn back. He cannot unsee the vision.

POINT III. *Consider the bold career of his Apostleship.*

 a. His own knowledge of the Jewish Scriptures sprang up into a new flood of Light. Dark words began to burn with fire.

 b. He had experienced the transforming power of God upon his own frame, bringing Him out of death. No infirmity of his outer nature could be of any hindrance to God working in Him.

 c. He felt the greatness of that Christian Truth into which he was baptized; and could not do otherwise than seek to bring all to its knowledge.

AFFECTIONS. Death to the world, and life unto God through Christ.

PRAYER.

O God Almighty, grant, we beseech Thee, that as Thine Apostle S. Paul was changed by Thy grace from being a persecutor, so I may be delivered from those sins whereby after many years of regenerate life, I am yet so miserably dishonouring Thy Holy Name, and may be sanctified through Jesus Christ our Lord. Amen.

APOSTOLIC PREACHING.

PRELUDE. *He of the Apostles that was last, is by his preaching first.*

ii. S. Paul in old age contemplating the crown of glory.

POINT I. *Consider the greatness of his labours.*

　a. Their extent. He is the Apostle of the Gentiles, and feels himself a debtor to all. They whom Christ has redeemed are to him as claimants in Christ's Name.

　b. Their toil, both natural and supernatural, mental and bodily, in much suffering and danger.

　c. Their success. God wrought mightily by him. He did not baptize his thousands as some Missionaries of later days, but he founded Churches in many places living with Christ's Life.

POINT II. *Consider the greatness of his revelations.*

　a. He had visions of God implying far more than ordinary closeness of fellowship.

　b. His contemplative life was not a hindrance to his active life, but was the very strength of it.

　c. His life with God did not merely elevate the aim of his ministerial labour, but it obtained for him a vast increase of spiritual power.

POINT III. *Consider the greatness of his temptations.*

　a. A thorn in the flesh was given him by reason of the greatness of his revelations, to keep him humble.

　b. He was exposed to violent persecutions in the world, and many kinds of death.

　c. He had the sore grief of bearing calumnies, and witnessing the decline of many of the Churches which he had established.

AFFECTIONS. Zeal. Diligence. Patience. Expectation of suffering as a token of Christ's love.

PRAYER.

O Lord Jesu Christ, Who didst call Thy Holy Apostle S. Paul to follow Thee in so much suffering, grant that I may have grace to bear whatever discipline Thou mayest ordain for me, and although I be unworthy of the revelations which were granted to him, enlighten me, I beseech Thee, with such necessary experiences of Thy Holy teaching as may best enable me to live to Thy Glory; Who with the Father and the Holy Ghost reignest God for evermore. Amen.

THE CHOSEN VESSEL.

PRELUDE. i. *Let us celebrate the Conversion of S. Paul the Apostle, for to-day he that had been a persecutor became a chosen vessel. Therefore Angels and Archangels rejoice and praise in heaven the Son of God.*

ii. Saul and his companions on the way to Damascus and the Light of the Glory of Jesus shining suddenly upon them.

POINT I. *Consider God's election of His special instruments.*

a. God's work is beyond natural power, but natural gifts are to be consecrated for supernatural work. What God gives He means to be used, and multiplied by Himself while being used by us.

b. If we cultivate our natural gifts for God's glory as best we can, He will use them in due time. He wastes nothing.

c. God chooses none because of natural gifts unless there be a supernatural aim in the life.

POINT II. *Consider the special hindrances to their acceptance.*

a. God's greatest gifts of nature are ever met by the greatest assaults of Satan.

b. When we feel any powers or desires for God within ourselves, we must expect special difficulties and temptations. God gives internal power, but generally external weakness.

c. When we see persons violently opposing the truth, we ought to feel that probably there is some great good in them, which Satan is turning aside to evil. They may yet be rescued from Satan.

POINT III. *Consider the Triumph of Grace.*

a. It is omnipotent. God will overcome all external obstacles, if we are true to him, acting according to our knowledge.

b. It is harmonious. God's purposes may be very different from what we expect, but the development of His Truth will always be in harmony with His Truth. Saul was overthrown, but the law for which he was so zealous was glorified in Saul by the grace of Christ, as its true fulfilment.

c. It is proportionate. If difficulties are greater than we expected, the developments of glory from God will be greater too.

AFFECTIONS. Diligence in God's service. Praise for His goodness. Confidence in His government.

PRAYER.

Grant, O Lord God, that as Thy servant Saul was reclaimed from his blindness to serve Thee in Thy Truth, so I, dedicating myself to Thy service, may attain to fuller experiences of Thy Truth, and may be transformed into an instrument of Thy glory, worthy of Thine eternal purpose; through Jesus Christ our Lord. Amen.

THE LORD COMING TO HIS TEMPLE.

PRELUDE. i. *The Lord Whom ye seek shall suddenly come to His Temple; even the Messenger of the Covenant Whom ye delight in: behold, He shall come, saith the Lord of Hosts.*

ii. The Child Jesus brought in.

POINT I. *Consider the hiddenness of the Divine Glory.*

a. He comes as the Messenger of the Covenant, and therefore upon an equality with those to whom He comes. It is a covenant of grace, not a manifestation of irresistible might.

b. He entereth His Temple. No Temple made with hands could contain the glory of the Lord of Hosts. Therefore no manifestation within the Temple could be worthy of God.

c. The Divine Presence is not less there because it is hidden. Human sense cannot perceive it. The eye of faith can.

POINT II. *Consider the Divine Person Who comes.*

a. He is the Lord. He created the whole world, and yet does not dwell therein. This Temple is the symbol of a holy habitation in which He ever dwells, even His Body.

b. In that Temple wherein He dwells He acts Personally, and never will be separated from it.

c. In that Temple of His Body He enters into this external temple, that He, the Only-begotten Son, may be presented before God the Father as the Representative of mankind, whose worship He comes to perfect by His mediation.

POINT III. *Consider the preparation which had been made for His coming.*

a. He came suddenly, because men were not faithful in looking for Him. There was no suddenness in Himself.

b. The presentation of the first-born for many generations had been a preparation for His coming. They had needed to be redeemed He comes as the Redeemer.

c. The time had long ago been proclaimed by the Prophets, and faithful hearts waited, like Simeon, to welcome Him.

AFFECTIONS. Delight in gazing upon Divine Mysteries. Preparation of heart so as to be able to welcome Christ.

PRAYER.

O Lord God, Who hast sent Thy Son to take upon Himself our nature and purify our actions, while we draw near to Thee by the virtue of His Holy mediation, grant that I may recognize His Presence under the veil of the Mysteries of Grace, and may evermore present Him unto Thee dwelling in my heart, so that I may be presented unto Thee as one of His true children, by Him Who liveth and reigneth with Thee and the Holy Ghost, God for ever and ever. Amen.

THE HUMILIATION OF GOD.

PRELUDE. i. *But who may abide the day of His coming?
And who shall stand when He appeareth? For He is like a refiner's
fire, and like fuller's sope.*

ii. The Child Jesus.

POINT I. *Consider the Majesty of Divine humiliation.*

   a. The humiliation of God. God using our feebleness, is more
heart-searching than when we lose our feebleness in the
paralyzing sense of His splendour.

   b. He humbles Himself in order to search us; He is present
as a Judge wherever He is. By coming He makes Himself
the measure of His creatures.

   c. If the Child Jesus be the True Worshipper in the Temple,
how can we worship rightly? Who can do that which God
humbles Himself to do, in order that it may be done in a
manner worthy of His acceptance?

POINT II. *Consider the certainty of the Manifestation.*

   a. God does not part with His glory by laying it aside. It
remains truly His. He will claim it in the end.

   b. The humiliation is not a mere transitory act. As an act of
God, it abides in God, and adds to the glory of the manifestation which is to follow.

   c. If we would stand when the glory of God is manifested, we
must lay hold upon the glory of God while it is hidden.
Lay hold upon Jesus by faith, that we may welcome the
sight of Him.

POINT III. *Consider the transforming power of the Presence.*

   a. As fire transforms into itself whatever contains it, so should
the Presence of Christ, filled with the Fire of God, burn out
our earthliness, and fill us with His Heavenly glow.

   b. If we are not purified by this Fire, we must be destroyed
thereby. It will transform us into evil beyond remedy, if it
do not transform us in His own goodness, so as to be beyond
danger of loss.

   c. The Presence of God separates between the good and the
evil. We must take our choice. If we cling to that which
He would purge off, we must become separate from Himself.

AFFECTIONS. Homage. Expectation. Humiliation. Self-
surrender.

PRAYER.

*O God, Who hast given Thine only Son to be amongst us, that in
our nature we may behold Thy glory, grant us so to welcome His
approach in the fulness of grace, that we may be presented by Him
in the end, pure and without offence, and may be worthy to share in
the glorious Fellowship of Thy Holy Temple for ever in Heaven?
through the same Jesus Christ our Lord. Amen.*

HIS HUMILIATION OUR PURIFICATION.

PRELUDE. i. *He shall sit as a refiner and purifier of silver; and He shall purify the sons of Levi.*—Mal. iii. 3.

ii. The Son of God watching the hearts of His worshippers, until He sees His own likeness produced therein.

POINT I. *Consider the Presence of Jesus Christ.*

a. He has come to His Temple to abide. He presents Himself in His Temple before the Father continually. His Presence is a Light, making the whole Temple to be manifest to the Divine scrutiny.

b. He gives grace by being present. He brings men not only to God's judgment, but to their own.

c. He calls men to be like Himself, and therefore to repentance as strict as His judgment will be hereafter.

POINT II. *Consider the patience of Jesus Christ.*

a. Great was His patience towards the Jews. Greater is it to us Christians, even as His gifts to us are greater. ·

b. He sits as a Priest upon His Throne interceding for us; and giving us the necessary gifts for our sanctification.

c. He waits until hearts are conformed to Himself by the power of His Holy Spirit; the gift of His grace and the discipline of outward suffering. By His hidden coming He would purify them for His manifestation.

POINT III. *Consider the Final Advent of our Lord J. C.*

a. Those will abide His coming then, who have felt its terror now. To fear *that* coming is vain. Fear *this*!

b. It is His coming now which gives terror to His coming then. So He says to the Jews: "Now have ye seen and hated Me and My Father."

c. He comes to purify the whole Church, by instituting a Priesthood to make the offering in righteousness, of His Body in the Holy Eucharist, as the means whereby the whole Body of the faithful are purified, the "better sacrifices" of "the Heavenly places."—Heb. ix. 23.

AFFECTIONS. Fear. Penitence. Preparation for Christ's Coming. Gratitude.

PRAYER.

O Lord God, grant that I may so truly acknowledge the Majesty of Thy grace, contemplating my vileness in the Light of Thy mysterious Presence, that I may have my share in the righteousness of Thy Holy Oblation, and may find acceptance with Thee in the great day of manifestation; through the merits of Jesus Christ Thy Son our Lord. Amen.

BISHOP OF SEBASTE IN ARMENIA.—A.D. 316.

INNOCENCY IN CHRIST.

PRELUDE. i. *Theirs is the Kingdom of Heaven who have despised the life of this world to gain a reward in the kingdom, and have washed their robes in the Blood of the Lamb.*—Rev. vii. 14.

ii. S. Blasius being torn to pieces by iron combs.

POINT I. *Consider the Martyrs as clothing Christ's Body.*

　a. As the wool grows upon the sheep, and is yearly shorn, so, from age to age, Martyrs are found clothing the Church of Christ. By the violence of man the Church is shorn.

　b. Woollen garments, outer clothing, symbolically represent the external life; as linen, the inner, the spiritual life.

　c. The wool is sprinkled with oil and carded. So the Martyrs, anointed of the Holy Ghost, are torn with tortures. Natural clingings are destroyed, and the fibres of the whole nature are reduced to the service of God.

POINT II. *Consider the tearing of the body in torture.*

　a. The wool requires to have its fibres separated, so as to be ready for the loom. So we need to have all the elements of our humanity presented perfected for God's use one by one.

　b. They who give their bodies to torture are most like to the Lamb of God, Who is their True Life, and suffers in them.

　c. Though not called to martyrdom, we must offer our bodies a living sacrifice. Bodily temptations serve to show whether we are of the fleece of the spotless Lamb.

POINT III. *Consider the innocency of the Lamb of God.*

　a. Wool, as representing what is animal, represents naturally what is sensual. But the Son of God is Incarnate yet sinless. His Humanity is most pure. Hearts washed in His Blood are full of Heaven. This wool is pure.

　b. The Lamb of God is content to be despoiled in silence. We cannot share His innocency unless we share His meekness.

　c. Of the Ancient of Days we read, that the hair of His Head was as the pure wool, as white as snow. That which grows from His Body on earth is pure as that which comes down from His Godhead in Heaven.

AFFECTIONS. Acceptance of pain. Meekness under spoliation.

PRAYER.

O Lord Jesu Christ, the Lamb of God, grant that by the discipline of Thy Providence every natural longing may be made subservient to the purposes of Thy grace, so that I may no longer live unto myself, but may be transformed according to Thy holy will, Who didst suffer upon the Cross for me, Who now livest and reignest with the Father and the Holy Ghost, one God, world without end. Amen.

5

A.D. 251.

GIFT OF SELF TO CHRIST.

PRELUDE. i. *When the Bridegroom came, they that were ready went in with Him to the marriage.*—S. Matt. xxv. 10.

ii. S. Agatha led out to torments, and saying, O Jesu Christ, Lord of all things, take as Thine own all that I am.

POINT I. *Consider the necessity of giving oneself wholly to Christ.*

   a. We are His by Creation and Redemption. Without our will He can claim us. He has given us a will on purpose that we may give ourselves to Him.

   b. We cannot retain possession of ourselves. Not a moment is really our own.

   c. There is none but Christ to Whom we can give ourselves. All others are dependent upon Him; and if any creature claim us, the act is but the greater rebellion.

POINT II. *Consider the reality of a gift made to Christ.*

   a. We must put away all sense of our own power. To belong to Him is more than merely concurring in His will. It is the surrender of our own.

   b. He must require us to do things which are against our own will. Else the gift would be only nominal.

   c. The whole discipline of life is as a nailing to His Cross. We can only be given to Him Who has died by dying to the world.

POINT III. *Consider the blessedness of being given wholly to Christ.*

   a. The more we are given to Him, the more do we experience the joy in which He lives. We cannot know that joy save by entering into the life beyond the grave wherein He lives.

   b. The risen Nature of Christ fills our nature with its own joy, if we give each faculty to abide in the sympathy of His new life.

   c. If we would live in His sympathy, we must accept His Sovereignty, and that is by completely giving ourselves to His Will.

AFFECTIONS. Heartfelt devotion to Jesus. Absorbing sense of His dominion.

PRAYER.

O God, Who hast given to us Thine own Love, that we might live through Him, grant that I may give myself wholly to Him in this time of grace, and may abide in the eternal joy of Thine Elect; through His merits, Who liveth and reigneth with Thee and with the Holy Ghost now and for ever. Amen.

THIRD CENTURY.

FELLOWSHIP WITH SUFFERING SAINTS.

PRELUDE. i. *Theirs is the Kingdom of Heaven who have despised the life of this world to gain a reward in the kingdom, and have washed their robes in the blood of the Lamb.*—Rev. vii. 14.

ii. Valentine assisting the Martyrs in their necessities.

POINT I. *Consider the honour which is due to those who are leaving this world for Heaven.*

    a. The glory of faith shines out in the heart of those who suffer, and should shine in ours who witness. A dying Saint should be to us as a looking-glass reflecting Heaven.

    b. We learn to honour the Kingdom of Christ by fellowship with those who are dying. The furnace slew those who would cast the Three Children into it. In the light of Heaven we die to the world while we assist the dying.

    c. S. Valentine assisted the Martyrs. We may not have Martyrs to assist. We must however honour their memory.

POINT II. *Consider that in ministering to the suffering people of Christ we minister to Christ.*

    a. The glory of the Saints is not merely derived from Christ. It is Christ's glory. They have no glory but His.

    b. Christ lives in His people, and therefore He reciprocates every act of love that we can render.

    c. If in acts of charity to God's people we pray to God, we are lifted up into the Heavenly mansions.

POINT III. *Consider that we gain the reward in the Kingdom by losing this lower life.*

    a. We die to the lower world first by grace. The presence of death, especially of saintly death, ought to make us dead to the world in the consciousness of Heaven.

    b. Mortification in this world quickens the capacity of Heavenly joy. If we would really accompany the dying into the Presence of Christ, we must mortify all of our nature which cannot be taken into that Presence.

    c. Christ will make manifest with Himself those who have died unto the world by much persecution and reproach; and those also who have been companions of their affliction.

AFFECTIONS. Affection to those that are in suffering. Desire for the higher world. Fellowship with Christ.

PRAYER.

O Almighty God, grant that as I reflect upon the precious death of Thy Saints, I may have my heart stimulated by their fellowship to live in Christ, and may so experience in this world the sweet return of His Love, that for love to Him I may rejoice to part with all that can hold me back from Him, and may attain to the Life with Him in glory; through His merits Who liveth and reigneth with Thee and the Holy Ghost now and for ever. Amen.

252   Feast of S. David.

FELLOWSHIP WITH CHRIST.

PRELUDE.   i. *Well done, thou good and faithful servant; thou hast been faithful over a few things, I will make thee ruler over many things: enter thou into the Joy of thy Lord.*—S. Matt. xxv. 21.

ii. S. David labouring in silence with his monks.

POINT I.   *Consider the faithfulness of lengthened preparation.*

    a. Resolutions to be faithful when greatness is attained are useless. Faithfulness is needed, while powers are small. God tries therein our fitness for great things by small things.

    b. We are not to be careful about self-culture, merely because we see what to expect, but out of love to God.

    c. The day of small things may be a long day, but the results which follow shall be all the greater. Our Lord during thirty years prepared Himself for a ministry of little more than three. Prepare more, attempt less: more will be done.

POINT II.   *Consider the faithfulness of silence in little matters.*

    a. Religious persons spent their time in hard manual labour, and never spoke except for purposes of necessity. The hand is faithful in toil; the tongue, more often, in silence.

    b. How often does the tongue prevent work by forwardness, hinder work by idleness, destroy work by falsehood. Others besides monks need to learn the rules of silence.

    c. It is especially in small matters of conversation that people need to be careful. Oftentimes the great truths people utter are marred by little vices of daily talk.

POINT III.   *Consider faithfulness in doctrine.*

    a. Silence should strengthen our communion with God; and if we speak less to man, we ought to value Divine Truth all the more.

    b. To talk even about Divine Truth with man too often secularizes our grasp of that truth. Silence trains men to see and maintain Divine Truth in its integrity.

    c. When there is a call to come forward and maintain truth, the Holy Ghost will give utterance and wisdom, and power to those who live habitually hidden with Him.

AFFECTIONS.   Self-discipline. Dependence upon God.

PRAYER.

O *Almighty God, Who hast permitted Thy Saints to be trained in much secrecy and lengthened devotion for the victories of faith to which they should afterwards be called, grant that I may be careful not to hasten unbidden to any work of Thy grace, but to prepare myself with all diligence for whatever Thou mayest desire; through Jesus Christ our Lord.* Amen.

BROTHERLY LOVE.

PRELUDE i. *Well done, thou good and faithful servant; thou hast been faithful over a few things, I will make thee ruler over many things: enter thou into the Joy of thy Lord.*—S. Matt. xxv. 21.

ii. S. Chad assisting S. Cedd in his monastic foundations.

POINT I. *Consider the sanctification of family life.*

    a. What a joy to Heaven is a family of brothers, all leading lives of prayer and devotion. The sympathy of kindred ought to intensify the individual love of Christ.

    b. How diligent ought men to be in prayer for their own kindred. S. Paul desired to be anathema for Israel. His prayer was answered by his successes among the Gentiles. Many fail abroad, because they neglect duties at home.

    c. How fully must God's Blessing rest upon the works of charity in which a natural family unite.

POINT II. *Consider sanctification through humiliation.*

    a. Humiliation, even if we suffer wrongfully, should always be made a matter of thankfulness.

    b. It should always bring us to penitence. If the humiliation be on some point undeserved, yet upon how many points do we deserve to be humbled even more.

    c. Gladly may we lose the outward tokens and occasions of honour which are so apt to injure us if we the more fully attain to that honour which cometh from God only.

POINT III. *Consider the sanctification of heavenly communion.*

    a. Events of nature, which to the natural heart speak only in fear, serve to the faithful as opportunities of renewed devotion. The lightnings and clouds bless the Lord when they waken us to faith and prayer.

    b. Much more should political disturbances, the storms of nations, lead us to retirement, hope, and prayer. Lift up your heads, says our Lord. We must lift up our hands also.

    c. God is ready to speak to those who speak constantly to Him. He will in many ways warn us by angel voices of that which it is well for us to know. The thought of death fills us with joy if we hear God warning us in all daily occurrences.

AFFECTIONS. Brotherly affection. Self-forgetfulness.

PRAYER.

O Almighty God, grant us to recognize Thine Almighty Presence in all things, that we may act in fellowship with Thy Holy will, submit to Thy Providence with cheerfulness, glorify Thee in the majesty of Thy Judgment, and rejoice in the expectation of Thy call; through Jesus Christ our Lord. Amen.

DETACHMENT.

PRELUDE. i. *The mother was marvellous above all, and worthy of honourable mention, because of the hope she had in the Lord.*

ii. A golden ladder reaching to Heaven with a dragon at its base, and sharp iron instruments on either side; so narrow, also, that only one can go up it at a time.

POINT I. *Consider how solitary is the act of death.*

a. Kindred cannot join with us in death. The mother cannot take her sucking-child along with herself. Those who are nearest in devotion cannot go with us. Those who die at the same moment are as much separated from us as any others.

b. Each one undergoes the individual scrutiny of the Divine Judgment. Each step of the ladder corresponds with some act of previous life.

c. In the act of death we first feel to the full our solitary responsibility, and the necessity of acting according to God's will. All the support of the world, even in appearance, will be taken away.

POINT II. *Consider the devil making us shrink from God's call.*

a. He would keep men from the Martyrs' ladder, but he would have them die by a death all the more terrible, although its terrors be more hidden.

b. He seeks to keep men from mortifications during life. The power of ascending the ladder does, as it were, gather up into itself the powers enacted in detail during life. We must practise death while preparing for it.

c. The dragon will not devour us if we obey God's call in climbing the ladder; but if we shrink from the ladder, we shall perish in the jaws of the lion.

POINT III. *Consider the ladder of death.*

a. It has instruments of terror on either side. Satan has the power of death, and he will not let the soul escape which is capable of being wounded by these sharp instruments.

b. The steps are of gold. If we come in obedience to God's call, we find in the greatest sufferings the support of His Love. By His Love we are sustained in mortification. By His Love we are drawn to Life.

c. The top reaches to Heaven. God calls us when we die. Blessed are they that hear His call.

AFFECTIONS. Preparation for death. Refusal to follow the world. Detachment even from ties of nature.

PRAYER.

O God, Who speakest within the soul, calling us to die, grant me so to obey Thy holy calls to mortification, that I may joyously hear that call which none can disobey. Through the merits of Thy Son Jesus Christ our Lord. **Amen.**

BISHOP OF ROME.—A.D. 604.

MISSIONARY ZEAL.

PRELUDE. i. *Well done, thou good and faithful servant; thou hast been faithful over a few things, I will make thee ruler over many things: enter thou into the Joy of thy Lord.*—S. Matt. xxv. 21.

ii. S. Gregory seeing the English slaves for sale in the market.

POINT I. *Consider the blessedness of Missionary zeal.*

a. A worse bondage than human slavery holds down souls which know not Christ. Were we alive to this, how could we rest until we had done our utmost to rescue them from Satan? Man was made in God's image, we ought to long for his deliverance.

b. If we desire anything for God, we should ourselves do what we can. If it is not our own duty, we should try and obtain the help of others. God delights to bless the co-operation of those who work together in love for His glory.

c. The love which S. Gregory felt for a few slaves has put itself forth in a vast ecclesiastical polity, which has spread through the world. How must we hope and pray over the beginning of missionary enterprise.

POINT II. *Consider the edifying power of Holy Scripture.*

a. A true desire or capacity for giving God's Truth to others must be nourished by a constant study of God's Truth for ourselves. Holy Scripture is the stay of our thoughts.

b. Holy Scripture speaks with a depth proportionate to the love wherewith we embrace it. The Spirit of love gives intuition of analogies hidden from the world's eye.

c. God will speak through the words of Holy Scripture to those who listen for His voice in devout meditation.

POINT III. *Consider how music and ritual should be appreciated in Divine worship.*

a. If we approach God intelligently we shall be careful to approach Him reverently. Externals of religion are not small matters. Interior religion requires a seemly exterior.

b. The devout heart shrinks from worldliness in the sanctuary. The external exists for what is interior.

c. Acts of devotion suffer much through want of preparation. Tranquillity of appointed order shelters the intensity of spiritual energy. If we do not guard this, we lose it.

AFFECTIONS. Zeal for the furtherance of the Gospel. Care in the heartfelt appreciation thereof.

PRAYER.

O God, Who hast been pleased to make known to us Thy Truth, grant that we may be diligent in communicating the same, and watchful so to observe its purity, and accept its laws, that our lives being strengthened in communion with Thee may be conformed to Thine Image; through Jesus Christ our Lord. Amen.

KING OF THE WEST SAXONS.—A.D. 979.

STRENGTH ATTAINED THROUGH MEEKNESS.

PRELUDE. i. *Theirs is the kingdom of Heaven who have despised the life of this world to gain a reward in the kingdom, and have washed their robes in the Blood of the Lamb.*—Rev. vii. 14.

ii. The boy king meekly bearing with the hatred of his step-mother.

POINT I. *Consider the joys of a Heavenly kingdom.*

  a. Free from envy. All hearts open to our joys, delighting in what is ours as if it were their own: our own joy to know it.

  b. Free from danger. Won by dangers past, but now unassailable. The will, strengthened by dangers in the toil, is established in the Holy Ghost as its reward.

  c. Free from care. Earthly sovereignty is exerted in repressing evil: heavenly sovereignty in manifesting good.

POINT II. *Consider the estrangement from the world by which this kingdom is attained.*

  a. We must learn maxims different from the world's, in the school of Saints who have themselves lived apart from it.

  b. The world is to us a bitter stepmother, anxious for her own offspring to get the day. The world will love her own. We must not be surprised.

  c. Goodness instead of winning the world's favour will only aggravate. The world cannot understand it.

POINT III. *Consider the violence by which this kingdom must be won.*

  a. In proportion as we have grasped the things of this world, so must we suffer violence in parting. What we love, wounds us in its removal. It avenges our despising it.

  b. We are one with the world by nature; and there must be a violation of our nature in tearing ourselves away.

  c. We are enslaved to the world by enjoyments; and every earthly joy has to be changed into spiritual, as it were in a furnace, ere we can be truly fashioned for what is heavenly.

AFFECTIONS. Meekness. Endurance. Hope.

PRAYER.

O God, strengthen me, I pray Thee, so to live for Thee amidst the opposition of this evil world, that I may rejoice at every suffering which the world inflicts as being a help to me that I may live the more closely united to Thee; through Jesus Christ our Lord. **Amen.**

A.D. 543.

RETIREMENT WITH GOD.

PRELUDE. i. *Well done, thou good and faithful servant; thou hast been faithful over a few things, I will make thee ruler over many things: enter thou into the joy of Thy Lord.*—S. Matt. xxv. 21.
ii. S. Benedict in prayer.

POINT I. *Consider the temptations to which God's people are subject.*

    a. We do not escape temptations by retirement from the world. When the world is away, Satan's immediate assaults may be more. Witness our Lord in the wilderness.

    b. We must not be disheartened because assaulted, nor wish to choose our own temptations. Temptations which grieve us most are best for us.

    c. Temptation is to sanctify us. All great Saints have gone through great temptations, though of various kinds. Our sanctification is a victory. A victory implies a struggle.

POINT II. *Consider the power of holy retirement.*

    a. Those who fly from the world rule the world. If we want to see our power, it soon evaporates before our eyes. What is unseen lives with God.

    b. We must live with God if we would live for ever. All that rests upon worldly support must perish. The sword, money, influence, individual genius, all alike fail to give lasting power.

    c. Retirement must be with God, if it is to have the Life of God. We cannot exercise God's Life apart from Himself. We must be hidden, even from ourselves in God.

POINT III. *Consider the abiding character of Life with God.*

    a. We outlive ourselves even while in the flesh, if we have by grace died to ourselves. Wonderful happiness of life! "To lose the soul for Christ's sake, so as to find it" in Him.

    b. We outlive our natural life. For the consequences of a life spent with God, a life which is the life of God in us, and not our own, last as long as the Church of God lasts.

    c. We outlive the world. If we have lived with God in the world, then when Christ, Who is our Life, shall appear, we also shall be made manifest with Him in glory.—Col. iii. 4.

AFFECTIONS. Passive reliance upon God. Deadness to the world. Acknowledgment of the power of faith.

PRAYER.

O Almighty God, grant that I may live so hidden from the world, so separate from self, in union with Thee, that I may be preserved amidst all the assaults of Satan, strengthened for the accomplishment of Thy work, and perfected in the Life that passeth not away; through Jesus Christ our Lord. **Amen.**

THE COMING OF THE HOLY GHOST.

PRELUDE. i. *The Holy Ghost shall come upon thee, and the power of the Highest shall overshadow thee. Therefore also that Holy Thing which shall be born of thee shall be called the Son of God.*—S. Luke i. 35.

ii. The Angel appearing to the Blessed Virgin.

POINT I. *Consider the descent of the Holy Ghost.*

a. He comes from the Father, from the very Being of the Father, not merely from His Presence. In Him the perfect energy of God is present, without any created limitation.

b. He comes from the Son. As the S. is One God with the F., the H. G. proceeds by an act of eternal identity, not collaterally, but primarily from the F., and derivatively from the Son.

c. He comes as the Bond of Both, in the Act of the Divine Life. He proceeds mutually from the Father and the Son in the act of eternal Love, whereby they abide One God.

POINT. II. *Consider the time of the descent.*

a. Still future when the Angel spake. Already the Holy Ghost sanctified her by many graces, yet these avail not for the purpose of the Incarnation.

b. The operation shall be the work of the Holy Ghost, not of the Blessed Virgin Mary. She must be simply passive, yielding herself to God's power.

c. The descent of the Holy Ghost shall effect a real combination of the two natures in an identity of life.

POINT III. *Consider the Person of the Blessed Virgin Mary.*

a. She remains in her earthly nature. The graces poured upon her do not make her different from other women.

b. She becomes the channel of a true Divine energy. The Child is not merely raised by an external impulse to a condition supernatural. The fulness of Godhead passes through her humanity to become enshrined in the Child.

c. The substance of the newborn Child is truly hers, although the Life of the Child be the Life of God. The Incarnate Son has no element of humanity save what He received from Adam through her. She is truly the Mother of God.

AFFECTIONS. Self-consecration to the Holy Ghost. Worship of God's Majesty. Praise for His condescension.

PRAYER.

O God, Who didst send Thy Son to be made of a woman that He might accomplish Thy work amongst men, through the power of the Holy Ghost, grant that I may always act in the power which Thou hast given unto me as one of His members, and in the confession of my own nothingness may exercise the fulness of Thine Almighty Grace; through the same Jesus Christ our Lord. Amen.

THE POWER OF THE HIGHEST.

PRELUDE. i. *The Holy Ghost shall come upon thee, and the power of the Highest shall overshadow them: therefore also that Holy Thing which shall be born of thee shall be called the Son of God.*—S. Luke i. 35.

ii. The Angel appearing to the Blessed Virgin.

POINT I. *Consider the power of the Highest.*

    a. The fulness of the Divine Energy is involved in this Conception; for the Child is the Son of God. The whole Godhead of the Father acts without diminution or change.

    b. No created substance is added to the nature of the Blessed Virgin Mary, but the Divine Power in spiritual glory comes upon her, a Substance truly Divine, a pure power.

    c. This power is the undivided Power of the Eternal Trinity. God is undivided in His action, for He is without parts.

POINT II. *Consider what the overshadowing is.*

    a. It is external to the nature of the Blessed Virgin Mary. She is overshadowed. That which is born of her is the Light of God. As the Holy Ghost took of her substance He filled it with Light. It ceased to be hers.

    b. The nature of the Blessed Virgin Mary was not annihilated or transformed, but it became full of glory as it became the nature of her Child.

    c. This overshadowing protects from all external hurt coming from contact with a sinful world.

POINT III. *Consider the singularity of this prerogative.*

    a. However great may have been the sanctification of any in former time, yet none had approached this overshadowing Presence. There had been types. Here is the Power.

    b. Although in future time many shall be taken into a union with God by grace which, as being illuminative, shall be higher in kind, yet shall none be so entirely subject to the Divine Power as passive instruments of God's Will.

    c. The glory remains, although the child-bearing be over. Humanity is perfected hereby passively in the child-bearing, that it may be subsequently glorified in the living fellowship of the Word made Flesh.

AFFECTIONS. Praise to God for Divine grace. Worship of the Incarnate God.

PRAYER.

O God, Who hast exalted our nature to such perfection, that it might become the instrument of Thy Holy Will in the Incarnation of Thine Only-begotten Son, grant that I may act in the power of Thy grace so as to attain to that glory for which thou hast created us in Life Eternal; through the same Jesus Christ our Lord. Amen.

THE HOLY OFFSPRING.

PRELUDE. i. *The Holy Ghost shall come upon thee, and the power of the Highest shall overshadow thee. Therefore also that Holy Thing which shall be born of thee shall be called the Son of God.*—S. Luke i. 35.

ii. The Angel appearing to the Blessed Virgin.

POINT I. *Consider the Holy Thing which is conceived.*

  a. The Child lives with the Life of God, a Life above human nature, by which the life of the Humanity is sustained.

  b. The Humanity, passive under the Divine operation in the Mother, becomes active with Divine sanctity in the Child.

  c. Out of the darkness of the overshadowed Humanity comes the Humanity bright with the glory of indwelling Light.

POINT II. *Consider the relation between the Mother and the Child.*

  a. It is a true relationship of transmitted nature. The glory of the higher nature does not destroy what is assumed.

  b. He will never cease to acknowledge that the Humanity wherein He lives has been received from her. The Election to be the Mother of God brings responsibilities, but it remains as a prerogative that is inalienable.

  c. It was by the Power of the Child, that the Mother was raised to the glory of this maternity. What He took from her was nothingness.

POINT III. *Consider the Incarnate Son of God.*

  a. The nothingness of the creature enshrines henceforth the glory of the Creator. The Divine Image seals the assumed nature with the true and living Likeness of the Father.

  b. The Holy Ghost is not Incarnate. He, the Bond of Mutual Love Eternal, proceeds from the Father and the Son. He could not rest in a created manifestation of Himself without losing this property of His Person.

  c. As He proceeds from the Person of the Son, He does not merely bring the Godhead of the Son into the Manhood to leave it there, but He takes the Manhood into the Godhead to be the instrument through which the Love of the Son towards the Father shall be manifested by His anointing.

AFFECTIONS. Faith in Jesus. Reverence towards all operations of the Holy Ghost. Self oblation in Christ to God.

PRAYER.

O God, Who hast caused our nature to be presented before Thee in the fulness of Thine own true Love by the power of the Holy Ghost, grant that I may rejoice to yield myself to the impulse of this renewing grace, and by the Power of the sanctifying Spirit may be raised to dwell in the Unity of the Divine Life; through the same Jesus Christ our Lord. Amen.

BISHOP OF CHICHESTER.—A.D. 1253.

SANCTIFICATION OF DAILY LIFE.

PRELUDE. i. *Well done, thou good and faithful servant; thou hast been faithful over a few things, I will make the ruler over many things: enter thou into the Joy of thy Lord.*—S. Matt. xxv. 21.
ii. S. Richard attending to his brother's estate.

POINT I. *Consider the blessing upon faithfulness in secular affairs.*

    a. Secular matters are a great sphere of devotional work, if undertaken in a devotional spirit. Many have been trained for God by being kept working at what seemed unprofitable.

    b. If we cannot find God in ordinary secular duties, we shall not find Him anywhere. If our work seems to keep us from God, it is plain that something does—but probably not our work.

    c. God leaves us immersed in secular duties, in order that we may learn to do them in a spiritual manner. Our nature is not fit for the Resurrection Life until we can do the things of this life in the power of the Resurrection.

POINT II. *Consider the sacredness of family duties.*

    a. The relationships of nature ought to develope within us the germs of those relationships which will last on in the Resurrection. They need to be spiritualized before they are fit to be raised.

    b. Our toil for others is of most spiritual use to ourselves, when we seem to get no good from it, but yet do it all in a manner worthy of the Name of the Lord Jesus.

    c. We must gladly recognise natural calls as the utterance of God's Providence. All things may be sanctified if we listen for the voice of God in them.

POINT III. *Consider that liberality must be without covetousness.*

    a. We give most freely when we are most free from the desires of earthly wealth. Losses of worldly advantage are sent by God to cure our covetousness.

    b. If means are wanting, we must not think complainingly of God. A little, with love of God, will go further than much more if we are out of unity with Him.

    c. However great be the demands of temporal necessity, our souls must long for retirement with God. We cannot use anything properly with God, without desiring to give it up in order to obtain God.

AFFECTIONS. Energy in worldly business.. Detachment from worldly aims.

PRAYER.

O God, of Thy great goodness, enable me so to serve Thee in earthly things that I may find Thee as the true Life of my soul; through Jesus Christ our Lord. Amen.

JUDICIAL FIRMNESS.

PRELUDE. i. *Well done, thou good and faithful servant; thou hast been faithful over a few things, I will make thee ruler over many things: enter thou into the Joy of thy Lord.*—S. Matt. xxv. 21.

ii. The child crying out in the assembly, "Ambrose, Bishop."

POINT I.—*Consider the duty of justice.*

a. We cannot rise to the higher virtues of the Christian life, save by the careful exercise of natural virtues. Grace ennobles and perfects nature, but does not supersede it.

b. The various relationships of outward life ought to call forth so many exhibitions of Divine grace. Grace is one in itself, but manifold as our natural relationships.

c. Natural society is under the ordering of Divine Providence as truly as the Communion of Saints in the order of grace.

POINT II. *Consider the power of tenderness.*

a. The greatest characters will be the most tender. God is Almighty, and God is Love. Tenderness is one of the greatest instruments of true power. Untender firmness may hold back, but not subdue. To subdue we must love.

b. Tenderness is to great as well as to small; removes the sense of superiority, whether in ourselves or in others; calls forth, by sympathy, the Divine Love, which all need alike.

c. Tenderness is as individual as it is universal. It is ready to act towards all, appreciating each case with a discrimination which Divine Love alone can teach.

POINT III. *Consider the necessity of boldness.*

a. The few things in which our faithfulness is tried are often small things. The boldness of faith arises from seeing the greatness which belongs to them, because they belong to God. Perverse stubbornness is not boldness.

b. The things which require our boldness are few, but sufficient to test us. If we fail on those few occasions, we shall not be able to claim the just reward.

c. Boldness is needed in dealing with the good as well as with the vicious. We must not let discipline be relaxed.

AFFECTIONS. Constancy in considering the great judgments. Sympathy in penitence.

PRAYER.

O God, Who requirest us to have mercy upon others, considering our own need of mercy at Thy hands. Open my heart in sympathy towards the necessities of others, and in bold avowal of Thy Sovereign truth, so that I may in all things fulfil the requirements of that justice wherein alone can perfect love be exercised; through Jesus Christ our Lord. Amen.

ARCHBISHOP OF CANTERBURY.—A.D. 1012.

FEARLESSNESS.

PRELUDE. i. *Theirs is the Kingdom of Heaven who have despised the life of this world to gain a reward in the Kingdom, and have washed their robes in the Blood of the Lamb.*—Rev. vii. 14.

ii. The Saint surrounded by the Danes in the massacre at Canterbury.

POINT I. *Consider the Christian's dread of great position.*

a. The worldly heart delights in worldly power as its natural instrument. The Christian regards it a natural enemy, and fears to be weakened thereby.

b. We shall fail of becoming Saints, if we think to become saints by making saints of others. A hermit ruling himself is better than a great leader who fails in self-discipline.

c. We must sanctify all positions of power by much prayer and fasting. Public honours demand great mortification.

POINT II. *Consider the fearlessness of the faithful amidst great dangers.*

a. We must despise the life of this world when it is threatened, rejoicing if it can be offered up to God on behalf of any whom God has entrusted to us.

b. We must urge others to fearlessness by our sympathy and example. If we cannot save life, let us teach how to die.

c. If we would gain the rewards of the Kingdom, we must commend all that we love to the care of the King. Our earthly prayers must outlast our lives, that we may pass to a life of prayer with Jesus in Paradise.

POINT III. *Consider the Vision of the future which is present to the minds of the faithful.*

a. A life of contemplation will read the signs of the times in many ways different from the world at large. The worldly heart is blinded to the future by its worldly hopes.

b. How little should we regard the victories of the wicked if we considered how shortlived they would be. "Fret not thyself." (Ps. xxxvii.)

c. We ought to see future power hidden in present weakness, if we suffer in any way of duty. Suffering loses reward, if we fail to look for it; pain is valueless without faith.

AFFECTIONS. Retirement from the world. Boldness in encountering the world. Hope in God.

PRAYER.

O God, I beseech Thee to grant me so to shrink from all which this world loves, that I may never fear to encounter the hatred of the world in the fellowship of Thy Love, which abideth for ever; through Jesus Christ our Lord. Amen.

CONFLICT WITH SATAN.

PRELUDE. i. *Theirs is the Kingdom of Heaven who have despised the life of this world to gain a reward in the Kingdom, and have washed their robes in the Blood of the Lamb.*—Rev. vii. 14.

ii. The soldiers of Christ in conflict with Satan.

POINT I. *Consider the boldness of expostulation with persecuting power.*

    a. It should not be thought a hard thing to give up any office for the sake of conscience, but rather a blessed thing if we have the opportunity of doing so.

    b. The natural heart finds it hard to suffer at the hands of those who are its paymasters—friends, relations, and the like—yet thus we prove our loyalty to Christ.

    c. Many who are bold towards strangers become dumb, through fear, in their own position. We must speak without fear when duty calls, and be silent when it does not.

POINT II. *Consider our fight with Satan.*

    a. He is an enemy not the less real because he is purely spiritual. When we fall into sins which we hate, it must be our encouragement, as well as our warning, to see in this sin some special nearness of the Evil One.

    b. All are subject to many temptations of the world, and suffer by natural necessity; but Satan especially assaults those who are living closest to Christ.

    c. God shall bruise Satan under our feet shortly, but we must be faithful in the fight as long as it lasts.

POINT III. *Consider the duty of being Christ's soldier everywhere.*

    a. A soldier cannot always choose his battle-field. Christ's soldiers generally fight at a disadvantage against the world.

    b. The object of our fight is not to win the world, but to shake it off. There is always great danger of our being tempted to win it back, when we have nearly rejected it.

    c. All the powers in the world are not so great as Satan, and Satan himself is not so great as Christ. By the power of the Cross we can always claim our freedom, and conquer Satan if we will be true to God.

AFFECTIONS. Courage. Reliance upon God. Perseverance to the end.

PRAYER.

O *Almighty God, grant me so to grasp the Sword of Thy Holy Spirit, that by His Divine Power I may put the enemy to flight, and so to bear the Cross at all times, that I may destroy the power of his tongue when he would swallow me up, and in the end may be found safe in the Kingdom of Thy Love; through Jesus Christ our Lord.* Amen.

THE BEAUTY OF THE RESURRECTION LIFE.

PRELUDE. i. *Thy Saints, O Lord, shall flourish as a lily. Alleluia! And they shall be as a sweet-smelling savour unto Thee. Alleluia!*

ii. A lily planted in the sanctuary of God.

POINT I. *Consider the beauty of the Resurrection.*

a. The body of the Saint comes out of the earth, derived from that which was buried therein, but rising up to the Light of Heaven in new form and colour.

b. The flower is different from the root and from the bud. So the manifestations of the highest life are different in order from those of the present earthly life.

c. The glory of the bloom or of the fruit is the true purpose of the root; and all the excellences of our present nature are only given with a view to their final development in the higher order of the Resurrection.

POINT II. *Consider the identity of the root and of the flower.*

a. God "gives to every seed his own body." The blossom springs from a special law of life inherent in the roots, and so there are special glories in the resurrection corresponding with the special graces possessed below.

b. We cannot trace the identity, nor judge of the one from the other. The most uncouth root may have the loveliest blossom.

c. The identity is one of life. It is not merely a regular succession of phenomena. The Holy Ghost is the Life whereby real grace developes into its proper glory.

POINT III. *Consider the value of the plant.*

a. It does not exist for its own sake, but for the husbandman. So the Saints of Christ do not exist merely in order to be happy, but for the glory of God.

b. The skill of the husbandman is manifest in the culture of the plant. Much more, the glory of God in the beauty of the Resurrection of His Saints.

c. They are made to grow by nourishment that seems altogether alien from their beauty. So the culture of earth differs far from the blossom of Heaven.

AFFECTIONS. Hope of Resurrection. Trust in God's care. Dedication to God's glory.

PRAYER.

O God, Who makest Thy Saints to grow up before Thee upon the earth according to the law of Thy grace, that they may share in the participation of Thine own uncreated loveliness everlastingly, grant me so to cherish Thy Grace, that I may be perfected in Thy will, and find blessing with all Thine Elect according to the special form of Thy predestinating Love; through Jesus Christ our Lord. Amen.

T

THE BLESSEDNESS OF DIVINE LOVE.

PRELUDE. i. *Blessed are the folk that He hath chosen to Him to be His inheritance.* Alleluia!—Ps. xxxiii. 12.

ii. God bidding an angel wait through ages for some soul yet unborn.

POINT I. *Consider the Blessedness of Predestinating Love.*

a. The natural man lives in the opinion others have of him. The new man lives in the knowledge which God has of him. What God knows us to be, that we are.

b. How we rejoice if we find our loved ones long occupied, unknown, in some act of love to us. God has watched us with Love from eternity. Sweet surprise to come to know this! We speak of it here: we shall know it hereafter.

c. Joy is great when prodigals return to love and be loved at home. Great our joy to know God's joy over us in that we come back to what He meant for us.

POINT II. *Consider the Blessedness of the Evangelical Message.*

a. The Evangelists wrote in the power of the Holy Ghost to make known God's covenanted Love in Christ.

b. They tell its blessedness as summed up in Christ, the Head of the Covenant.

c. They tell its blessedness as resulting in a life which is eternal in Christ. Because He lives we shall live also.

POINT III. *Consider the Blessedness of knowing God's Satisfaction in us.*

a. God's knowledge of us is a transforming knowledge. His knowledge makes us what we are. His curse is expressed in the words, "I know you not."

b. Joy is great if a prodigal returns to a loved or loving home. Great our joy to know God's joy at our return to what He so long has purposed for us.

c. If it is a joy to please our earthly parent, how much more to please God.

AFFECTIONS. Childlike love of God. Dependence upon God. Adoration of the Divine wisdom.

PRAYER.

O Almighty God, Who knowest with the contemplation of eternal joy all those to whom Thou makest Thyself known in the fellowship of the Divine Life, grant that I may always remember that Thou hast called me out of the world, so as evermore to live in the power of that Life which Thou hast given; through Jesus Christ our Lord. Amen.

DIVINE CONTEMPLATION IN GLORY.

PRELUDE. i. *Blessed is the people, O Lord, that can rejoice in Thee. they shall walk in the light of Thy countenance. Alleluia.*—Ps. lxxxix. 16.

ii. The pillar of fire a symbol of God's Light irradiating His people.

POINT I. *Consider the Blessedness of the Divine Vision.*

a. The highest enjoyment of man is the contemp.....ion of Truth. Here the fallen intellect is independent of the affections, yet the affections demand a basis of truth. There the truth will be the object of our affections.

b. Here the joy of intellect is in the acquisition of Truth. There our spiritual joy will be in its perfect possession.

c. Here the object of intellect is external—dead. There the truth is the ever-living source of our own life.

POINT II. *Consider the Blessedness of the Divine Reciprocity.*

a. Created truth is not personal; does not rejoice in being a joy to us. God does rejoice in being known and loved by us.

b. This has no power of self-manifestation to those who search into it. God does manifest Himself by His Holy Spirit to those who seek Him.

c. Increasing knowledge here makes man feel increasingly his littleness. Every increase in Divine knowledge brings to us fresh powers of hope. We grow in God, by knowing God.

POINT III. *Consider the Blessedness of the Divine Energy.*

a. God is full of joy in His own Life, by reason of the perfect relationships in which the Divine nature acts eternally.

b. God makes that joy known to us as we contemplate Him in the power of the Holy Ghost. To see His joy, however imperfectly, is our highest joy.

c. God takes us into the Divine Nature at our Baptism, that we may be enabled to contemplate His Light in the true fellowship of His children.

AFFECTIONS. Homage to each Person of the Blessed Trinity. Gratitude for the Manifestation of God in the Flesh. Desire of Heavenly Vision.

PRAYER.

O God, in Whom alone our mind can find the Truth personally manifested as the source and object of Love, grant us so to praise Thee for the Gospel of Thine Only-begotten Son, that we may finally attain to Thy perfect fruition ; through the same Thy Son Jesus Christ our Lord. Amen.

PARADISE.

PRELUDE. i. *O ye spirits and souls of the Righteous : bless ye the Lord.* Alleluia.

ii. The Light of Jesus surrounding the faithful departed.

POINT I. *Consider the Blessedness of Grace remembered.*

  a. They praise God for all that He has done for them, in creation, redemption, and sanctification.

  b. They praise God for the discipline of earth, by which He has drawn them away from the world.

  c. They praise God for all that He has done in them, acknowledging every good thing in their past life to be His, not theirs. What in them is His remains : what was theirs is gone.

POINT II. *Consider the Blessedness of Security possessed.*

  a. They praise God for having brought them safely out of the land of the enemy, wherein they were so often in danger.

  b. They praise God for sheltering them in so much peace, while their brethren are accomplishing their struggle upon the earth.

  c. They praise God for the vision of that security which, amidst the struggles of earth, is so often clouded by unworthy fears.

POINT III. *Consider the Blessedness of Glory contemplated.*

  a. They praise God for the manifestation of His own Triune Glory as far as they behold it ; the glory which God has in Himself.

  b. They praise God for the spiritual faculties which operate within them freely, now that the incumbrance of the flesh ceases to clog them.

  c. They praise God for the glory wherein their flesh shall be glorified as the Flesh of Christ, in Whom even now their souls are living, and rejoice to wait for the resurrection.

AFFECTIONS. Spiritual Life in Christ. Desire to be with Him. Love of the faithful departed.

PRAYER.

O God, Who bringest the souls of Thy faithful ones out of the misery of earth to wait in Thy glory unto the day of resurrection, then to receive the reward of that which Thou hast wrought in them, grant us so to join our prayers and praises to those of Paradise, that in the end we may praise Thee with all Thy Saints in Thy Heavenly Kingdom ; through Jesus Christ our Lord. Amen.

REST.

PRELUDE. i. *There remaineth a rest for the people of God. Alleluia.*—Heb. iv. 9.

ii. The blessed souls, conscious of the Light around them as being the arm of God which sustains them.

POINT I. *Consider the end of toil.*

a. The end of vexation. Here the faithful soul must ever be as Lot, vexed at the sins around. In Paradise is rest.

b. The end of temptation. Here our enemies tempt us, specially they who seem our friends, to forsake God. There no one even in thought goes away from Him.

c. The end of struggle. Here we have to serve God in a constant war. There no enemy comes near.

POINT II. *Consider the Sabbath of the Blessed.*

a. The Sabbath of joy wherein the Creator ever dwells is the contemplation of that which He has done.

b. God hallowing this Sabbath. The faithful must partake of the Divine holiness while resting therein. There is perfect energy, but no weariness.

c. The sweetness of present repose, as contrasted with previous struggle.

POINT III. *Consider the people of God who enter in.*

a. God has chosen them, and called them out of the world.

b. They have chosen God, and have not shrunk from the terms of His Covenant.

c. God has dwelt in them upon the earth, and makes them now to know the joy of reposing upon Him as their centre.

AFFECTIONS. Diligence to gain admission. Rest in God's Promises. Tranquillity in anticipation.

PRAYER.

O God, Who hast provided a holy rest in Thyself for all Thy Saints, grant me so to exert the powers which Thou hast given me for Thy service here, that I may find my repose in the welcome of Thy glory there; through Jesus Christ our Lord. Amen.

ETERNAL LIGHT.

PRELUDE. i. *Light Eternal shall shine upon Thy Saints*, O Lord, *and length of days.* Alleluia.

ii. The glory of God filling the Heavenly temple.

POINT I. *Consider the Light of the Resurrection.*

    a. The mysterious life of the Saints who rose with Christ during the Forty Days. They were pilgrims on earth before He came. Now earth is no more a home for them than before. They live in the light of God, and the darkness is past.

    b. The Light of grace, which fills the souls of the baptized. There is the light of the body and the light of the intellect, and the Light of grace. The two former pass away. The last is eternal.

    c. The Light of glory. As the darkness, the moonlight, starlight, twilight, give way to the full day, so the darkness of earth to the Light of Heaven. Grace is glory begun.

POINT II. *Consider the Eternity of this Light.*

    a. It is eternal in itself, unchanging. With God there is no variableness neither shadow of turning.

    b. With us it is conditional. We must abide in the Light, otherwise we shall lose it. We abide in it by the exercise of the spiritual faculties which deal with it.

    c. This Light shall be our eternal glory if we continue in it. Our nature must be perfected in the fellowship thereof.

POINT III. *Consider the joy of this Light.*

    a. To our imperfect nature its brightness is dazzling. We can only by degrees attain to conceive it. We shrink from it. It is not a perfection of nature, but above nature.

    b. While our nature remains imperfect, we are incapable of its fulness. Even the souls of the Blessed cannot have it in its perfection until the Resurrection. Yet even we on earth have a real participation in it.

    c. Humanity shall be perfected in superhuman joy as befits the members of the Incarnate God, by the true fruition of this Light continually. In my flesh shall I see God. We shall be like Him, for we shall see Him as He is.

AFFECTIONS. Joy in union with the risen Saviour. Anticipation of the Eternal Joy of God's Presence.

PRAYER.

O *God, Who hast formed me to be perfected in the contemplation of Thine Eternal glory, grant that I may approach Thee in the fulness of the power of the Resurrection of Thine Only-begotten Son, according to the blessed invitation of Thy grace, so that I may rise to the perfect apprehension of Thy glory hereafter, according to the full purpose of Thy Love; through Jesus Christ our Lord.* Amen.

MAN'S DESIRE FOR GOD.

PRELUDE. i. *Lord, show us the Father, and it sufficeth us. Alleluia.*—S. John xiv. 8.

ii. S. Philip addressing these words to our Lord.

POINT I. *Consider the natural desire of man to see God.*

a. As man was made in God's Image, he feels his own want, unless he truly reflect the glory of God, which ought to be his life.

b. The nearer we come to God, the more shall we feel this need. Christ's presence with His Apostles awakened this longing more intensely than it ever was felt before.

c. Philosophy seeks to know the law of causation. Love desires to know the Father, the Blessed Fount of Godhead, and the Author of all creation.

POINT II. *Consider the belief in Christ's power to show the Father.*

a. Christ's Presence could not have awakened the desire unless there were in Him a true capacity of declaring the Divine Nature. The Word is Co-equal with the Father.

b. The Glory of God is actively present in Christ, not as a Truth shut up in a Book, but as a Life filling all His faculties, and perfectly known by Himself while He acts in this power.

c. He comes on earth on purpose to declare the Father to us, the Word Incarnate, speaking in our flesh,—engrafted, speaking individually in those whom He makes His members. (S. James i.)

POINT III. *Consider the sufficiency of that Vision to satisfy the soul.*

a. As man is created in God's Image, there is no element of desire within him which does not find its satisfaction in the sight of God.

b. The soul of man has desires which reach out infinitely. They are not indefinite. They are for God. The infinite glory of God gives them rest.

c. God is the source of all created joy; and the creatures find their joy in proportion as they attain to the knowledge of Him. He gives all joy, and is greater than any of His gifts.

AFFECTIONS. Desire for God. Looking to Christ. Disregard of all else except as a means of seeing Him.

PRAYER.

O Lord God, Who hast filled our souls with the deep longing for Thy manifestation, grant us so to look to Thine Only-begotten Son, that we, receiving the revelation which He brings, and rejoicing in the hope to which He calls us, may at length attain to the full vision of Thy glory, and rest in Thee as the true End of our Being; through the same Jesus Christ our Lord. Amen.

CHRIST SATISFYING MAN'S DESIRE.

PRELUDE. i. *He that hath seen Me, hath seen the Father.* Alleluia.—S. John xiv. 9.

ii. Christ speaking these words.

POINT I. *Consider what it is to see Christ.*

a. Those alone see Christ who see Him as Christ, know what He is. The mere external vision of human fellowship is only blindness.

b. The relationships which exist within the Eternal Trinity are not accidental to the Divine Persons as human relationships are to us. Their Personality consists in these relationships, and we cannot see any one of the Divine Persons alone, as if existing separately from the other two.

c. We do not see Christ unless we know Him as the Son of God, and united with the Father in the Person of the Holy Ghost Who proceeds from Them Both.

POINT II. *Consider the Consubstantial Godhead of the Father and the Son.*

a. Their Eternal Unity is a Unity not of weakness and sterility, but of power and fruitfulness.

b. It is a Unity of perfect mutual delight. If we would see the Son, we must come to the knowledge of the ineffable delight which the Father takes in Him.

c. The Son of God were not worthy of this delight, if He were not truly one in substance with the Father, for the Father cannot give His glory to any one who is apart from Himself.

POINT III. *Consider the power of the Holy Ghost, whereby alone the Father can be seen.*

a. Only by the power of the Holy Ghost can we know the things of God, and the glory of the Eternal Mysteries.

b. Not by change on God's part, lowering Him to us, but by change in ourselves, elevating us to Him, must we come to see the things of the Holy Ghost.

c. The Godhead which is in Christ, the Holy Ghost "takes and shows" unto us, by making us partakers of the Divine Nature.

AFFECTIONS. Gratitude for our Divine adoption. Energy in the exercise of this Holy Sonship.

PRAYER.

O God, Whose Blessed Son was manifested in our nature, being conceived by the Holy Ghost, grant that I may contemplate His glory in Thyself, and by the power of the same Eternal Spirit may be led onward to live in oneness of life with Him, so that in Thine undivided glory I may find the perfect fruition of Thy Love; through the same Jesus Christ our Lord. Amen.

THE MEDIATION OF CHRIST.

PRELUDE. i. *I am the Way, the Truth, and the Life*; *no man cometh unto the Father but by Me.* Alleluia.—S. John xiv. 6.

ii. The Body of Christ as an Orb of living Light, in which the soul is drawn onward to the full brightness of its central principle.

POINT I. *Consider our need of access to God.*

a. It is not enough to see God afar off. Such vision only teaches man how utterly he is outcast.

b. Man must come near to God. God has shown himself to man, coming in the Flesh. Now man must rise above his natural position. God's humiliation is useless without man's elevation.

c. All whereby we seem to rise in creation only shows us how incapable we are of really coming any nearer to God. We only see the intervening steps of creation the more clearly.

POINT II. *Consider the impossibility of coming to God except through Christ.*

a. No creature can lay hold upon God, and therefore no creature can help his neighbour to lay hold upon God.

b. All that come before Christ are thieves and robbers, making professions which ensnare their followers, but incapable of bringing them to salvation.

c. Many attempt to come to God without Christ, but the sincerity of their pious purpose does not avail to accomplish a result which is beyond their strength.

POINT III. *Consider the true Life whereby Christ brings us to God.*

a. He is the Way, not merely a connection between us and God, but a Way; so that being joined to Him we are led onward till we are perfected in God.

b. He is the Life, the living Way, so that as we advance in the Way, we advance to a higher manifestation of Life with God.

c. He is the Truth, the true, the only Life. What seems like Life outside of Him is only reflection of His glory. The only true Life is the Life of, and in, the Only-begotten Son.

AFFECTIONS. Praise to Christ for His mediation. Desire of fuller knowledge of Christ's Life.

PRAYER.

O God, in Whom alone true Life is to be found, grant us so to approach Thee, through the grace of Thine Only-begotten Son, that we may attain to live with Thee eternally as Thy true children, to the glory of Thy Holy Name; through the same Thy Son Jesus Christ our Lord. Amen.

THE VOICE OF RIGHTEOUSNESS.

PRELUDE. i. *O ye spirits and souls of the righteous, bless ye the Lord.* Alleluia.

ii. The Blessed Spirits in the Throne and round about.

POINT I. *Consider the joy of the righteous souls.*

a. They feel the Life of God filling them. The Just in Christ live by faith. When they leave the Body, they find that Life which the corruptible Body oppressed before.

b. They feel the wisdom of God illuminating them. They not only live, but they know what it is to live. The Divine Consciousness fills them.

c. They praise the Father. They live with the Life of the Son of God, and therefore are ever mindful of the Father as the Fountain of their life.

POINT II. *Consider the utterance of the Righteous Souls.*

a. They speak with the Spirit of Christ, whereby they are justified. Their righteousness is itself an uncontrollable utterance of praise.

b. The Spirit of Christ is the Holy Ghost. The Righteousness of Christ wherewith they live is an energy worthy of God, for it is truly Divine.

c. The Holy Ghost Who thus speaks through them in the very act of their Life is the Bond of the Eternal Trinity. They bless God in the utterance of the Eternal Love.

POINT III. *Consider the Object which the Righteous Souls address.*

a. It is God Himself. They praise God, as they know that they come from Him. Cry of gratitude ! Whatever be their outward condition, it is glorious with the glory of God.

b. Their praise reaches the Ear of God, for it is spoken in the power of the Spirit of His Only-begotten Son.

c. It is a changeless utterance of Eternal Life, never wearying, never exhausted, never capable of silence : for silence were death, and death is sin.

AFFECTIONS. Praise to God for Divine life in Christ. Fellowship with the Saints.

PRAYER.

O Lord God, in Whose praise the Righteous live for evermore, grant me so to show forth Thy praise in this condition of earthly life, that I may find every longing of earth perfected in the blessed song of the Redeemed, and praise Thee hereafter with an utterance worthy of Thyself; through the same Jesus Christ our Lord. Amen.

CONTINUANCE IN CHRIST.

PRELUDE. *i. If ye abide in Me, and My words abide in you, ye shall ask what ye will, and it shall be done unto you. Alleluia.*—S. John xv. 7.

ii. The soul as a mouthpiece of the Body of Christ through which the Holy Ghost speaks.

POINT I. *Consider what it is to abide in Christ.*

a. We must abide in Christ with our whole nature, not merely with fruitless aspirations, but with integrity of conduct.

b. Christ's words must abide in us as the constraining law of our being, in all the power of the Holy Ghost.

c. This mutual indwelling is a real identity of Life, whereby we live in oneness of thought and desire along with Jesus.

POINT II. *Consider the power of prayer.*

a. Prayer in Christ is the utterance of praise calling forth the manifestation of the Divine power.

b. We can will nothing but what is Christ's will: else we should cease to abide in Him. Our will calls the will of Christ into action externally. He prays in us, and He fulfils our prayer.

c. Prayer is the voice of Christ, Who speaks universally through His Body, but it is uttered according to the individual need of each soul that lives conscious in Him.

POINT III. *Consider the Father's blessing on the Righteous Souls in Christ.*

a. What they desire, He gives. They cannot desire what is evil. He cannot withhold what is good.

b. The more we ask, the more God is glorified.

c. The energy of prayer will depend upon the perfection of active discipline, whereby the soul has been brought into the fellowship of the Life of Christ.

AFFECTIONS. Gratitude. Desire. Obedience.

PRAYER.

O Almighty God, Who givest whatsoever we ask in Thy Son's Name, grant us so to live in the Truth of that Sonship, that by the merits of His Passion we may obtain the gifts of glory which Thou hast foreordained, so that the kingdom of Thy dear Son may be hastened, and we and Thy Saints may have our perfect consummation and bliss; through the same Jesus Christ our Lord. Amen.

THE MANSIONS PREPARED.

PRELUDE. i. *Let not your heart be troubled: ye believe in God, believe also in Me. In My Father's house are many mansions. Alleluia.*—S. John xiv. 1, 2.

ii. Our Lord Jesus speaking these words.

POINT I. *Consider the joy of heart which belongs to a true reliance.*

 a. God will watch as carefully over those whom we love though they die, as if they lived. In fact they do live more truly. We who live to this dead world are dead.

 b. Their leaving us must only serve to quicken our expectation of that better life which awaits us.

 c. Every form of trouble shall have its specialty of reward in the life which is to come. Pains pass away from the children of God; the glory which they effect abides for ever.

POINT II. *Consider the Divine Sonship.*

 a. The Son is Lord over His Father's House. All that belongs to the Father is His.

 b. The Christian revelation only makes the same demands upon our faith which natural religion does. Our relation to God by nature is no more manifest to sense than is our relation to Christ by grace. In both cases we must accept the unseen.

 c. The knowledge of God without Christ must be to us a source of trouble. The knowledge of Redeeming Love gives peace and joy.

POINT III. *Consider the abiding character of the rest which remaineth.*

 a. The present life is not a mansion. It is only a temporary state of discipline. Our hearts demand that which is permanent.

 b. Our relation to Christ cannot be a transitory one; for though we are so changeable, yet the Son abideth for ever. He makes us, therefore, partakers of His unchangeableness by uniting us with Himself.

 c. If our relation to Christ were a matter of natural sense, it would be transitory. It is eternal, because it is a matter of faith, even as all our relations to God.

AFFECTIONS. Rest in Christ. Hope. Detachment.

PRAYER.

O God, Who hast given Thine Only-begotten Son to be associated with us in the things of earth, that He may bring us by His Resurrection to the fellowship of that Life which endureth for ever, fill our hearts, we beseech Thee, with joy and peace, that we may find rest amidst our present difficulties, in the hope of attaining to Thine eternal glory; through Jesus Christ our Lord. Amen.

GLORYING IN THE CROSS.

PRELUDE. i. *The Kingdom of Heaven is like unto a treasure hid in a field.* Alleluia.—S. Matt. xiii. 44.

ii. As in the Parable.

POINT I. *Consider the hiddenness of the Cross of Christ.*

a. Christ has a cross for us. It is buried in the earth, as that which S. Helena found. We have to find it, each for himself, amidst the events of the daily life. Life were indeed worthless without this.

b. We must look for the cross of Christ in daily life, not shrinking from it as an evil, but welcoming it as a treasure.

c. A Queen discovered the Cross of old. We are now made kings and queens by finding it. If we suffer, we shall reign with Christ. We honour it truly if we suffer thereon.

POINT II. *Consider the manifestation of the Cross of Christ.*

a. By nature we are diseased. The Cross of Christ effected universal redemption. If we find the Cross, we shall be healed.

b. To find the Cross of Christ is the great Wisdom. We need supernatural grace to see it. When it is found it becomes to us a source of constant illumination. Fellowship with Christ in His Passion, teaches us more than can be learnt otherwise.

c. The Cross of Christ shall be manifested in the great day as the glory of all who have suffered thereon whilst here.

POINT III. *Consider the glory of the Cross of Christ.*

a. While we are in this world, it involves us in shame. The world knows it not, nor us, nor Him Who hung thereon.

b. We have to choose the glory of the world, or the glory of the Cross. Satan will often try and deceive us.

c. When its glory shall be manifested in the great Eastertide of the Resurrection, it is a glory which shall never pass away. Treasures of earth are then lost. The treasure whereby we are set free from earth lasts on for ever.

AFFECTIONS. Glorying in the Cross. Thankfulness. Desire to follow Christ.

PRAYER.

O *Blessed* Lord, *Who gavest Thyself to be for us a perfect sacrifice upon the Cross, and didst call us to be conformed to Thine example of suffering while sharing in the benefits of Thy redemption, grant that I may never shrink from the Cross, but rather may esteem it as my richest treasure amongst all the things of earth, and may be accepted by the Father to suffer along with Thee, by the power of the Holy Ghost, even as Thou by the same Spirit didst offer Thyself for me, and hast purchased on the Cross a Kingdom where Thy faithful followers shall reign with Thee for ever; for Thy mercies' sake.* Amen.

THE MARTYR-BAPTISM.

PRELUDE i. *The Apostle John, being plunged into a vessel of boiling oil, by Divine mercy came forth unharmed.* Alleluia.

ii. The miracle as narrated.

POINT I. *Consider S. John's devotion to Martyrdom.*

a. He had accepted our Lord's appeal to him, and had vowed himself ready to share the Martyr's baptism. This he did, trusting in the grace by which our Lord Jesus Christ would strengthen him.

b. He knew that he could not have the nearness to Christ hereafter, without that fellowship in suffering here. ·

c. He had used the grace which Christ had given him, so as to persevere hitherto, and was now looking forward to seeing again the Lord he loved.

POINT II. *Consider him now being cast into a cauldron of boiling oil.*

a. The oil symbolized to his mind the gift of the Holy Ghost, and the fervour of Divine love. He was indeed to be anointed.

b. He could not shrink from the pain, for he knew it to be the fulfilment of his Lord's covenanted promise, and it therefore contained for Him an assurance of victory.

c. He looked to Jesus to come and help him, in such way as should be best.

POINT III. *Consider his deliverance.*

a. Not for his own sake, but for God's glory. The brief remnant of life which was left, was not of value to him in itself. Rather he would have rejoiced to go to Jesus.

b. He was left a while on earth, to suffer yet more.

c. The intimations of prophecy must be verified. Jesus Christ was to come to him to fetch him. Therefore he must be delivered by Divine Providence from any danger of violent death, however imminent.

AFFECTIONS. Zeal. Trust. Love to Jesus. Contempt of the world.

PRAYER.

O Lord Jesu, open Thou mine eyes in every time of difficulty to look up to Thee, that I may fearlessly encounter every opposition, assured that Thou canst give me deliverance, and may joyfully accept whatever Thy Providence shall determine, content to bear the struggle of life on earth if Thou ordain it, but longing to depart and be with Thee in Thy glory as soon as Thou in Thy great mercy shalt appoint; Who with the Father and the Holy Ghost livest and reignest, one God, world without end. Amen.

ARCHBISHOP OF CANTERBURY.—A.D. 988.

CHRIST OUR LIGHT.

PRELUDE. i. *Light Eternal shall shine on Thy Saints, O Lord, and length of days.* Alleluia.

ii. The Blessed in the glory of Christ's Presence.

POINT I. *Consider the Light of Christ's Body.*

a. The glory of God shines from Him. All the Angels shine in His brightness. His lustre fills the Heavenly Jerusalem.

b. It is a sustaining Light. Instead of consuming that wherein it shines, it is the power which preserves all from decay.

c. It is a quickening Light. It is the Life of men. Those who abide therein are elevated to a consciousness of glory proportionate to their participation therein.

POINT II. *Consider the Light of holy souls.*

a. The souls of the faithful are not separated from the Body of Christ, although they are separated from their own bodies for a season. This is the House not made with hands wherein they dwell, the City of Holy Light.

b. As they dwell in this Light, so they shine therewith. The outer nature hid its glory on earth. Now the corruptible body is removed, and the glory of Jesus shines.

c. In this Light they glorify Him. They clung to Him by faith when they were on earth. Now they rejoice in a more perfect fellowship of Love.

POINT III. *Consider the Light of the Resurrection Body.*

a. This Light shall shine through their resurrection bodies yet more brightly. The soul without the body lacks the proper instrument of expression, although it abides in the glorious Body of Christ.

b. The acts done in the body upon earth constitute the measure of perfection wherein the risen body shall be able to show forth the glory of Christ eternally.

c. In the Resurrection it will be manifest how the Body of Christ infused into our bodies at Baptism, and our Food in the Holy Eucharist, lives in each of His members, so that they have no life but His being one with Him.

AFFECTIONS. Exultation in Christ. Longing for Christ's Kingdom. Love to all that are in Christ.

PRAYER.

O Almighty God, grant that I may rise up in holy contemplation to the glory wherein Thou hast called me to live ; and although I cannot now behold Thy Light, strengthen me to walk so worthily of Thy children by the power of Thy grace, that in the great day I may rise in the glory of that Heavenly Light; through Jesus Christ our Lord, Who liveth and reigneth with Thee and with the Holy Ghost one God for ever and ever. Amen.

ARCHBISHOP OF CANTERBURY.—A.D. 604.

THE GLORY OF THE FAITHFUL IN CHRIST.

PRELUDE. i. *Light Eternal shall shine on Thy Saints, O Lord, and length of days.* Alleluia.

ii. The members of Christ's Body manifest in their eternal relationships of glory.

POINT I. *Consider the blessedness of having made ventures for Christ.*

a. Each act of faith lives on in the Resurrection as an act whereby the Life of Christ has been exercised and His glory appropriated.

b. The life of faith is beyond the understanding of the world, but the rewards of that life shall be manifest to the eyes of all men.

c. The Love wherewith the faithful shall rejoice in Christ eternally, is the consummation of that Love which has grown to its perfection by repeated acts on earth.

POINT II. *Consider the blessedness of having brought souls to Christ.*

a. Those who have spoken in Christ's Name will be in Heaven with all who have received His word at their lips, and all will abide in one community of holy joy.

b. There will be a closer fellowship between those who are thus related in the Heavenly Life than there is between earthly parents and their offspring upon earth. Here there is separation. There the individual life remains in a perfect unity of corporate life.

c. The joy of Christ, which is the strength of all, is the bond of all, and circulates through the abiding relationship of those who are the members of His glorified Body.

POINT III. *Consider the Eternity of this Blessedness.*

a. The activity of the Body of Christ never wearies. The Love which binds its members together operates for ever and ever with a ceaseless delight of mutual contemplation.

b. Christ Himself, as the Head of the Body, makes His Light to shine through all His members with a living consciousness of His Divine glory as their Bond of unity.

c. The Love wherewith the Father loveth the Son is communicated to each one of His members, so that they rejoice in the glory of the Eternal Trinity by the power of the H. G.

AFFECTIONS. Joy in the Divine Life. Abasement before the Divine Love. Confidence in the Divine call.

PRAYER.

O God, Who hast called us out of darkness into the kingdom of Thy dear Son, grant that I may ever abide in the Truth of Thy Heavenly Kingdom, and, serving Thee faithfully upon earth, may attain to the perfect joy of Thy Love for ever in Heaven; through Jesus Christ our Lord. Amen.

A.D. 735.

LEARNING.

PRELUDE. i. *Light Eternal shall shine on Thy Saints, O Lord, and length of days.* Alleluia.

ii. The Saints praying to God while studying His Truth.

POINT I. *Consider the value of human learning.*

a. Not for sake of distinction amongst men, but for the purpose of approaching God with true devotion.

b. In itself valueless : if used for heavenly purposes, beyond all value.

c. Created things are God's work, and our knowledge of them must be a real help towards knowing Him. Else it is no true learning.

POINT II. *Consider the energy of true learning.*

a. It is the Light of the living day, cheered with the glory of the risen Saviour. Things are known truly, when they are known in the Light of the Eternal.

b. A life of true learning is like the Vigil of the Ascension, on which Feast V. Bede died. It waits to be changed into the Vision of the glory which it anticipates.

c. True learning strengthens the soul for prayer. It makes all life to be a Rogation day. What we know of God's works makes us long for further manifestations of His power.

POINT III. *Consider the Eternity of true learning.*

a. We learn truly only by spiritual experience. The learning of the natural mind has no hold upon Truth. What we learn must be our Life. We know it not unless we live by it.

b. We may lose Eternal Life, because we have not fully grasped it. But, then, whatever we have known about it, we have not learnt it, for we are not transformed into it.

c. False ideas of truth, however sincere, hinder the soul. The experiences of true Divine learning are the very beginnings of the Eternal fruition and Vision of God.

AFFECTIONS. Zeal for truth. Joy in possessing it. Diligence in communicating it.

PRAYER.

O God, Who hast given Thy truth to be the delight of our hearts, that we may live thereby, grant that I may diligently seek Thee, so that by the power of Thy Holy Spirit, I may live for ever in the satisfaction of Thy Heavenly Vision; through Jesus Christ our Lord. Amen.

U

(Date doubtful.)

MUTUAL VISION OF SAINTS.

PRELUDE. i. *Light Eternal shall shine on Thy Saints, O Lord, and length of days.* Alleluia.

ii. The joy of Saints living in Christ.

POINT I. *Consider the absence of mutual knowledge upon earth.*

a. How many are isolated by sickness, poverty, social circumstances ! Yet solitude does not separate any from the Communion of Saints, the Life of the Holy Ghost, in the Body of Christ, if they only live with Christ in God.

b. Of those who know one another, how few possess true knowledge. The knowledge vouchsafed to us in Christ shall no longer be superficial.

c. Time or distance separate many, so that we know not one another even by name. All such hindrance will be no more. We shall know all even as Christ knows all.

POINT II. *Consider the interest which the members of Christ take one in the other.*

a. All feel together, as members of one Body. The joy of each is the joy of all. There are no selfish interests or desires.

b. Their joy in themselves is by reason of the Holy Ghost, the Spirit of Christ, Who shines forth within them everlastingly.

c. Their joy in one another is by the Divine knowledge which the Holy Spirit effects, binding them together with more intimate communion than any human experience.

POINT III. *Consider how all are known to God.*

a. However obscure their earthly position, they are the children of the Light, and abide in the fulness of the Divine consciousness.

b. The Light of the Divine Presence is the loving knowledge wherewith God welcomes them to be made perfect in Himself, as they live with the Life of the Only-begotten Son.

c. The Light wherewith they see is the very same indwelling Light whereby they are manifest to others. They rejoice in the Life of God, which they possess, by the very same act wherewith they rejoice in one another. All are one in Christ Jesus.

AFFECTIONS. Joy in the Saints. Gratitude for the Life of God. Thanksgiving for the children of Light.

PRAYER.

O Everliving God, Who hast called me into the fellowship of Thine Eternal Light in the Body of Thine Only-begotten Son, grant that I may so abide in Thine illuminating grace, that I may attain to the glorious knowledge of Thy Love, manifested in all Thy Saints; through Jesus Christ our Lord. Amen.

ARCHBISHOP OF MENTZ.—A.D. 755.

MISSIONARY ZEAL.

PRELUDE i. *Light Eternal shall shine on Thy Saints, O Lord, and length of days.* Alleluia.

ii. Boniface setting sail from Hampshire for Friesland.

POINT I. *Consider the Divine impulse of Missionary Enterprize.*

    a. It is for the communication of Eternal Life, the manifestation of Eternal Light to men, who are sitting in darkness.

    b. It can only be by the Holy Ghost. It is in vain to speak of light to the blind. So to preach of Christ is vain without the Holy Ghost sent down from Heaven, Who will open their eyes to see that of which the preacher tells.

    c. The light which dawns in the work of Missions, is the very same which shall shine in the Noonday of Eternity.

POINT II. *Consider the co-operation of the Holy Ghost in all Mission Work.*

    a. His eternal Procession constitutes the Personal glory of God the Son, in union with the Father. Therefore, whatever the Son does, He does by the power of the Holy Ghost. The Holy Ghost proceeding from His Person anoints His members, His acts, His ministers.

    b. Mission Life is quickened by His Presence acting in all things, not merely blessed by His consecration of the ministration when done.

    c. The person of the Mission Priest is, as it were, the dress with which the Holy Ghost clothes Himself, in order to communicate the gift of life.

POINT III. *Consider the Blessedness of Mission Life.*

    a. In its origin. The Holy Spirit proceeds. He is a self-diffusing Spirit, even as the light which symbolizes Him. We cannot know this Spirit unless we live true to His law of diffusion. .

    b. In its power. Earthly acts may fail. The power of the Holy Ghost is all-sufficient. We can never fail if we work with Him.

    c. In its issue. The manifestation of the Divine Light on earth prepares us for the fruition of the Divine Light eternally in Heaven.

AFFECTIONS. Zeal for the spread of the Gospel. Confidence in the all-sufficiency of the Holy Ghost.

PRAYER.

O God, Who hast sent down the Spirit of Thy Son into our hearts, grant that as I know Thee now in the fellowship of this Holy Spirit, so I may bring others to the same Fellowship, and may hereafter have my full participation in the glory of Thine Eternal Light with all Thy Saints ; through Jesus Christ our Lord. Amen.

A.D. 303.

HOSPITALITY.

PRELUDE. i. *Theirs is the Kingdom of Heaven who have despised the life of this world to gain a reward in the Kingdom ; and have washed their robes in the Blood of the Lamb.*—Rev. vii. 14.

ii. The stream dividing to let the Saint pass to his Martyrdom.

POINT I. *Consider his welcome of the Priest.*

   a. The welcome of shelter. He was not kept from receiving him by any fear of danger or scorn.

   b. The welcome of regard. He could reverence the devotions of his guest even before he had come to accept his religion. By seeing how God was loved, he came to love God himself.

   c. The welcome of life. He gave his life for Jesus and saved the life of his guest. Truly he obtained the promise for receiving a Prophet, and received a Prophet's reward.

POINT II. *Consider his Confession of Christ.*

   a. Before the judge. He recognized a tribunal of greater power and authority than the Roman Emperor.

   b. In the endurance of pain. The scourging did not shake his constancy, but rather served to develop within him a supernatural joy.

   c. Before the vast multitude. How will they all behold him at the last day !

POINT III. *Consider his Martyrdom.*

   a. The throng of people that follow. Few knew that they were leading him forth to Paradise. Blessed they who could see the Divine power glorifying him in this struggle.

   b. The stream drying up for him to pass over, symbolizes his death as a new Exodus. Surely now did the terrors of the stream of death dry up before Him.

   c. The executioner becomes a convert. As he rejoiced to share his earthly home with the Priest, so he rejoices to bring the soldier to his heavenly home.

AFFECTIONS. Generosity. Boldness. Love of Truth.

PRAYER.

O God, Who hast called Thy servants by laying down their lives to bear witness to thy Holy Name, grant that we may not shrink from confessing Thee through fear of aught that man can do against us, but rather may rejoice to look upward to Thee for the manifestation of Thy power; through Jesus Christ our Lord. Amen.

HONOURS TO THE DEAD.

PRELUDE. i. *Theirs is the Kingdom of Heaven who have despised the life of this world to gain a reward in the Kingdom, and have washed their robes in the Blood of the Lamb.*—Rev. vii. 14.

ii. The young King's body receiving the honours of stately burial.

POINT I. *Consider how God honours His Saints.*

a. He rewards after death those who have not received their reward during life. Why are we so anxious to prevent God rewarding us, by seeking honours during life from fellow-men?

b. Even worldly honours are in God's disposal, and He can give them as may suit His purposes.

c. He cannot reward any but the dead, for unless we are dead to the world, its honours are to us as the devil's gifts, not God's. We should regard the world's honours as a State funeral.

POINT II. *Consider the changeableness of outward power.*

a. Whether it be for us or against us, it will soon pass away. We shall be judged not by its actions to us, but by ours to it.

b. The tyranny of the wicked passes away. When we see posthumous honours given to the good, we must think of the greater honours of Paradise.

c. The only lasting good thing which the world can do to us, while living, is to kill us. What are its honours to the dead?

POINT III. *Consider the translation of the dead body.*

a. From one tomb to another. How heedless it is of its resting-place! What a type of Christian life!

b. It remains but a mass of corruption wherever they carry it. No worldly honours can make us better than we are.

c. The Resurrection will be a change not so much of place as of state. The bodies of the Saints shall be glorified in the Body of Christ for ever.

AFFECTIONS. Disregard of the world. Deadness to its honours. Hope of resurrection.

PRAYER.

Grant us, O Lord, we beseech Thee, so to be dead to this evil world that, our souls being detached from it now, our bodies may also be translated out of it by Thy power in the glory of the Resurrection; through Jesus Christ our Lord. Amen.

THE FULNESS OF TIME.

PRELUDE. i. *Elizabeth's full time came that she should be delivered, and she brought forth a son, John Baptist, the Forerunner of the* Lord.—S. Luke i. 57.

ii. As in the Gospel.

POINT I. *Consider the order of Nature.*

a. Even when exerting special powers, God subjects them to the order of nature. The Birth of the Baptist was miraculous, but it must be in the fulness of time.

b. We are not to doubt God's working with us because things seem to move but slowly.

c. God knows when anything will be wanted, and He sets things in motion sufficiently long beforehand to ensure all being ready at the fitting time.

POINT II. *Consider the insufficiency of natural result.*

a. A child born. How ordinary, how insignificant an event! Who can tell how the child shall grow? God knoweth.

b. God endued this child from the very first with the qualities which should naturally develope, so as to meet the requirements of his position. We must trust in God to give what is wanted, however He may hide it.

c. God's working in grace is as imperceptible as it is in nature. Man likes startling changes. God acts in quietness.

POINT III. *Consider the relation between Nature and Grace.*

a. The barrenness of nature must be acknowledged before God will give special grace. We must not look for grace to perfect nature, but to supplant it.

b. Men must be true to God in the way of nature if they would witness the germination of grace.

c. God uses each age as the forerunner of some greater future, if only we are faithful to act in the power of the Holy Ghost.

AFFECTIONS. Hope. Quietness. Reverence for small indications of God's will.

PRAYER.

O God, Who didst send Thy servant John Baptist to be wonderfully born, grant that we may always look to find the abundance of Thy grace in the hour of greatest need, and in forms of smallest appearance, so that we may recognize Thy will as it is declared to us by the events of Thy Providence; through Jesus Christ our Lord. Amen.

THE GIFT OF GRACE.

PRELUDE. i. *They made signs to his father, how he would have him called: and he asked for a writing-table, and wrote, saying, His name is John.*—S. Luke i. 62, 63.

ii. The name of John : *i.e.*, the grace of God.

POINT I. *Consider the necessity of preventing grace.*

a. Its supernatural origin. We should not be fit to receive Christ unless there were the Mission of S. John to prepare the way for Him. The powers of man do not avail of themselves to approach to God.

b. Its teaching power. We cannot accept atoning Love unless Divine grace points to the Lamb of God. Penitence else were blinded in pride.

c. Its cleansing power. Divine grace trains us in penitence that we may give ourselves up to be the true followers of the Lamb. Contrition is the work of grace, and without contrition we cannot come to Christ.

POINT II. *Consider the promise of grace.*

a. The Angel had announced the birth of this child, and the name which belonged to him by Divine appointment. Grace will be promised to us in ways which seem to be impossible. God will effect what He foretells.

b. If we fail of corresponding with the promises of grace, punishment is a mercy. We must not distrust God because of it, but rise up in faithfulness when the time comes.

c. God's promises to us are the outgrowth of promises made to us long before.

POINT III. *Consider the acknowledgment of grace.*

a. As God promises are fulfilled, we must ever acknowledge His grace. In our dumbness we must write, His Name is John.—So shall we receive Divine grace to sing God's praise.

b. As we acknowledge God's sovereignty, so shall we find our own joy. We must delight in everything in proportion as we own God's power therein.

c. We must confess God in such way as best we can. Friends will not understand what we do. God will bless us in the doing.

AFFECTIONS. Penitential gratitude. Homage to the Divine Sovereignty.

PRAYER.

Almighty God, enable us, we beseech Thee, so to acknowledge Thy grace, that we may rise out of the weakness of our present condition, and abide in the joys of Thy ceaseless Benediction ; through Jesus Christ our Lord. Amen.

THE JOY OF GRACE.

PRELUDE. i. *Thou shalt call his name John: and thou shalt have joy and gladness, and many shall rejoice at his birth.*—S. Luke i. 13, 14.

ii. Zacharias writing down the name.

POINT I. *Consider the joy of Zacharias.*

  a. How this nativity answered the prayers of his long-continued Priesthood, and went beyond all that he had prayed for.

  b. The discipline by which he had been punished prepared him to rejoice all the more in the consciousness of the Divine Power which was effecting so great a result.

  c. This child would indeed be another Isaac, bringing the gladness of a Saviour's Love.

POINT II. *Consider the joy of the many.*

  a. They must learn to bewail their sins at his bidding ere they could know the joy of his message. The penitent would rejoice in being made ready for the Lord.

  b. They must share the discipline of his life ere they could have their joy fulfilled in sympathy with him.

  c. They would rejoice in him, by being handed over to One greater than him. Earthly objects give us true joy as they vanish and leave Christ to take their place.

POINT III. *Consider the growth of this joy.*

  a. There was great rejoicing throughout the neighbourhood at this birth. All could see it to be beyond nature. None could appreciate its purpose.

  b. There would be much sadness as the life developed in struggle with a sinful world, but those who could accept this joy, would not shrink from that sadness.

  c. The joy would die out in a greater joy. Its very growth was an alienation from earth. The less of earth the more of Heaven. Such was its law.

AFFECTIONS. Praise to Jesus, the Lamb of God. Grateful acceptance of pardon.

PRAYER.

O God, Who didst give joy to many by the birth of Thy Servant John Baptist, grant that we may rejoice by giving heed to his teaching, and may follow Thy Son Jesus Christ with truly penitent hearts, so that our joy may be perfected in Thy Love; through the same Jesus Christ our Lord. Amen.

SUPERNATURAL GROWTH.

PRELUDE. i. *He shall be great in the sight of the* Lord : *and shall drink neither wine nor strong drink: and he shall be filled with the Holy Ghost even from his mother's womb.* —S. Luke i. 15.

ii. The Angel speaking these words.

POINT I. *Consider the fulness of the Holy Ghost.*

a. The Holy Ghost inspired him with wisdom and joy even before his birth.

b. The Holy Ghost had marked him out as a special object of prophecy by reason of his nearness to our Lord Jesus Christ.

c. The Holy Ghost filled him with joy as earthly sorrows thickened round him, for his joy was fulfilled by the coming of Jesus.

POINT II. *Consider the ascetic training.*

a. The special sanctification of the Holy Ghost did not exempt him from the austerity of self-discipline. On the contrary, the greatness of his gifts made the greater austerity needful.

b. The exhilaration of earth was to be put aside that the soul might long for the exhilaration of Heaven, as it should be given by the Presence of Jesus. Noah in a renewed earth was ensnared by the wine of earth. S. John in a corrupt world would prepare the Way by abstinence for man to drink the wine of Heaven.

c. Many Nazarites had observed the rule. He first should experience the joy. As the Bridegroom's friend, he would find the water turned into a better wine than at the Marriage of Cana.

POINT III. *Consider his greatness before God.*

. *a.* A predestined greatness, announced before his birth, as Divinely prepared for him.

b. A supernatural greatness, effected by the Holy Ghost, habitually operating upon him.

c. An accepted greatness, in that his own will and effort were habitually correspondent with the Divine intention.

AFFECTIONS. Resolution to act always with God. Self-restraint in worldly indulgence. Longing for Jesus.

PRAYER.

O my God, grant that I may so put away from me those pleasures which are apt to ensnare my affections, that I may receive the inspirations of the Holy Ghost without hindrance, and may rejoice in the predestination of Thy grace ; through Jesus Christ Thy Son our Lord. Amen.

THE PROPHETIC PREPARATION.

PRELUDE. i. *He shall go before Him in the spirit and power of Elias; to turn the hearts of the fathers to the children, and the disobedient to the wisdom of the just; to make ready a people prepared for the Lord.*—S. Luke i. 17.

ii. As before.

POINT I. *Consider the Supernatural character of the Mission.*

a. God Who had so wonderfully removed Elias from the earth, would as wonderfully send the Baptist. The interval of time would not destroy the real connection between the two ministries, as it existed in the Divine purpose.

b. This Mission was immediately connected with the Incarnation, and therefore had a dignity superior to all others:—in the power of Elias, but with greater honour.

c. It was only a transitional ministry, but the glory was not the less on that account. The glory was in the brightness to which it led. It died not so as to perish, but to live.

POINT II. *Consider the Moral aspect of the Mission.*

a. Renewal of social obligations. If we do not recognize the bonds of family duty, we cannot recognize our higher duty to God nor welcome Christ.

b. The loss of family affection is one of the great sins of the last days.—2 Tim. iii. 3.—We must have an Elias.

c. None can welcome Christ unless they have learnt the necessity of moral restraint. Self-will in every form must die out before His Sovereignty can be acknowledged.

POINT III. *Consider the Spiritual end of the Mission.*

a. The object of man's discipline is that he may accept Christ. The preaching of repentance would be valueless without this.

b. The people are to be prepared for the Lord, and must die to themselves. How greatly do we need such preparation.

c. The wisdom of the just must rule our hearts, and it will teach us to rise beyond the demands of natural life to the glory of the Life of Christ.

AFFECTIONS. Glory in union with Christ. To seek God in social duties as well as in private.

PRAYER.

O God, mercifully look upon Thy servants, and grant us so to put away all self-will that we may be found ready and waiting when Thy Son our Lord Jesus Christ shall be revealed from Heaven, and may find acceptance with Thee through His merits Who liveth and reigneth with Thee and the Holy Ghost; one God, for ever and ever. Amen.

PENITENTIAL PRAISE.

PRELUDE. i. *And his father Zacharias was filled with the Holy Ghost, and prophesied, saying, Blessed be the Lord God of Israel.*—S. Luke i. 67, 68.

ii. The aged Priest blessing God.

POINT I. *Consider the name of Zacharias.*

  a. "God remembereth." He may seem to forget, but He is unchangeable and true. What He does for us, He does not by impulse but by eternal purpose.

  b. God sends His Angel to every Zacharias, *i.e.*, to those who live in the joy of His remembrance. The wicked who forget God are cast out of His remembrance also.

  c. The memory of God must be the parent of penitence. We must remember God's command, God's promises, God's law; then we shall know ourselves.

POINT II. *Consider the fulness of the Holy Ghost.*

  a. The dull, dead memory of man were worthless without the inspiration of the Holy Ghost.

  b. Zacharias said, His name is John. We cannot be filled with the Holy Ghost, save by acknowledging "God's grace."

  c. Blessed was that long-continued dumbness, which should at length be changed into such an utterance of the Holy Ghost. Words of pride end in dumbness. The dumbness of penitence in benediction.

POINT III. *Consider the outburst of praise.*

  a. The praise of this nativity is given to God. The first utterance of penitence must be to glorify Him.

  b. This wonderful child is regarded only in reference to One Greater Who shall come after him.

  c. The penitent dumbness of the Temple is changed into a song of praise, which shall be sung without ceasing throughout the ages of the Church.

AFFECTIONS. Wonder at Divine Grace. Self-surrender to the Holy Ghost.

PRAYER.

O God, forasmuch as no words of ours can ever be worthy of Thy praise, grant that the power of Thy Holy Spirit may so fill our hearts with gratitude, that we may attain to that glory which Thou hast prepared for us; through Jesus Christ our Lord. Amen.

APOSTOLIC FELLOWSHIP.

PRELUDE. i. *Now Peter and John went up together into the Temple at the hour of prayer, being the ninth hour.*—Acts iii. 1.
ii. As in the Narrative.

POINT I. *Consider the duty of united worship.*
- a. Christ is the Head, and no one can have solitary fellowship with Him, apart from the members of His Body.
- b. The promise of Christ's Presence, and of miraculous answer to prayer, is to two or three of the Apostles when they are gathered together, not to any one alone.
- c. We must go up together to the earthly Temple if we would be sharers together in the ministering of Heavenly consolation.

POINT II. *Consider the ancient hour of prayer which they observed.*
- a. They associated themselves with the generations of their forefathers who had observed the same hour from ancient times.
- b. They knew that the faithful observance of God's promises surrounding that holy House was the surest way to obtain His more recent promises, made to themselves as the new place of His abode.
- c. They went up for the ordinary duty of prayer, not knowing what wonders God would work through them.

POINT III. *Consider the new associations of that hour.*
- a. The hour of our Lord's Death. They saw the way into the holiest opened, and His Blood ministered within the veil.
- b. The evening sacrifices were outshone, as they gazed upon them by the glory of the True Sacrifice which had already taken their place.
- c. They knew that the prayer of God's Church rose up now through the Person of the High Priest in Heaven, and became efficacious through Him.

AFFECTIONS. Love of united intercession and brotherly union in prayer. Union of heart with past ages. Unity of life with Christ in Heaven.

PRAYER.

O Lord God, Who callest us to dwell together in unity that we may be partakers of the Unction which rests upon Jesus Christ our High Priest and Head, grant us so to persevere in habits of devotion received from our fathers, that we may obtain those gifts of grace which are promised to us in Thy Son Jesus Christ our Lord. Amen.

APOSTOLIC POVERTY.

PRELUDE i. *Silver and gold have I none; but such as I have give I thee.*—Acts iii. 6.

ii. As in the Narrative.

POINT I. *Consider the Apostolic poverty.*

  a. Christ had not this world's wealth while He was upon the earth. He did not leave it to his Apostles. They did not look for it.

  b. They " are not to me." They are non-existences, for they have no power to effect that which belongs to my true sphere of life.

  c. The Apostle did not think himself worse off for not having them. Many had given the poor man alms : had these alms helped him ?

POINT II. *Consider the Apostolic power.*

  a. It was a real power, capable of making itself felt upon the external world, requiring certain conditions of the outer world, but operative of itself.

  b. It was a personal possession, not a mere confidence that God would answer prayer, God had already bestowed personally upon His Apostles this inherent co-operation of the Holy Ghost.

  c. It was a joint possession, exerted by one Apostle, only as mouthpiece of the community in whom it resided. " Look on *us.*"

POINT III. *Consider the Apostolic beneficence.*

  a. What power they had was a trust for the good of others. As such S. Peter exercised it.

  b. It was a power given, not merely an act done. The power was the power of the Holy Ghost. This the Apostle had. This he gave.

  c. It required a certain disposition upon the part of the lame man to receive it, shown by his obedience to the Apostle's words.

AFFECTIONS. Dread of wealth as being inconsistent with Apostolic power. Confidence in God's power.

PRAYER.

O Lord God, Who hast given Thy Son to be Head over all things to Thy Church, grant that we may so walk in the power of the Spirit which He has given, that we may experience the efficacy of His operations to the glory of Thy Name; through the same Jesus Christ our Lord. Amen.

ANGELIC MINISTRATIONS AROUND THE CHURCH.

PRELUDE. i. *And the Angel saith unto Peter, Cast thy garment about thee and follow me.*—Acts xii. 8.

ii. As in the Narrative.

POINT I. *Consider the ministry of Angels.*

a. S. Peter saw: but they wait upon us, who are the heirs of salvation, to do what is needed, and we do not see.

b. While we live as we do, by material agencies of power, money, and the like, we cannot expect to have the ministry of Angels in manifest attendance.

c. The Angel comes to those who recognise this world as a prison, that he may make them free with the Life in God.

POINT II. *Consider the preparation of dress.*

a. Ere we can follow the Angel's bidding, we must have "risen up" loosed from the fetters of sin. No absolution avails for those who remain sluggishly as they were before.

b. We must have " girt ourselves "—*i.e.*, with dogmatic truth —Eph. vi. 14—holding in true faith the substance of unseen verities, and " bound our sandals " on our feet—*i.e.*, the preparation of the Gospel of peace in the twofold law of love to God and man.

c. Then will the Angel bid us " cast our garment about us, *i.e.*, the outer garment of resurrection glory wherewith we shall enter the streets of the Heavenly Jerusalem.

POINT III. *Consider the following of the Angel.*

a. The Angel watches the sleeper. Our flesh is bound in slumber by two chains—original and actual sin. Two soldiers guard us—the world and the devil.

b. We must follow the Angel through the first ward—*i.e.*, life in this world. Then comes the second ward—*i.e.*, the intermediate state. Then will the iron gate open of its own accord, that we may enter into the Golden City.

c. Outward difficulties do not hinder angelic assistance. Rather they invite them. Angels cannot bring us securely through the dangers of life unless we follow them, seeking to do God's will as they do it.

AFFECTIONS. Gratitude for God's Angels, and reverence in the thought of them. Imitation of their obedience.

PRAYER.

O God, Who hast given to us the gift of Thy Holy Spirit, that we may serve Thee in newness of life, and hast committed us to the external guardianship of holy Angels, that the powers of the world may be unable to harm us, grant that we may so serve Thee in our lower station according to the perfection of their obedience, that we may attain to that greater glory wherein Thou wouldest have us be perfected in Thyself; through Jesus Christ our Lord. Amen.

THE RESTORATION OF THE PENITENT.

PRELUDE. i. *Simon, son of Jonas, lovest thou Me ?* Lord,
Thou knowest all things: *Thou knowest that I love Thee.* *Feed
My sheep.*—S. John xxi. 11.

ii. As in the Narrative.

POINT I. *Consider the love of the Apostle.*

   a. It was ardent. Like everything in his character, it was
   impetuous. He was fully conscious of it.

   b. It had failed. Yet the failure did not make the Apostle
   mistrust it for himself. Now that Jesus was with them
   again, the denials and the paroxysm of tears seemed to
   belong to a dream, leaving the reality of this love as it was
   before.

   c. How different will be the tender, persevering Love which
   the Holy Ghost will awaken in his heart ere long, the supernatural love so conscious of past sin, self-distrustful,
   patient.

POINT II. *Consider the need of investigating this love.*

   a. Jesus did indeed know all things. It was not for His own
   sake that He asked the question. God deals with us so as
   to awaken proper dispositions in us.

   b. The impetuosity of this love made inquiry very irksome to
   the Apostle. Having failed to learn self-distrust, he could
   not bear to be distrusted by Jesus.

   c. Seeing Jesus as if nothing had happened, he lost the sense
   of any wrong done to Jesus which needed reparation.

POINT III. *Consider the necessity of giving proof of love.*

   a. Love must be proved by active devotion. Restoration to
   apostleship is not enough without restoration to saintliness.
   Saintliness must be proved by diligence in the work of
   apostleship.

   b. Diligence must be stimulated by penitence for the past.
   The threefold dedication corresponds with the threefold
   denial.

   c. Jesus questions now in order that S. Peter may act hereafter. Self-examination must always lead to active amend-
   ments.

AFFECTIONS. Love to Jesus. Zeal for souls. Desire to
repair past sin.

PRAYER.

*O Lord God, Who requirest us to love Thee with a perfect heart,
grant that in mindfulness of past sin, we may be truly thankful for
every trial whereby our integrity may be assured, so that whatever
be our calling in Thy Church, the diligence which Thy grace
inspires, may enable us to regain by penitence the approval which
our self-will had forfeited. Grant this, we beseech Thee, for the sake
of Jesus Christ our Lord. Amen.*

APOSTOLIC FOUNDATIONS.

PRELUDE. i. *Thou art Peter, and upon this Rock I will build My Church.*—S. Matt. xvi. 18. ii. Our Lord speaking these words.

POINT I. *Consider the building of the Church.*

a. There are twelve foundation-stones, having their individual character and lustre.—Rev. xxi. 14-19.

b. They are a combined foundation.—Eph. ii. 20.—Not merely of outward support but of interior Life, as the main branches of a Tree.—S. John xv. 5.

c. Of these S. Peter was nominated "the first," but warned lest by negligence he became "the last."—S. Matt. xix. 30.

POINT II. *Consider the Rock whereon the Church is built.*

a. "That Rock was Christ." The Rock always symbolizes the Divine Nature. "There is no Rock like our God."—1 Sam. ii. 2.

b. This Divine Nature underlies His Manhood. Christ—Heb. iii. 6—digged deep, and laid these foundation-stones in the wounds of His glorified Humanity upon the Rock—S. Matt. vii. 24—so that they cannot be shaken—Heb. xii. 23—by the violence of Hell.

c. This Rock is Life-giving The "lively stones"—1 S. Peter ii. 4—have a new birth—Deut. xxxii. 18—as members of Christ by the unction of the Holy Ghost, "the oil out of the Rock."—Deut. xxxii. 13.

POINT III. *Consider where this Church is built.*

a. "He founds upon the Holy Hills"—Ps. lxxxvii. 1—*i.e.*, upon the Heavenly Life of God, no earthly centre like the old Jerusalem—Heb. xiii. 14. The Seven Hills, the temporal power, of the degraded city, seem to be the mystical contrary of the Seven Gifts of the Divine Life. So the Foundation is also a corner-stone.—1 S. Peter ii. 7. The building reaches downward, not upward.

b. The whole building is Heavenly—Amos ix. 6—growing with Spiritual power, to do the work of God, and will be revealed coming out of Heaven from God.

c. It lives secure with the Holy Ghost, by whose Apostolical communication the Body of Christ is built.—Eph. iv. 12. This Spirit resting upon the whole Body makes it to be the habitation of God.—Eph. ii. 22.

AFFECTIONS. Reverence to the Divine Indwelling. Gratitude for Sacramental Grace. Faith in the Holy Church.

PRAYER.

O Almighty God, Who hast built Thy Church upon the Holy Apostles that by the indwelling of Thy Holy Spirit we may manifest Thy Divine power, grant me so to abide firmly established in the Mystical Body of Thy dear Son, that I may be Thine in the day when Thou shalt count up Thy jewels; through Jesus Christ our Lord. Amen.

APOSTOLICAL AUTHORITY.

PRELUDE. i. *Whatsoever thou shalt bind on earth, shall be bound in Heaven, and whatsoever thou shalt loose on earth, shall be loosed in Heaven.*—S. Matt. xvi. 19.

ii. Our Lord speaking these words.

POINT I. *Consider the twofold character of the Apostles.*

a. Their outward life is upon the earth, in social intercourse with mankind, sanctified, not destroyed by the Holy Ghost.

b. Their inward life is in the Kingdom of Heaven. There is to be not a subsequent confirmation of their acts, but an immediate identification of the heavenly life with the earthly organ of life.

c. Their outward acts, having this spiritual character, have lasting results. By the exercise of the keys, Heaven is shut up or opened, so that grace flows through the Kingdom or is restrained accordingly.

POINT II. *Consider their representative character.*

a. They minister in the Person of Christ, the One Head. He acts and rules through them all.—S. Luke x. 16; S. John xx. 21.

b. The Holy Ghost, Who spreads Life throughout this Kingdom, ministers on earth through them and fills their acts with Divine power; while they act not individually, but collectively.

c. The real character of their action is to be estimated not by man's acquiescence, but by the inspiring Authority.

POINT III. *Consider the associated character of the Apostles.*

a. The Holy Ghost was not given to any one of the Apostles separately. The twelve Apostles are the life-transmitting foundations of this Kingdom while acting in their corporate unity: "Receive ye the" One "Holy Ghost."—S. John xx. 22.

b. The promise of the keys was not given to S. Peter outside of the kingdom. The kingdom does not receive life or authority from him. He is one of its organs.

c. The ministry of grace in the whole Body is valid in each Sacrament of Christ's Institution, although schism destroys much of the individual power of the ministry in spontaneous acts.

AFFECTIONS. Gratitude to God for an Apostolic Church. Sense of union with all the faithful in Christ in spite of every separation, whether by death or by schism.

PRAYER.

O Almighty God, Who hast gathered together Thine Elect in the Body of Thine Only-begotten Son, to be a Kingdom not of earth, but of Heaven, grant that we may so praise Thee for the ministration of grace through Apostolic Ordinances, that we may attain to the joy of Thy people when the unity of Thy Holy Spirit shall be manifested in them; through the same Jesus Christ our Lord. Amen.

x

SYMPATHY IN HOLY JOY.

PRELUDE. i. *Rise up, my love, my fair one, and come away; for, lo! the winter is past, the rain is over and gone; the flowers appear on the earth.*—Cant. ii. 10-12.

ii. The meeting between Mary and Elizabeth.

POINT I. *Consider the impulse of congratulation.*

a. The Blessed Virgin hearing of what had happened to her aged relative, could not but rejoice with her exceedingly. Hence she rises up with haste.

b. Our Lord Christ is the true cause of congratulation to all mankind. He strengthens us to congratulate others. No object deserves congratulation save by reference to Him.

c. If earthly things lead the children of the world to congratulate one another, much more ought the things of the Kingdom of Heaven to draw devout souls into fellowship.

POINT II. *Consider the energy of Spiritual renewal.*

a. As the sense of renewed strength in the body, so in the whole nature the sense of Divine Life bursting forth, is like an irrepressible spring.

b. We must share God's gifts with those who can appreciate them; those who dwell in a city of Juda, in the hill country of Divine Praise.

c. In the fellowship of Saints we shall delight to lie hidden. The B. V. M. waited for the Forerunner's birth to return to Nazareth.

POINT III. *Consider the joy of sympathetic expectation.*

a. What great events did both of these Mothers look forward to, by reason of their children.

b. The barren winter of sin is past, and germs of heavenly life begin to show. This visit begins with the song of the Virgin, and ends with the Priest freed from dumbness to celebrate its close.

c. The Birth of the Baptist, honoured by so great a visitor, happened when the days were longest. " There hath not risen a greater than John the Baptist." Man seemed to rise to his highest dignity in Him. Jesus was born when days are shortest. Then they lengthen. He took man's nature in its misery to perfect it with the glory of God.

AFFECTIONS. Praise to God for all that He does for ourselves or for others. Desire to impart spiritual joy.

PRAYER.

O Lord God, Who hast called us to rejoice in that which Thou doest for others as for ourselves, grant us so to praise Thee in holy sympathy, as members of one Body in Christ, that hereafter we may abide with Thee in the Eternal fruition of Thy glory; through the same Jesus Christ our Lord. Amen.

LOVE TO THOSE IN SUFFERING.

PRELUDE. i. *Well done, thou good and faithful servant, thou hast been faithful over a few things, I will make thee ruler over many things: enter thou into the joy of thy Lord.*—S. Matt. xxv. 21.
ii. The grand ceremonial of removing his body to its new resting-place.

POINT I. *Consider the Saint's abhorrence of persecution.*

a. The first capital punishment for heresy was in the case of Priscillian, by Maximus. S. Martin and S. Ambrose refused to communicate with the Bishops who were a party to it.

b. He does not fear death for himself who fears to injure others.

c. To save the lives of others S. Martin promised the Emperor to communicate with the Bishops guilty of persecution. He now had greater difficulty in working miracles. God withdraws heavenly powers when we bend to earthly ones.

POINT II. *Consider the poverty of his life.*

a. Great is the joy of sharing all things with the poor. So only can we share with Jesus Christ.

b. His uncouth dress made the Bishops refuse him when the people chose him to be Bishop. Yet their grandeur led them into sin, and he sat with Jesus on His Throne.

c. When dying he refused to lie otherwise than on sackcloth and ashes, rejecting all bodily comfort. Yet he could rejoice to live in the world and pray for life so long as God had anything for him to do.

POINT III. *Consider the abiding sumptuousness of his grave.*

a. His body was translated to a church of greater glory than at first received it. Oh that we could see the increasing glory of the blessed dead who rest in Christ!

b. His grave became for ages the centre of special devotion in France. Let us see that we are close followers of his example, seeking not his dead body but his living spirit.

c. Unbelievers desolated his grave, yet the spot became glorious again with holy memories. Saints are truly translated while we seek to imitate them. The virtues of their followers are a shrine which no man can lay waste.

AFFECTIONS. Confidence in God. Mercy to the ignorant and sinful.

PRAYER.

O God, grant that I may always rely on Thee alone, and finding in Thee the satisfaction of my heart, may refuse no toil which Thou givest, and seek no power which Thou givest not, but may rejoice in the mercy which comes from Thee, while I exercise mercy according to Thine inspiration towards all that do me wrong; through Jesus Christ our Lord. Amen.

x 2

A.D. 862.

LOVE OF POVERTY.

PRELUDE i. *Well done, thou good and faithful servant, thou hast been faithful over a few things, I will make thee ruler over many things : enter thou into the joy of thy* Lord.—S. Matt. xxv. 21.

ii. S. Swithun going barefoot, as was his wont, to dedicate a Church.

POINT I. *Consider the Love of Poverty.*

a. Precious are the poor in the sight of God, and yet men rejoice in external gifts which only hide the soul.

b. Riches do not perfect the Image of God which they hide: nor will they profit in the day of death. Too often they injure the soul, like a wrapper sticking to a varnished picture, and making the picture valueless.

c. Poverty which hinders many works in this world, will not hinder the soul's glory when this world is passed away.

POINT II. *Consider the love due to the Poor.*

a. Jesus Christ took upon Himself our poverty, that we might have better riches by fellowship with Him. We cannot be like Him if we value men for what they have, and not for what they are.

b. As Jesus Christ clothed Himself with poverty, we ought to recognise in the poor the special likeness of Jesus Christ. They may not be as like Him as they ought to be; but do we regard their poverty as He regarded it?

c. Love to the poor helps to make us feel how many superfluities we ourselves possess. We cannot complain of small wants if we know their great wants.

POINT III. *Love to poverty in ourselves.*

a. We cannot value poverty and keep aloof from it. Rather we shall feel pained at being so much involved in wealth.

b. We shall tremble at riches as really tending to choke the Divine grace which would otherwise work within us.

c. We shall not mind if the world despises us for our poverty. The poor in spirit do not wish for praise. Christ's work will go on. To shrink from poverty forfeits His help.

AFFECTIONS. Fear of riches. Joy at suffering want. Reverence for the poor.

PRAYER.

O Lord Jesu Christ, Who didst condescend to suffer want as one of the sons of men, though all the world was Thine own possession, yea, Thy creation, grant that I may never shrink from suffering along with Thee, but in every time of want may look to Thee to supply whatever is lacking; Who with the Father and the Holy Ghost livest and reignest God, for ever and ever. Amen.

THE POWER OF THE CROSS.

PRELUDE. i. *When the Bridegroom came, they that were ready went in with Him to the marriage.*—S. Matt. xxv. 10.

ii. S. Margaret, according to the symbolism of the legend, escaping from the jaws of the dragon by the power of the Cross.

POINT I. *Consider that we are all swallowed up of Death.*

a. Death is like a mighty monster, in whose belly all mankind are inclosed, as Jonah in the whale's belly.

b. We have no power of escaping from this estate of death by nature. We are born dead, and what men call death is only a change in the form of death.

c. Men are unconscious that they are thus swallowed up of Death, and therefore neither know nor desire the blessed liberty which constitutes true Life.

POINT II. *Consider the destruction of Death by Christ.*

a. Christ by death destroyed him that had the power of death. The jaws of death into which He entered could not close upon Him, for He had a Divine Life, and never lost it.

b. Death could not hold Him, for although His earthly nature was subjected to the separating power of Death, yet He had the power of the Holy Ghost, which Death could not master.

c. When He escaped, He destroyed Death itself, so that Death must yield up all the carcases it has swallowed, and Death will itself, with all its prey, be cast into the lake of fire.

POINT III. *Consider the power of the Cross.*

a. Those who cling to the Cross cannot be held by Death. The Cross is a bond of Divine Love between the faithful and their Redeeming Lord. They rise up in the power of His Life, by holding to the trophy of His Death.

b. The Cross is the Sign of the Son of Man, and it affrights the Angel of Death with remembrance of defeat.

c. The Cross appeals with all the merits of the Passion to God the Father on our behalf. But it must separate us from the world as dead, if it is to unite us to God in Life.

AFFECTIONS. Exultation in the Cross. Contempt of Death. Anticipation of Risen Life.

PRAYER.

O God, Who hast called us into the fellowship of Thine Only-begotten Son, that we being crucified to the world, may live unto Thee, grant that I may abide in the glorious liberty of Thy children, wherein we are set free from the tyranny of Death, so that in the end I may have my portion in the Book of Life; through His merits Who died upon the Cross, even Thy Son Jesus Christ our Lord. Amen.

THE LOVE OF THE PENITENT.

PRELUDE i. *Instead of the thorn shall come up the fir tree, and instead of the brier shall come up the myrtle tree ; and it shall be to the Lord for a name, for an everlasting sign that shall not be cut off.*—Isa. lv. 13.

ii. Jesus appearing to Mary in the garden.

POINT I. *Consider her courageous love.*

a. She was not afraid to hear the taunts of the Pharisee while she exhibited her love to Jesus.

b. She trusted in Jesus and did not let her past sin hold her back from doing Him homage.

c. She did not think that death should hold her back, and she recognized His voice as the call of a Master, though He spake from the other side of the grave.

POINT II. *Consider the liberality of her love.*

a. She anointed our Blessed Lord's feet. She heeded not the grudging scorn of those who would be more offended with her charity than with her sins.

b. She ministered to our Lord of her substance as He went upon His travels, rejoicing that others should be partakers of a like deliverance.

c. She gave her whole heart to serve Jesus. She had been delivered by His power. She acknowledged Him by her homage as being the source of all the gifts He gave.

POINT III. *Consider the blessedness of her recovery.*

a. She was standing beside the Cross. The penitent must come humbly to the Cross. In vain had Jesus cast the devils out, unless by death he had destroyed their power.

b. She was the first to welcome our Lord when He rose from the dead. Although she was not permitted to touch Him, yet she was permitted to become His messenger. She repined not at the denial, but rejoiced at the message.

c. How complete is the transformation which grace effects in the soul. The greatest sin will be blotted out if we love much. The smallest will be our ruin if we love little.

AFFECTIONS. Gratitude to Jesus. Penitent boldness in acknowledging Him. Watchfulness for His Second Coming.

PRAYER.

O Lord Jesu, Who didst accept the homage of the sinner, and didst choose Mary Magdalene to be the first witness and messenger of Thy Resurrection, grant that I with true contrition of heart may love Thee as my Deliverer, own Thee as my Master, and worship Thee as my God, so that when Thou comest in Thy glory I may be enabled to lay hold upon Thee, not as now, under sacramental veils, but in the fulness of Thy Glory ; for Thy Mercy's sake. Amen.

THE CARE OF CHILDREN.

PRELUDE i. *Who can find a virtuous woman? for her price is far above rubies.*—Prov. xxxi. 10.

ii. S. Anne teaching the Blessed Virgin.

POINT I. *Consider the love of S. Anne for the child.*

  a. How ought we to rejoice in beholding a child growing up in holiness. It is a blessed thing to live in ties of natural affection with those who find favour with God.

  b. Blessed are those parents whose children truly have the Lord for their portion. Death perfects for them a fellowship with their children far beyond all they can have here.

  c. How little could S. Anne know of the high destiny of her child, yet how mysteriously was her love drawn out by the preventing grace which led her child onward to it.

POINT II. *Consider the blessedness of training children.*

  a. God sanctifies a child before it can speak. How ought we to recognize that sanctity in our dealings with them.

  b. We know not who it may be whom we train in the way of grace, but we ought to expect the result of grace to be worthy of God the Giver Whom we do know. It is man's fault that baptismal grace is so generally given in vain.

  c. If the germ of Divine grace is developed into a blessed maturity by our care, we shall be partakers of the Blessing.

POINT III. *Consider the future relations of a child.*

  a. We know not with whom a child may have to deal. S. Anne could not imagine how her child would live in close intimacy with Messiah. Let each child be trained to wait upon God.

  b. We know not the future office or work to which a child may be called. Yet in training a child, be those words remembered, Whosoever doeth the will of My Father Which is in Heaven, the same is My brother and sister and mother.

  c. We know not how a child may come to die. We know that Heaven awaits that child for eternity.

AFFECTIONS. Reverence to Christ in children. Trust in God for them.

PRAYER.

O God, Who didst call one Child of our race to become after the flesh the Mother of Thine own Son, begotten of Thyself in Consubstantial Godhead from all eternity, grant us in the acknowledgment of this Mystery not only to praise Thee for Thy goodness manifested to the Blessed Virgin Mary, but also to consider the dignity of the Vocation wherewith Thou vouchsafest to call every child of Thy Covenant to partake of Thy Divine Life by incorporation into the Body which Thy Blessed Son hath assumed; through the same Jesus Christ our Lord. Amen.

CALMNESS AMIDST PERSECUTION.

PRELUDE i. *The same night Peter was sleeping between two soldiers, bound with two chains.*—Acts xii. 6.
ii. As in the History.

POINT I. *Consider S. Peter sleeping.*

   a. The quietness and confidence with which we are to rest amidst external danger. " So He giveth His beloved sleep."

   b. The freedom of the Spirit abiding in fellowship with God. Although there be outward bonds, nevertheless we must rest in elevation of soul contemplating God. Our repose must be the repose not of idleness but of devotion.

   c. While Peter was thus sleeping, watchful prayer was being made by the Church for him. We must praise God for the grace of which He makes us partakers in the Communion of Saints by the prayers of all our brethren.

POINT II. *Consider the strictness of the imprisonment.*

   a. The powers of the earth strive to make their prisoner sure; but the Church of God has a life beyond their grasp.

   b. The two soldiers may be taken as representing the world and the devil, who keep watch against the Church. The chains of our sins bind us in their power, but the Angel who shall loose the chains will set us free from these tyrants.

   c. It was night time. God will effect the deliverance of His Church just when all are unsuspecting.

POINT III. *Consider the prayer of the Church for him.*

   a. The safety of those who are bound is linked with the energy of the whole Body of Christ. No member of Christ has security and strength apart from the whole Body.

   b. The safety of the Church does not consist in a charm which supersedes her own efforts, but in the power of the Holy Spirit of Love wherein she ever lives in active correspondence with God.

   c. Dangers as they develope the prayer, so they develope the life of the Church.

AFFECTIONS. Trust in God. Prayer. Mutual Love.

PRAYER.

O God, Who hast sent Thy Holy Spirit to be the Life of Thy Church, that acting in His strength we may not be destroyed by any devices of the enemy, grant unto us, Thy servants, that with all boldness we may look up to Thee and seek Thy help in every time of need, so that the oppression of the evil world may only serve to make manifest Thy glorious power, and to perfect our co-operation with Thy Love; through Jesus Christ our Lord. Amen.

CHRIST THE CENTRE OF ALL CONTEMPLATION.

PRELUDE. i. *Jesus taketh Peter, James, and John his brother, and bringeth them up into an high mountain apart, and was transfigured before them : and His Face did shine as the sun, and His raiment was white as the light.*—S. Matt. xvii. 1, 2.

ii. As in the Gospel.

POINT I. *Consider the transfiguration of Christ's Body.*

a. The features of our Lord's countenance remained unchanged, although shining with a glory not visible before.

b. It was during the night. All is morally dark throughout the world when Christ appears in His glory. We must not be discouraged by darkness, but look for the Divine Light.

c. It was on a high mountain apart. We must be apart from the world if we would see Christ as He is.

POINT II. *Consider the transfiguring Light.*

a. It was from within. The Light of Christ is not derived from the world, and needs no worldly assistance for its manifestation.

b. His countenance was as the sun. He is Himself the Sun of Righteousness, and the glory of the new world shines from His own Person.

c. His raiment was as the Light. The Saints are His raiment, shining with His brightness, the humanity of the redeemed wherein He is glorified.

POINT III. *Consider the Spectators.*

a. The three Apostles : Peter representative of the active life; James, of the martyr host; John, of contemplative Love. In action, in death, and in contemplation we must be sustained by seeing the glory of Jesus.

b. Moses from the depth below, having died. Jesus calls him, for Jesus is Lord of the dead and of the living.

c. Elias from the height above, who never yet had died, reserved to gather Israel together at the last day, as Moses had gathered them together in the Exodus from Egypt.

AFFECTIONS. Delight in Christ's glory. Communion with Saints. Hope of resurrection.

PRAYER.

O God, Who didst cause the glory of Thine Only-begotten Son to be made manifest upon the Holy Mount, open Thou mine eyes that I may behold the hidden glory whereof I am made partaker by the mystery of Thy grace, and may so abide therein during the night-season of this earthly life, that I may be partaker of the fulness of glory when Thy Blessed Son shall be revealed from Heaven in the sight of all men ; through the merits of the same Jesus Christ our Lord. **Amen.**

THE GLORY OF THE MEDIATOR.

PRELUDE. i. *God also hath highly exalted Him, and given Him a Name which is above every name : that at the Name of Jesus every knee should bow, of things in heaven, and things in earth, and things under the earth.*—Phil. ii. 9, 10.

ii. The Host of Heaven worshipping the Incarnate God.

POINT I. *Consider that the Name which God gives expresses the Truth of that which exists in His Presence.*

a. All creatures exist by the Word of God, and the truth of their nature consists in their correspondence with the Divine Vocation, the predestination from which they spring.

b. All the Heavenly Host looked upward in the consciousness of One in Whom creation was to be perfected, greater than themselves and equal with God.

c. Jesus at His Ascension was exalted far above all Heavens, that He might fill all things ; above them, in an order of nature above their comprehension, much more above ours.

POINT II. *Consider wherein the exaltation of Jesus consists.*

a. He is exalted above all Heavens. The Heaven of Heavens cannot contain the glory manifested in His exaltation. Rather His glory contains and sustains the Heavens.

b. He is exalted to the Right Hand of God. As God eternally acts through His Only-begotten Son, His Word, so now He acts through the Manhood which His Son has assumed.

c. Jesus is thus the Mediator between God and all His creatures. The glory of God streams forth on all creation from the Body of Christ, as the Temple wherein it dwells.

POINT III. *Consider the worship of Jesus by all creation.*

a. All things, Heaven, earth, and hell, acknowledge His Sovereignty. He reigns by the unchangeable necessity of Divine Power. All depend upon Him.

b. The Blessed worship Him as the Manifestation of the Divine Love from whence their being springs: Angels as their Creator ; men, as their Redeemer.

c. The Lost also own Him, hating themselves, and blaspheming that Love of God which they can neither see nor know. The more God's Love is manifested, the more terrible it is to those who are blind of heart.

AFFECTIONS. Love of Jesus. Acceptance of grace.

PRAYER.

O Blessed Jesu, let Thy Name ever fill my heart with its sweetness! Yea, let me welcome every assault of the enemy, that the power of Thy Name to heal and save may be the more manifest within me! So grant me to learn in this world the truth of Thy power that in the world to come I may rejoice in the glory of Thy Manifestation ; for Thy great mercy's sake. Amen.

A.D. 258.

LIVING FOR ANOTHER WORLD.

PRELUDE. i. *Gold is tried in the fire, and acceptable men in the furnace of adversity.*—Ecclus. ii. 5.

ii. S. Lawrence being laid upon the gridiron over a slow fire.

POINT I. *Consider the Love which is due to the poor.*

    a. The devout poor are the treasure of the Church. These are they whom God hath chosen. We must look for the manifestation of the grace of Christ in them.

    b. Nowadays poverty is not holy, but riches are not less sinful. If we look to earthly riches, can we expect the poor to rejoice in poverty? We cannot be sanctified if we love riches.

    c. Riches which a man keeps for himself separate him from the Church, which hath all things in common by the law of Divine Love. The more we live for others, the more do we receive the grace which is bestowed upon all.

POINT II. *Consider the Honour due to God's Sanctuary.*

    a. The holy Deacon cared for the precious vessels of God's House. Their dedication made him value them more than the jewels that adorned them.

    b. He parted with them to feed the poor. He would have those vessels minister to the bodily necessities of God's people which could no longer minister the gifts of Heaven.

    c. He was not afraid to incur the wrath of the Roman Prefect, rather than surrender what he had in trust.

POINT III. *Consider the desire of Martyrdom.*

    a. Bodily weakness and suffering give occasion for patience, and possess the highest advantages. So did he regard the sorrows of this life. What he loved in life became the glory of his death.

    b. We are not rightly desiring martyrdom if we shrink from a continued life of suffering. We cannot be martyrs if we are impatient.

    c. We cannot value suffering truly in others, if we draw back from it in ourselves. A mortified life is the necessary preparation for a martyr's death.

AFFECTIONS. Contempt of the world. Love of that which the world hates. Longing for Christ.

PRAYER.

O Lord, I pray Thee, let my whole nature be consumed by the fire of Thy Love, that my carnal self may be entirely destroyed by constant mortification both of flesh and of spirit, and the transfiguring power of the Holy Ghost may enable me so to contemplate Thy glory, that I may be perfected in Thy likeness; through Jesus Christ our Lord. Amen.

A.D. 430.

THE DEVELOPMENT OF INTELLECT.

PRELUDE. i. *Well done, thou good and faithful servant; thou hast been faithful over a few things, I will make thee ruler over many things : enter thou into the Joy of thy Lord.*—S. Matt. xxv. 21.

ii. S. Augustine contemplating his youthful doubts.

POINT I. *Consider the natural intellect in its pride.*

   a. Pride of superiority. The empty boast of knowing more than others, not the solid satisfaction of knowing truth.

   b. Pride of capacity. Our knowledge grows indefinitely : therefore the intellect claims to be infinite. But the Infinite eludes it. Our boast ends in disappointment.

   c. Pride of criticism. As men think themselves able to understand the laws of what is beyond their grasp, so they think themselves warranted in judging God's Acts.

POINT II. *Consider the natural intellect in its humiliation.*

   a. The mind finds evil all around it as a fact, and spends its energies in seeking to evade it, but all in vain.

   b. However many discoveries are made in nature, yet the world we live in contains a multitude of secrets which defy all possible solution by experiment.

   c. Man finds his intellectual development nothing worth in the real amelioration of his own condition. He may live longer in suffering, and be more ingenious in crime, but is no better in what makes him worth the name of man.

POINT III. *Consider the natural intellect in its inspiration.*

   a. Intellect rises out of despair into hope by the discipline of the faith, and rejoices to recognize and to exercise the Love of God. To see God is the fulness of joy.

   b. The human intellect must contemplate the things of God by the illuminating energy of the Supernatural Life, not by the power of nature. It gains a new order of perception.

   c. The intellect raises man to a higher dignity when he comes to know himself as partaking of the Divine Nature by the regenerating Spirit. Inspiration illuminates the intellect from within by purifying and quickening the heart. We know God in proportion as we love Him.

AFFECTIONS. Desire of Divine Knowledge. Self-distrust.

PRAYER.

O God, Who by the power of Thy Love dost call us to the knowledge of Thyself as the true Satisfaction of our nature in the Fellowship of Thy Supernatural Life, teach me so to contemplate Thy goodness that I may be ever moved by the holy energy of Thy Divine Spirit, and rejoice in the growing expression of Thy Love; through Jesus Christ our Lord. Amen.

CHRIST GAINED BY DEATH.

PRELUDE. i. *Herod himself had sent forth and laid hold upon John, and bound him in prison for Herodias' sake, his brother Philip's wife; for John had said unto Herod, It is not lawful for thee to have her.*—S. Mark vi. 17, 18.

ii. The Saint receiving the order of decapitation.

POINT I. *Consider that nearness to Christ involves death to the world.*

    a. He who was the Forerunner, preparing the way in this world, must go down also to the grave before Christ. He must decrease to the nothingness of death.

    b. He must lose the head of his natural body, but Christ is the Head of the Body wherein he hopes to live eternally. We must lose what is of earth in order to have Christ.

    c. All men must die as sinners, even though sanctified like S. John Baptist. To die near to Christ is to die in protesting against sin.

POINT II. *Consider that death does not separate us from the love of Christ.*

    a. God sent His Son into a world that was already dead by sin. Outward death, which is the consequence of sin, does not remove us from God, but shows that we are by nature removed from Him.

    b. We cannot know the love of Christ in its fulness until we are wholly dead to this world of darkness and ignorance.

    c. The Holy Ghost was with the Body of Christ in the grave, and with His Soul, when living separate from His Body. Before Christ came, the souls of the righteous were in the Hand of God by predestinating Love. Much more since Christ came is it impossible for death to separate us from the Love of God in Him.

POINT III. *Consider the weakness of the sword.*

    a. The soul is not destroyed, but freed, by martyrdom.

    b. The voice of rebuke may be quenched by violence, but it is changed into a voice of accusation rising up before God, and though man heeds not the rebuke, God hears the cry.

    c. The lips speak feebly, but a life of suffering, the Martyr's death, makes the whole nature a mouthpiece of the Holy Ghost.

AFFECTIONS. Boldness in Christ. Resistance to evil. Joy in death.

PRAYER.

O *Lord God, grant me the spirit of ghostly strength evermore to resist the evil which is in the world around, that I may not fear to lose anything that is in the world, but may rejoice by every loss to gain a fuller participation of Thine endless Love; through Jesus Christ our Lord. Amen.*

LOVE OF SOLITUDE.

PRELUDE. i. *Well done, thou good and faithful servant; thou hast been faithful over a few things, I will make thee ruler over many things: enter thou into the Joy of thy Lord.*—S. Matt. xxv. 21.
ii. The hind taking refuge from his pursuers at S. Giles' feet.

POINT I. *Consider the danger of worldly applause.*
  a. If we fly from men, we must do so in humility, as from danger, not in pride or disregard.
  b. The best things which God has given us, learning and piety itself, may turn to evil, if the applause of men leads us to rely upon human approbation. We must look to God alone.
  c. We are tempted to think we are doing good to men if they praise us, whereas they rather are doing us harm. We must be hidden if we would have our work prospered.

POINT II. *Consider the blessings of solitude.*
  a. Uninterrupted communion with God. Those who are much alone must learn to abide in constant prayer. Without the practice of God's Presence silence will be gloomy.
  b. Clearer sight of the worthlessness of the goods of this present life. It is difficult to realize their emptiness while we are in the midst of them.
  c. Growing apprehension of Heavenly Truth. Divine Truth is developed in the soul according to the care with which it is cultivated. We must live up to each thought if we would have fuller intuitions.

POINT III. *Consider the dangers of solitude.*
  a. In solitude we are exposed to special assaults of Satan. If God calls any to solitude, whether by sickness, religion, or other circumstances, He will give them grace if they seek it.
  b. Our nature is fitted to expand by sympathy with others, and we are in danger of shrivelling up, when left alone. We need constant fellowship with God, and with His Saints, the members of Christ's Body like ourselves.
  c. Contemplation may die out in dreaminess. Our double nature requires both body and soul to be exercised. Idleness ruins devotion. Activity of spirit must drive it away.

AFFECTIONS. Retirement with God. Activity of soul. Shrinking from the world.

PRAYER.
O God, Who revealest Thyself in solitude to those whom Thou dost call away from the world, grant that I may find my chief delight and highest energy in blessed communion with Thyself, so that amidst the distractions of the world I may find Thee to be my Refuge, Whose praises shall be the all-sufficient occupation of my solitude; through Jesus Christ our Lord. Amen.

A.D. 340.

THE WORLD'S IGNORANCE OF SAINTS.

PRELUDE. i. *Well done, thou good and faithful servant: thou hast been faithful over a few things, I will make thee ruler over many things : enter thou into the Joy of thy Lord.*—S. Matt. xxv. 21.

ii. The Saint welcoming the inspiration of the Holy Ghost.

POINT I. *Consider the world in which our faithfulness is tested.*

   a. The world hates Christ, and thus makes our faithfulness to be approved. There were no merit in serving Christ if the world served Him too.

   b. The world recognizes our faithfulness to Christ as a declaration of war. We must fight against the world, if faithful to Him. We must fight on until the world be destroyed.

   c. The world passeth away. Our relation to it ceases soon ; we have to live in the sight of Christ, longing for the world to pass away.

POINT II. *Consider the approbation of God.*

   a. It is not given by any tokens of outward glory. The more we are approved of Him, the less will the world account of us.

   b. It is not attended by worldly praise. The actions which live in the remembrance of God are not cherished in the annals of the world. The world cannot understand them.

   c. The individual soul lives in the brightness of God's Love, receiving His Eternal Benediction according to the fulness of the Divine knowledge of the service rendered upon earth, although the world forget all but the name.

POINT III. *Consider the reward in God.*

   a. God Who is the Strength of all our actions is Himself the Life of our reward. We see God, because we live with the Life of God, and know Him as dwelling in ourselves.

   b. The reward of the Divine Life is not a mere vague immensity of joy. It is that communication of Divine Joy which is proper to the special exercise of Divine energy, whereby the soul has co-operated with grace.

   c. The inner life of the soul is perfect in the Divine knowledge, although altogether lost to sight of man.

AFFECTIONS. Hiddenness. Joy in contemplation. Disregard of worldly fame.

PRAYER.

O God, in Whose holy keeping Thy Saints lie hidden and secure, grant me so to live a hidden Life with Thee upon the earth, that by Thee I may be kept secure from all evil, and find my Joy in the manifestation of Thy Love eternally ; through Jesus Christ our Lord. **Amen.**

DIVINE SECRECY.

PRELUDE. i. *A little fountain became a river.*—Esther x. 6.
ii. Her father taking her up, and praying for her to be Blessed.

POINT I. *Consider the Divine knowledge.*
- *a.* Mary was born in the midst of a degraded population; but God knew the destiny of grace whereby she would be sheltered from the evil around, so as to be fitted for her mysterious calling.
- *b.* With God nothing is small, for the smallest things are the objects of His greatest Love. Things are great not by man's recognition but by God's Love.
- *c.* God knows all things in their future from the very first of their beginning. We should consider what God means us to be, not what we are, as the true measure of ourselves. So should we rise up to the Divine knowledge.

POINT II. *Consider the ignorance of the world.*
- *a.* The world only pays honour to that which is accidental. What the world honours passes away, and so. does the world's homage.
- *b.* The world cannot appreciate the collapse of its own greatness, nor the growing greatness of that which is united to Christ.
- *c.* The world is death. Christ is life. The world cannot see any glory save that of death. True life, true glory, are hidden from the world.

POINT III. *Consider the patient submission of the faithful.*
- *a.* If we live in the security of God's knowledge, we can wait God's time. We know that nothing is impossible except for things to continue as they are. The world must change.
- *b.* We know that God's work is a growing work, and therefore no smallness of beginning can discourage us.
- *c.* God's promises are not made to the world, nor effected by the world's dead machinery. We cannot heed worldly appearances. Greatness in the world is no token of spiritual growth.

AFFECTIONS. Humility. Love of hiddenness. Fear of worldliness.

PRAYER.

O God, Who didst choose a lowly Virgin to be the Mother of Thine Incarnate Son, grant that we may abide in Thy Love by lowliness and purity, and eschew the greatness of the world which is dead to Thee. Grant this for the sake of Jesus Christ Thy Son our Lord. Amen.

A.D. 629.

THE CRUCIFIED LIFE.

PRELUDE. i. *The Kingdom of Heaven is like unto treasure hid in a field. Alleluia.*—S. Matt. xiii. 44.

ii. The Emperor carrying the Cross barefoot through Jerusalem.

POINT I. *Consider the loss of the Crucified Life in our days.*

  a. The first Christians honoured the Crucified Life. The Cross in its silver case may symbolize this for us. Alas! we live for the world.
  b. Satan has robbed us of this treasure, and hinders us from carrying out the law of self-sacrifice. He has surrounded us with maxims of worldly business and pleasure, and we are in a far-off land under his tyranny.
  c. Without the Crucified Life we cannot be true to Him Who died upon the Cross.

POINT II. *Consider the importance of the Crucified Life.*

  a. Only thereby can we exercise the supernatural Life which belongs to Jesus. The Cross is the gate of Heaven, whereon we must hang if we would know the glory of the Life beyond.
  b. By the Crucified Life of Jesus we were redeemed, and by a Life crucified with Him our sanctification is perfected.
  c. No faculty that we possess in the world can be offered to God except upon the Cross. Our energies are often our destruction. It is by dying to the world that we really live to God.

POINT III. *Consider the recovery of the Crucified Life.*

  a. It must be with much effort carried out in a spirit of true faith.
  b. We must attack the enemy in his own country, by setting ourselves against those worldly maxims which carry away the Cross, and prevent its being the standard of our lives.
  c. We must carry the Cross with the bare feet of poverty through the Heavenly Jerusalem. The outward poverty of the Cross must be our glory in the Communion of Saints.

AFFECTIONS. Love of the Cross. Holy zeal. Cherishing of poverty.

PRAYER.

O Lord God, Who hast given Thine only Son to triumph upon the Cross for our sakes against the Evil One, grant that I may so learn to take up my Cross and follow Him, that I may enter into the Heavenly Jerusalem in the full joy of Thy triumph with all Thy Saints; through the same Jesus Christ our Lord. Amen.

Y

A.D. 709.

FORTITUDE.

PRELUDE. i. *Theirs is the Kingdom of Heaven who have despised the life of this world to gain a reward in the Kingdom, and have washed their robes in the Blood of the Lamb.*—Rev. vii. 14.

ii. The Saint unwillingly accepting the responsibility of the Episcopate.

POINT I. *Consider Fortitude in exercising discipline.*

a. We are not all sent to call others to penitence, but a Christian, living fearlessly in the observance of holy discipline, strengthens others by example and sympathy.

b. How many fall away because those who are over them are not firm. True charity sustains dependents, and does not enfeeble them.

c. Fortitude will always be accompanied by tenderness and consideration. We need to know from God what is the limit to be observed. He strengthens and softens those whom He teaches.

POINT II. *Consider Fortitude in obedience.*

a. Divine Authority recognised by obedience should strengthen us to fulfil commands from which we might else shrink.

b. Divine grace will always assist us in doing what is rightfully enjoined.

c. In obedience we exercise sympathy, rejoicing to act in union with another. Human nature is formed to act most vigorously in association. God binds us together by holy obedience.

POINT III. *Consider Fortitude in death.*

a. Fortitude is not recklessness, but it arises from a contemplation of a glorious issue, even though it wait to find this issue beyond the grave.

b. Fortitude regards every overthrow not in itself, but as a step by which some greater reward may be obtained.

c. Fortitude rejoices in the example of Christ, and is ever ready to suffer violence rather than to avenge self for any wrong however great.

AFFECTIONS. Boldness in duty. Desire to strengthen others. Dependence upon God for strength.

PRAYER.

O Lord God, strengthen me amidst the manifold devices of the Evil One, that I may be stedfast in the fulfilment of Thy holy commands, and patient in the endurance of all things according to Thy will, resting evermore in the assurance of Thy wise government, and looking forward to the triumph of Thy loving purposes in a world that is beyond all pain; through Jesus Christ our Lord. Amen.

THE SYMBOLICAL CREATURES.

PRELUDE. i. *And the four beasts had each of them six wings about him.*—Rev. iv. 8.

ii. The Vision described in the Apocalypse.

POINT I. *Consider the four living creatures.*
  a. They symbolize a multitude, all the members of the Living Body of Christ; a multitude having an organic unity of which Christ is the Head.
  b. They all live with one Life, and that Life is the true Life, the Life of God which is in His Son.
  c. The various manifestations of the Living Body of Christ move with one impulse.

POINT II. *Consider the six wings.*
  a. Six is the number of created perfection. The wings cannot bear up the creatures save by the power of the uncreated life which they breathe.
  b. The wings are in pairs, for all the acts of the Body of Christ are wrought in the power of the Spirit of Divine Charity, and move therefore in love to God and man.
  c. There are twenty-four wings in all, corresponding with the twenty-four Elders, the heads of the courses of the Priesthood. The successive arrangement of David is now gathered into one combined ministration of the Holy Ghost in union with Christ the Head of all.

POINT III. *Consider the signification of the four creatures.*
  a. The lion symbolizes the royal, as the ox the sacrificial, character of Christ. The Face of a Man signifies His Humanity, as the Flying Eagle His Divine Nature.
  b. That which belongs to Christ the Head belongs to His members, as partakers of His Life.
  c. The fourfold character signifies the universality of Redemption, as the city lying four square, and the four corners of the Cross.

AFFECTIONS. Joy of Heavenly Unity. Reverence for our new Life in Christ.

PRAYER.

O God, Who hast made us to be partakers of a new Life in the Body of Thine Only-begotten Son in union with all Thy Saints, grant that I may always walk as befits this heavenly character, and may show forth Thy Holiness by acting faithfully in accordance with Thine inspirations; through Jesus Christ our Lord. Amen.

THE ILLUMINATED LIFE OF THE FOUR.

PRELUDE. i. *And they were full of eyes within.*—Rev. iv. 8.
ii. The vision as before.

POINT I. *Consider the interior Vision of the Blessed.*

    a. They have God within them, according to the promise, " I will dwell in them and walk in them." " We are built together for an habitation of God by the Spirit."

    b. Being one with Christ they have the power of seeing God's glory which illuminates them. The king's daughter is all glorious within.

    c. Every faculty of their nature is an eye, wherewith they behold God, for they have an experience of God's indwelling in every sense.

POINT II. *Consider the Purity of their Vision.*

    a. " Blessed are the pure in heart, for they shall see God." The faculties are altogether purified, so that nothing impedes their exercise.

    b. Being dead unto the world, they are freed from the obstruction of all objects which could come between them and God. They see into the inmost depth of the life which they possess, for the Spirit which animates their faculties searches into all things, even the deep things of God.

    c. There is no dullness attendant upon their vision, for their faculties are sustained and kept free from all possibility of weariness by the Life which inspires them.

POINT III. *Consider the Blessedness of their Vision.*

    a. The Divine Life is the joy of all who behold it, for it cannot be seen without a real union of energy whereby it becomes a sweet experience.

    b. It is a blessedness which, as it is an infinite energy, is not exhausted by a momentary contemplation, but satisfies the whole nature with changeless delight.

    c. The Infinite Joy of the Blessed which is to be revealed hereafter in us is given to us already as a principle of Life, to be cherished and developed, for if it be lost it cannot be regained.

AFFECTIONS. Joy in the Divine Life. Carefulness in preserving it. Desire for its perfection.

PRAYER.

O God, Who dost reveal Thy glory to all whom Thou callest into the fellowship of the Body of Thine Only-begotten Son, grant me so to live in the remembrance of that Life which I cannot see, that hereafter I may rejoice in the full manifestation of Thy predestinating Love; through the same Jesus Christ our Lord. Amen.

THEIR CEASELESS PRAISE.

PRELUDE. i. *They rest not day and night, saying, Holy, Holy, Holy, Lord God Almighty.*—Rev. iv. 8.

ii. The Vision as before.

POINT I. *Consider the unbroken utterance of song.*

a. It is an energy of created nature, a real resurrection of those faculties which constitute humanity.

b. It is a Divine inspiration sustaining that nature. In this world the Divine impulse is but imperfectly identified with the creature. There it is the only life.

c. It is a joy whereof the nature never wearies. As it has the Divine Word for its only life it acts with the perfect simplicity of God.

POINT II. *Consider the Divine origin of that song.*

a. It is the communication of the Voice of God. The utterance of creation is only the return of the Voice of God to Himself. Hence the great dignity of speech, and the sacrilegious character of evil words.

b. It is the manifestation of the Eternal Word in the mysterious harmony of His own individual utterances to each soul. The perfection of the combined utterance flows from the unity of the original impulse.

c. It is the complete expression of the Divine Manifestation as far as created energy is capable of correspondence with it.

POINT III. *Consider the mutual joy of the multitude by whom this song is uttered.*

a. The joy of utterance. By pouring forth the Divine Word we feel its sweetness. So often does the Psalmist express his delight.—Pss. xix. 10; cxix. 103.

b. The joy of hearing. As we hear so we speak. Hearing will not imply imperfection, but correspondence of life.

c. The joy of sympathy. Here we hear the words of others. There we shall hear the Word of God in others, which is the very Word Who speaks in ourselves. The Life of each is the Life and the Joy of all.

AFFECTIONS. Delight in Divine Praise. Joy in the knowledge of God's goodness to others.

PRAYER.

O Lord God, holy in Thyself, Who makest Thy holiness manifest in the sanctification of Thy creatures, grant that I may so serve Thee in holiness, acting here according to the greatness of Thy power, that I may hereafter rejoice in Thy holiness as my everlasting portion and infinite joy; through Jesus Christ our Lord. Amen.

THE ETERNITY OF GOD.

PRELUDE. i. *Holy, Holy. Holy, Lord God Almighty, which was, and is, and is to come.*—Rev. iv. 8.

ii. As before.

POINT I. *Consider the creatures as living with the Eternal Life.*

  a. Being partakers of the Eternal Life, they are able to praise God for His Eternity with a consciousness which we cannot have in this world while compassed about with the body of death.

  b. They feel within themselves the power of God by which they live and rest in its changeless security.

  c. The predestination of God finds its perfect expression in their consciousness.

POINT II. *Consider the manifestation of God's Holiness within them.*

  a. They experience the Divine goodness by an entire correspondence therewith.

  b. The glory of the Divine holiness shines out before them triumphant over all the difficulties by which it was obscured from sight in the lower world. The illuminated will of the creature becomes perfectly one with the wisdom of Divine Providence in recognizing the righteousness of God.

  c. In their own redemption from the power of evil they find the greatest display of the Divine power and goodness.

POINT III. *Consider the Immutability of God.*

  a. That which He has been from eternity He is to all eternity to come. The act of the Divine Life whereby the Three Persons are evermore One God, remains unchanged.

  b. The development of creation changes not the eternal relationships of God. That which in prescience He predestinates, He in accomplishment beatifies.

  c. The future is present to His prescience. The past does not die away from His power. All things receive order, sustenance, retribution from His Love. Their experience of Him changes, His knowledge of them is ever the same.

AFFECTIONS. Repose in God. Adoration. Confession of ignorance.

PRAYER.

O Eternal God, Who in Thy wisdom ordainest all things from the beginning, that Thou mayest manifest to all Thy Love, grant me so to praise Thee with holy confidence in this season of ignorance, that I may attain to joy in the contemplation of Thy wisdom when the kingdom of Thy dear Son shall be established; through the same Thy Son Jesus Christ our Lord. Amen.

A.D. 258.

DISCIPLINE.

PRELUDE. i. *Theirs is the kingdom of heaven who have despised the life of this world to gain a reward in the kingdom, and have washed their robes in the Blood of the Lamb.*—Rev. vii. 14.

ii. S. Cyprian warning his flock against laxity under persecution.

POINT I. *Consider the strictness of Holy Discipline.*

a. The laws of grace must be as unalterable as those of nature, since they come from the same Author. The result will be equally beneficial in both cases, for both are organized by Infinite Wisdom.

b. The Church must live true to her prerogatives, by carefully fulfilling her obligations. Human will is admitted into the development of the Kingdom of Grace, so as to elevate what is human, not to set aside the law which is Divine.

c. Human power should never set Divine law aside. Holiness never can, for, if it did, it would cease to be holy. Relaxation must be with prudence; then it is charity. If it be merely for personal ends, it results in death.

POINT II. *Consider the sweetness of Holy Discipline.*

a. If we practise the law of God we may look to experience the love of God.

b. Discipline perfects the Church in the harmony of Heavenly Life; and as we live thereby we must find the joy of the Heavenly Choirs binding us all in one.

c. The energies of the individual life are developed by holy discipline, for God has ordered the wellbeing of society and of the individual so that they help one another.

POINT III. *Consider the security of Holy Discipline.*

a. That which lacks discipline must perish. All the parts of the system tend to destroy one another if they are not acting under law.

b. Every part of the body becomes helpful to the other parts, if all are controlled by one unchanging law.

c. That which is governed by a law superior to itself rises to energies and purposes superior to itself. By the very principle of subjection it grows to perfection.

AFFECTIONS. · Love of unity and order. Thankfulness for repression. Joy in obedience.

PRAYER.

O God, Who art the Author of order, brightness, and love, binding all Thy works together in the living Unity of Thine own All-wise Predestination, grant that I may always accept Thy discipline with meekness, praising Thee alike for Thy revelation, Thy chastisements, Thy promises, and Thy grace, and looking forward through the unchangeableness of Thy counsel to attain to the unchangeableness of Thy Life; through Jesus Christ our Lord. Amen.

THE ANGELIC PRAISE.

PRELUDE. i. *To Thee all Angels cry aloud: the Heavens and all the Powers therein.*

ii. The Vision of the Heavenly Host.

POINT I. *Consider the glory of the Angel Choirs.*

    a. The Spirit of God moves them with a ceaseless utterance. Their glory is a derived, created glory; not inherent, not independent, but continuous as the Divine Love.

    b. The varied Powers utter God's praise in perfect harmony. Amidst the multiplicity of creation there is a unity of purpose combining all the energies of all that live.

    c. There is a progress of praise as God's work advances. Creation is continually developing ; not stationary, but growing to perfection in the manifestation of the infinite purpose of God.

POINT II. *Consider the Object of their Praise.*

    a. They cry out unto God. Themselves created by His Word, they by the power of that Word respond to Him.

    b. God to Whom they cry is One : but their knowledge of God is varied, as their own natures vary.

    c. God delights in the utterance which is thus addressed to Him. Creation is not an addition to God, but a manifestation of that Eternal Power which constitutes His changeless Bliss.

POINT III. *Consider the joy with which they thus cry out to God.*

    a. It is not the cry of want, but of fulness; not of wearied satiety, but of ever fresh fruition.

    b. It is the irrepressible cry of their life. They live in praising God. As their life is not in themselves it cannot rest in themselves, but returns in praise to its true source.

    c. They cry aloud, for their whole being is absorbed in the utterance. There is no dumbness, no faculty not filled with praise.

AFFECTIONS. Union with the Angels in Praise. Joy in their fellowship. Self-forgetfulness in God.

PRAYER.

O God, Who hast filled the Heavenly Host with glory to show forth Thy Praise, grant that I may glorify Thee in the fellowship of their glory, and attain to that glory in the perfect manifestation of Thyself within me, for which Thou hast subjected me to this discipline of struggle with the darkness; through Jesus Christ our Lord. Amen.

ANGELIC MINISTRATION.

PRELUDE. i. *I am Raphael: one of the seven holy Angels which present the prayers of the Saints.*—Tobit xii. 15.

ii. The Angels round about the Throne of God.

POINT I. *Consider the Angels ministering to the Body of Christ.*

a. They sustain the functions of nature for the demands of grace. So our Lord was strengthened by an Angel as man, though speaking to the F. in the fulness of the H. G. as God.

b. The seven Angels of natural presentation correspond with the sevenfold spirit of Divine inspiration. Creation does not merely symbolize, but it subserves the Incarnation.

c. Their ministries are as vials, which Divine grace rejoices to fill with odours.

POINT II. *Consider their assistance in driving away evil.*

a. As the veil of the Cherubim shut in the Holy Place, so the holy Angels shut in the Body of Christ, that we His members may not be hurt by the assaults of Satan.

b. The Holy Ghost fills the mind with holy thoughts, but the holy Angels guarding us, lest we dash our foot against a stone, keep off evil thoughts which hinder our prayers.

c. Gifts of grace are destroyed by material and by spiritual agents of evil. So angels and sacraments conduce to our restoration, and save us from forfeiting the gift of Divine Life.

POINT III. *Consider the joy which we ought to take in these Heavenly surroundings.*

a. The Angel hosts as a glorious temple enshrine the Body of Christ, manifested in the Living Creatures. If ritual of earth can cheer, how much more should this Heavenly glory do so.

b. As the wonderful order in which we and they are combined is of God's Creative Love, how must we welcome our Father's Glory and Love in those who minister with us, around us, to us !

c. Their worship is a ministration to us, and our worship is the instrument of their own perfection. They help us that we may pray. They do not supersede our prayer.

AFFECTIONS. Heavenly Joy. Rapture of Divine Worship. Gratitude for all Divine appointments.

PRAYER.

O God, Who hast called me to approach Thy Majesty in the Body of Thine Only-begotten Son, and with the participation of all the Heavenly Host, enable me so to worship Thee now amidst the darkness of this fallen world, that I may hereafter worship Thee in the manifest glory wherein Thy blessed ones behold Thy Face for ever; through Jesus Christ our Lord. Amen.

ANGELIC PROCLAMATION.

PRELUDE i. *And I saw the seven Angels which stood before God, and to them were given seven trumpets.*—Rev. viii. 2.

ii. The Angels ready to sound when God shall speak.

POINT I. *Consider the manifestation of Divine Power.*

a. They manifest God's work to His Saints. As in the Old Testament, so in the New. God sends His angels to His servants.

b. They manifest God's power through the world; but the world does not see the Vision or hear the Voice.

c. They carry on the war of God, fighting against the enemies of the Church, although unseen by man.

POINT II. *Consider the progress of Divine Judgment.*

a. They hold back the self-willed, as they did Balaam; staying the instruments which they would use in the prosecution of their evil.

b. They bring visitations of anger, pestilence, and other punishments, as when David had numbered Israel.

c. They will come in full assembly along with our Lord Jesus Christ, when He shall appear for the Judgment of the Great Day.

POINT III. *Consider the anger of the nations.*

a. The Angels hasten the consummation of Christ's Kingdom. They develope the laws by which God's work in this world, in opposition to Satan, is carried to its completeness.

b. They proclaim its approaching glory. But the world is only maddened, thinking to triumph, while yet they announce that the kingdoms are become the kingdoms of God and of His Christ. So shall sudden destruction come upon the world.

c. The reapers in the Last Day will be the holy Angels, who will gather the tares in bundles to burn them.

AFFECTIONS. Trust in God's Providence. Expectation of results beyond natural power. Joy in having such allies.

PRAYER.

O *God, Who hast surrounded us with oly Angels, who   e ever carrying out Thy holy will, suffer me not to be blinded by outward things, so as to find in them occasion either for hope or fear, but ever to look for the glory of Thy Truth to be manifested in such ways as Thou shalt ordain; through Jesus Christ our Lord.* Amen.

ANGELIC BLISS.

PRELUDE. i. O *ye Angels of the Lord, bless ye the Lord, praise Him and magnify Him for ever.*
ii. The Angel choirs.

POINT I. *Consider their consciousness of the Divine glory.*
 a. They proclaim the blessedness of the Lord because they find themselves to be blessed in the power of the Divine Life.
 b. As they do God's will, they rejoice in His glory. They know that their own work is but the manifestation of His power, and that they themselves are nothing.
 c. By the joy of the strength given to them, they learn the glory of the strength from which their own strength is derived.

POINT II. *Consider their joy in making it manifest.*
 a. To behold it and not to utter it would be a condition of spiritual death. While the intelligence is moved with its joy it partakes of its Life.
 b. They know that they were created for its manifestation, and rejoice in the Joy which God Himself takes in what they do.
 c. They find a joyous sympathy in the admiration of their fellow-creatures, not taking it to themselves, but rejoicing that God should be acknowledged and glorified.

POINT III. *Consider the perpetuity of this joy.*
 a. There is no intermission. As they breathe the Life of God continually, so from the first moment of their creation they bless Him.
 b. There is no end. The praise of God must ever sustain them, for it is itself exhaustless. While there is any Divine perfection to praise, the intelligence which lives in its contemplation must find sustenance for its life.
 c. There is a communicated eternity. If the glory of God were not made known in its eternity, it would not be made known in its truth ; but it cannot be made known in its eternity except by the gift of an eternal power of contemplation and union. The knowledge of God is eternal Life.

AFFECTIONS. Joy in union with the holy Angels. Desire to glorify God in like manner.

PRAYER.

O God, before Whom the holy Angels exult in the glory wherewith Thou hast endued them, contemplating Thy glory from Whom their strength proceeds, grant that I may so constantly abide in Thy Presence here with joyful homage, that in Thy Presence I may find the fulness of joy for evermore ; through Jesus Christ our Lord. Amen.

ANGELIC UNITY.

PRELUDE. i. *With Angels and Archangels, and with all the company of Heaven, we laud and magnify Thy glorious Name.*

ii. All the Heavenly Host 'around the Throne of God.

POINT I. *Consider the Love which unites the Heavenly Hierarchies.*

> *a.* The will of God binds them in one impulse. Each order has its several work to do, but all act with perfect oneness of mission.
> *b.* The glory of God binds them in one aim. Their existence has a special purpose as conducing to the one great result, the manifestation of God.
> *c.* The Spirit of God binds them in one consciousness of joint endeavour. All rejoice in the work of each.

POINT II. *Consider the assumption of the redeemed into the fellowship of their Love.*

> *a.* Man was created to supply the vacancy caused by the fall of the angels.
> *b.* Man is called to serve God in unison with the Heavenly Host, although not seeing them.
> *c.* Man shall attain to visible fellowship, being more gloriously filled with the Holy Ghost than any of the Angels.

POINT III. *Consider the increase of joy in Heaven by reason of our exaltation.*

> *a.* The manifestation of God in man is the object for which all creation yearns, waiting for the redemption of our body. —Rom. viii. 23.
> *b.* They ascend and descend upon the Son of Man, and exult in every manifestation of the Divine Life of the Church.
> *c.* They will gather round the Throne of the glorified Saviour, and find eternal joy in His Praise.—Rev. v. 12.

AFFECTIONS. Diligence. Obedience. Self-restraint. Hope.

PRAYER.

O God, Who hast appointed to each of Thy creatures that special work whereby Thou wouldest have them serve Thee, grant me so to fulfil Thy will within the limits appointed for my discipline, that I may attain with all Thy Saints and holy Angels to behold Thy glory according to the fulness of Thy Truth; through Jesus Christ our Lord. Amen.

ANGELIC GUARDIANSHIP.

PRELUDE. i. *Take heed that ye despise not one of these little ones; for I say unto you, That in Heaven their Angels do always behold the Face of My Father Which is in Heaven.*—S. Matt. xviii. 10.

ii. The holy Angels welcoming the regenerated child as shining with the communicated Life of God.

POINT I. *Consider the loving care of the Angels.*

    a. The love of God in which they are called to live is the bond of love which binds them to the objects of their trust. Their love is not less but greater, as springing from Divine command.

    b. It is an absorbing love, from which they never turn by any distraction or forgetfulness.

    c. It is a love which draws them onward to God, so that they look for the manifestation of the Divine Life in those they guard, for God to be manifest in their flesh.

POINT II. *Consider the intelligence with which they contemplate the loving Predestination of God for His children.*

    a. The Angels desire to look into the glory of the work of redemption. The manifold wisdom of God shall at length be manifested to them through the Church. God chargeth His Angels with folly. The glory of His purpose they cannot know until it be accomplished.

    b. Those intelligences shine with Divine Light according to the measure of God's gift. Satan's intelligence retains its capacities but is separated from the Truth, so that he remains in darkness.

    c. All the orders of holy Angels act in subordination as God has fixed their conditions, each having that intelligence which is needed for his own proper functions.

POINT III. *Consider the desire which they have to see that Predestination manifested.*

    a. They minister to the Incarnate God, and develope the successive eras of the world, but they long for the end, that God may be manifest.

    b. They carry on the war of ages without weariness, holding Satan back.

    c. They look for Christ to drive Satan away by the struggle of the Church, the sufferings of the Saints.

AFFECTIONS. Thankfulness. Heavenly Fellowship. Desire for Christ's appearing. Love to Christ's members.

PRAYER.

O God, Who hast appointed Thy holy Angels to be our guard, having united us to the Body of Thine Only-begotten Son, grant that we may always look up to Thee, so that in the Light of Thy countenance we may act as befits Thy holy Love ; through the same Jesus Christ our Lord. **Amen.**

A.D. 420.

BIBLICAL CRITICISM.

PRELUDE. i. *Well done, thou good and faithful servant: thou hast been faithful over a few things, I will make thee ruler over many things: enter thou into the Joy of thy* Lord.—S. Matt. xxv. 21.

ii. The Saint studying Hebrew.

POINT I. *Consider the Voice of God in Holy Scripture.*

a. If we praise God for speaking, we must take care that we do not suffer any negligence of ours to make us fail of apprehending what God says.

b. The Word of God to one age needs to be translated into new languages, and applied under differing circumstances, but its moral teaching is the same to all, and at all times.

c. God speaks to us through men of former generations, but He has given us His Holy Spirit that we may patiently search what He has said.

POINT II. *Consider the necessity of various studies in order to understand God's Word.*

a. All learning is sanctified by being used as a handmaid to Divine knowledge. God would have our whole life thus consecrated. Learning is true joy when undertaken for God's glory.

b. God's will touches upon every domain of action, and therefore He would have us search into nature, which is His handiwork, to understand the full scope of His Revelation.

c. Nothing is worth knowing unless it helps us towards doing God's will.

POINT III. *Consider the retirement in which God's Word must be studied.*

a. In life amongst men we are apt to be led astray by their maxims, so as to translate God's truth by their imaginations.

b. We are in danger of seeking man's praise for what we have learnt, rather than holiness, without which we cannot learn anything truly.

c. We cannot hear God's Voice speaking to us through His Word unless the soul be truly listening with prayerful devotion.

AFFECTIONS. Desire to sanctify natural powers. Reverence for God's Sovereign Truth. Attentiveness to the Divine Message.

PRAYER.

O God, Who in Thy Holy Scriptures dost speak to us as the Creator of all things, teaching us to use all to Thy glory, give me understanding, that I may rightly and reverently search into Thy Revelation, and may be conformed to Thy will; through Jesus Christ our Lord. Amen.

LONGEVITY.

PRELUDE. i. *Well done. thou good and faithful servant:
thou hast been faithful over a few things, I will make thee ruler
over many things: enter thou into the Joy of thy Lord.*—S. Matt.
xxv. 21.

ii. The Saint when past ninety years of age.

POINT I. *Consider the weariness of lengthened life.*

    a. The weariness of bodily decay. Who could endure it, save
for the knowledge of a work to be done for God in offering
the body more perfectly to be a sacrifice than had been done
in time of health?

    b. The weariness of the mind. If the mind can forecast, yet
the body cannot execute. The will serves but to mock us,
unless we have learnt to give the will wholly to God.

    c. Social weariness. How sad it were to outlive the friends
and hopes of youth, if we could not live in the Communion
of Saints. Old age is misery if there be no foretaste of
Heaven. Why do we not rather desire Heaven than old age?

POINT II. *Consider the vicissitudes of lengthened life.*

    a. This is a world of evil, and success can only be measured
by the evil which we have met and overthrown.

    b. The calm development of the inner life in the contempla-
tion of God belongs not to the length of years. It is perfected only by death.

    c. How needful is sorrow here, even to give zest to joy. Why
do we hug sorrow instead of longing to be absorbed in God?

POINT III. *Consider the success of lengthened life.*

    a. Our sufferings are the true offering which we give to God.
Outward wealth is not ourselves, and God heeds it not.

    b. To have succeeded much is to have suffered much; and in
contemplating worldly success we set our eyes on that which
must soon be taken away.

    c. Success and lengthened life were an Old Testament pro-
mise, for then the grave was darkness. Now the faithful in
dying go to Jesus. That is a better success, a joy that ends
not.

AFFECTIONS. Dedication of life to God. Desire to see
Jesus. Detachment from the world.

PRAYER.

*O God, Who hast ordained this life to be a preparation for that
which is to come, grant me so to live here simply for Thy service,
that in dying I may lose nothing, but may gain the Vision for which
in life I have longed; through Jesus Christ our Lord. Amen.*

THIRD CENTURY.

SIMPLICITY OF FAITH.

PRELUDE. i. *When the Bridegroom came they that were ready went in with Him to the marriage.*—S. Matt. xxv. 10.

ii. The Virgin, arrayed by her Mother, coming forth to the Judge.

POINT I. *Consider the calling of the faithful.*

 a. The soul that is betrothed to Christ in faith must be a virgin soul, unspotted by the world, however much assailed thereby.

 b. The soul must know the Voice of the Beloved. The sense of duty as an abstract principle does not suffice to the faithful soul. We must in all matters hear Him that speaketh.

 c. Our Christian Name must be a pledge of holiness of life. It symbolizes for us every virtue, since it expresses our union with Christ.

POINT II. *Consider the trial of faith.*

 a. Our Christian Name is to us a pledge of suffering, for it is only by suffering that our virtue can be made manifest. A holiness with only joy would not be a holiness suited for those who have to escape from a world of sin.

 b. Our faith must consist in a real identification with the world that is beyond; otherwise it would not be the substance of the things hoped for, even though it might be a result of the heavenly hope.

 c. Hope must spring from faith : not faith from hope; for faith has a supernatural experience of Divine things, whereas hope only recognizes the development of our experience.

POINT III. *Consider the issue of faith.*

 a. Faith exults in natural sufferings, for the pain we bear is the measure of the consciousness of hidden life, by which we triumph.

 b. Faith sets us free from all external enemies. These cannot touch that inner realm of eternal life, which is the home of faith.

 c. Faith presses onward to the Love of God. It feeds upon hidden treasures of Divine Love, and finds a joy that is ever near.

AFFECTIONS. Faith. Boldness. Joy.

PRAYER.

O God, Who callest us to lay hold upon Thy glory now by faith, grant that the outer nature may be destroyed in conflict with the world, and the inner life perfected in faith according to Thy holy purpose, so that we may be superior to all worldly fears, and rejoice in the fellowship of Thy changeless Love; through Jesus Christ our Lord. Amen.

DELIBERATION.

PRELUDE. i. *Theirs is the Kingdom of Heaven who have despised the life of this world to gain a reward in the Kingdom, and have washed their robes in the Blood of the Lamb.*—Rev. vii. 14.

ii. S. Paul standing on the orator's stone before the assembly on Mars' Hill.

POINT I. *Consider the calmness of the judicial character.*

a. How impartially does the Judge watch the development of the case which is being tried before him. How much more calmly ought we to listen to a voice pleading for God.

b. Our anxiety by reason of the greatness of the issue will make us quick to discern the real bearings of the question, not hasty so as to evade the real urgency of the arguments.

c. We must not be moved from the calm consideration of Divine Truth by the mockery or flippancy of others.

POINT II. *Consider the reverence due to deliberation on Divine things.*

a. S. Paul was called out by the earnest listeners from the throng of the market-place to the hill-top of judgment. Let us retire from the world to listen to God's Voice.

b. On the hill-top of Divine Contemplation the Divine Speaker will bring home to our conscience the insufficiency of our natural thoughts, our hopeless ignorance.—Acts xvii. 22, 23.

c. From the dignity inherent in our own nature, even though fallen, God will make known to us the claims of His own glory and truth.—Acts xvii. 29.

POINT III. *Consider the necessity of adhering to Truth.*

a. The world regards the Apostle of Christ as a babbler ; for he tells of things which the world cannot understand. The world's mockery must not drive us away.

b. The habit of exercising judgment must make us stedfast in our allegiance to Truth as we come to know it more and more.

c. High station does not commend us to Christ, but we must praise God when we see any in high station who are enabled by His mercy to give up the world and cling to Him.

AFFECTIONS. Desire for Truth. Independence of the world. Loyalty to God.

PRAYER.

O God, Who callest us all into Thine own Presence, that we may be judged according to Thy Truth, grant us so to recognize Thy Voice speaking within us as the power whereby we may judge ourselves, that we may evermore be stedfast in our allegiance to Thee, and order all our thoughts and ways according to Thy glorious Revelation; through Jesus Christ our Lord. Amen.

z

A.D. 1066.

ROYALTY.

PRELUDE, i. *Well done, thou good and faithful servant: enter thou into the Joy of thy Lord.*—S. Matt. xxv. 21.

ii. The Sovereign seated in the Chair of the Confessor

POINT I. *Consider the sacredness of royalty.*

   a. It is the expression in earthly government of the eternal Sovereignty of God, in Whose Name it is exercised.

   b. It is the expression of national unity in its personal reality before God as the source of domestic relationships, and the stay of family love.

   c. It is the channel of Divine utterance, so that God makes it to be a mark of His displeasure against a nation when He appoints those to rule who are morally and physically unequal to the task.

POINT II. *Consider the responsibility of government.*

   a. All government, whether supreme or subordinate, and even the smallest, exists by God's permission, for the purposes of His Will, so that those who exercise authority have their primary duty towards Him, as the source of their office and power.

   b. The individual is created in God's image. The control of the individual man has primary reference to the glory of God in that individual.

   c. Those in authority have to execute God's will with forethought and care. It does not suffice that they abstain from contravening it.

POINT III. *Consider the inheritance of honour.*

   a. The glory, much more the holiness, of those from whom we are sprung ought to form a consciousness of Divine covenant, pledging our fidelity to Him Who blesses the thousand generations of the faithful.

   b. The knowledge of noble deeds done by the help of God should make us realize what we can do who have the same natural constitution and the same Divine grace.

   c. Honours, which come to us by Divine Providence without human counsel, violence, or fraud, demand a special acknowledgment to be given to God. This is true in all positions with respect to all faculties of mind, body, or estate.

AFFECTIONS. Reverence for authority. Care for the memory of ancestors. Self-dedication to God.

PRAYER.

O God, Who ordrest the affairs of mankind from one generation to another, grant that we may recognize Thine authority in those who rule by Thy grace, and may give ourselves wholly to Thee in the exercise of every faculty which of Thy bounty we receive; through Jesus Christ our Lord. Amen.

VIRGINITY OF HEART.

PRELUDE. i. *The* Bridegroom *came, and they that were ready went in with Him to the Marriage.*—S. Matt. xxv. 10.

ii. The Saint ministering to the Religious Community at Ely.

POINT I. *Consider the blessedness of Virgin Love to Christ.*

    a. The soul which seeks Christ as its only portion, enjoys the Presence of Christ with unsullied delight.

    b. The corruptible body weigheth down the incorruptible spirit. The Divine Spirit in the glorified Body of Christ, raises us out of the dominion of our lower nature, if we are wholly His.

    c. If we are united to Christ in undivided love, we shall hear Him speak in our hearts with blessed revelations of truth. As a touch prevents the ring of a bell, so the world's touch prevents the soul vibrating with that heavenly voice.

POINT II. *Consider the reward of Christ for those who despise all things for His sake.*

    a. Christ will manifest His Love to us proportionately to the value which He sees us to set upon it.

    b. He despised earthly things for our sake ; and if we would share in His reward we must follow Him in the Life of the Cross by dying to the world.

    c. If we have exerted our will by Divine inspiration to set aside earthly things, we shall find the hunger of our souls increased ; and as we hunger more, so God fills us more.

POINT III. *Consider what the world is which we have to set aside for Christ.*

    a. It is little to set aside the sinful indulgences of the world. These we must renounce by the necessity of God's Justice ; yet God's Love does welcome those who obey His Justice.

    b. So if sorrows drive us away from the world, there is little reason why Jesus should value our appeal to Him. Yet He does use sorrow as a means of drawing us to Himself.

    c. To put the world away for God, even in things not sinful, seeking to hold communion with God more unreservedly in Christ, is a sure way of finding Him. Acting in pure love to Him, we find His Love to us.

AFFECTIONS. Separation from the world. Union with Christ.

PRAYER.

O God, Who hast called us to share the kingdom and patience of Thine Only-begotten Son Jesus Christ, grant that I may find my joy in waiting patiently upon Thee ; and, holding myself aloof from the joys of this transitory world, may experience the sweet foretastes of the Eternal Kingdom, where Thou callest us to reign with Thee in the perfect manifestation of Thy glory ; through the same Jesus Christ our Lord. Amen.   z 2

A.D. 287.

LABOUR.

PRELUDE. i. *Theirs is the Kingdom of Heaven, who have despised the life of this world to gain a reward in the Kingdom, and have washed their robes in the Blood of the Lamb.*—Rev. vii. 14.

ii. The two noble brothers making shoes by night.

POINT I. *Consider the duty of labour.*

a. God has appointed labour. "If a man will not work neither should he eat." High station may exempt from the necessity, but not from the duty. Pleasure itself becomes by God's judgment a toil, if men will not earn it by labour.

b. No gifts of nature can be sustained in a worthy manner except by proportionate labour. Honours are inherited by providence, but appropriated by labour.

c. Labour is of various kinds, but the highest pleasures are proportioned to the pain of the toil. The pleasure of sanctity demands the sharp struggle of penitential discipline.

POINT II. *Consider the fruitfulness of labour.*

a. If we labour for the Love of God, God will send a Blessing on what we do far superior to anything that we could get by our own desires.

b. Labour appropriates God's gifts, but the gifts which we thus appropriate, multiply beyond the measure of our toil, according to the indwelling energy of the Life of God.

c. It is the Passion of Christ which gives fruitfulness to all toil. It communicates to our toil the fructifying power of the Holy Ghost, whereby it was itself accomplished.

POINT III. *Consider the sanctification of labour.*

a. No toil is fruitful without holiness : for no seeming fruitfulness can be abiding without the Holy Ghost.

b. The sanctifying power of the Holy Ghost must be continuously sought for by prayer. We must look towards God in devotional exercises if we would work with God and for God in any profitable service.

c. Labour does not hinder prayer but multiplies it, if it be done in a prayerful spirit.

AFFECTIONS. Industry. Prayerfulness in work. Expectation.

PRAYER.

O Lord God, Who hast ordained that we should eat bread in the sweat of the face, grant that I may labour for that Bread which endureth unto everlasting Life, and seeking amidst all toil the continual help of Thy Holy Spirit may be sanctified in the work which Thou givest me to do ; through Jesus Christ our Lord. Amen.

THE MULTITUDE OF THE SAINTS.

PRELUDE. i. *I beheld, and lo, a great multitude which no man could number, of all nations, and kindreds, and people, and tongues, stood before the Throne.*—Rev. vii. 9.

ii. As in the Apocalypse.

POINT I. *Consider the nations of the world, whence they are gathered.*

> *a.* They come from all nations. Each had their own difficulties to encounter, unlike those of others. In varied tongues they spake the one Divine Word of witness for the Truth.
>
> *b.* They were scattered, and knew not of one another upon the earth; yet one life was in them, wherein they now dwell in mutual love.
>
> *c.* Whatever their earthly relations were, they were separated from them. The call of the Lamb separated them from the world as a call of Death, and therefore the call of Death was to them the call of the Lamb uniting them together.

POINT II. *Consider the multitude.*

> *a.* No man can number them. Yet their number is known to God; He has formed them and redeemed them, that they may fill up the vacant numbers of the Heavenly Host. Not one is wanting, not one superfluous.
>
> *b.* The multitude is formed of individuals, each having had his own special discipline from God.
>
> *c.* Life on earth has been to all of them "the great tribulation." They came out of it not as a triumphant organised army, but as individual sufferers. Now shall their organization in the Body of Christ be made manifest.

POINT III. *Consider their standing before the Throne.*

> *a.* It has been the object of their hope. How the joy of fruition is enhanced by the discipline of expectation! Man's nature requires the virtue of hope for its final happiness.
>
> *b.* The robe of their humanity, once defiled, now shines with the bright life which the Blood of the Lamb communicates.
>
> *c.* As they behold the Lamb upon the Throne, they behold the glory of the Passion, whereby their hope was animated during their earthly suffering.

AFFECTIONS. Largeheartedness. Hope. Contempt of the world. Reverence for the Blessed Dead.

PRAYER.

O God, Who hast gathered unto Thyself a number greater than the thought of man, to live with the glory of Thine Only-begotten Son, participating in the reward of His Passion, while they praise Him eternally, for Love of Whom they rejoiced to suffer on the earth, grant that I may be in such wise partaker of His sufferings here, that of Thine ineffable bounty I may then share with them in His Joy; through the same Jesus Christ our Lord. Amen.

THE FELLOWSHIP OF SAINTS AND ANGELS.

PRELUDE. i. *And all the Angels stood round about the Throne, and about the Elders and the four beasts, and fell before the Throne on their faces and worshipped.*—Rev. vii. 11.

ii. As in the Apocalypse.

POINT I. *Consider the joy of the blessed Angels, as they behold the Church of the Redeemed and their glory.*

    a. For this they have waited. The Angels understand not God's manifold wisdom until they see the Church's triumph. Why do we miserable men perplex ourselves about God's judgments, which are much more out of our sight?

    b. They have ministered to these chosen ones in their great tribulations: in their glory they find their reward.

    c. As creatures they find their own natures exalted, for the Divine glory shines upon them through a perfected manifestation of created life in the fulness of the Body of Christ.

POINT II. *Consider the subjection of the blessed Angels.*

    a. Here we are made "lower than the Angels." Angels hold us up when we through weakness fall. How mindful we ought to be of the glory of their ministrations!

    b. Then the Church of the Redeemed will be "crowned with glory and worship." We shall judge angels. The Voice of Jesus speaks in His Elect, in prayer now, in lordship then.

    c. The Redeemed are standing before the Throne, for in union with Jesus they are the Priesthood of the Universe. The Angels fall down and worship through this mediation.

POINT II. *Consider the sevenfold song of Angelic Praise.*

    a. Blessing is the Father's Voice in the Eternal Generation of the Word. Glory is the Divine Nature. Wisdom is God's Personal Knowledge of Himself, which is now manifested to the Angels by the glorification of the Church.

    b. Thanksgiving, or Eucharist, is the praise which the members of Christ offer to the F. through Christ their Head. Honour is the homage of all creation to the Incarnate God.

    c. Power is the energy of the H. G. as the eternal bond of the All-glorious Trinity; and Might is perhaps the communication of that same Power to the glorified Humanity, which triumphs through the indwelling of the Holy Ghost.

AFFECTIONS. Reverence for the Blessed Angels. Joy in the Divine Triumph.

PRAYER.

O God, Who hast made us subject to Angels in this world, having nevertheless a glorious hope of Exaltation to the Throne of Thy Divine Glory, grant me so to carry out the law of obedience in the power of the Holy Ghost, that by His glorious might I may be perfected in glory; through the Mediation of Jesus Christ our Lord. **Amen.**

THE PRAISE OF THE REDEEMED.

PRELUDE. i. *Thou hast redeemed us to God by Thy Blood out of every kindred, and tongue, and people, and nation.*—Rev. v. 9.

ii. As in the Apocalypse.

POINT I. *Consider the cost of the purchase.*

a. Jesus has purchased us with His own Blood. The Life is in the Blood. This voluntary Bloodshedding of Jesus was a submission to the law under which man was placed.

b. That Blood is the Blood of God. By shedding it, all the energy of the Life of God was exercised in struggle with Him that had the power of death.

c. All the power of the enemy was exerted in vain to destroy Him. That Blood given to us in the Sacraments of Grace remains for ever as a power beyond his control.

POINT II. *Consider from what we are redeemed.*

a. From the curse of the law.—Gal. iii. 13.—The law could not remove the curse, for it could not give life. The curse had not power to destroy the Divine Life of Jesus. It could only touch upon His outer nature.

b. From amongst men. Therefore we are not to be led astray by the habits of men, nor by the maxims of the world.

c. From the hand of the enemy. All nations were in bondage to the Prince of this world. Now the Gospel of Christ is preached to all nations, and there can be no power anywhere to hold us down. Satan may inflict many a blow as we escape, but he cannot claim our life.

POINT III. *Consider the result of the purchase.*

a. Jesus becomes our Master, having bought us for Himself. —2 S. Peter ii. 1.—We were enslaved in enmity against God, and could not love God by nature. We need not know how this redemption affected any power that held us down. Enough that we now belong to Him that bought us!

b. We are His for ever. He bought us by the manifestation of His Love. By love we must own Him as our Master.

c. He has freed us from the power of the Devil: He has freed us from the weakness of the flesh: He has freed us from the falsehood of the world: that we may henceforth be wholly His. We lose our freedom when we fail to acknowledge His Sovereignty.

AFFECTIONS. Self-surrender to Jesus. Gratitude. Love.

PRAYER.

O Blessed Jesu, Who hast purchased us unto Thyself to be a peculiar people, zealous of good works, grant that I may ever rejoice to acknowledge Thee as my Lord and Master, seeking in all things to do Thy will, and satisfied in Thy Love; Who, with the Father and the Holy Ghost, livest and reignest God, for ever and ever. Amen.

THE PRAISE OF CREATION.

PRELUDE. i. *O ye Angels of the Lord, bless ye the Lord: praise Him, and magnify Him for ever.*—Song of the Three Children.

ii. The Church appealing to the Angels that are round about her.

POINT I. *Consider the Angels, as the mouthpiece of Creation, praising God,*

    a. They praise God, not with empty song, but with full harmony of active Life, accomplishing His will in perfect obedience throughout all the realms of space.

    b. Our material world is but the crust of Creation. The various orders of Angels keep all in blessed unity, of which we in this outer region of existence can form no idea.

    c. They minister to us not as if we were the noblest beings in creation, but in order to give glory to God.

POINT II. *Consider the Church as calling upon the Angels to glorify God.*

    a. Here, our prayers to God set Angels in motion to accomplish towards us His holy purposes, so that He is glorified.

    b. There, the Church, filled with Divine glory, will manifest to the Holy Angels the hidden mysteries ot Divine love.

    c. The Church wakens their praise to God, by the utterance of the Divine indwelling Word, which calls forth of necessity a response of praise from every intelligence which lives in the manifestation of the Eternal Light.

POINT III. *Consider the Eternity of the Praise.*

    a. The Word which speaks from everlasting speaks to everlasting. The Church, as the Body of the Incarnate Word, gives the universe a summons to praise, which must be co-extensive with the existence which the same Word sustains.

    b. The will of the Blessed Angels is fixed in changeless union with the glory of God which the Church proclaims.

    c. The glory of the Incarnate God is the Law of Creation. Those who refuse this glory find themselves eternally at war with Creation, and the laws thereof only serve to perpetuate their anger while they experience eternal doom.

AFFECTIONS. Desire for the manifestation of Christ's glory. Joy in the anticipation of Christ's kingdom.

PRAYER.

O God, Who hast revealed to us the consummation of all Thy works in the manifestation of the glory of Thine Only-begotten Son, hasten, we pray Thee, the day of His triumph, and grant us of Thy mercy so to be sanctified according to Thy will, that we may attain to the position which Thou hast prepared for us therein; through His merits Who liveth and reigneth with Thee One God, world without end, ever the same Jesus Christ our Lord. Amen.

THE GLORY OF GOD'S PRAISE.

PRELUDE. i. *All His Saints shall praise Him: even the children of Israel, even the people that serveth Him; such honour have all His Saints.*—Pss. cxlviii. 13 ; cxlix. 9.

ii. The Saints rising in glory.

POINT I. *Consider who they are that praise Him.*

   a. The children of Israel, gathered into covenanted relation with Him, born into the fellowship of supernatural life.

   b. The people that serveth Him, walking in the terms of that covenant, and obedient to the law which He has given.

   c. They who serve Him, or literally those who are near Him. By acts of holiness we abide near to God, for it is while we act in holiness that God acts within us. Our weakness is the vehicle of His power.

POINT II. *Consider the union of Saints in praising God.*

   a. Saints speak one to another while they speak to God. The praise which they offer to God binds them in an intense unity of action, which perfects the natural law of human sympathy.

   b. The will of the individual man is stablished in the one collective will of the Body of Christ. Each one is taken out of his own individual defectibility. All the Saints praise God with a consciousness of undivided intelligence.

   c. Each one shall then delight in the various discipline by which God has been training others as well as himself. No one will repine because his own vocation has been different from that of others.

POINT III. *Consider the honour of the Saints.*

   a. God's glory is the honour of the Saints ; not what they have done, but what He has done. His victories are the cause of their exultation.

   b. They seek their honour in glorifying Him. Gratitude is one of the noblest principles of human nature ; and it is the ennobling principle of Heaven.

   c. Each act of Divine Love that the soul can recognize becomes a fresh vocation, whereby God calls the soul to be bound to Himself in the conscious participation of His glory.

AFFECTIONS. Adoration. Gratitude. Love.

PRAYER.

O God, Who callest Thy Saints to praise Thee, that in the utterance of Thy praise they may find the glory of Thy Life, grant me so to praise Thee for thy goodness, as Thou dealest lovingly with me upon the earth, that I may attain hereafter to praise Thee in the perfect knowledge of Thy glorious Love; through Jesus Christ our **Lord. Amen.**

THE VARIED SONG OF SAINTLY PRAISE.

PRELUDE. i. *The glorious company of the Apostles; the goodly fellowship of the Prophets; the noble army of Martyrs; the Holy Church throughout all the world, doth acknowledge Thee, O Holy, Blessed, and Glorious Trinity.*

ii. The Blessed in Heaven.

POINT I. *Consider the various orders of Praise.*

  a. The form of earthly service determines the specialty of praise in Heaven. Individuality remains, although perfected by identity of Life in all.

  b. Every element of power in the Body of Christ abides as a living glory in the Company of Heaven.

Earthly purposes which developed individuality are passed away, but every faculty thus developed finds its true fulness in the fruition of God, Who thus communicates Himself by means of the many to the perfect consciousness of the undivided Body.

POINT II. *Consider the Divine Spirit of Praise.*

  a. All have lived in the power of the Holy Ghost, and have become perfected as members of the Body of Christ, to speak as He has formed them.

  b. All abide in the power of the Holy Ghost, so that each one breathes forth the fulness of the undivided Spirit.

  c. All are carried onward by the Holy Ghost to the fuller knowledge of God, as they rise up to Him in loving Praise.

POINT III. *Consider the Divine Love which receives their Praise.*

  a. It inspires their song. God rejoices in the Praise which they give, as being what He has Himself empowered them and taught them to give.

  b. It cheers their song. As they praise God they know how God delights in their praise : and while they rejoice in His Love, they rejoice to retain His Love by uttering their love to Him.

  c. It receives their song into the fulness of the Divine Life. God dwelleth in the praises of His people. Their words die not on the air around. Enshrining the Consubstantial Word as Inspired by the Holy Ghost they return into the Ear of that Love from whence at first they came.

AFFECTIONS. Sympathy with all Saints in Divine Love.

PRAYER.

O God, Who by the Spirit of Thy Son hast taught us to praise Thee, teach me to rejoice in Thy Praise as the true end of my being, that I may find eternal Life in the welcome which Thou givest to those who love Thee; through Jesus Christ our Lord. Amen.

FREEDOM.

PRELUDE. i. *O ye holy and humble men of heart, bless ye the Lord; praise Him, and magnify Him for ever.*—S. of the 3 Children.

ii. S. Leonard asking for the deliverance of prisoners.

POINT I. *Consider the freedom of the soul in holy retirement.*

a. The world is a prison-house. The soul of man longs for a freedom which it cannot find here. The maxims of the world are chains which keep souls back from rising to the freedom of Christ, unless we be dead to it.

b. God calls some away from the world by vows of religion. In order to profit by them we should find a real freedom of spirit therein. The same is true of various religious obligations. They should bring to us a holy freedom.

c. Whatever separates us from the world should produce the same effect. The solitude of a sick man should be welcomed not as a time of confinement, but of liberation.

POINT II. *Consider the charity of visiting prisoners.*

a. Their sins which have brought them under the penalties of the law should not remove them from the sympathy of brotherly love.

b. Though we may be unable to obtain for them a mitigation of the sentence by an earthly judge, yet we may bring them to such a knowledge of God, as will by His mercy give them the true freedom which alone is important.

c. God can free their hearts, even though their bodies be bound. Blessed are they who work along with Him in this gift of freedom.

POINT III. *Consider the attainment of true freedom.*

a. We must know what our bond is, otherwise we shall not seek aright to get free from it.

b. We must seek Divine grace. Nothing else can really set us free, though other things may make the bondage easy for a little while.

c. We must go on in our endeavour to get free, and not rest satisfied in the holiness of things around us, unless our soul rise up to the full freedom of the holiness of God.

AFFECTIONS. Charity to others. Zeal for God. Estrangement from the world.

PRAYER.

O God, Who callest us to walk in holy freedom, that the bonds of sin being burst, we may rise to the full enjoyment of Thy glory in holiness of life, grant me so to flee from the world, that my heart may experience the blessedness of Thy children, and exult in the energy of Thy boundless Love; through Jesus Christ our Lord. Amen.

A.D. 397.

GENEROSITY TOWARDS GOD AND MEN.

PRELUDE. i. *Well done, thou good and faithful servant;*
thou hast been faithful over a few things, I will make thee ruler
over many things : enter thou into the Joy of thy Lord.—S. Matt.
xxv. 21.

ii.   S. Martin, as yet a Catechumen, dividing his cloak with the
beggar.

POINT I.   *Consider zeal in temporal mercy.*

   a. The misery of our fellow men shivering in nakedness, is a
symbol of the miseries of souls.   If we are not moved by
what we see, how can we rise up to understand that which
it symbolizes?

   b. We are members one of another.   If we do not feel in the
body for the bodies of men, our souls can scarcely become
identified with their souls.

   c. God does not withhold His temporal benefits in this world
even from the evil.   We cannot expect to share His glory
in the next world if we do not care to act like Him in this.

POINT II.   *Consider the bravery of Christ's soldiers.*

   a. If we would save others from suffering, we must not fear
to suffer ourselves.   Relieve sorrow by self-sacrifice.

   b. The overthrow of the idol-temples and false worship was
effected by prayer and suffering.   We need much boldness
to fight with Satan as well as to convince mankind.

   c. S. Martin would not flatter the Emperor, but rebuked the
sins by which he had obtained his dignity.

POINT III.   *Consider the quickness of spiritual apprehension.*

   a. It is not the learning of this world which can solve the
mysteries of Heaven.   The wisdom of God can only be
learnt by living the Life of God.

   b. If we live closely with God we shall see in all God's outer
works parables of spiritual admonition respecting His
Heavenly Kingdom.

   c. A life of devotion in intimacy with God fits the soul to
answer difficulties of dogma and casuistry.   It were a sin
to neglect learning : yet God loves to use the unlearned.

AFFECTIONS.   Love.   Courage.   Self-denial.

PRAYER.

O God, Who hast made all men of one blood, and callest all man-
kind to the higher unity of the Eternal Life in the one Body of Thy
dear Son, by the power of the One Sanctifying Spirit, grant that I
may fear no worldly loss, knowing the greatness of my Heavenly
calling, but may rejoice to communicate to the temporal needs of all
whom Thou callest to share with me in Thine Eternal bounty;
through the same Jesus Christ our Lord.   Amen.

A.D. 444.
CONVERSION.

PRELUDE. i. *Well done, thou good and faithful servant; thou hast been faithful over a few things, I will make thee ruler over many things: enter thou into the Joy of thy Lord.*—S. Matt. xxv. 21.

ii. The Saint reflecting upon the laxity of his early life under the government of S. Martin.

POINT I. *Consider the triumph of grace.*

a. We must not despair of the conversion of any because of their long-continued resistance to grace. We must pray for others. We must pray for ourselves.

b. If God calls any one, He also gives the means of rising up to fulfil that calling. We must seek to develope the inward grace of which the outward calling is an assurance.

c. The H. G. carries on a secret work in those whom He calls. However great may be man's sin, He can triumph.

POINT II. *Consider the responsibility of holy example.*

a. We may be with saintly persons, and their holiness, instead of communicating itself to us, only makes our sin more apparent. So also with intercourse by books and otherwise.

b. The examples of others are specially given us by God in order to lead us to holiness. God's will must be recognized herein, acting with individual love to ourselves.

c. We should think of meeting hereafter. How shall we tremble to see them glorified and Christ glorified in them, if now we have not cared to see Christ drawing us to Himself through them !

POINT III. *Consider the difficulty of conversion.*

a. Conversion must be complete, directing all the energies of soul and body to the glory of God.

b. Conversion is the work of God the Holy Ghost, and we must be converted not merely by passive submission, but by a true correspondence of subordinate co-operation.

c. The conversion of the intellect from carnal prejudice is a difficult matter, as with S. Paul. The conversion of the heart from sluggishness to energy in correspondence with truths long known is a harder and a slower work.

AFFECTIONS. Self-oblation. Emulation. Zeal.

PRAYER.

O Lord God, Who by Thy Holy Spirit drawest unto Thyself the hearts of those whom Thou callest, grant me grace to correspond with this holy attraction that I may obey Thy call, and being wholly withdrawn from the world and turned to Thee, may be enabled to show forth Thy glory in every action; through Jesus Christ our Lord. Amen.

A.D. 565.

FAITHFULNESS IN VARIED RELATIONSHIPS.

PRELUDE. i. *Well done, thou good and faithful servant; thou hast been faithful over a few things, I will make thee ruler over many things: enter thou into the Joy of thy Lord.*—S. Matt. xxv. 21.

ii. The Saint seeking to rouse his relaxed monks to devotion.

POINT I. *Consider the blessedness of holy relationships.*

  a. This Saint had many close kinsmen who were also Saints. How are we helped by the prayers of those we love!

  b. The family ought to bring home to us the unity of the Church with Christ for its Head, and it is sanctified by symbolizing so great a mystery.

  c. How many Saints have been our fellow-countrymen, our kinsfolk, of whom the world knows nothing. Those are great whom God knows. Man's knowledge is worthless.

POINT II. *Consider the opposition of relaxed persons.*

  a. In his monastery S. Machutus is said to have kindled coals in his bosom when the monks strove to hinder his lighting the lamps for service. We may take this as symbolizing the triumph of true devotion amidst all opposition.

  b. The fire of Divine Life in the heart must kindle our worship, or the sanctuary will remain dark.

  c. The coldness and darkness which are around must make us look the more earnestly to hold communion with God, and that which is interior will light up what is external.

POINT III. *Consider the honours given to him in death.*

  a. Honours profit not the dead. The world can only honour us in that body which ought to be dead even now by grace. How can the world's honours attract us?

  b. A Saint's name may remain, but it affects him not whether the world honours him for real or for legendary actions. Our true honour is from God. He knows us as we are.

  c. God honours Himself by making men honour His Saints for lives unknown. A holy life is a nucleus of history by God's power. Men compass it with legends, and seek to hide spiritual glory by material marvels.

AFFECTIONS. Delight in prayer for kindred. Fervour. Simplicity. Hiddenness.

PRAYER.

O God, Who dost glorify Thy Saints by hiding them from the praise of men, that they may receive that honour which cometh from Thyself alone, grant us amidst the waves of this troublesome world to rest securely in Thy worship, and in the darkness of this world to have both our hearts and our words enkindled by Thy Heavenly fire; through Jesus Christ our Lord. Amen.

A.D. 1200.

FIRMNESS.

PRELUDE. i. *Well done, thou good and faithful servant; thou hast been faithful over a few things, I will make thee ruler over many things : enter thou into the Joy of thy Lord.—*S. Matt. xxv. 21.

ii. The Saint making protest against the King.

POINT I. *Consider the universality of firmness.*

a. Firm towards all men. This firmness comes from a life rooted in the very being of God, and alien from the world. If we be dead with Christ, the world cannot move us.

b. Firm under all circumstances. The dead are not moved by considerations of expediency. If we could see things as the Blessed do from Paradise, hope and fear would vanish.

c. Firm within ourselves. It is not enough to resist the attacks of others. We must have an active firmness in pursuit of our fixed aim of life.

POINT II. *Consider the sympathy of firmness.*

a. Dead and impervious to all assaults, nevertheless to live outside of ourselves in a loving consciousness of the needs of others.

b. To appreciate the variety of characters with which we deal. The Lord Jesus met those around Him in the way most suited to each, for He loved them all.

c. To bring others to firmness of conduct by contact with ourselves. Unsympathising rigour will never quicken.

POINT III. *Consider the capacity of firmness.*

a. The intellectual and moral energies must all combine to effect our purpose. We must know what we are working for. Our Lord Jesus came to bear witness unto the truth, and He had the Cross always in view.

b. Plans must be developed, and all resources gathered together to effect our purpose. " What was there more that I could have done unto My Vine ?"

c. Life in God makes us dead to the world, and gives unity of aim. Whether our natural faculties be great or small, they must all be set in motion by this power.

AFFECTIONS. Striving for God's glory. Disregard of transitory failure. Desire to bring others to God.

PRAYER.

Grant, O Lord, I pray Thee, that stedfastly seeking for the advancement of Thy glory, I may so faithfully use those faculties which Thou hast given me, that by the co-operation of Thy grace I may bring others to own Thee as their only end, and at last may have my portion in the victory of faith ; through Jesus Christ our Lord. Amen.

A.D. 870.

SELF-SACRIFICE.

PRELUDE. i. *Theirs is the Kingdom of Heaven who have despised the life of this world to gain a reward in the Kingdom, and have washed their robes in the Blood of the Lamb.*—Rev. vii. 15.

ii. S. Edmund tied to a tree and covered with arrowshots, is at length beheaded by the Dane.

POINT I. *Consider the source of self-sacrifice.*

    a. We must learn self-sacrifice in the school of Christ. S. Edmund spending one twelvemonth in Retreat, learnt by heart the Psalter, and in the Psalter learnt the true Spirit of Christ.

    b. Self-sacrifice is not the mere act of physical courage, but shines with the grace of Christ in characters which are naturally feeble.

    c. It is required of us all, and we must seek the strength of Divine grace that we may be enabled to practise it when occasion arises. The mortified spirit rejoices in the small acts of daily self-sacrifice by which it may grow up to greater ones.

POINT II. *Consider the royalty of self-sacrifice.*

    a. Jesus our King gives Himself a Sacrifice for us. None can rule truly who do not join with Him in self-sacrifice.

    b. Self-sacrifice is the true measure of greatness. He who is enabled by God to sacrifice himself, shows thereby the dignity of his relationship as guardian of others.

    c. We show what we are living for, by dying for it. If we hold back, we show that we regard it as existing for us, not ourselves for it.

POINT III. *Consider the necessity of self-sacrifice.*

    a. We pass into the Presence of God triumphantly, if having loved unto the end that which He gave us, we have suffered in order to preserve it from harm.

    b. We cannot set forth God's glory, except in so far as we give ourselves up in the hope of attaining to it hereafter.

    c. We cannot suffer for God in Himself, but as being represented by that deposit which He has given to our care. It may be some principle of faith or duty, some gift of grace, some persons or flock.

AFFECTIONS. Thankfulness in suffering. Stedfastness. Praise.

PRAYER.

O God, Whose Blessed Son came to be a sacrifice for our sins, grant that we may learn so to be conformed to His Self-sacrifice, that in exercising the power of His grace, our hearts may be enlightened to see the Blessed Vision of Thy Triumphant Love, wherein we seek to find our reward; through the same Jesus Christ our Lord. Amen.

Feast of S. Cecilia. U. ♄ ♍. 345

MUSIC.

PRELUDE. i. *When the Bridegroom came, they that were ready went in with Him to the marriage.*—S. Matt. xxv. 10.
ii. The Saint singing the Psalter.

POINT I. *Consider the power of Music.*

a. Our nature is formed to feel its influence, as the inarticulate utterance of a higher world conversing with us.

b. Debased music is the most pleasing to our fallen nature. The truest utterances of a fallen world are plaintive.

c. Divine music expresses the longing of the soul for things beyond this life, and strengthens the soul to rise up to those longings with energies beyond the reach of words. O my God, do I thus rise to Thee as befits our sacred song?

POINT II. *Consider the converse of the soul with God.*

a. Man's voice should have been a constant voice of song, as much beyond the song of birds as his mind is beyond their consciousness. The Fall has ruined the instrument.

b. How musically does the voice express the best sensations of the heart. O what a sweet music was it to the ear of the penitent when Jesus said unto her, Mary!

c. How careful should we be in the use of sacred music that the uplifting power, which should excite a craving within us, does not become a deceitful, satisfying power. Our songs here are the beginning of a worship which must have no perfect cadence until it swell out in the "Amen" of eternity.

POINT III. *Consider the preparation for Heaven.*

a. Melody represents the individual life of the Saints: Harmony, the collective life of the Body of Christ.

b. Let us sing God's praises upon earth, so as to die out in the living voice of the Eternal. The human voice shall rise again, as well as the affections and the understanding.

c. Let "the voices of many waters," the multitude of the regenerate, be the constant accompaniment of our divine worship, strengthening, softening, sweetening, the cry of our hearts, whether in prayer or praise.

AFFECTIONS. Joy in Divine Praise. Elevation of heart. Purity of soul. Discipline of life.

PRAYER.

O God, Who hast given us the faculty of speech, that we may approach Thee in the power of the Holy Ghost, as the members of Thine Incarnate Word, grant me so to utter Thy praise with all Thy Saints in the unity of that law of sanctification whereby Thou requirest us to be perfected for Thy worship upon the earth, that in the ages of eternity my whole being may be made worthy to rejoice in the celebration of Thine infinite glory; through J. C. our Lord. Amen.

HOPE BEYOND THE GRAVE.

PRELUDE. i. *Theirs is the Kingdom of Heaven who have despised the life of this world to gain a reward in the Kingdom, and have washed their robes in the Blood of the Lamb.*—Rev. vii. 14.
　ii. S. Clement thrown into the sea bound to an anchor.

POINT I. *Consider the anchor of Christian Hope.*
　a. Thrown into the deep, we hope for that which we see not. The security of Divine Hope cannot be known without the ventures of Faith.
　b. Firmly fixed upon the Truth of the Divine Nature. Nothing save the Life of God can keep us secure amidst the buffeting of the world.
　c. We are kept secure not for the sake of the voyage, but of the Home whither we are going.　There are waters above the firmament, and the soul abides safely on the Heavenly height, if it hold fast this heavenly Hope amidst the storms and dark depths of the world.

POINT II. *Consider what it is to be bound to this Anchor.*
　a. Our whole being must be detached from all else, and bound to that whereby our Hope shall be attained.
　b. We must feel the bond which binds us.　If we do not know now the tightness of the discipline of faith, we cannot have the Life for which this discipline leads us to hope.
　c. We must die to the world, holding fast our Hope, that therewith we may live in God,

POINT III. *Consider the entering into new Life.*
　a. The watery grave symbolizes the spiritual grave of Holy Baptism.
　b. The violence of the fling is as the force which is necessary in order to separate us from the world, on which our natural footing rests.
　c. We do not cast this anchor into the deep in order that we may be left riding on the waves of this world, but that the perishing of the flesh may be the preservation of the Life of the Spirit.

AFFECTIONS. Hope in Christ. Separation from the world.

PRAYER.

Grant, O Lord, that as it hath pleased Thee to write our names in the Book of Life, we may always be looking forward to the attainment of Thy Promise, and may have our portion in the Joy of Thine elect; through Him Who died for us and rose again, Thy Son Jesus Christ our Lord.　Amen.

A.D. 311.

THE SANCTIFICATION OF WISDOM.

PRELUDE. i. *When the* Bridegroom *came, they that were ready went with Him to the marriage.*—S. Matt. xxv. 10.

ii. The philosophers yielding to S. Catherine's arguments, and confessing themselves Christians.

POINT I. *Consider how the chains of nature are broken by the touch of Divine Wisdom.*

    a. The course of natural events is like those four spiked wheels on which the Saint was to have perished. Life is a revolving series of difficulties, given us to try our faith.

    b. Satan binds together various forms of trouble for our hurt. God snaps the chain, and sets those free who trust in Him. They who have Divine wisdom in their hearts fear not for their outward life.

    c. The triumphs of the faithful become the glory of the Church for future generations, through which heavenly joy shines on countless worshippers. By fellowship with Divine Wisdom we see that these troubles cannot hurt.

POINT II. *Consider the transporting joy of Divine Wisdom.*

    a. If we would live as angels, we should carry to our homes the memory of those who have known God.

    b. If we are truly dead to the world, Divine wisdom transports us from the place of our suffering to the mountain of God, from the Egypt of sin to the Sinai of holiness.

    c. Divine wisdom transports the hearers from the desire of living for the world, so to contemplate God, that henceforth they are dead to it, and live with the wisdom they receive.

POINT III. *Consider how natural wisdom is glorified by union with Divine revelation.*

    a. Natural wisdom in itself is dead. Religious souls find a sanctuary for it amidst the heights of revelation, tracing out with holy wisdom the analogies of nature and grace.

    b. The purpose of all true wisdom is that we may fulfil the moral law with spiritual power, and rise to the Righteousness of God. Angel-wisdom is nought without angel-service.

    c. The contemplation of Divine Wisdom does not save us from temptation and danger. The children of wisdom must die to live. Blessed philosophers who were martyrs!

AFFECTIONS. Love of contemplation, Superiority to the world. Fellowship of life with all the hosts of Heaven.

PRAYER.

O Lord God, Who hast given us wisdom that we may contemplate Thy Truth, grant us by the same wisdom to live in Thy Love, dying to all the pleasures of this world, and by Thy grace rejoicing to render Thee a ceaseless service, in union with all the company of Heaven; through Jesus Christ our Lord. Amen.

2 A 2

MEDITATIONS

ON

THE SONG OF ZACHARIAS.

THE DUMBNESS OF NATURE.

PRELUDE. i. B*lessed be the Lord God of Israel.*
ii. The longing of the aged Priest to utter God's praise.
POINT I. *Consider the dumbness of natural incapacity.*
  a. The Word is God, and without the Divine Word man cannot come forth to man out of the prison-house of his own self. Speech is self-communication, man's prerogative, as being formed in the Divine image.
  b. Much less can man come forth to God by his own will. Speech is a gift from God, implying the covenant of Divine Love, by which God is willing to attend to what we say.
  c. When man by sin refused to listen to God's commands, he forfeited all claim upon God to listen to his own requests. The supernatural link was broken. The Incarnate Word is the medium whereby prayer and praise are restored.
POINT II. *Consider the dumbness of natural unbelief.*
  a. With the loss of speech man lost the power of hearing God's Word perfectly. He could not recognize God's coming forth to himself. He doubted when God spoke to him.
  b. Losing this experimental knowledge of God's Word, he lost the sense of God's Personal power throughout creation. Laws of nature came as general abstractions between him and the Personal Will of God. Nature became to him a dead machine.
  c. God's promises died out. Man had no hope of supernatural devotion, unless God's voice spoke to him again as a supernatural principle of peace. Adam trembled to hear God's voice in Eden.
POINT III. *Consider the dumbness of the Jewish dispensation.*
  a. Abraham had been called to a special fellowship with God, speaking and hearing. His blessing remained with his posterity in proportion as they could rise to the like fellowship.
  b. God's Word was promised as about to come amongst men. In the Temple services, man was called to recognize the gradual expansion of this promise until the Truth should come.
  c. Zacharias, though blameless according to the Law, failed of hearing this Voice latent amidst the daily duties of his office. The earthly angel knew not the heavenly angel. Not hearing God's Voice, he could not bless in His Name.
AFFECTIONS. Reliance on God's Personal Love. Lifting up of heart beyond the sphere of nature. Desire for God.
PRAYER.
O God, Whose Word ruleth all things, and worketh in all, grant me so to recognize Thy Personal Presence, that I may always act in the power of Thy Holy Will through Jesus Christ Thy Son our Lord. Amen.

THE MOUTH OPENED BY GRACE.

PRELUDE. i. B*lessed be the Lord God of Israel.*
ii. Zacharias having written the name of John bursts forth in praise.

POINT I. *Consider the discipline of silence.*
   a. Zacharias had asked for a sign of the truth of God's messenger, and it was given him by the manifestation of his own weakness.
   b. In this time of silence his heart was drawn the more fully towards God, waiting for the blessing to be given that the penalty might be removed.
   c. He was taught his own unworthiness by this long-continued penalty. We cannot become fit to receive God's blessing unless we patiently bear His discipline for those faults by which we deserved to lose it.

POINT II. *Consider the utterance of preventing grace.*
   a. He wrote the word "John," the grace of God. At the name of the Precursor, who represents preventing grace, his mouth was opened immediately, according to the angel's word.
   b. If we are true to preventing grace, we shall be led onward. He did as the angel bade, and he was at once filled with the Holy Ghost and prophesied.
   c. The thought of the child John is only subordinate to the thought of God Himself coming to His people. Preventing grace suffices not in itself, but leads us to Christ.

POINT III. *Consider the utterance of illuminating grace.*
   a. The other John declares God's Blessedness in His own consciousness and Love. By illuminating grace we see and hear the Word of Life, so as to praise God for what He is.
   b. The Word of Divine Life is revealed as giving to us that Life which He has in Himself.
   c. God is Blessed in Himself with a Blessedness which only His own word can utter. Our praise of Him is by the illumination of that Word. The Life is the Light of men.

AFFECTIONS. Penitence. Dependence upon God. Patient waiting for Christ.

PRAYER.

O Lord God, pardon my unworthiness, and lead me onward in Thy Love, that I may welcome Thy visitation, prepare for Thine appearance, and, rising in the Light of Thy Presence to the knowledge of Thine eternal glory, may be perfected according to the truth of Thy Word; through Jesus Christ our Lord. Amen.

III.—THE DUTY OF PRAISE.

PRELUDE. i. *Blessed be the Lord God of Israel.*
ii. Zacharias having written the name of John, bursts forth in praise.

POINT I. *Consider that man was formed to praise God.*

　　a. Our outer faculties contemplate God's works. Our minds cannot rest in them, but travel onward to the Maker. Otherwise it is conscious of being baulked.

　　b. We were formed not merely to feed upon external nature, but to refashion it. All we do ought to be an act of homage to the Creator. As created persons we feebly exercise our will in subordination to His more glorious Personal Agency.

　　c. God delights to be praised by man, for man being formed in God's image, rises by praising God to the truth of his own nature in the knowledge and love of God.

POINT II. *Consider that man partakes of the Divine Nature whilst praising God.*

　　a. Man reaches beyond creation by faculties of reason, imagination, moral intuition, desire. He is dead : creation is his tomb : unless he do reach out to God the Life. No finite exercise of powers lets him breathe. His nature demands the infinite.

　　b. Man rises to the infinite in proportion as he approaches the excellence of God. His own life developes by each fresh perception of God.

　　c. God's Eternal Word was made flesh by the Holy Ghost. Man rises up to the infinite demands of his nature—lives— by the Holy Ghost enabling him to lay hold upon the Word of Life. We praise God while the Holy Ghost, the Eternal Love of the Father and the Son, speaks through us.

POINT III. *Consider man's eternal joy in praising God.*

　　a. When the finite is passed away, the faculties by which we hold communion with God, will be set free to act in their infinite scope, so as to approach God in a worthy manner.

　　b. Our nature will act in perfect unity of Life with that which we contemplate. Intellection and action will be one. The joy of Heaven will be an appreciative Love of God.

　　c. This joy will never weary, for the faculties wherewith we praise God and the glory which we praise are both one.

AFFECTIONS. Hope. Joy. Love.

PRAYER.

O Lord God, Who hast formed me to utter Thy praise, grant that I may so contemplate Thy glory, that in the power of Thy Divine Light I may make manifest the truth of Thy Love; through Jesus Christ our Lord. Amen.

THE PERFECTION OF PRAISE.

PRELUDE. i. *Blessed be the Lord God of Israel.*

ii. Zacharias having written the name of John, bursts forth in praise.

POINT I. *Consider that praise comes primarily from God.*

  a. It is the utterance of the Divine Word making His own perfections manifest.

  b. The only true praise which man can receive is the Voice of the same Word, approving him as being conformable to the Divine Image.

  c. The only true praise which man can give is the utterance of the same Divine Word raising our faculties to apprehend and acknowledge the true excellence which is in God and from God.

POINT II. *Consider that praise is an act of union with God.*

  a. God alone is good, the law of goodness to all His creatures. To discern what is worthy of praise is an act of Divine intelligence.

  b. God alone is good, the source of goodness. To experience anything which deserves our praise, is an experience of His favour.

  c. God alone is good, the recipient of all the glory and goodness which comes forth from Himself. To acknowledge God's perfections in what we praise is an act of Divine Love.

POINT III. *Consider that praise ennobles our faculties.*

  a. The more we acknowledge God in His works, the better we shall do so. Searching out His works, we see more and more of His excellencies.

  b. The more we praise God, the more does the energy of the Divine Word of Blessing raise our consciousness into correspondence with the Divine Power.

  c. The more our faculties rise to God in praise, the more does the inspiration of the Holy Ghost absorb them into the blessing of God, and purge off their earthliness.

AFFECTIONS. Contemplation. Thankfulness. Ecstacy.

PRAYER.

O God, Who although needing nothing in the All-sufficiency of Thine own Glory hast nevertheless created us so to praise Thee that in praising Thee we may grow in perfection by the exercise of Thy Love, grant me so to praise Thee amidst the difficulties of time, that in Thy praise I may find the glory of eternity; through Jesus Christ our Lord. Amen.

THE DIVINE CONSCIOUSNESS.

PRELUDE. i. *Blessed be the* Lord *God of* Israel.
ii. The joyous inspiration of Zacharias.
POINT I. *Consider the rapture of Divine Love.*

   a. The act of Divine Praise takes us away from self. We do not bless God by contrast with our own misery, but by the substantive knowledge of His own excellence.

   b. The consciousness of Divine Joy becomes our own. We praise God for what He is, while we experience the joy of the Divine Being. We praise Him as possessing in Himself that which He calls us to share.

   c. This sense of Divine Joy is a fruit of the Holy Ghost, a power giving new faculties to the life, making our dumbness to pass away by its incontrollable inspiration.

POINT II. *Consider the fellowship of Divine Love.*

   a. We must personally know God in order to praise Him. His glory as a mere abstract quality, were an empty imagination. We must know the Personal Activity of His glory.

   b. We must know this glory in its Eternal Personal Relationships. If we do not know God in the Substantive Relationships of His Triune Life, we only know Him by His negative Relationships to our own misery.

   c. We must know this glory as taking ourselves up into the Communion of Divine Life. We can only know the essential Relationships of the Three Persons by this participation in the Covenant of Life whereby we live in their Name.

POINT III. *Consider the repose of Divine Love.*

   a. The infinite acquisition of Divine glory. As we are the sons of God in the Only-begotten, there is nothing left for us to desire. All which God is, is ours.

   b. The infinite future of Divine glory. The glory depends not on the struggles of a life of chance. The glory which we have received must calmly develope itself within us if we will continue in that Love

   c. The infinite security of Divine glory. God has taken us into Himself by the act of His own Eternal Truth. He loves us, not because we, who are changeable, love Him, but by His own spontaneous unchangeable Love.

AFFECTIONS. Transporting Joy. Gratitude. Wonder.

PRAYER.

O God, Who quickenest our hearts to love Thee by the Spirit of Thy Wellbeloved Son, grant us so to praise Thee for Thy goodness, that we, being transformed according to Thy will, may receive Thy Love, and rest therein according to the fulness of Truth wherewith Thou callest us thereby to abide in Thyself; through Jesus Christ our Lord. Amen.

THE BLISS OF GOD.

PRELUDE. i. *Blessed be the Lord God of Israel.*
ii. The Host of Heaven praising God in the Light of His Joy.
POINT I. *Consider the Blessedness of God.*
> *a.* A personal Blessedness. God is the Source and Archetype of all Personal existence, but having a Personality far beyond the creature.
> *b.* A conscious Blessedness, not a mere negation. Lower forms of life would be superior to the true Life, if God were a mere abstraction. The highest Life must be the highest consciousness.
> *c.* An essential Blessedness. God knows and declares His own Blessedness by the eternal generation of His Consubstantial Word. The Divine Persons are not necessary One to the Other as external, supplemental objects of delight, but as the co-essential manifestation of an undivided energy. The word here used [Blessed] is used of God alone.

POINT II. *Consider God as the Only Blessed One.*
> *a.* Others may be happy. "All generations shall call me happy." Others receive blessing from God. " Blessed art thou among women." God is Self-Blest, "to be blest."
> *b.* Blessedness in God is far beyond our words or thoughts, the joyous utterance of His own Infinite Being.
> *c.* Others may lose blessedness. Human personality is empty, dependent on circumstances. God is Blessedness to Himself by the exhaustless energy of His Personal Substance.

POINT III. *Consider the communication of the Divine Blessedness.*
> *a.* God by His Eternal Word does not speak to vacancy. The Word whereby His Personal Blessedness is imaged forth lives in the Joy of the Eternal Love. The Blessed Word remains One with the Father in the Unity of the Holy Ghost.
> *b.* God by His Word calls created vacancy into being, in order that He may fill each creature according to his measure with the joy of perception or reflexion, for itself or for others.
> *c.* God calls those who hear His Word to rise up by grace to dwell in the consubstantial joy of Eternal Life in the knowledge of Himself.

AFFECTIONS. Adoration. Joy. Largeness of Heart.

PRAYER.

O Lord God, *Who art Blessed for evermore, in Thine own Eternal energy, and callest us, miserable creatures of time, defiled with sin, to rise into the purity of Thy Life, grant me so to rejoice in Thy Divine Joy that I may be strengthened for the glory of Thine immortality; through Jesus Christ our Lord.* Amen.

THE LORD.

PRELUDE. i. *Blessed be the Lord.*

ii. All creation acknowledging the Divine glory.

POINT I. *Consider the Divine Self-existence.*

    a. God is the Lord because He exists by His own Sovereign Will. He rejoiceth in the glory of His own Being, from whence is derived all else that is.

    b. This Sovereign Will excludes all possibility of evil. Whatever is not worthy of that Divine glory, cannot be His Will, and therefore cannot touch Him.

    c. If He were liable to anything harmful, there would be a power independent of Himself. He exists independently of all, and therefore as He wills.

POINT II. *Consider the changeless Eternity of God.*

    a. His own Nature cannot change, for if it did He would possess perfections at one time which would be wanting to Him at another.

    b. His essential Relationships cannot change. The Three Persons of the Godhead dwell eternally in the Unity of the Divine Substance. No relationship can spring up therein without making a change in the Divine Perfection.

    c. He is not changed by His relation to the created universe, for creation is but the manifestation of what exists eternally in His Mind. All created goodness is but the effluence of His own eternal purpose.

POINT III. *Consider the Sovereign Dominion of God over all.*

    a. Whatever excellence or power any creature possesses, it can only come from God. He is Almighty because He is the Author of all might.

    b. The power of using is as much His gift as the thing which is used. The gift of a free will enables us to use or to refuse God's gifts, but not to change them.

    c. To choose as God wills is our supreme good. To refuse His will is our destruction. His gifts are our ruin unless used according to the law of His Will.

AFFECTIONS. Obedience. Thankfulness. Worship.

PRAYER.

O Almighty God, Who rulest according to Thy will throughout all the universe of Thy creatures, grant me so to follow Thy will in the use of what Thou hast given, that I may attain to the knowledge of Thyself, Who art the chief and only good of those whom Thou callest to the participation of Thine Eternal Life; through Jesus Christ our Lord. Amen.

THE COVENANT GOD.

PRELUDE. i. *The* Lord *God of Israel.*

ii. The Divine cloud resting upon the Camp of Israel in the Wilderness.

POINT I. *Consider God anciently choosing His people.*

　a. "He chose our fathers."—Acts xiii. 17.—Fallen man has no claim upon God. God chose a covenant people not so as to limit to them His Blessing, but to use them for its communication to others.—Gen. xii. 3.

　b. He did not cease to be their God by reason of any external troubles. God did not ease them from trouble. Rather they were exposed, as God's people, to Satan's special hatred.

　c. He would not let them fall without hope of recovery. His gifts and calling are without repentance. At last they rejected God, and fell under a curse, yet God has His special purposes for Israel at the end of the world.

POINT II. *Consider God watching over His people.*

　a. The Birth of the Forerunner is an evidence of God's watchful care and truth. His coming was foretold as attendant upon Messiah, and the Jews accepting him ought to have been saved from rejecting Messiah.

　b. It is an evidence of purposes which God is about to bring to fulfilment. "John did no miracle," but he was a miracle. People felt the force of his preaching.

　c. This people will now stand out distinct from all the nations of the world by the glorious fulfilment of the promises of their God, separated hitherto from man. Henceforth they will be united to God, for of them, as concerning the flesh, Christ comes.

POINT III. *Consider God manifesting His glory amidst His people.*

　a. "They glorified the God of Israel." The glorious Majesty of their God was upon them. They shone with His glory.

　b. His power was a present help in time of trouble. When things were darkest, Israel's God acknowledged His people.

　c. His power was pledged to them for eternity. His mercies, so great now, could not fail. Our God must be accepted as "our Guide unto death."

AFFECTIONS. Joy in union with God. Praise for His Covenant. Self-surrender to Him.

PRAYER.

O *God, Who hast been graciously pleased to call me into the number of Thy Covenant people, grant that I may always acknowledge Thy goodness, and praise Thee for the greatness of the Love wherein Thou dost bind me unto Thyself; through Jesus Christ our Lord.* Amen.

THE DIVINE VISITATION.

PRELUDE. i. *He hath visited His people.*
ii. Jesus weeping over Jerusalem.

POINT I. *Consider that God visits man.*

a. "What is man that Thou visitest him ?"—Heb. ii. 6.—Man was formed to hold communion with God, but has fallen away from the union of life wherein he should have dwelt with God.

b. Man lost a natural delight in that communion by his sin. He trembles now to hear God speak. He cannot see God and live.

c. God's lovingkindness to man effects his salvation. The Dayspring from on high visits them that are in darkness, clothes Himself with our darkness that He may lift us up to His Light.

POINT II. *Consider God visiting the world.*

a. God visits for judgment.—Gen. xviii. 21. S. John ix. 39.— He comes to see, for His Presence shows what is in man. Man rejects God, and is condemned by so doing.

b. God visits with plagues. He makes men feel the power of His wrath, in order that He may bring them to the joy of His Love.

c. God visits for selection.—Acts xv. 14.—He will not condemn men except by the law which they have received. He cannot save any unless they are brought into the power of His own Life-giving Name whereby He visits them.

POINT III. *Consider God visiting His chosen ones.*

a. In their trouble, as in Egypt. The times of greatest outward sorrow and persecution are those in which God will show His glory in His Church.

b. With mercy to individuals in their sorrow. As to the widow of Nain.—S. Luke vii. 16.—We can hardly look for Divine manifestations while all is outwardly prosperous. When the world is against us we may. God's loving care acts individually and discriminatingly.

c. In the time of final dispersion. When His judgments are in all the world, the Good Shepherd will not suffer any individual soul to perish through His neglect.

AFFECTIONS. Reliance upon God. Praise for His condescension. Acceptance of His offers.

PRAYER.

O Lord God, Who dost mercifully gather unto Thyself from all the nations of the world those that will seek Thee in humility and truth, grant that I may ever be watchful for the tokens of Thy Presence, so that I may profit by the invitation of Thy Love; through Jesus Christ our Lord. Amen.

REDEMPTION.

PRELUDE. i. *He hath made redemption for His people.*
ii. God sending Moses to call His people out of Egypt.

POINT I, *Consider Moses as a redeemer.*

  a. He came with the power of the Angel who appeared to him in the bush. He was only a type of the great Redeemer Who should exercise God's power as His own.—Acts vii. 35.

  b. He smote the Egyptians with a great destruction. Man is enslaved to a real power. Zacharias knew that Israel still needed redemption from the power which Egypt typified. Death and Hell shall be cast into the lake of fire.

  c. He set Israel free by causing the Paschal lamb to be slain. All Israel, as God's first-born, were mystically dead. The blood of the lamb sealed the doors of their houses.

POINT II. *Consider the redemption by Christ.*

  a. It is here attributed to God the Father, for He sent His Son to be the propitiation for our sins. By Redeeming Love the Father and the Son act in the oneness of the Holy Ghost to deliver creation from vanity, by glorifying the Body of the faithful in the fulness of the Divine adoption.

  b. Christ is the Lamb of God, by Whose precious Blood we are redeemed. The Redeemer must by dying destroy the power of death over all that were under death. Earthly life, however prolonged, could not become life eternal. We must die to this in order to enter into that.

  c. He is the ancient hope of Israel.—S. Luke xxiv. 21.—God had set Him forth as the object of hope long before, but man did not know from what he needed to be redeemed.

POINT III. *Consider the character of this redemption.*

  a. From the vain conversation of the fathers.—1 S. Pet. i. 18. —Death wastes all the energies of natural life. The best things of this world cannot satisfy us any more than the worst. We have an instinct which demands an eternal joy.

  b. An eternal redemption.—Heb. ix. 12-15.—It is efficacious for ever, so that the old claims of death cannot revive. By this redemption we gain an eternal inheritance.

  c. So as to purify the redeemed as a peculiar people unto Himself, zealous of good works.—Tit. ii. 14.—This world is at variance with God's law, a world of iniquity.

AFFECTIONS. Desire of Eternal Life. Joy in the Cross.

PRAYER.

O God, Who by Thine Only-Begotten Son hast redeemed us from all iniquity that we may serve Thee here in hope of the glory ready to be revealed, grant us to set all our affections upon heavenly things, and to keep ourselves unspotted from the world, so that we may be worthy as Thy children by adoption and grace to receive the inheritance to which we are called; through the same Jesus Christ our Lord. Amen.

THE PEOPLE OF GOD.

PRELUDE. i. *Blessed be the Lord God of Israel, for He hath visited and redeemed His people.* ii. As before.

POINT I. *Consider the bondage in which they were.*
  a. Mankind as the Elect race were the object of Satan's special envy and hatred. In proportion as man knows the dignity of his predestination he feels the tyranny. To be blind to it is the very worst bondage of all.
  b. Those who were drawn to God from the rest of mankind were ever under bondage to the seed of the Wicked One.
  c. This bondage is the penalty of sin, because they abide not in the truth.—Psalm cvii. 4; S. John viii. 34.—The truth makes those free who walk in its power.—Rom. viii. 2.—We escape by the supernatural life of grace.—Gal. v. 1.

POINT II. *Consider the abiding Love of God to them.*
  a. God does not cast off His people though they forsake Him. The redemption is effected for all mankind, for God is willing that all should be saved, inasmuch as all are created in His own Image.—1 S. John ii. 2; 1 Tim. ii. 4.
  b. God appoints their very difficulties as the means of bringing them to know His Love, and to estimate their own unworthiness. He ever makes for them a way of escape.
  c. God beholds in the people whom He calls those whom He has foreknown. Though the many reject Him, there is ever in the midst of them a remnant elected by grace—Rom. ii. 5—whom God will build up for the satisfaction of His everlasting Love.—Jer. xxxi. 3.

POINT III. *Consider their response to His Love.*
  a. They are found worthy in the day of His power. When He calls, they hear.
  b. They acknowledge their faults, and turn towards the Covenanted Temple of God, which is the centre of their hopes, even the Body of Christ in His Glory.—1 Kings viii. 47-49.
  c. Their response is a newness of Life into which they enter by coming to Him. They are transformed—Rom. xii. 2—and live—S. John v. 40—by coming to Jesus in the covenant of grace.—S. John viii. 37.

AFFECTIONS. Love to God. Confidence in His Protection. Hope of perfect fellowship with Him.

PRAYER.

O God, Who didst create us to be Thine own people, that we might glorify Thy Name, and triumph over the enemy, fill us with holy gratitude for Thy predestinating Love, and strengthen us that we may walk in Thy truth, and press onward to attain Thy promises; through Jesus Christ our Lord. Amen.

2 B

SALVATION.

PRELUDE. i. *He hath raised up a mighty salvation for us in
the House of His servant David.*

ii. A bright light within the dwelling, to which all may fly from
the perils of darkness outside.

POINT I. *Consider that Salvation is Life.*

a. Redemption from the power of death would be of no avail
without the gift of life. Death loses its power, and we can
" depart in peace " if " our eyes " have seen the salvation
of God.—S. Luke ii. 30.

b. So had the prophet declared respecting the future covenant
of salvation, " The just shall live by faith."—Hab. ii. 4. The
Law could not give life, and therefore could not save.

c. In the New Covenant, the saved are born again. " He
saved us by the washing of regeneration."—Tit. iii. 5.

POINT II. *Consider that Life is fellowship with God.*

a. " Behold, God is my salvation."—Isa. xii. 2. God goeth
forth for the salvation of His people, anointing with power
those whom He calls near.—Hab. iii. 13.

b. The people of God are those who dwell in the true Jerusalem. " I will be their God in truth and righteousness."
—Zech. viii. 8. The Life is the Light of men.—S. John i. ;
and their salvation.—Ps. xxvii. 1.

c. " Those who are written in the Lamb's Book of Life "—Rev.
xxi. 27 — are heirs of salvation along with Christ and in
Him.—Heb. i. 14.

POINT III. *Consider the joy of this salvation.*

a. It has been long " waited for."—Isa. xxv. 9. The devices
of the serpent shall not destroy it.—Gen. xlix. 18. In
the darkness of the world, the salvation which cometh out
of Zion will be as a lamp that burneth.—Isa. lxii. 1.

b. It is a secure abiding-place. " Salvation will God appoint
for walls and bulwarks."—Isa. xxvi. 1.

c. It is for ever. " The Lord shall be thine everlasting
Light."—Isa. lx. 20. The salvation and the righteousness
which Christ gives, are for ever.—Isa. li. 6.

AFFECTIONS. Hope. Joy. Praise.

PRAYER.

*O God, Who savedst us when we were lost, grant that we may
walk in the power of Thy salvation, and abide in the glory of Thy
Light, so that we may have our perfect portion with Thy redeemed
in the Blessed Vision of the Heavenly City; through Jesus Christ
our Lord. Amen.*

THE HORN OF SALVATION.

PRELUDE.　i. *He hath raised up an horn of salvation for us.*
ii. The sinner pursued by enemies, but grasping the Cross.

POINT I. *Consider the Divine character of this horn.*

　　a. The title is applied to God by David.—2 Sam. xxiii. 2 ;
Ps. xviii. 1.—God raises up the horn of salvation by sending
His own Son.

　　b. The horns belong to the head, and signify the Divine power
of Jesus, the Head of the Church.

　　c. The ram offered instead of Isaac was caught in the thicket
by the horns, and thus was expressed the twofold law of
Love, whereby the Son of God was made to offer Himself a
Sacrifice on behalf of mankind.

POINT II. *Consider the horn as an emblem of Royalty.*

　　a. So it is constantly in the visions of Daniel. The horn of
our salvation comes with royal power to bear witness to the
Truth. "Now is come salvation, strength, and the kingdom
of our God, and the power of His Christ."—Rev. xii. 10.

　　b. This salvation is the work of a King, even the Lord mighty
in battle. He is the King, just, and having salvation.—
Zech. ix. 9.

　　c. It is a salvation in which He watches with royal care over
those whom He gathers into His kingdom. The power
whereby it began is the power round which His people
must rally continually.

POINT III. *Consider the horn as an emblem of Priesthood.*

　　a. The horns of the altar are for the fastening of the victims.
This horn of salvation is the Life of those who, being bound
thereto, are offered as sacrifices to God, and become dead unto
the world.

　　b. Thither the guilty fly for refuge. Our accusers cannot
claim us for death if we take refuge in the Sacrifice of
Christ.

　　c. The sign of the Son of Man, the horn of the Anointed, is
the Cross,—a threefold horn. " He had horns coming out
of His Hands, and there is the hiding of His power."—
Hab. iii. 4.

AFFECTIONS. Trust. Supplication. Obedience. Self-
sacrifice.

PRAYER.

*O God, Whose Blessed Son was manifested as the Horn of Salva-
tion, whereto we may fly for refuge, grant us, rejoicing in His
protection, to abide evermore safely in the Covenant of Eternal
Life whereunto Thou hast called us by His Mediation; Who with
Thee and the Holy Ghost liveth and reigneth evermore, one God,
world without end. Amen.*

2 B 2

THE HOME OF SALVATION.

PRELUDE.   i. *He hath raissd up a mighty salvation for us in the house of His servant David.*

ii. The Branch from the Tree of Jesse that was cut down.

POINT I.   *Consider the Covenant made unto David.*

    a. David desired to build a House for God, but God promised rather to establish the House of David himself, and to make thereof His own Eternal Temple.—2 Sam. vii. 16.

    b. According to His old promise, God would deliver His people Israel out of the hand of all their enemies by the hand of His servant David.—2 Sam. iii. 18.

    c. The promise of a Man to sit upon the throne of Israel for ever, rises in Christ to its eternal fulfilment.—2 Sam. vii. 13 ; 1 Kings viii. 25.—The covenant with David could not be broken, for it had the predestined glory of Christ for its foundation.—Jer. xxxiii. 20.—God fulfils His word in a manner greater than our expectation.

POINT II.   *Consider the fallen state of David's House.*

    a. No feebleness of present condition could destroy God's promises.   So Ahaz was admonished to trust in God by the developed promise, that a Virgin should conceive.—Isa.. vii. 13.—God's presence makes all sure.

    b. Its low estate ought rather to encourage the hope of an uprising : for so it had been prophesied that a Branch should come out of the Tree of Jesse which had been cut down.   God's manifestations imply preceding overthrow.

    c. David's House had lost its honour as a matter of temporal regard, but the eye of faith still reverenced it as the Home whence Divine power was to issue for deliverance.

POINT III.   *Consider the promises for the future.*

    a. The Horn of Salvation is a living Divine Presence within the House of David, whereby the Jews shall eventually be brought back to God.   They shall then be as David the Beloved.—Zech. xii. 8.

    b. God has promised one Shepherd to the House of Israel, even His servant David.—Ezek. xxxiv. 23.—Who has also other sheep not of that fold, and makes " both one."

    c. The Son of David shall sit upon the Right Hand of God, waiting till His enemies be made His footstool.   The glory of earth passes through death into Eternal Glory.

AFFECTIONS.   Belief in God's Promises.   Spiritual anticipations.   Patience amidst outward desolation.

PRAYER.

O God, grant us so to remember the sure mercies of Thy Covenan; that we may patiently endure all that is appointed by Thee for the discipline of our faith, and may have our portion in the glorious fulfilment of Thy Word, which surpasseth all our desire; through Jesus Christ our Lord. Amen.

THE HOUSE OF THE BELOVED.

PRELUDE. i. *The House of His servant David.*
ii. The bright light of God's Presence filling the heart.
POINT I. *Consider the fellowship with God.*

  a. God comes to dwell with him who keepeth His word—
  S. John xiv. 23—for He loveth those that love Him.

  b. The love which obtains His abiding is but a response to
  the love which gave the original call. " We love Him because
  He first loved us."

  c. The beloved of the Lord shall dwell in safety by Him—
  Deut. xxxiii. 12—and though the enemy will compass the
  beloved city—Rev. xx. 9—yet the fire of God shall destroy
  the enemy. God dwelling in Sion makes her secure for ever.

POINT II. *Consider that this House is built in Divine Love.*

  a. Jerusalem is the city at unity with itself, because the One
  Holy Spirit binds it in one indissoluble life. The power
  which builds is the Spirit of Love.

  b. God loved those whom He chose to be His covenant people
  by a predestinating Love, foreseeing in them His Only-
  begotten Son Who should take His earthly nature of their
  substance. They were beloved as containing Him Who is
  the Only-beloved. The shout of an unborn King was
  among them.

  c. The Love which is given is an abiding Love whereby the
  House shall live eternally. The voice of joy and health
  shall never cease therein. That which is built is the Body
  prepared for the Only-beloved.

POINT III. *Consider the glory of Divine Love which fills this
House.*

  a. This Love was often hidden, so that they were tempted to say,
  What shall this Birthright profit me? But its glory was sure.

  b. In due time the glory of the Lord should fill the House.
  The dedicating glory of Solomon's Temple was but a type
  of the Divine glory belonging to the True Temple. All
  nations should be built as lively stones therein.

  c. In this House God would be glorified eternally, for He
  would manifest Himself therein to all the host of Heaven,
  even by the glory of the Lamb.

AFFECTIONS. Praise to God for calling me into His House.
Separation from the world. Contempt of its glory.

PRAYER.

*O God, Who by Thy Love dost build us together in the unity of
the Body of Thine Only-begotten Son, grant us so to love Him Whom
Thou hast given, and to keep His word, that we may be kept by
Thee, and may be found worthy to be Thine eternal habitation;
through the same Jesus Christ our Lord. ˒Amen.*

THE WARRANT OF PROPHECY.

PRELUDE. i. *As He spake by the mouth of His Holy Prophets.*

ii. The Prophet speaking in God's Name.

POINT I. *Consider the encouragement of prophecy.*

   a. The Divine promises led men's hearts to look beyond the limits of their own day, in the consciousness of the great developments of God's work which were to be in some manner their joy even after death.

   b. The accomplishment of immediate prophecies made them sure of the truth of the larger prophecies which demanded their simple faith.

   c. The glorious things which were foretold, cheered their hearts with confidence amidst present distresses, for they knew the House of David could not perish until those glories were attained.

POINT II. *Consider the importance of prophecy to ourselves.*

   a. The details of prophecy show us that Christ did not come into the world as an after-thought, but as the culminating glory of a long-prepared scheme of Divine power.

   b. He Who fulfilled His word so accurately in time past, will equally fulfil all His promises to us.

   c. The fulfilment often seemed near and was delayed, yet the time was fixed. So now we may be disappointed in our expectations, but, in His due time, God's work will be done.

POINT III. *Consider the development of prophecy.*

   a. God's promises are ever enlarging. As they become more special to individuals, they become more glorious to all.

   b. They have their fresh starting-points of development in seasons of danger, decay, and seeming death. God makes as if He had forgotten His people in order to develope their desire for Him to speak anew.

   c. They lead the soul onward to seek spiritual results, and not to be satisfied with merely earthly greatness.

AFFECTIONS. Trust in God. Expectation of Divine interposition. Patient waiting for God.

PRAYER.

O God, Whose Word never faileth, grant me to live in constant reliance thereupon, and gladly to accept all disappointment, whatsoever I may have expected, knowing that by Thy power it shall turn to greater results than I had dared to contemplate, for Thy glory and my own sanctification; through Jesus Christ our Lord. Amen.

THE DIVINE SPEAKER.

PRELUDE. i. *He spake.*

ii. The Spirit of God coming upon the Prophet.

POINT I. *Consider the utterance coming direct from God.*

    a. "God spake unto the fathers by the Prophets," just as truly as "in these last days He has spoken unto us by His Son."

    b. It was by the power of the Holy Ghost that He thus spake, as the Nicene Creed asserts.

    c. The Holy Ghost spake in the Prophets as being the Spirit of the Eternal Word. The Word of God could not come forth without the Holy Ghost, else had the Word become external to the Godhead, and would have been a dead word. Prophecy was not merely man's utterance about God, but God's living utterance through man.

POINT II. *Consider God's mercy in speaking through man.*

    a. The Israelites besought God not to speak to them in His glory, lest they should die. God yielded to their desire.

    b. He used their brethren not merely to announce His commands, but to disclose His purposes.

    c. The glory of prophetic mediation culminated in the Great Prophet, even His Only-begotten Son, Who should not only utter the Divine Word in transitory articulation with human lips, but should be the Word made Flesh, speaking in our nature for ever.

POINT III. *Consider the effect of Divine speech.*

    a. Each Divine utterance, although occasioned by an accidental detail, contains a changeless law, for God's method of action is unchangeable. The immediate occasion only helps forward the universal manifestation.

    b. The Divine utterance contains mysteries which the hearers upon each individual occasion fail to recognize. Yet these mysteries may be brought to light in future time.

    c. All the words of God point onward to the Incarnate Word. "The testimony of Jesus is the Spirit of prophecy."—Rev. xix. 10.

AFFECTIONS. Reverence for God's Word in every form. Contemplation. Docility.

PRAYER.

O God, Who hast spoken to us by Thine Only-begotten Son, Who being Thy consubstantial Word, alone can fully reveal Thy Truth, grant me so to receive His teaching in the power of Thy Holy Spirit, that according to the fulness of Thy Truth I may be transformed, and live to Thee; through the same Jesus Christ our Lord. Amen.

THE MOUTHPIECE OF THE HOLY GHOST.

PRELUDE. i. *He spake by the mouth of His Holy Prophets.*
ii. The Prophet falling down powerless.

POINT I. *Consider the Holy Ghost coming upon the Prophets.*

a. He came unsolicited. His seizure was a violent one, unexpected, as in the case of Saul.—1 Sam. x. 11.

b. When He had taken possession of a Prophet His Presence might be invited by various means, *e.g.*, ascetic discipline, sacred music.

c. He did not give the Divine Life to those whom He used for the Divine utterance. He spake by their mouths, but as instruments only, not as living organs. The higher utterance could not be until the Incarnation.

POINT II. *Consider the ignorance of the Prophets.*

a. The voice being external to their nature did not convey necessarily any illumination of the Holy Ghost for them to understand their own words.

b. They spake " in the Spirit," as our Lord says of David, and therefore with a real Divine Power.

c. They needed to obey this Holy Spirit, although not themselves rising up to the meaning of what they spake. Their very utterance was an act of faith in spite of the unbelief and ignorant contempt with which their prophecies were received.

POINT III. *Consider the Divine efficacy of their words.*

a. Their words came with comfort of the Holy Ghost to faithful hearts. However feebly understood, yet they brought the hope of Israel near to men's hearts.

b. They were to the condemnation of those who, because they did not understand them, rejected them as meaningless parables. The hearers would know that a Prophet had been among them.

c. Their words live on with power to all generations. They test us as they did their contemporaries. They did not merely foretell the earthly future, but they disclosed Divine mysteries.

AFFECTIONS. Reverence for prophecy. Desire of the Divine Will. Patience.

PRAYER.

O God, Who didst cause Thy Prophets of old to reveal mysteries which should have power for us though they knew not their meaning, give me grace; I beseech Thee, to meditate upon these Divine utterances that I may the better prepare myself for Thy most strict judgment; through Jesus Christ our Lord. Amen.

THE SANCTIFICATION OF THE PROPHETS.

PRELUDE. i. *His Holy Ones.*

ii. The Prophet waiting upon God in a long fast.

POINT I. *Consider the holiness of a Divine Messenger.*

  a. God does not find men holy, but He makes them so, if He wants to use them for holy purposes. They must have power beyond that of man, if they are to do God's work.

  b. The mere utterance of holy words does not constitute a Divine Messenger. The preacher must be sent—Rom. x. 15. He is sent by God's Presence going with him.   .

  c. The Prophet must live according to his vocation, or his office will be his own destruction. The Presence which accompanies him demands from him homage and subordination, to worship and to minister.

POINT II. *Consider the effects of this holiness.*

  a. As the Messenger honours God, so will God honour him. Compare Saul and Solomon with David and S. Paul.

  b. The neglect of the Messenger does not destroy the holiness of the power wherein he is sent; but it may make the Messenger guilty, if those to whom he goes reject his message through his fault.

  c. The power of holiness will strengthen the Messenger for the closer walk with God, if he cultivate it within himself, although seeing that his Message is rejected by others.

POINT III. *Consider the higher sanctity of the Kingdom of Heaven.*

  a. The holiness given is proportioned to the work which God has for His servants to do. The prophets spake of God, but nothing more. Therefore their sanctification was external, the gift of the Spirit occasional.

  b. The ministers of righteousness in the Christian Church have not merely to speak of holy things, but to communicate God's Holy Spirit. Therefore they have the Holy Spirit as a new Life in themselves by regeneration.

  c. Hence the need of personal preparation for God's work, that the holiness given may be duly exercised. "Separate unto Me Barnabas and Saul." We need a separated life.

AFFECTIONS. Reverence to the Holy Ghost. Joy in the Hidden Life.

PRAYER.

O God, Who hast called Thy servants to be separate from the world by the power of Thy Life-giving Spirit, grant that they whom Thou sendest may ever live true to the remembrance of Thy Love, which goeth forth along with them; through J. C. our Lord. Amen.

THE PREDESTINATION WHICH THE PROPHETS DISCLOSE.

PRELUDE. i. *His Holy Prophets which have been since the world began.*

ii. God speaking to Adam.

POINT I. *Consider the Divine Predestination of which they are the organs.*

    a. Prophecy discloses to us the unseen purpose of God. God makes the future known to us not merely as certain, but as springing from His own will, His Sovereignty.

    b. God ordains events for us with the very same Love wherewith He causes those events to be made known for our good.

    c. No one speaking from a merely earthly standpoint can make this will known; and it must be received in the same power of Divine Love wherewith it is proclaimed. God's children must love what their Father in Love declares.

POINT II. *Consider the first announcement of the promise.*

    a. The hope of glory was given to man as his birthright. His position in Paradise was probationary and initiative. God's command given to him then was a conditional promise.

    b. Immediately almost upon his fall, God spoke to him of restoration through his own offspring, an elevation from within the race of man carrying out the original purpose.

    c. God would not let man think that His work was to be a failure, however much it seemed to be thwarted by man's sin. He would still use the Seed of the woman to triumph over His enemy the Prince of this world.

POINT III. *Consider the continuity of prophetic utterance.*

    a. The Eternal Voice was a constant companion of the development of history. While facts seemed to be adverse, God recalled His people to the knowledge of what He was really purposing as the true result of those facts.

    b. Man was to live for the higher world, whence the Voice of promise came to him: not for this lower threatening world.

    c. The appearance of events in this world is ever fluctuating. The prophetic Voice from the Eternal Will is ever sure. Man is fitted to receive God's promises by believing in them.

AFFECTIONS. Delight in God's word. Hopeful obedience. Fearlessness in danger.

PRAYER.

O God, Who from the very beginning hast-declared to us Thine unchangeable will, grant us so to walk in obedience to Thy commands, with loving confidence in Thy promises, that our desires may be stimulated by Thy promises, and our lives perfected through Thy commands to attain that which Thy Sovereign will has ordained; through Jesus Christ our Lord. Amen.

THE PERFECT SALVATION.

PRELUDE. i. *Salvation from our enemies.*

ii. The Christian hidden in the grave of Christ from all enemies.

POINT I. *Consider that Christ is salvation.*

    a. The horn of salvation which is raised up is Christ; and Christ is the very salvation which He brings. He gives Himself to us, and salvation in Himself, not as a mere result of His sufferings, but as the essence of His Life.

    b. The name of Jesus signifies salvation. The promised Seed was to be a Jesus to the ends of the earth.—Isa. xlix. 6; Acts xiii. 47.—The Apostles endured all things, that the Elect might obtain the salvation which is in Christ Jesus with eternal glory.—2 Tim. ii. 10.—We ought to suffer with the same object in view.

    c. " There is not salvation in any other."—Acts iv. 12.—Salvation is not by a doctrine, but by a Life, and Life cannot be without personal union, membership with Christ.

POINT II. *Consider that salvation is an accomplished fact.*

    a. It was a matter of prophecy. The prophets searched diligently what the salvation should be.—1 S. Pet. i. 10.—No wonder if it still surpasses our comprehension !

    b. " Now is the day of salvation." " The grace of God that bringeth salvation hath appeared unto men."—Titus ii. 11.

    c. The fruits of our life must be such as " accompany salvation."—Heb. vi. 9.—Worthy of the vocation wherewith we are called.

POINT III. *Consider that it is a perfect salvation.*

    a. God does not prove us by imperfect help, to see whether He shall save us in the end; but He saves us by union with Christ, in order that He may prove us in the use of that Life, so as to obtain the rewards of glory.

    b. " How shall we escape, if we neglect so great salvation ?" The threats were fully accomplished against those who had the imperfect deliverance. The promises shall be as fully accomplished towards us if we are faithful.

    c. It is an eternal salvation.—Heb. v. 9.—For the Life in Christ is eternal.—1 S. John v. 11. Union with Him is given conditionally, but the effect of that union is complete from the first.

AFFECTIONS. Thankfulness. Holy Desire. Diligence.

PRAYER.

O God, Who hast saved us by Thy grace, grant that we may ever abide in Thy salvation, and strive to attain Thy promises ; through Jesus Christ our Lord. Amen.

OUR ENEMIES.

PRELUDE. i. *Salvation from our enemies.*
ii. Jesus driving back all that assault us.
POINT I.   *Consider who are our enemies.*

  a. Probably Zacharias thought mainly of Herod the great
  tyrant, but he spake by the Holy Ghost, and so his words
  are not limited by his thoughts.

  b. Jesus delivers us from the greater enemy, Satan. The
  temporal deliverance of one nation from a galling bondage,
  would be of little value. A few years and it would be over.
  This salvation, this redemption, is eternal.

  c. Our three great enemies, the Devil, the world, and the
  flesh, are the true objects which the prophet-priest must
  allude to in his song of deliverance.

POINT II.   *Consider how many our enemies are.*

  a. Satan, and all the multitude of the fallen angels.

  b. The world, ever powerful both in wealth and numbers to
  oppress the people of God. Herod, and the Roman Empire,
  to which Herod himself paid tribute, were but the actual
  representatives of the world-power ever strong against the
  Church, though with varying names.

  c. The flesh, and its many necessities, appetites, lusts. Every
  instrument of Divine Service requires to be snatched from
  the hand of the enemy who would hold us captive thereby.

POINT III.—*Consider our personal suffering under this hatred.*

  a. We have to fight our way, one by one, out of this tyranny.
  They are enemies, not merely oppressing the race, but
  seeking to destroy the individual.

  b. We cannot be saved, except by their overthrow. To
  live in friendship or peace with these enemies is to be an
  enemy of God.

  c. We are naturally under their dominion. Our knowledge
  of the salvation of Christ will be in proportion as we have
  died to the outer life in which these enemies meet us.

AFFECTIONS. Love of Mortification. Contempt of the
World. Renunciation of Satan.

PRAYER.

*O God, Who hast delivered us from our enemies, by calling us to
live unto Thyself, being quickened for Thy service by the Blood of
Thine Only-begotten Son, grant that I may eschew that friendship
of the world which is enmity against Thee, and in the strength of
Thy renewing Love, may bear with patience all the violence of
diabolical assaults; through Jesus Christ our Lord. Amen.*

THE TYRANNY OF OUR ENEMIES.

PRELUDE.　i. *The hand of all that hate us.*

ii. Death as a mighty monster, having all mankind in his grasp.

POINT I.　*Consider the actual tyranny of Satan.*

 a. He tempted our first parents in Eden, hoping to enslave them. We are subject to his power externally as soon as we are born.

 b. He stirs up the corrupt flesh to seek those things which are opposed to God's law. He can poison and intoxicate our fleshly nature by manifold forms of injurious delight, now that, by eating of the forbidden fruit, it has become subject to decay and death.

 c. He rules the world and organizes its powers for the over-throw of God's people, whether by persecution or flattery.

POINT II.　*Consider the activity of his hatred.*

 a. His hand is not slack. He goes about with eagerness to carry out his plans against us, and these are vastly greater than we can measure.

 b. He acts with the most subtle intellect, knowing what are our weakest points, and laying plans to meet us accordingly.

 c. All our enemies hold us by one grasp, for all are made one by subordination to Satan as their combined leader. Whether it be the world or the flesh which prominently assails us, it is really one hand, *i.e.*, Satan's.

POINT III.　*Consider the loosing of his grasp.*

 a. Christ saved us from the hand of Satan by dying for us. "By death He destroyed him that had the power of death."

 b. Christ saves us now from his power by sanctifying mortifi-cation, so that the very instruments whereby he would retain us, become instruments whereby we may die to him and live to God.

 c. He saves us also by giving us the gifts of a higher Life which Satan cannot touch, so that although externally exposed to him, we can ever find a sure place of refuge if we will seek it diligently. Satan cannot follow into that glory whereinto Christ is entered.

AFFECTIONS.　Watchfulness against Satan. Trust in Christ.

PRAYER.

O Lord God, Who hast sent Thy Blessed Son to destroy the works of the devil, and to set us free from his bondage, grant that by the exercise of Thy grace we may praise Thee for delivering us from his tyranny ; through the same Jesus Christ our Lord. **Amen.**

THE CAUSE OF THEIR HATRED.

PRELUDE. i. *All that hate us.*

ii. The dragon waiting to devour the Offspring of the mystical Woman.

POINT I. *Consider the envy of the Devil.*

  a. He forfeited Divine joy because he forfeited Divine sanctity. The loss of the one involves the loss of the other, for us as for him. Then hatred of God takes the place of God's love.

  b. He hates man because man is called to abide in the Joy and Love of God.

  c. He hates men in proportion as he sees them to be dwelling in God's love, both because they love God and because God loves them.

POINT II. *Consider the hatred of the world.*

  a. Satan fills the world with an intense hatred of God, and therefore of all who love God.

  b. The world naturally hates the people of God, because their lives are a witness against the world. So did Cain.

  c. Also because their hopes are fixed upon another object. The attainment of Christian hope is the overthrow of what the world hopes for. A Christian is to the world like a corpse in a banqueting hall.

POINT III. *Consider the changelessness of this hatred.*

  a. Satan watches for the woman [mankind] to bring forth the Seed that he may destroy it. He cannot destroy it: nor does it destroy him until the end.

  b. The supernatural power of the Church does but intensify his hatred with every fresh manifestation. He hates not chiefly the evil, but the good, that is the Church.

  c. The world naturally loves natural good, but Satan fills the world with a necessary hatred of the supernatural good. "For the love that I had unto them, lo, they take now my contrary part."—Ps. cix. 3.—Because Satan blinds their spiritual understanding, and misleads them.

AFFECTIONS. Patience. Gentleness. Love of enemies. Intercession.

PRAYER.

O God, Who callest us to abide in Thy Love, lest we perish by the malice of the devil, grant us so patiently to endure whatever he may stir up against us, that in patience and meekness we may be approved of Thee, and in the exercise of Thy Love towards all enemies may find increase of fervour in Love to Thyself; through Jesus Christ our Lord. **Amen.**

THE ACCOMPLISHMENT OF DIVINE MERCY.

PRELUDE. i. *To show mercy upon our forefathers.*
ii. The Soul of Christ shining amidst the dead when He descended to Hell.

POINT I. *Consider the prisoners of hope.*
   a. They died in faith not having received the promises.—Heb. xi. 19.—Abraham " rejoiced " not because he saw the day of Christ, but " in order to see it."
   b. They went down into silence in the grave. Life seemed profitless by reason of the grave, but the faithful looked forward for their glory to sing praise in the resurrection.
   c. Christ came to proclaim liberty to the captives.—Isa. lxi. 1.—Zacharias contemplates the joy of his forefathers at Christ's appearing, before thinking even of his own joy.

POINT II. *Consider their deliverance as an act of mercy.*
   a. Of them the world was not worthy. Nevertheless they were justly bound under Satan's power. They could not claim deliverance as an act of justice due to themselves. No law could give life, for none could give righteousness.
   b. It was an act of goodness and mercy by which He restored their souls, and led them forth from the valley of the shadow of death, the pit wherein was no water.
   c. The refreshment which they had during their time of expectation—S. Luke xvi. 25—was an anticipation of the joy of welcoming Christ to deliver them, Whom they had seen afar off.—Heb. ii. 13.

POINT III. *Consider wherein this mercy consisted.*
   a. First Christ "bound the strong man," their enemy, the Prince of Darkness.
   b. Christ made the Light of the Divine Presence to shine upon them, whereas they were in darkness until the true Light came to them.
   c. Christ brought them with Himself, perfected for the heavenly glory, the hosts who followed Him into the angelic choirs.—Ps. xxiv. 10.

AFFECTIONS. Joy in contemplation of the blessed dead. Imitation of their faith. Gratitude for the opening of Paradise.

PRAYER.

O Lord Jesus Christ, Who didst say that whosoever liveth and believeth in Thee should never die, grant that as Thou hast showed Thy mercy to our forefathers of the elder covenant, so I may walk in Thy grace, that I may not die, but may have my portion with Thy Saints, and a joyful resurrection in the day of Thine appearing; for Thy mercy's sake. Amen.

GOD'S MINDFULNESS.

PRELUDE. i. *To remember His Holy Covenant.*

ii. The name Zachariah, *i.e.*, God remembereth.

POINT I. *Consider the living eternity of God's Word.*

  a. God cannot forget. We must consider the years of the Right Hand of the Most Highest.—Ps. lxxvii. 9.—The Word by Whom God speaks is the Right Hand by Whom He acts.

  b. God's words do not die out as our words. His word does not leave Himself as a mere vibration. It is consubstantial with Himself, living, and life-giving.

  c. Our words pass away from ourselves, and therefore from our memory. God's Word abides in Himself. What He has spoken He speaks with an unalterable power of Life.

POINT II. *Consider the vicissitudes of God's people.*

  a. Often it seems as if God's Word must be sure to fail, but that is only to try our faith.

  b. God's people are exposed to outward buffeting like others. God does not cast them off, but waits for all else to fail before He shows Himself.

  c. When things are darkest God makes His Light to shine again. He remembereth that we are but dust. He never swerves from the purpose of His Love whereby He seeks to transform us into His glory.

POINT III. *Consider God's renewed manifestations of Himself.*

  a. Zacharias had doubted, but his very name ought to have made him watchful for the Divine appearance.

  b. The time of God's visitation was fixed, and the priest ought to have been expecting that which was so carefully revealed. God remembered the time which He had announced,

  c. Whatever blessings come by Christ were contained within the limits of the original promise. All fresh triumphs manifest the Eternal Word in some new form.

AFFECTIONS. Trust in God. Study of his Word. Indifference to outward change.

PRAYER.

O *God, Who art ever true and faithful, yea! Thy Word is unchangeable, and Thou canst not deny Thyself, grant me always so to repose in the security of Thy promises that I may serve Thee without fear amidst the vicissitudes of the outer world; through Jesus Christ our Lord. Amen.*

THE COVENANT.

PRELUDE. i. *To remember His Holy Covenant.*
ii. God speaking to Abraham.

POINT I. *Consider the Covenant as God's unalterable Promise to Abraham and his Seed.*

    a. This Covenant is an appointment by Almighty God, independent of any act whereby the creature in future time should be considered as obtaining for himself the gift. It is a pure promise.—Eph. ii. 12.

    b. There cannot be any alteration made therein. It remains in its original simplicity, resting upon the Truth of God.

    c A man's appointments are liable to be cancelled by him until he die. God cannot alter His promise without ceasing to live. He is the unchangeable Truth.

POINT II. *Consider that Christ is the true ultimate Seed.*

    a. Abraham had a double offspring : one by nature, the other the Supernatural Seed. It is to the latter that the Promise is made. Ishmael is of nature. Isaac is above nature.

    b. That offspring which began miraculously in Isaac, has a still more miraculous elevation awaiting it in Christ. The promises, therefore, sum themselves up in Him.

    c. The Supernatural gifts of God come to Him, not only as the Chief Development of the race, but as the Sole Inheritor of those gifts. Some possessed them as types of Him : others as His members : none except in union with Him.

POINT III. *Consider the Israelites as the Children of the Covenant.*

    a. As Abraham's children, the family of whose substance Christ should be born, they stood in a different relation to God from what the Gentiles possessed.

    b. The Gentiles were strangers to the Covenant of Promise. They could not win the promised gift by their own effort.

    c. The offer of the Gospel was made first to those to whom it was promised, and was not made to the Gentiles until they rejected it. If God calls us near, he will not neglect us. It is our own fault to neglect Him.

AFFECTIONS. Reliance on God's Truth. Expectation of great gifts in store. Dependence on God's free gift of Love.

PRAYER.

O God, Who hast created man in Thine own Image to receive the fulness of glory by the Incarnation of Thine Only-begotten Son, grant that we may evermore praise Thee for Thy goodness, abide in Thy law, wait for Thy promises, and attain the purposes of Thy Love, which surpass all that we can desire ; through Jesus Christ our Lord. Amen.

THE THREE COVENANTS.

PRELUDE. i. *To remember His Holy Covenant.*
ii. God speaking to Abraham.
POINT I. *Consider the Eternal Covenant.*
> *a.* The Covenant of the Kingdom of Christ. "My Father hath appointed unto Me a kingdom."—S. Luke xxii. 29.— "I have set my King upon My Holy Hill of Sion." This kingdom of the Incarnate Son was pre-ordained eternally, in the generation of the Word by Whom all things were made.
> *b.* The Covenant of universal Heirship. Christ is the Heir of all things.—Heb. i. 2.—As the husbandmen of the vine-yard said, "This is the Heir."—S. Matt. xxi. 38.—His Possession is an inalienable Birthright.
> *c.* The Covenant of indissoluble Life. Christ is the consub-stantial Son of the Father. "All things that the Father hath are Mine."—S. John xvi. 15.—The Covenant is bound in the unity of the Eternal Spirit.

POINT II. *Consider the legal Covenant.*
> *a.* It was ordained for a time until the coming of Christ, Who was the Heir of the promise.
> *b.* It was an earthly transitory covenant, having a worldly sanctuary, but not a holy life. It symbolized that which was to take its place.
> *c.* It is the old Covenant, not by reference to the Eternal Covenant between the Father and His Incarnate Son, but by reference to the New Covenant which God promised to establish through Christ.

POINT III. *Consider the New Covenant.*
> *a.* It is new as being developed in active power, so as to take the place of the old which prepared the way for it.
> *b.* It springs out of the old, but with a new power. The Commandment of Love is old according to the letter, but new according to the spirit; so is this Covenant one with the old, but superior to it.
> *c.* It is a manifestation of the Eternal Covenant within the limits formerly occupied for a season by the old or legal Covenant, and spreading beyond those limits to all the human race.

AFFECTIONS. Trust in God. Dignity through union with Christ. Acknowledgement of Divine claim.

PRAYER.

O God, Who hast called me to partake of the Love whereby Thou hast given all things to Thine Only-begotten Son, grant that I may so praise Thee for calling me near, that I may never lose the Life whereinto Thou hast called me; through Jesus Christ our Lord. Amen.

THE TOKENS OF THE OLD COVENANT.

PRELUDE. i. *His Holy Covenant.*

ii. The Priest blessing the child when he was presented before the Lord.

POINT I. *Consider the initiatory token, Circumcision.*

　　a. It symbolized the Divine acceptance. It was the mark of God upon the bodies of His Covenanted people, sealing them as His own.

　　b. It symbolized death. The gift of the Covenant was to be made sure by the testator's death: but also it required that those who received it should die to their old relationships in order to enter into the possession.

　　c. It symbolized the purity which is required in God's Covenant, putting off the body of the sins of the flesh by the Circumcision of Christ.

POINT II. *Consider the sustaining token of the Covenant, Sacrifice.*

　　a. It symbolized the Redeemer Who having died should call His worshippers by feeding upon His everliving Body to receive the glorifying Food of another Life.

　　b. It symbolized the state of the worshipper; he cannot find favour with God unless he be identified with the Victim who has died.

　　c. It symbolized the Divine acceptance; for the fire which consumed the Victim showed that it was acceptable with God, and consequently those who fed there must be partakers of the same acceptance.

POINT III. *Consider the administrative token of the Covenant, Priesthood.*

　　a. The Priest represented the people, as being a suppliant before God ; but in his action towards the people he represented God freely and sovereignly bestowing His gifts.

　　b. He symbolized a more perfect Mediator; for unless his office rose to a truer fellowship with God, it remained useless. It was only a dumb show.

　　c. As he manifested the Personal character of the glorious Mediator Who should take his place, so he manifested the Personal character of God Whom that Mediator represented, and with Whom He dwelt in an eternal Covenant.

AFFECTIONS. Reverence for Divine ordinances. Desire of spiritual profit.

PRAYER.

O God, Who hast made Thy Covenant with man by means of outward tokens to assure us of Thy purpose, grant me so to approach the ordinances of Thy grace with sincerity and truth, that I may experience the blessed manifestations of Thy truth and power in the fulness of the Holy Ghost; through Jesus Christ our Lord. Amen.

2 c 2

THE PROMISES OF THE OLD COVENANT.

PRELUDE. i. *His Holy Covenant.*

ii. The Angel of the Lord speaking to Abraham.

POINT I. *Consider the inheritance of the world.*

  a. This is primarily the Birthright of the Incarnate Word, the Creator of the world.

  b. This Promise inherent in the Eternal Sonship, became conditioned through the family of Abraham. Abraham was joined in the Promise to his seed that he should be the heir of the world.—Rom. iv. 13.—God takes mankind into the Covenanted glory of His Son.

  c. Adam had to subdue the earth that He might be assumed into the Sonship. Jesus has manifested His Sonship by subduing the Prince of this world, and now He waits to receive it from His Father. We have been assumed in order to subdue.

POINT II. *Consider the Promise that all families of the earth should be blessed in him.*

  a. There could be only one Mediator of Blessing between God and man. No man could be a blessing to the rest, save by participation of the Divine Nature. Abraham by this covenant was separated with a view to the Incarnation.

  b. His one family was separated for many ages to abide in the Divine Covenant, in preparation for that Divine Seed which should be the Mediator for the benefit of all.

  c. Israel was looking forward to the one man whom God had ordained. With Him the Covenant was sure, and the mercies of David were sure as being established upon Him.

POINT III. *Consider the promise of Divine Communion.*

  a. The primary Covenant of worship, "I will be their God, and they shall be My people." This Divine relationship cannot exist truly without adoption into Divine Life. God is separate from all that is merely of earth.

  b. The promise developing into paternity: "I will be his Father, and he shall be My Son."—2 Sam. vii. 14.

  c. The fulness of Divine Love accomplished by the Incarnation. The Covenant between God and the Chosen Seed becomes perfect in the bond of the Holy Ghost.

AFFECTIONS. Large-heartedness. Spirituality. Filial Love.

PRAYER.

O *God, Who hast given Thine only Son to be the Mediator in Whose Person all Thy gifts are made sure to us, grant me so to be true to Him, that in Him I may find the true glory of Thy Heavenly gifts; through the same Jesus Christ our Lord.* Amen.

THE NEW COVENANT AND THE OLD.

PRELUDE. i. *His Holy Covenant.*
ii. The old Temple as a symbol of the Heavenly one.

POINT I. *Consider the contrast of duration.*

a. The Old Covenant ordained for a temporary purpose, pointed onward to its successor. The New, the Everlasting Covenant, does not tolerate the thought of any after dealings between God and man.

b. The O. C. by its local enactments was suited only for a time such as actually belonged to it. The N. C. has the adaptability necessary for a religion which should be co-extensive with the world in area and in duration.

c. The O. C. attests both its own truth and the truth of its successor by vanishing away just when it did, in fulfilment of its own prophecies.

POINT II. *Consider the contrast of power.*

a. The O. C. reminded of sin, but could not take sins away. The Temple required to be hallowed yearly on the Day of Atonement. The N. C. provides access for us to the Holy of Holies, putting away all sin.

b. The O. C. warned man of sin, but did not help him to resist it. The N. C. gives grace to triumph over sin.

c. The O. C. did not raise man above his natural position. The N. C. has the gifts of the Spirit, that we may therein partake of the Nature of God.

POINT III. *Consider the contrast of purity.*

a. The O. C. provided a cleansing of the flesh, that men might draw near to God in typical ordinances. The N. C. provides the answer of a good conscience before God, that men may draw near to Him in spiritual purity.

b. The O. C. had a temple which being earthly was itself in need of cleansing. The N. C. has for its Temple the Body of Christ, which is the principle of purity for all.

c. The O. C. had sacrifices which were offered in a state of death, consumed by fire. The N. C. has One Living Oblation to bring before God, even the Body of Christ Who has risen from the dead.

AFFECTIONS. Heavenly-mindedness. Gratitude for Blessings in Christ.

PRAYER.

O Lord God, *Who hast taken away the Old Covenant, that Thou mayest establish with us a New Covenant of Everlasting Life, grant me so to walk before Thee in newness of life, that I may obtain the glorious promises which Thou hast given unto us therein; through Jesus Christ our Lord.* Amen.

THE NEW COVENANT INTIMATED BY THE OLD.

PRELUDE. i. *His Holy Covenant.*

ii. Moses contemplating the heavenly reality while he arranges the earthly representation thereof.

POINT I. *Consider the Everlasting promise.*

    a. God promised to establish His Covenant for an everlasting Covenant with the seed of Abraham, but the provisions of the old Covenant contemplated its abolition.—Gen. xvii. 7.

    b. Shiloh was to be the culminating point of the Old Covenant, and the nations were to be gathered to Him. Then should begin a kingdom, not local and temporary, but universal and eternal.

    c. The Priesthood which was handed from one generation to another was too glorious for itself. It needed something greater to justify its solemn acts before God.

POINT II. *Consider the prosperity promised by the Old Covenant.*

    a. Great were the promises, and yet through many generations they failed of any earthly fulfilment. But devout hearts knew that spiritually they must come true.

    b. The phraseology indicates that what is promised externally is intended to bring with it a spiritual meaning, for which in the older dispensation there was no place.

    c. The seed of Abraham was to be a blessing to all the world. But this could not be without higher gifts than worldly prosperity could contain. None can be a blessing to the nations of the earth without belonging to a higher order of life than that of earth.

POINT III. *Consider the Divine Fellowship which was promised.*

    a. The Promised Seed was to be the Son of God, and God was to be His Father. This was a Sonship not inherited but predicted. The Eternal Son should Himself be given.

    b. God would dwell in His people and walk in them. So would He be their God, and teach each one of them.

    c. God would call to Himself Priests and Levites from all the nations of the earth, ministering in eternal righteousness.

AFFECTIONS. Trust in Divine Promises. Expectation of Heavenly developments. Fixed regard of Christ.

PRAYER.

O Lord God, Who didst promise earthly things to the fathers, and hast given us those heavenly realities which were therein foreshadowed, grant that as they looked forward to the Heavenly City, so we who dwell therein may be preserved from looking backward to the world, and may rejoice in Thy Truth; through Jesus Christ our Lord. Amen.

THE HOLINESS OF THE COVENANT.

PRELUDE. i. *His Holy Covenant.*
ii. The Holy Ghost filling the members of Christ with Divine Life.

POINT I. *Consider the Covenant of God worthy of God in its end.*

> *a.* Holiness belongs to God alone. The Covenant originates in the Divine Promise, and must rise up to the Divine Life.
> *b.* The Covenant binds us to God; and nothing can bind us to God which is not itself participant in the Life of God. The O. C. had the watchword: "I said ye are gods."
> *c.* There is no power superior to God. He is not bound, save by His own will. But the will of God cannot rest on any object short of His own true essential glory.

POINT II. *Consider the Covenant of God as worthy of God in its means.*

> *a.* The Eternal Covenant, the appointment of God, is given to man without any mediation, simply by promise. It is to Abraham and his Seed, which is our Lord Jesus Christ.
> *b.* The O. C. made with Israel, did not raise man above this lower world. Yet was the law holy, because it was sustained by a Divine intention pointing onward to the living Righteousness of the Faith.
> *c.* The means of the N. C. have a higher holiness, for they contain Christ. They are a real ministration of the Holiness of God.

POINT III. *Consider the Covenant of God as worthy of God in its virtue.*

> *a.* The virtue of the Covenant is proportionate to the recipient. To the All-perfect One it is manifest in its perfection, even the glory of the Consubstantial Sonship which makes the Name of Jesus to be above every other name.
> *b.* The virtue of the O. C. wrought conformably to the requirements of that age of expectation, fencing the people in, so as to be kept for Christ.
> *c.* The virtue of the N. C. is a living virtue proceeding in the Body of Christ; even the Holy Ghost, Who as He proceeds from the Person of Christ eternally, necessarily inheres and acts in all the members of His Body.

AFFECTIONS. Reverence for our calling in Christ. Self-surrender to live for God. Humiliation for continuing infirmity of nature.

PRAYER.

Grant, O Lord, that being gathered into Thy Covenant of Israel, I may ever walk worthy of this Holy Vocation; through Jesus Christ our Lord. Amen.

THE PROMISES OF THE NEW COVENANT.

PRELUDE. i. *His Holy Covenant.*
ii. The glory of Heaven shining forth from the Throne of Jesus and encircling us with Holy Light.

POINT I. *Consider that they are worthy of the Giver.*

a. God's promises in Christ are true, sure, abiding. As Christ glorified the Father by His own Life upon the earth, so these promises are to the glory of God by us.

b. They required the complete surrender of His Humanity, so as to become an instrument of unimpeded action to His Godhead. If He had not died to earth by being entirely given to God, He could not act towards earth so as to communicate the Life of God.

c. The glory of His Mediatorial Kingdom, in the homage received from creation, is only expressive of that Life which it is His glory to give because He has it in Himself.

POINT II. *Consider that they are the transmission of what He has Himself received.*

a. The promise was made to Christ that He should be the Heir of the world. The Righteousness of faith which was in Abraham rises to a supernatural development in Christ.

b. The promise is to Abraham and his Seed; but it is to the Seed first, and through Him to Abraham. "He rejoiced that he might see My day."

c. He is Mediator, not the primary Source of the Divine Life. That which He receives consubstantially He communicates ministerially alike to Jew and Gentile.—Rom. xv. 8, 9.

POINT III. *Consider that they are necessary in order to raise man to his proper dignity in Creation.*

a. Knowledge of Christ is not enough without the gift of the Holy Ghost. The Apostles must tarry in Jerusalem until the ascended Saviour sent down the promise of the Father.

b. Only by Resurrection in Christ can man truly live unto God. If Christ were not raised, we should be yet in our sins, but His Resurrection is the germ of ours.

c. Man needs a tabernacle sanctified for ever from all remembrance of sin, as his abiding Home with God. But that must be a Heavenly tabernacle, sanctified by the Blood of the Covenant in the power of the Spirit of Grace.

AFFECTIONS. Gratitude. Hope. Deadness to the world.

PRAYER.

O God, Who hast fulfilled to us such exceeding great and precious promises in the Covenant of Thy dear Son, grant that we may walk worthy of that which Thou hast given, so that we may be perfected for the manifestation of Thy glory; through the same Thy Son Jesus Christ our Lord. Amen.

THE LEGISLATION OF THE NEW COVENANT.

PRELUDE.　i. *His Holy Covenant.*

ii. The living Creatures about the Throne of Christ glowing with Divine Life.

POINT I.　*Consider the legal organization of the Old Covenant.*

　　a. It was incidental.　The promise to Abraham's Seed was not overruled by it.　The law only prepared the way for it.

　　b. It was typical, for all things were to be arranged by Moses according to the pattern of Heavenly things.　Hence Isaiah speaks of the Priests and Levites to be gathered from the Gentiles, typified in the Aaronic ministry.

　　c. It was transitory, founded upon the Priesthood of the tribe of Levi.　But the true, the great High Priest, was to be of the tribe of Judah.　A change was therefore necessary whenever Christ should come.—Heb. vii. 11.

POINT II.　*Consider the legal organization of the New Covenant.*

　　a. It is based upon Christ.　He is the High Priest Who remaineth for ever, with promises proportionate to Himself.—Heb. viii. 6.

　　b. It is a living organization.　The Church is the Body of Christ, from Whom, as its Head, it receives nourishment and compactness by the joints and bands of an appointed ministry, and increases with the increase of God the Holy Ghost dwelling within.

　　c. It is eternal.　The Church not being a preparatory but a distributive organization, never can lose her office as long as the Life lasts which binds the members of Christ in one.

POINT III.　*Consider the beatific promises which glorify it.*

　　a. The promises which this legislation contemplates are exceeding great and precious—2 S. Pet. i. 4—even to be partakers of the Divine Nature.

　　b. That promised gift is transforming us from glory to glory into the Image of Christ while we contemplate Him.

　　c. The old law was organized with surroundings of glory, although transitory.　The organization of the Church has an inalienable glory, for it is a Body which abideth for ever—2 Cor. iii. 11—wherein we are to attain to be like Christ in very truth, for we shall see Him as He is.

AFFECTIONS.　Joy in the use of Christian Sacraments. Praise to the Holy Ghost, the Giver of Life, Determination to rise as He calls.

PRAYER.

O Lord God, Who in Thine Only-begotten Son hast made us partakers of Thy Life-giving Spirit, grant that we may so walk in His power that we may be made perfect in His Love; through the same Jesus Christ our Lord. Amen.

THE HEIRS OF THE COVENANT.

PRELUDE. i. *His Holy Covenant.*
ii. Jesus upon the Throne of God.

POINT I. *Consider the natural heir.*

a. The Son of God is the only Heir. He has inherited a Name greater than that of any Angel.—Phil. ii. 9.

b. This inheritance was assured to Him by the Father's appointment from the very beginning. All things were made by Him and for Him.— Col. i. 16.

c. It is inalienable. The Throne of the Son of David is eternal as the Covenant of Divine Sonship wherewith it is associated. The Son shall deliver up the kingdom to God the Father; not so as to part with it, but rather to reign with the more manifest perfection of Divine power.

POINT II. *Consider the Mediatorial Extension of the Old Covenant.*

a. The Old Law did not touch the inheritance, but was a treaty made between God and the people by the hand of a Mediator, and with Angels attendant upon it.—Gal. iii. 19.

b. It was to last until the promised Seed should come. The people needed external mediation to uphold them in their inheritance : none of them could claim the birthright.

c. Association with the 'law was only valuable in so far as it signified association with Him Who should fulfil the Law and perfect the promises, the true Heir of all things.

POINT III. *Consider the Mediatorial Extension of the New Covenant.*

a. The gifts of the New Covenant are given not by the Hand of Christ as a mediating servant such as Moses was, but in the Body of Christ as a sanctifying organization wherein we are builded together so as to partake of His Life.

b. The Promise had no Mediator. He who is sole Heir of the Promise is sole Mediator, distributing God's gifts. Angels cannot order them. He is the High Priest of our Profession.

c. This true and living Mediation gives us Eternal Life in Christ, so that we become partakers of the eternal inheritance promised to Him, being freed from death.—Heb. ix. 15.

AFFECTIONS. Exaltation in union with Christ. Contempt of the world. Hatred of sin.

PRAYER.

O Lord Jesus Christ, Who hast vouchsafed to become the Mediator of the New Testament that we might live with Thy Life, grant me so to experience Thy grace that I may joyfully take up Thy Cross in the confidence of Thine all-sustaining glory ; Who with the Father and the Holy Ghost livest and reignest God for ever and ever. **Amen.**

THE MEDIATOR OF THE NEW COVENANT.

PRELUDE. i. *To remember His Holy Covenant.*
ii. The Son of God in the midst of the golden candlesticks.

POINT I. *Consider Christ as the Mediator of the New Covenant.*

a. Equal to the Father. Moses was Mediator of old, but only as a servant, acting in God's Name. God had put the work in his hand. Christ acts in His own Name, not having power in His hands for a time, but in His own Person for ever.

b. Acting in the fulness of Divine Power. Christ shows the fulness of His power by the fulness of His gift. "Receive ye the H. G." Moses gave not this Spirit, for he had it not.

c. Appointing for us the inheritance which He has Himself received. "I appoint unto you a kingdom, as My Father hath appointed unto Me." Christ acts as the Head. He took the form of a servant, and humbled Himself to be the Minister of the Circumcision, but He performs His mediation, acting as Head over all things to the Church.

POINT II. *Consider the Mediatorial Kingdom of Christ.*

a. God appoints the Kingdom to Christ by supernatural birth. Christ appoints it to us by new birth.

b. To Abraham the promise was given, as it were, through a grave, from whence in a figure he received Isaac back to life. It is given to us through a grave. We must die to the world.

c. The Kingdom which He gives is not the old world as it was, but a new world perfected in righteousness and eternal life.

POINT III. *Consider the Mediatorial legacy of Christ.*

a. Death shows that the gift of Christ is irreversible. He who is unchangeable passes out of this world of change, leaving this testament behind.

b. Christ by dying destroyed death. The inheritance which Christ gives is valid not only by the seal of death, but against the power of death.

c. Death separates a natural parent from his heirs. Christ, in the unchangeableness of the Divine Will, by the power of the Holy Ghost, gives efficacy to the dispositions which before dying He had made as Man.

AFFECTIONS. Faith. Acceptance of death. Detachment from this present world.

PRAYER.

O Lord Jesu Christ, Who art entered into the Presence of God with the offering of Thine own Blood, that it may thence flow down upon us in the fulness of lifegiving power by the ministration of the Holy Ghost, grant that I may live in entire detachment from that world to which Thou hast died, and rejoice in the risen Life of Thy Kingdom, Who with the Father and the Holy Ghost livest and reignest God for ever and ever. Amen.

388 𝔖𝔬𝔫𝔤 𝔬𝔣 𝔷𝔞𝔠𝔥𝔞𝔯𝔦𝔞𝔰.—XXXVIII.

THE COVENANT CONFIRMED BY DEATH.

PRELUDE. i. *His Holy Covenant.*
ii. The High Priest carrying the Blood of the Victim.
POINT I. *Consider the Death which symbolically hallowed the Old Covenant.*

a. The O. C. did not transfer from death to life; but its pro--
mises symbolised the Life, its solemnities the death, of
Christ. The victim perished in death because he could not
find Life; but it showed forth a death which should give
Life because the Victim would not perish.

b. Everything was hallowed by death, being sprinkled with
blood. There could be no remission without death.

c. The High Priest entered into the holy place with blood, for
otherwise the Covenant would have remained precarious by
reason of the changeableness of all things living. The blood
showed the completeness of man's gift to God, the security
of God's gift to man.

POINT II. *Consider the death of Christ which gives validity
to the New Covenant.*

a. He became obedient unto death, offering the Body which
the Father had prepared for Him as the perfect oblation.

b. It was so perfectly offered in death by the power of the Holy
Ghost, that it derived no taint from death, saw no corruption.
His blood does not stagnate in death, but lives with the H. G.

c. He gives His Body and Blood sundered as under the form
of death, but powerful with the reality of eternal life to communicate to us the gifts of the Covenant.

POINT III. *Consider the Eternal Life of the New Covenant,
springing out of the Death of Christ.*

a. The promises of the N. C. belong to another world. Although
communicated in this life, they cannot be known except in
proportion as we are dead to this world.

b. Even Christ being in this world of death, could not enter
upon the gifts of the better world save by the surrender of
the life which held him down in this. He, the Life, must
die, ere He, as Man, could exercise the glory of the Life.

c. His reward is a final reward. He cannot forfeit the heavenly
glory, nor can death itself separate us from the love of God
if we are abiding in Him.

AFFECTIONS. Glorying in the Cross. Deadness to the
world.

PRAYER.

O *God, Who hast confirmed to us the Covenant of Thy Love by
the precious death of Thy dear Son, grant that we may be dead unto
the world, and live in the power of Thy Holy Love; through the
same Jesus Christ our Lord. Amen.*

THE BLOOD OF THE COVENANT.

PRELUDE. i. *His Holy Covenant.*
ii. The High Priest going into the Holy of Holies.

POINT I. *Consider the Covenant Blood of Atonement.*

    a. The High Priest could not enter the Holy of Holies without the Blood which he had to sprinkle there, in order to sanctify the place for worship during the coming year. The Temple needed to be consecrated yearly.

    b. Blood was sprinkled on the worshipper in order to cleanse him from legal pollution.

    c. None might drink of the Blood. Being sprinkled, it was the symbol of cleansing. In itself it was the Blood of death and could not avail to cleanse the conscience.

POINT II. *Consider the Atoning Blood of Christ.*

    a. He goes in with His own Blood. Once there, He still has power, although He has shed it. For He does not live by it. Rather it lives by Him. It is living Blood wherever it flows, and it attests His Life.

    b. This Blood does not cleanse by the fact of its being shed upon the Cross. It cleanses that whereon it is sprinkled.

    c. It is sprinkled not upon the surface of our nature, but upon our hearts and consciences, communicated in sacraments, as an interior Life-giving principle. We are to drink it.

POINT III. *Consider the difference of the Old and the New.*

    a. The Old typified the New, but it was death typifying Life. The Old took the worshipper into the fellowship of a dead Victim, but that was only fellowship in expectation, looking for a real perfection to be given hereafter.

    b. The New fulfils the expectations which belonged to the type. The Blood of Jesus in the Sacraments of the Church gives fellowship with Him Who died and is alive again.

    c. The Blood of those helpless victims must taint those who drank it. The Blood of the Almighty Victim glorifies those who drink worthily, and gives them the Divine Life which it contains. The Blood of Calvary consecrated the Covenant. The Blood administered from Heaven cleanses, regenerates, renews, purifies the conscience for acceptable service.

AFFECTIONS. Devotion to the Blood of Jesus. Joy in the consciousness of having received it.

PRAYER.

O Jesu, Who hast shed Thy Blood for my sins, and givest me to drink thereof that I may rejoice in Thine Eternal Life of holiness, grant me always to act in the power of Thy holy impulses, that I may attain to Thy Divine glory ; Who livest and reignest with the Father and the Holy Ghost for ever and ever. **Amen.**

THE OATH OF THE COVENANT.

PRELUDE. i. *The Oath which he sware unto Abraham.*
ii.   God appearing to Abraham on Mount Moriah.
POINT I.   *Consider the Eternal Truth of God.*

    a. The Truth of God is the warrant of all oaths that are taken by the creature. He is the Truth, and things are true in proportion as they are conformable to His will.

    b. His will is not a changeable will as is the will of imperfect beings. It is a universal Will, comprehending all things with a perfect harmony of purpose. The law of His Being and the law of His action are alike unchangeable.

    c. The fixity of God's working in nature, developing in spite of the imperfection of the instruments through which He developes His eternal purposes, depends upon the fixed perfection of the nature of God in Himself.

POINT II.   *Consider God's Word pledged to the creature.*

    a. By an oath we pledge our honour before God to the Truth of our words. That honour involves our salvation, our union with God. God swears by Himself, making His whole glory to rest on the fulfilment of His promise.

    b. God pledges His Word to the creature, by subjecting His Word to the creature. God gives us His Word. His Word is made Flesh. We thereby acquire a claim upon God.

    c. The creature, as God's instrument, is thus taken out of its changefulness into the unchangeableness of the Divine Nature by Hypostatic Union, and by the Incarnate Word God effects His revealed purpose.

POINT III.   *Consider the purpose of God's taking the Oath.*

    a. Abraham for fulfilling God's Word received that Word as His reward. The blessing resting hitherto upon him externally became an interior principle of Eternal Life.

    b. Abraham received the imputed righteousness of the Covenant by his faith—Gen. xv. 6; Rom. iv. 3.—He received the Oath after probation upon obedience.—Gen. xxii. 16-18; James ii. 21.

    c. This oath was further developed by the Oath respecting the High Priesthood of the Chosen Seed, by whose ministrations the communicated Life should operate for the sanctification of others.

AFFECTIONS. Trust in God. Joy in Obedience. Patience.

PRAYER.

O God, Who hast bound Thyself to us by the gift of Thy Word to take upon Himself our nature and to share our needs, grant me so to live in union with Him that I may receive the Blessed Vision of His Divine glory; Who liveth and reigneth with Thee in the unity of the Holy Ghost, one God world without end. **Amen.**

THE OATH TO ABRAHAM.

PRELUDE. i. *The Oath which He sware unto Abraham.*
ii. The Angel appearing in answer to Abraham's sacrifice.

POINT I. *Consider the Oath of Multiplication.*

    a. The seed was supernatural in its origin : for Abraham's body was, as it were, dead when Isaac was born. That birth was an intervention of the Divine Word allying itself with human nature by a law of election.

    b. The multiplication should be as supernatural as the origin. The stars of heaven are the symbol not only of the number, but of the heavenly character of the offspring.

    c. The sand represents the barrenness as well as the numerical infinity of the offspring. The sea is symbolical of sacramental grace established by the Oath of God, so that the offspring, dead to this world, may live to God.

POINT II. *Consider the Oath of Possession.*

    a. The Divine Oath confers on this seed that which His enemies now possessed ; not a simple inheritance, but a birthright obtained by conquest.

    b. Those enemies must be proportionate to the terms of the promise, *i.e.*, the Prince of this world and His angels. This refers to the enmity between the Seed of the woman and the seed of the serpent.

    c. This Oath is the beginning of the promise that the Gates of Hell shall not prevail against the Kingdom of Christ.

POINT III. *Consider the Oath of Benediction.*

    a. The Word of God being the source of all benediction, is pledged by this Oath to use the Seed of Abraham as its instrument for blessing mankind.

    b. That Oath is a promise of energy proportionate in power to the extent of the promised sway. His Life should be the manifestation of God.

    c. The Divine reality of Blessing received is shown by the Divine power of Blessing exercised towards all nations.

AFFECTIONS. Reliance upon God. Power in God.

PRAYER.

O God, Who hast sworn that Thy Word shall not fail, being pledged through the Seed of Abraham to bless the world, grant me so to live in the power of Thy Covenant, that I fail not to rejoice in its manifestation ; through Jesus Christ our Lord. Amen.

THE DEVELOPMENT OF THE OATH.

PRELUDE. i. *The Oath which He sware unto Abraham.*
ii. The institution of a Royal Priesthood by God's Oath to David's Heir.

POINT I. *Consider the Oath renewed to David.*

    a. The sure mercies of David are not a fresh covenant in addition to the old, but a germination of the original covenant in fulfilment of the Oath.

    b. God made a covenant with Abraham and sware an Oath [with reference] to Isaac. The living Oath should manifest itself according to the developing law of human life.

    c. The living Oath must rise to a personal centre of maturity from whence to distribute itself. Up to David's time the Blessing is simply one of passive security.

POINT II. *Consider the Mediatorial glory of the Vocation.*

    a. The active glory of the Blessing shows itself in the royalty wherewith the Beloved begins to gather the nations under His sway.

    b. The royalty of Blessing is a Priestly Royalty. Its character could not be inferior to the character of Melchizedec. He who blessed Abraham exhibited typically the future glory of the Blessing which Abraham's Seed should give.

    c. The promise of the world to this Seed was not a promise of wealth to be received, but of poverty to be relieved. The world's necessities would show the Divine resources inherent in the Mediator, the Priestly King.

POINT III. *Consider the Divine glory of the End.*

    a. The Oath of God, personified in the coming Child, would make its Blessings to flow in exhaustless fulness of Divine Life.

    b. The development would be gradual, but there never would be any recession. The features of Blessing once exhibited by the Seed would live eternally.

    c. The Oath would therefore have no limit until it found itself perfected in the glory of God, showing forth that glory from whence it proceeded, which the Incarnate Word had with the Father before the world began.

AFFECTIONS. Repose in Divine Mystery. Expectation of growing developments. Spirituality of Desire.

PRAYER.

O God, Who hast given Thy Blessed Son to be the Mediator in Whom we may have access to Thee, grant us to praise Thee for that which Thou hast revealed, by looking forward to the glory which remains to be manifested; through the same Jesus Christ our Lord. Amen.

Song of Zacharias.—XLIII. 393

THE OATH OF EXCLUSION.

PRELUDE. i. *The Oath which He sware unto Abraham.*
ii. God's wrath against Israel in the wilderness.
POINT I. *Consider the exclusion of the whole generation.*
  a. The Oath was the manifestation of a Blessing which needed to be accepted by faith. The want of faith in receiving it would change the Divine action into a curse.
  b. God's great deliverance of the people from Egypt in fulfilling the promise, became a curse because they did not rise up to it. He sware that they should not enter into His rest.
  c. The manifestation of the Divine Seed in earthly surroundings was for the purpose of drawing away from earthly repose those who would seek fellowship therewith.
POINT II. *Consider the exclusion of Moses and Aaron.*
  a. Fellowship with this Seed in holy ministration demands a proportionate appreciation and acknowledgment of its Divine All-sufficiency.
  b. God sware that Moses and Aaron should not enter into the promised land, because they glorified not Him.
  c. The Oath required a chosen Seed worthy of its inherent Benediction. Israel as a people, Moses and Aaron as conjointly exhibiting the royal priesthood, were set aside by the necessity of the Oath, for they had not the Divine intuition needful in order to accomplish its purposes.
POINT III. *Consider the Anathema of Christ.*
  a. The Oath rests upon Christ, separating off the supernatural Seed from all the rest of mankind. The Promise was sure, but it could not be given until He came Who was worthy to receive it.
  b. The Blessing promised upon Oath to the chosen Seed is therefore equivalent to an Anathema upon all that is outside of Him.
  c. The Blessing of the Oath is to be obtained only by union with Christ to Whom it belongs. It cannot be got from Him or through Him, except by being in Him.
AFFECTIONS. Thankfulness for covenanted gifts in Christ. Loyalty to Christ as the Head of the Church.

PRAYER.

O Lord Jesu Christ, in Whom are hidden all the treasures of he Divine Love, grant me so to abide within the sanctuary of Thy rovenanted grace. that I may escape the condemnation of those who relieve not, and may attain to behold with all Thy Saints the glory f Thine inheritance; Who with the Father and the Holy Ghost ivest and reignest God for ever and ever. Amen.

2 D

THE WORK OF GRACE FORESEEN.

PRELUDE. i. *That He would give us.*

ii. Angels watching, but unable to see what God in His inmost counsel had already ordained for His people.

POINT I. *Consider the foreknowledge of God.*

a. The gifts of God are not of the moment. He has through ages been purposing to give them, and all the events of the world have been preparing the way for the gift.

b. His gift is worthy of His foreknowledge, and abides in the Eternity of His Life.

c. One gift of God does not take the place of another, but perfects, developes, glorifies, whatever has been given beforehand.

POINT II. *Consider the fixity of God's operations.*

a. The variety of God's Providences is all operating in mysterious harmony towards the ultimate issue.

b. Apparent change only shows the capacity of God fo adapt His arrangements with triumphant success to the complications which arise amidst His creatures.

c. God's gifts may be delayed by man's sin, but He will not withdraw from His promise. He requires us to recognize His power ere He can fulfil to us His promise, and the difficulties from which we shrink are required in order to test our fitness.

POINT III. *Consider the necessity of waiting upon God.*

a. God waits to be gracious until He finds those who will wait for His grace. We must have an earnest desire, along with a patient confidence.

b. The promises of God are given for the purpose of awakening in us that expectation which is needed.

c. The hindrances of life are permitted in order that we may learn to rest in the assurance of His Truth.

AFFECTIONS. Patience. Self-discipline. Boldness in adversity.

PRAYER.

O God, grant that we, to whom Thou hast made such gracious promises, may ever abide in the security of Thine unchanging Word, and act in the confidence of Thine All-controlling sovereignty, so that we may at length obtain the gifts which Thy loving wisdom has ordained; through Jesus Christ our Lord. Amen.

FEARLESSNESS.

PRELUDE. i. *That we without fear.*

ii. Israel standing on the shore of the sea when the Egyptians were drowned.

POINT I. *Consider the holy fear of the redeemed.*

    a. We are to perfect holiness in the fear of the Lord; that is, the fear of incurring His displeasure if we fall away from our covenanted position.

    b. Such fear is external to our position, and does but enhance the energy with which we strive to fulfil God's will.

    c. That fear is the offspring of holy love, for our fear of losing the gift of grace will be proportioned to our acknowledgment of the precious Blood of our Redemption. So great the price! So terrible the loss!—1 S. Pet. i. 17, 19.

POINT II. *Consider the unholy fear of the enslaved.*

    a. Fear of violence arises from consciousness of inherent weakness. The promised strength will raise us above this.

    b. Fear of external assault implies a distrust of the Love of God; but this must be fully assured to us by the promise.

    c. Fear of Divine displeasure implies uncertainty as to the continuance of God's Love, and consequently a sense of imperfection in the actual state of covenant with Him.

POINT III. *Consider the deliverance from fear which Christ has effected.*

    a. Christ establishes us in security by the overthrow of our enemies. We must regard them as being utterly vanquished.

    b. Christ binds us to God in an indissoluble covenant. So that we have power to resist the assaults which our foes, though vanquished, may make upon us.

    c. Christ perfects us in God with a living communication of Divine gifts, so as to set us beyond the reach of evil powers, for Satan cannot intervene between us and God if we cling to Him.

AFFECTIONS. Reverence. Filial trust. Boldness against evil.

PRAYER.

O God, Who callest us to act without fear in the strength of Thy grace, knowing the All-sufficiency of Thy bounty, grant us so to rejoice in the freedom which Thy dear Son has obtained for us, that we may persevere in grace and be perfected in glory; through the same Jesus Christ our Lord. Amen.

CONSCIOUSNESS OF FREEDOM.

PRELUDE. i. *Being delivered out of the hand of our enemies.*
ii. The overthrow of the powers of darkness by the coming of Christ.

POINT I. *Consider the bondage fore-announced.*

   a. The accomplishment of freedom is not immediate. The enemy will rise up in power, ere he be shaken off. So Pharaoh ; so the world-power first against Christ at the Crucifixion, then against the Church in the last days.

   b. The length of permitted tyranny is fixed beforehand. Human foresight cannot assign a term to it. It is sure by God's decree.

   c. The enemy will not cease from his antagonism, but will perish in his power while he seeks to pursue us.

POINT II. *Consider the habit of confidence developed.*

   a. If we look to God, we cannot despond at any seeming impossibilities. It is when things seem most hopeless that He will interfere.

   b. This confidence is no sudden impulse. It needs discipline. We are each of us subjected individually to forms of Satan's bondage, in order to be perfected in patience and hope.

   c. As we have found the power of God in past deliverances, so we look for increasing difficulties as preliminary to future manifestations.

POINT III. *Consider the spiritual deliverance consummated.*

   a. The song of Moses on coming out of Egypt was as the first note of the Song of the Lamb in the glory of the resurrection.

   b. Though the assaults of Satan increase with successive triumphs, yet with each fresh bondage God provides some higher gift of grace.

   c. When grace is perfected in glory, then shall the deliverance be complete, and the accuser of the brethren will be cast out.

AFFECTIONS. Confidence. Opposition to the world. Endurance of Temptation.

PRAYER.

O God, Who delightest to recover Thy people from the thraldom of the enemy, grant us so to look to Thee that we may profit according to Thy purpose by the discipline of the outer life, and may abide patient amidst all suffering, waiting for the manifestation of Thy glory ; through Jesus Christ our Lord. Amen.

FILIAL WORSHIP.

PRELUDE. i. *That we might serve Him.*
ii. God's promise that Moses should bring Israel to that mountain to serve Him.

POINT I. *Consider God's desire for our worship.*

    a. In creation God desired to constitute man as the High Priest, bearing His own Image. He gave existence to man for this very purpose, to be the Priest and Ruler of the world.

    b. God trained His chosen ones taken from amongst mankind to receive the gift of His grace, that they might draw near for themselves and for others, and so prepared the way for Christ.

    c. God has called us out from among the heathen, on purpose that we may be partakers of His glory, and that He may take delight in us as the true seed of Abraham.

POINT II. *Consider our blessedness in God's service.*

    a. "I will be to Him a Father, and He shall be to Me a Son," is the law of the Christian Covenant—of Christ the Head, and of us His members. We must worship Him as His children.

    b. The promise of closer fellowship and spiritual worship belonging to the chosen Seed transcends the promise given under the earlier dispensation, which was only to last until the Seed should come.

    c. "If the ministration of condemnation were glorious, how much more doth the ministration of righteousness exceed in glory!" Our service is a service of righteousness by the power of the Holy Ghost given to us in Christ.

POINT III. *Consider the supernatural requirements of God's service.*

    a. We cannot serve God by nature. Therefore the chosen worshippers must be a regenerate seed, having the life of God. Abraham's seed was to be made God's seed (2 Cor. vi. 18 ; vii. 1), being developed through the One great promised Seed.

    b. The first Heir of the promise was born by a power above nature, according to God's Word. The final heirs of the promise must be taken into the nature of God Himself. The Word does not merely give them life, but is their Life.

    c. God seeketh true worshippers, who shall worship Him in the spirit and in truth.

AFFECTIONS. Dignity of Divine Fellowship. Elevation of heart to God with filial regard.

PRAYER.

Grant, O Lord, that as we are called into the glorious liberty of Thy children, over whom the powers of Hell can no longer exert their tyranny, we may rise to Thee with that intensity of desire which befits those who have been made to taste of Thy glory; through Jesus Christ our Lord. Amen.

PIETY.

PRELUDE. i. *Serve Him in Holiness.*

ii. A heart sheltered by the Divine Providence, and burning with the Divine Love.

POINT I. *Consider the separating power of the Divine call.*

    a. The Covenant has its origin in the sanctity of the Divine Love, the tender mercies of David.

    b. As the pledged Love of God binds Him in solemn obligations to His people, it distinguishes them from all others, and constitutes a sphere of Life in which they are to dwell.

    c. It is a living Covenant of real personal regard and Divine power, in which God claims from our whole heart the acknowledgment of the close intimacy vouchsafed to us.

POINT II. *Consider the fear of God engendered by the Divine deliverance.*

    a. If we fear not our enemies because of the greatness of the Divine power which protects us, we must fear that power lest we bring upon ourselves its curse by our negligence.

    b. Gratitude is of itself a form of pious fear. There must be a sense of awe towards one to whom our Eternal Life is due.

    c. Worship is the expression of that holy fear which befits the Divine Majesty in the confession of His glory and our nothingness.

POINT III. *Consider the Love of God which befits this Holy Covenant.*

    a. The love we have for the things of God will vary according to our appreciation of them as our own truest treasure.

    b. We can only claim them or love them while we use them. If unused, they become to us as if they were non-existent.

    c. We can only use them while we reverence their supreme majesty with holy submission and reverent care, for otherwise they turn against us.

AFFECTIONS. Reverence. Watchfulness. Love. Thankfulness.

PRAYER.

Grant, O Lord, that I may worship Thee evermore with holy worship; and trusting in Thy power for my deliverance, may set Thy glory before me as the only object of my hope; through Jesus Christ our Lord. Amen.

JUSTIFICATION.

PRELUDE. i. *Serve Him in righteousness.*

ii. Man set free from Satan and clothed with the brightness of the Holy Ghost.

POINT I. *Consider the Divine ideal in man's creation.*

    a. God created man with faculties capable of rendering Him an acceptable service in presenting His creatures before Him by the power of the Holy Ghost.

    b.' Man was formed for righteousness, but could not attain to it after he had forfeited the Divine Life by the Fall.

    c. God still requires of man that true justification of Life whereby His original purpose may be fulfilled. Deliverance from enemies had been vain, unless this Life were given with the power of supernatural righteousness.

POINT II. *Consider the freedom of man for the work of righteousness in Christ.*

    a. Now that this power of righteousness is restored to man in Christ—the power of God unto salvation—we must walk worthy of our vocation.

    b. The new man, created after God's Image in righteousness and true holiness, must be put on day by day.

    c. We must walk not after the flesh but after the Spirit, if the ministration of righteousness which that Spirit effects is to be of avail to us. The Old Covenant did not give Life. The New Covenant does give Life.

POINT III. *Consider the Divine standard of righteousness.*

    a. Man was formed in God's Image, and His righteousness must be the true, perfect, willing acceptance of the Mind of God.

    b. Christ is the end of the law for righteousness, exhibiting in His own Person that entire identity in will and work which constitutes Oneness with God, the righteousness of our nature.

    c. We are justified in Him by being taken into this Divine Oneness. Our atonement is not a mere external removal of stain, but an interior communication of Life.

AFFECTIONS. Self-dedication to God. Joy in God's law.

PRAYER.

O God, Who hast called us to live before Thee and accomplish Thy purposes as a royal Priesthood in the world, grant that we may so use the grace which Thou hast given us, that we may attain to the glory which Thou hast promised; through Christ our Lord. Amen.

THE DIVINE APPROVAL.

PRELUDE. i. *In holiness and righteousness before Him.*
ii. The Eye of Divine Watchfulness and Love.

POINT I. *Consider the Divine Presence as the law of perfection.*

 a. God said to Abram, Walk before Me, and be thou perfect. The consciousness of a Personal God watching us at all times must be our security against the vacillation natural to our conscience when left alone.

 b. God does not merely watch us as a spectator, but as a Governor. While He watches, He speaks. We cannot know Him as a dumb God. We must listen for His Word.

 c. God does not merely command; He empowers. As God sees, so He both speaks and loves. His Holy Spirit strengthens those who dwell before Him to do His will, whatever it be.

POINT II. *Consider the Divine Presence as the joy of holiness.*

 a. The Presence of a Father. As He rejoices in the work of His Providence, so must we rejoice to serve Him therein. Not because of the thing to be done, but from love to Him Who wills it.

 b. The Presence of All-sufficient power. Whatever we have to do, nothing can be wanting to us, if we are abiding under the eye of God. When we fancy something is wrong, it is because we have removed ourselves from His Presence.

 c. The Presence of perfect Goodness. Mere justice is dead and cold. Goodness stimulates the heart with energy of love—Rom. v. 7—but goodness can only be known in the personal perfection of God.

POINT III. *Consider the Divine Presence as the reward of service.*

 a. We dwell in God's Presence whilst serving Him, and we look to dwell with Him for ever when our work is done.

 b. Our joy in His Presence then shall sum up in remembrance all the experience of fellowship which we have had amidst the troubles of life on earth.

 c. The joy will not arise from attaining some common object of desire, but from the mutual Love wherein He ruled with Holy Providence, and we served with holy worship.

AFFECTIONS. Fellowship with God. Trust in Providence. Hope of Divine manifestation.

PRAYER.

O God, Who hast called me out of the darkness of sin, to serve Thee in the blessed Light of Thine All-holy Presence, grant that I may always remember Thy Presence, trust in Thy Power, rejoice in Thy Goodness, and accomplish Thy Will; through Jesus Christ our Lord. Amen.

PERSEVERANCE.

PRELUDE. i. *All the days of our life.*

ii. The aged Martyr saying before the heathen tribunal, eighty and six years have I served Him, and He hath never failed me.

POINT I. *Consider the necessity of prolonged trial.*

 a. Impulses for good are suggestions from God, and do not show what the individual character is: we need to act upon those impulses in the face of difficulty before we can claim any result from them.

 b. We need to undergo temptations, not only repeated but varied, ere we can be said to have really grasped one of those suggestions as our own true choice.

 c. We have to become conformed to God's Eternity. Our life needs to be tested at several points in order to claim such conformity.

POINT II. *Consider the growing power of habitual holiness.*

 a. The habit of choosing God becomes more and more sweet to the soul as we come by personal experience to know what it is to serve Him.

 b. In gradual resistance to evil the soul learns its own capacities and its need of good. Each fresh act opens to view the possibilities of something greater.

 c. The dignity of holiness becomes a sustaining power which the soul fears to forfeit.

POINT III. *Consider the Divine gifts by which holiness is developed.*

 a. God rewards us as we go on. He does not wait for the end. He gives increasing grace as He sees us using what He has given.

 b. The joy of such increasing spiritual experiences far exceeds the pain whereby they are won. We must be looking up to God for grace continually.

 c. Perseverance is God's gift, so that the soul is strengthened against the final struggle: and yet all the previous efforts of holiness are valueless without it.

AFFECTIONS. Stedfastness. Patience. Courage.

PRAYER.

O God, strengthen me, I beseech Thee, that I may continually rejoice in Thy power, and with strength renewed may glorify Thee more and more, until I come to the final experience of Thy victorious Love; through Jesus Christ our Lord. Amen.

INDIVIDUALITY.

PRELUDE. i. T*hou, Child.*

ii. The aged Priest gazing on the new-born Child.

POINT I. *Consider the individuality of our Person.*

  a. Personality is, as it were, a ray of glory from the Divine Life. It gives completeness to our existence in the sight of God. We cannot make any one else share it with us. We cannot cast it off.

  b. It is complete when we first breathe, and remains unchangeable amidst all developments of future life, nor does death destroy it.

  c. The Personality of God is not dependent as ours is. Our personality has no power save what is reflected from Him. His Personality is substantive, self-sustained, self-reproducing.

POINT. II. *Consider the responsibility of individual life.*

  a. As our life comes from God, we have to give account to Him respecting the conformity of our personal conduct to His.

  b. As it is a direct relationship between ourselves and Him, we must not think that others can lessen the inherent law of spontaneous activity, whereby we must correspond with God.

  c. Other things are given us only for a while, in order to develope the moral character of our individual life, but this remains when other things are gone.

POINT III. *Consider the individuality of God's Love for us.*

  a. He does not merely compassionate us as a race, but He loves each one as being a complete mirror of Himself, however imperfect in development.

  b. God loves each individual member of Christ with that Love which belongs to Christ the Head.

  c. God, by His love, would gather up all who love Him into Himself, that their life may be not only superficially from Him, but substantively in Him. To fail of this end is to die eternally.

AFFECTIONS. Reverence toward God. Watchfulness on the Divine Likeness in ourselves. Gratitude for grace.

PRAYER.

Grant, O Lord, I beseech Thee, that as I exist by Thy simple power, so I may enter in watchful correspondence with Thy will until I attain to become one with Thee in Love and Life Eternal; through Jesus Christ our Lord. Amen.

PREDESTINATION.

PRELUDE. i. *Thou, Child.*

ii. As before.

POINT I. *Consider the fixity of God's purposes.*

    a. God does not fashion His purposes to suit individuals, but raises up individuals for His works to suit His purposes.

    b. God has a special work for each individual, and we attain true greatness by seeking after that which God has thus marked out for us.

    c. Wonderful destiny of this Child! And yet if he was to prepare the way for Christ, every Christian has to abide in the unity of the Life of Christ. We little think how great our calling is!

POINT II. *Consider the concurrence of the individual will.*

    a. God does not predestinate us by reason of merit on our part, nor does He do so without our own will concurring. It is as moral agents, as persons, not as things, that we receive our predestination.

    b. The will must choose what God has marked out. We cannot exchange our predestinated glory for any other. It is set before us from childhood as the end for which our discipline shall fit us.

    c. Predestination does not force us to acquiesce. It involves a corresponding penalty if we fail.

POINT III. *Consider the sufficiency of grace.*

    a. God will not call us to a destiny beyond what He gives us grace to reach.

    b. The difficulties which meet us do not hinder our predestination, but are the stepping-stones by which we must attain it. By every difficulty we ought to rise higher.

    e. Since predestination involves our own effort in the use of grace, it can be no true destiny which we attain without labour and sorrow.

AFFECTIONS. Energy in union with God. Self-sacrifice. Hope.

PRAYER.

O God, Who hast created me for the manifestation of Thy Divine power in the weakness of man, grant me so to act in the fellowship of Thy grace, that I may attain the reward of Thy glory; through Jesus Christ our Lord. Amen.

VOCATION.

PRELUDE.   i. *Thou, Child, shalt be called.*
ii. The Child in the arms of His Mother.

POINT I.   *Consider the call of God.*

    a. God calls by external circumstances of Providential arrangement. God leads us in the ways most suited for His designs.

    b. God calls by inspirations of the Holy Ghost. This Child yet unborn showed forth the power of the Spirit which was leading Him. How carefully ought the movements of the Holy Ghost to be cherished in young children! How simply ought we to accept them in ourselves!

    c. God calls by the voice of authority. Internal inspirations are not trustworthy without some external warrant.

POINT II.   *Consider the attestation of man.*

    a. Mankind will often favour the outset of a Divine work, and shrink afterwards from accepting its progress.

    b. S. John Baptist was reverenced rather as a preacher of penitence than as pointing to Christ. Yet future ages have acknowledged him in this truer character, and thus he is truly known.

    c. The world will attest by rejecting if not by accepting. Those who are nearest to Christ must waken the fears of the world.

POINT III.   *Consider the reality of life.*

    a. We are—not what man calls us but—what God calls us. He calls us to be, by predestination. He calls us as being, by approval.

    b. We are—not what we appear to men but—what we are known to be amidst the Heavenly Host by the voice of God.

    c. All that is not true to His vocation is unreal. It is lifeless. God alone gives life. Success without His approval is nothing. Failure, if He approve, leads to real triumph.

AFFECTIONS. Firmness of purpose. Hatred of pretence. Communion of heart with the world unseen.

PRAYER.

O God, mercifully grant that I may so recognize Thy call, that I may follow Thee in the way of Truth, and being acknowledged by Thee may obtain the end for which thou hast created me; through Jesus Christ our Lord. Amen.

RELATION TO GOD IN CHRIST.

PRELUDE. i. *Thou, Child, shalt be called the Prophet of the Highest.*

ii. The Child in the midst of the wondering circle of spectators.

POINT I. *Consider what constitutes our true calling.*

   a. We are what we are in relation to God. Relation to other things is merely accidental, whatever effect it has in this transitory world, it leaves our eternal being unchanged.

   b. The words of men are of little avail whether good or evil. What are we called in the kingdom of grace, as seen by the Heavenly Host, the Church of the Redeemed, and by God Himself? That is the true Name and Praise which comes from God.

   c. Our relationship to God springs from the Love of God, and can be accepted by us only in the Love of God.

POINT II. *Consider the Mediation of Christ as determining our relationship.*

   a. By nature we were broken away from God. Sin puts an end to all active relationship between us and God.

   b. Christ calls us to participate in the Life of God by union with Himself.

   c. Our relation to God can have no feature of life save what it receives through the quickening grace of Christ, as necessary to every detail as to the whole.

POINT III. *Consider the dignifying power of this Mediation.*

   a. The fulness of the glory of God shines out upon us thereby.

   b. We are taken up into a real social relation with the Eternal, since He has been pleased to come and dwell amongst us in the relations of time.

   c. Our relation to Him is eternal as Himself, so that we retain for ever the glory of any act of union with Him done here.

AFFECTIONS. Reverence to Christ. Disregard of transitory things.

PRAYER.

O Lord God, Who hast called me into union with Thyself by the Mediation of Thy Son Jesus Christ, grant that I may learn to value the glory of the heavenly calling, and to act worthy of its demands ; so that finding in Him my strength and my repose while earth shall last, I may find in Him the eternity of joy, and contemplate Thy glory as my reward according to the measure of the expression of Thy Love; through the same Jesus Christ our Lord. **Amen.**

THE OFFICE OF THE FORERUNNER.

PRELUDE. i. *The Prophet of the Highest.*
ii. As before.

POINT I. *Consider the greatness of John the Baptist.*
   a. Our Lord says, among those that are born of women there hath not risen a greater than he.—S. Matt. ii. 11.—Yet his greatness was only to fit him to prepare the way for One that was greater. The greatest vocation can only lead to Christ.
   b. He was filled with the Holy Ghost even from his mother's womb.—S. Luke i. 15.—Yet he that is least in the kingdom of Heaven, being born anew by the power of the Holy Ghost, is greater than he.
   c. He was called to baptize Christ, that Christ might thus make righteousness complete, sanctifying water for the washing away of sin.—S. Matt. iii. 15.—Yet he had need to be baptized of Christ. He must decrease, passing away from the glory which he had, and must look to receive glory everlasting from Him that came after him.

POINT II. *Consider him as pointing to the Lamb of God.*
   a. Before His coming, he announces Him. He is content to lose all thought of self as a Nameless Voice in the wilderness. In truth our only name is that which we bear by reference to Christ.
   b. At His coming. To Him he refers his own disciples, that they may leave him and follow Jesus. In vain do we draw any to ourselves, unless it be as helping them to find Jesus.
   c. When his own death was near. He was in no way disappointed because Jesus brought to him no earthly deliverance. He had preached, and he looked for, a better salvation in the remission of sins.

POINT III. *Consider him as making the way straight.*
   a. Making the way straight for Christ, by levelling the obstacles of human pride through the preaching of penitence.
   b. Leading men straight to Christ, by exciting to penitence so that they may feel their need, and to moral effort so as to ensure the grace of Christ when they see Him.
   c. Calling men to take Heaven by force. There are mighty enemies to be encountered on the way, which can only be conquered not in the strength of the Baptist's teaching, but in the grace of Christ to Whom he guides.

AFFECTIONS. Looking to Christ. Self-forgetfulness. Holy Vengeance.

PRAYER.

O God, Who didst send the Forerunner to prepare the way in the wilderness, grant that my heart, even though by nature it be barren and worthless, may yet welcome the grace of Thy dear Son, and be enriched with holy abundance to Thy glory; through the same Jesus Christ our Lord. Amen.

CORRESPONDENCE WITH VOCATION.

PRELUDE. i. *For Thou shalt go before the Face of the Lord.*

ii. As before.

POINT I. *Consider the chances which await a child.*

a. What bright destinies rise before a child if we consider the possibilities of success!

b. How they vanish as time goes on, and various acts of sin darken the hopes of future life!

c. The vocation once forfeited never wholly returns. At the very best, a vocation when regained will have the sad colouring of penitence instead of the brightness of purity.

POINT II. *Consider the necessity of appreciating our vocation.*

a. Most persons are quite ignorant of their having any vocation. Yet every one must "serve God truly in that state of life in which it shall please God to call him."

b. Zacharias prophesied of the vocation of John. We must remember that the vocation awaiting us is quite as sacred as if it had been the subject of prophecy.

c. Our actions must gain a dignity from our consciousness of Divine vocation. If we act without God, our actions will become proportionately valueless.

POINT III. *Consider the blessedness of a life true to God.*

a. The Divine authority which calls us forth accompanies us and makes us triumphant.

b. As we listen to God's call, God will speak more and more familiarly with us, making known to us His will.

c. What we do with God we shall do with ease if we trust in Him. The sweetness of God will make our hearts exult in the midst of any hard and bitter struggle that we may endure.

AFFECTIONS. Diligence to make our calling and election sure. Love of God.

PRAYER.

O God, Who hast provided for us gifts of Divine strength that we may go forward to accomplish Thy will, in the fellowship of Thy Holy Spirit; grant that I may always be true to Thy guidance, hoping for Thy promises, resting upon Thy grace, secure under Thy protection; through the same Jesus Christ our Lord. Amen.

THE REVELATION OF GOD.

PRELUDE. i. *Thou shalt go before the Face of the Lord.*

ii. S. John Baptist and the Infant Saviour.

POINT I. *Consider the Image of God wherein man was created.*

   a. Man is a personal being. His person holds together all the elements of his nature. Without this personality there would be in him no continuity of life, no memory.

   b. Our circumstances are far removed from the Divine Life. Our person feels a capacity of entering into the contemplation of the Divine Life.

   c. However unlike to us God may be in all that surrounds His Personal glory, we feel that He must have a Personal character of infinite glory, sustaining the glorious attributes of His nature.

POINT II. *Consider the Personality of Christ.*

   a. Christ comes amongst us to act upon earth as man. We therefore see that the Personality of God is most truly akin to our own.

   b. He lays aside the glory of the Divine Nature, and the Personality wherewith He acts in our nature shows Him to be truly capable of feeling with our necessities.

   c. The Personality of Christ cannot be different from the Personality of God the Father, nor of God the Holy Ghost. He did not become a Person by being born on earth. He was a Divine Person Who came to us on earth.

POINT III. *Consider the glory of the Divine Persons.*

   a. The personality of man is created, and tells of dependence. It acts through its accidental surroundings. God's Personality is uncreated.

   b. The Personality of God being independent, self-existent, has the power of infinite activity co-equal with its own knowledge and will. So the Persons of the Son and of the Holy Ghost have their eternal origin from the Father's Person.

   c. The relationships of the Divine Persons differ. In nature and essence they are one and indivisible.

AFFECTIONS. Love to God. Praise for His Love.

PRAYER.

O God, Who hast sent Thine only Son to take our nature and act as Man amongst men, grant us to glorify Thee for Thy condescension, while we rise in heart to the adoration of Thine invisible glory; through the same Thy Son Jesus Christ our Lord. **Amen.**

THE PERSONAL ADVENT OF CHRIST.

PRELUDE.   i. *To prepare His ways.*
ii. As before.

POINT I.   *Consider the Person Who comes.*
- *a.* He is the Son of God. He comes to act in a dependent condition, but not to be subject as a dependent person.
- *b.* He comes forth from the Father with Whom He dwells in Eternity. His Person comes by acting under a created form, but He is not separated from the Divine Essence.
- *c.* He comes forth with the Holy Ghost, proceeding from Himself in every action. Thus the Divine Power is felt, although the. actions seem to be in no way different from those of other men.

POINT II.   *Consider how He comes.*
- *a.* He is born of the substance of an earthly Mother. He enters upon the pathway of human life in the most elementary form of being.
- *b.* He is conceived by the Holy Ghost. He lays aside the Majesty, but not the reality of the Divine glory. He cannot come if He lay aside this Life of God.
- *c.* He comes to all the varied accidents of human life. These only serve to show the unchangeable glory of His Person. The same yesterday and to-day and for ever.

POINT III.   *Consider the effect of His coming.*
- *a.* His ways are ways of renewal. By the power of the Life-giving Spirit He takes created things into God, while He comes to subject Himself to creaturely surroundings.
- *b.* His ways are ways of sanctification. The Spirit proceeding from Him purges off all that would defile, and gathers all into the holiness of Divine Life.
- *c.* His ways are ways of judgment. He comes to those that will receive Him, that they may become the sons of God in Him. He comes to others to mark them off as past all cure, because they do not recognise Him.

AFFECTIONS. Worship to Jesus. Welcome to Him. Dependence on Him.

PRAYER.

O Lord God, Who hast given Thy Son to come into the world and dwell with us, grant that we may look up to Him and walk in His ways, praising Thee with holy thankfulness for the gifts which He brings to us in Thy Name; Who with Thee and with the Holy Ghost liveth and reigneth God for ever and ever. Amen.

2 ʙ

THE NECESSITY OF PREPARATION FOR CHRIST.

PRELUDE. i. *Thou shalt go before the Face of the Lord to prepare His ways.*

  ii. The Baptist at the Jordan.

POINT I. *Consider the mode of preparation.*   .

  a. Man must be prepared for Christ by the preaching of repentance. The Preacher must be sanctified by the Holy Ghost for this work.

  b. Man must learn this need of reconciliation with God; otherwise he cannot accept Christ as bringing to Him such reconciliation.

  c. Man must learn to judge himself truly; otherwise he cannot accept Christ the Judge, nor rest in His judgments.

POINT II. *Consider the necessity of desiring Christ.*

  a. We must desire Christ in Himself; otherwise we shall not part with anything to welcome Him. But we can welcome none, much less welcome Christ, unless our hearts be emptied and hungering for the joy which comes.

  b. We must desire Christ for what He will do, raising us to a higher estate. If we are satisfied with what we can do for ourselves by nature, we cannot accept an offer which involves much difficulty.

  c. We must desire Christ simply and alone. The heart which longs for Him has no room for anything else.

POINT III. *Consider the prophetic announcements of Christ.*

  a. If God sends a messenger, we may be sure that He will make that messenger known; not leaving us merely to conjecture and research.

  b. The distant prophets guaranteed the truth of the immediate Forerunner whom they had foretold. God speaks to us through all ages with a voice that never dies.

  c. The unprepared heart will reject the teaching of the prophets respecting the suffering Lamb of God, and seek to anticipate the glory which is to follow.

AFFECTIONS. Hunger after righteousness. Abhorrence of self. Welcome to Jesus.

PRAYER.

O God, Who didst send Thy servant John Baptist to prepare the way for Thine Only-begotten Son when He came into the world, grant that I may so prepare my heart by true repentance in the use of Thy grace, that I may welcome the advent of Thy dear Son in every mode of His approach; and when He shall come again in His glory may find in Him the fulness of my joy; Who liveth and reigneth with Thee and with the Holy Ghost one God world without end. **Amen.**

INTELLECTUAL PREPARATION FOR CHRIST.

PRELUDE. i. *To give knowledge of salvation unto His people.*
ii. S. John pointing to the Lamb of God.

POINT I. *Consider the knowledge of salvation.*

a. This is Life Eternal, "to know the only True God, and Jesus Christ Whom He hath sent."—S. John xvii. 3.— Man is formed in God's Image, and Personality demands consciousness. He rises to the full exercise of Personal Life, in the consciousness of the Personal God.

b. This knowledge is the basis of all true action. What is done without exercise of this knowledge is not worthy to be called an action of life.

c. Man does not know God by nature, having forfeited the Divine Indwelling by his sin. Salvation consists in restoration to this fellowship. The human intellect must be informed so as to rise by grace to the Divine exercise of faith.

POINT II. *Consider the active power of Divine knowledge.*

a. The knowledge of God, which constitutes Eternal Life, is a consciousness of participation in the Life of God. It must, therefore, lead to Divine actions. We only know God while we act in Him.

b. We must recognize the supernatural character of such activity, as saving us from the stagnation in which nature must otherwise perish.

c. S. John came to point to the Lamb of God Which taketh away the sin of the world. The removal of the sin is the restoration of the knowledge of God.

POINT III. *Consider the gift of this knowledge.*

a. The preacher of penitence rouses to a sense of want, so as to make this knowledge desired.

b. The greatest of the prophets announces the accomplishment of all that those before him had foretold.

c. The Spirit of God must perfect the gift of knowledge in the heart; otherwise the external preaching will be of no avail to illuminate the understanding.

AFFECTIONS. Love of Dogmatic Truth. Reliance upon the Holy Ghost. Desire to know God.

PRAYER.

O Lord God, Whom truly to know is Everlasting Life, grant me so to experience the saving power of Thy Holy Faith, that, being ever ready to act in accordance with Thy heavenly will, I may praise Thee evermore for this great salvation; through Jesus Christ our Lord. Amen.

2 E 2

THE PEOPLE OF GOD.

PRELUDE. i. *To give knowledge of salvation unto His people.*

S. John pointing to the Lamb of God.

POINT I. *Consider to whom this knowledge is given.*

 a. The Ministry of the Baptist was to the Jews, as the people of God : as the Ministry of our Lord Jesus Christ Himself was to the lost sheep of the House of Israel.

 b. They were taught to look forward to this salvation of which prophets had inquired and searched diligently, while prophesying of the grace which is now come—1 S. Pet. i. 10—but which the prophets did not see.

 c. According to promise, this salvation was first preached to the chosen people, though they put it from them, and judged themselves unworthy of everlasting life.—Acts xiii. 46.

POINT II. *Consider God's faithfulness to His people.*

 a. He neglects nothing which may help them to estimate their privileges. "The baptism of John" left them without excuse in rejecting Him of Whom John spake.

 b. How many subsidiary acts of Divine Providence are vouchsafed in order to enable us to recognize the work of His grace in His loving guidance of our own selves.

 c. Casualties often deceive, for they look like Providential tokens. The Ministry of the Baptism was an ordained sign. We must look for God's promises, not for our own imaginations.

POINT III. *Consider how God desires to prepare His people.*

 a. God does not expect us to rise up to accept supernatural workings without a discipline of natural preparation.

 b. Each warning indicates something greater which is to follow. If the inferior sign is not recognized, much less will the heart be prepared to receive the greater manifestation.

 c. Each rejection is more terrible in its consequences. God does not withhold His manifestations because we neglect the tokens.

AFFECTIONS. Faithfulness to God. Watchfulness. Hope.

PRAYER.

O God, Who didst send Thy servant John Baptist to make known the coming salvation to Thy people Israel, grant that I, living in the fulness of that salvation, may accept its promises, and cherish its obligations with gratitude and holy fear; through Jesus Christ our Lord. Amen.

REMISSION OF SIN.

PRELUDE. i. *To give knowledge of salvation unto His people for the remission of their sin.*
ii. S. John pointing to the Lamb of God.

POINT I. *Consider that the Baptist proclaimed the approaching gift of pardon.*
    a. He had not power to give it. He preached the baptism of repentance which should lead to the remission of sins, not the baptism of grace conveying it.
    b. He proclaimed the Kingdom of Heaven as being near at hand in which remission should be given, which could not be under the old Covenant.
    c. Salvation is of the Jews: but they had need as much as others that remission of sins should be proclaimed to them through Jesus Christ, which their own law did not give.—Acts xiii. 38.

POINT II. *Consider the Blood shed for the remission of sins.*
    a. In the Old Covenant there was the typical Bloodshedding but no real forgiveness. John could point to the Lamb of God Who would take away the sins of the world.
    b. The blood of bulls and goats could not take away sin. No one might drink thereof.
    c. Our Lord Jesus Christ took the Cup and gave thanks, and gave it to them saying, " Drink ye all of it, for this is My Blood of the New Covenant, which is shed for many for the remission of sins."—S. Matt. xxvi. 28.

POINT III. *Consider the freedom following upon remission of sins.*
    a. The freedom wherewith Christ makes us free is the freedom of holiness, that sin may no more have dominion over us.
    b. By descent into Hell our Lord Jesus set free the faithful of the earlier dispensation, that all might share in His Resurrection.
    c. By causing us to be baptized into His death He calls us to rise into the freedom of a regenerate life, as those who are dead, and therefore are freed from sin.—Rom. vi. 7.

AFFECTIONS. Love of Holiness. Deadness to the world. Gratitude to Christ.

PRAYER.

O Lord God, Who hast called us to receive remission of all our sins in the Covenant of Grace which Thy Son hath ordained, grant that I may walk before Thee in newness of life, and show forth the power of Thy grace by ever abiding in deadness to the world through Jesus Christ our Lord. Amen.

THE TENDER MERCIES OF THE INCARNATE GOD.

PRELUDE. i. *Through the tender mercies of our God.*
ii. The Child Jesus.

POINT I. *Consider the Covenant Love of God.*

   a. These tender mercies imply a closer relationship than that which exists between God and all His works, although His love and mercy do in some sort rest upon all.

   b. By the Covenant, God enters into consanguinity with man —fully when the Covenant becomes complete through the Incarnation—even before the Incarnation, having a certain immanence within us by reason of predestinating love towards the human race.

   c. God, impassible in Himself, identifies Himself with our nature, that He may share all our sorrows, and feel our needs.

POINT II. *Consider the moving cause of our salvation.*

   a. Not our own righteousness, but the lovingkindness of God towards men—Titus iii. 4—acting according to a law of simple mercy.

   b. Not any abstract law of necessary restoration, but the personal operation of His Love towards us in particular, according to the riches of His mercy.—Eph. ii. 4.

   c. Not any separate movement of will in the Son of God, but the Love which the Father Himself had to us, Who sent His Son to be the Saviour of the world.

POINT III. *Consider the human manifestation of that Love.*

   a. God sent forth His Son, made of a woman, made under the law, to redeem them that were under the law—Gal. iv. 4.— The reality of the Divine Love to man could not be shown save in the nature of men.

   b. God hath laid upon Him the iniquity of us all. It had been no true mercy if God had simply done away our sin without providing for us the means of acting in righteousness.

   c. The sufferings of Jesus manifest both the Justice of God, Who would not restore man without an adequate propitiation, and also His Love Who was willing to give His Son, consubstantial with Himself, to suffer the full penalty of sin, in order to restore us.

AFFECTIONS. Gratitude for the Divine Love. Hatred of Sin. Acceptance of the Cross.

· PRAYER.

O God, as Thou didst love us when we were far away, so vouchsafe, we beseech Thee, to preserve us from forfeiting Thy Love by any neglect of the grace whereby Thou callest us to serve Thee ; through Jesus Christ our Lord. Amen.

THE DIVINE FATHERHOOD.

PRELUDE. i. *Our God.*

ii. God appearing to Moses.

POINT I. *Consider the paternal regard of God for His covenant people.*

   a. Israel was very unfaithful to God, but God was none the less true to them. He was pledged to them as the children of Abraham, and still more by the presence in the midst of them of the predestinated Humanity whereof His own Son should in due time take our nature.

   b. God regarded them as His own children, for He saw them in the Light of the yet future Christ.

   c. God regards us as His children because He sees Chiist actually within us by the gifts of Sacramental Grace, no longer an object of unaccomplished hope, but a present object, the hope of glory soon to be made manifest.

POINT II. *Consider the unchangeableness of relation between us and God.*

   a. We may walk unworthy of Him, but we cannot escape from the relation which binds us to Him. The prodigal son is still a son.

   b. This relationship sets before us the hope of our glorification. We shall not come to meet a strange God in Heaven hereafter. Earth becomes Heaven in proportion as we see God here.

   c. We must cherish this relationship abidingly, so as to develope the action of God's goodness towards ourselves. " This God shall be our God for ever and ever."

POINT III. *Consider the specialty of God's mercies.*

   a. Although God watches over all, yet He has a special love for His covenant people. We need to think more of His ever special care for them.

   b. To them the promises of God were first fulfilled in the sending of His Son. Israel was His own possession. To them, therefore, Christ was sent first of all.

   c. For us, now, the mediation of Christ is specially exerted. He died for the whole world, but He prays not for the whole world, but for those who are given to Him out of the world, by the goodness and will of the Father.

AFFECTIONS. Childlike trust. Desire to show forth God's Honour. Filial Imitation.

PRAYER.

O God, Who hast been pleased to call us out of the world into a special relation to Thyself, grant that we may abide in the covenant of Thy Love with childlike affection, and rely upon Thy Fatherly care to bring us safely to Thine Eternal Kingdom; through Christ our Lord. Amen.

THE CONSUBSTANTIAL GODHEAD.

PRELUDE. i. *The Dayspring from on high.*
ii. The Divine Nature as an Ocean of Light.

POINT I. *Consider the height from whence He came.*

   a. This Light comes from on high, from the very height of God's own dwelling, the Light that no man can approach unto.—1 Tim. vi. 15.

   b. The Father sent the Son. The love which brought Him to us was an impulse from on high.

   c. No man hath ascended up to Heaven but He that came down from Heaven. He could not raise us to a higher glory than that from whence He Himself came when He came to save us.

POINT II. *Consider the character of that height.*

   a. It was not from any mere elevation of place that He came down. It was from the height of an uncreated, a Divine, Nature.

   b. That Nature is not inert as is the dead material nature which we know. It is full of activity. It has a power of action, generation, procession, incarnation, inspiration, within itself.

   c. The Divine Nature is not confined by space. The action of God in coming forth is not a motion as from place to place; but from beneath the veil of nature and unfettered by place.

POINT III. *Consider the coming forth of Him Who yet abides.*

   a. He comes from the height where God dwells, but He does not leave it. He is all the while in Heaven, although upon the earth.

   b. The Divine Nature having the power of generation within Itself, He Who is begotten of the Father remains essentially one with Him, and when He becomes man He does not cease to be one with the Father.

   c. In all His actions upon the earth He accomplishes the Father's will, and abides in perfect moral unity with Him, being man, as in essential unity being God with Him.

AFFECTIONS. Reverence. Hope. Welcome.

PRAYER.

O God, Who hast given us Thine own Son, abiding ever one with Thee in Thy glory, to share our life of suffering upon the earth, grant that we may always remember Thy nearness, so that we may both confide in Thy protection and be restrained by Thy contemplation; through Jesus Christ our Lord. Amen.

THE INCARNATION.

PRELUDE. i. *The Dayspring from on high hath visited us.*

ii. Our Lord's Body as seen at the Transfiguration.

POINT I. *Consider the Divine Personality of the Saviour.*

    a. He is no created angel, for He comes from the height which is above all, as a Ray from the Eternal Sunshine of Divine Glory.

    b. He is not merely moved by the radiance of God, as an earthly object moving in the sunlight. He hath visited us, come to us from without.

    c. He is not a mere phantom, the sight of whom may raise us by kindling noble thoughts. He hath visited us, hath looked upon us.

POINT II. *Consider His Unity with the Father.*

    a. God the Father hath visited and made redemption for us and God the Son hath visited us so as to effect the purpose of the Father. The Father visits us by Him.

    b. He comes from the height, and therefore He is personally distin t from the Father, in Whose height of glory He dwellsc

    c. By the power of the Holy Ghost He comes. It is the procession of the Holy Ghost from Himself which makes Him to be an illuminating principle to the earth which He visits.

POINT III. *Consider His visitation of mankind.*

    a. He looked upon us with pity, for He knew we were but dust in our origin, but He also knew that we were formed in God's own Image with a heavenly predestination.

    b. He came to us to act among us with the intimacy of created life and kindred nature.

    c. He visits us so as to communicate the Divine Light of Life to those who receive Him.

AFFECTIONS. Adoration. Gratitude. Welcome to Jesus.

PRAYER.

O Lord Jesu, Who hast come near to us from the glory of the Father, grant me grace to welcome Thee in all the acts of daily life, that Thou mayest behold me and work alway with me according to the power of grace, so as to bring me in the end to the full contemplation of Thy glory ; Who with the Father and the Holy Ghost livest and reignest for ever and ever. **Amen.**

THE LIGHT OF LIGHT.

PRELUDE. i. *The Dayspring from on high hath visited us.*
ii. A bright ray from the sun as a symbol of the Incarnate Saviour.

POINT I. *Consider the Eternal Day.*

   a. God is Light, and in Him is no darkness at all. He is the true Light by the perfection of that knowledge whereby He knows and sees His own All-glorious Being without veil or imperfection.

   b. As He is the only true Eternal Being, and all creation springs from His Eternal Will, He is the Light making manifest the secrets of Creation, its substance, and its purposes.

   c. He has the Light in Himself, so that outside of Him all is dark. None can have Light from Him but by being in Him, one with Him.

POINT II. *Consider the manifestation of the Eternal Light.*

   a. The Eternal Son, the Light of Light, is the Dayspring to Whose brightness we must draw near if we would know God.

   b. He is consubstantial with the Father, and in coming forth from the Father He does not cease to abide in the Unity of the Eternal Essential Light.

   c. If He could be separated from the Father by coming to us, He would be unable to bring to man that Light which He needs. In Him was Light, and the Life was the Light of men.

POINT III. *Consider the uprising of the Light upon the darkness.*

   a. S. John Baptist was sent to bear witness of that Light. The blindness of the natural heart by reason of sin made such witness necessary.

   b. The Light shineth in darkness, but the darkness comprehended it not. No created power could behold the glory of the Divine Life, except through veils proportionate to its nature.

   c. Jesus came a Light into the world, that whosoever believeth in Him should not abide in darkness. By union with Him we enter into the Light.

AFFECTIONS. Joy. Gratitude. Calmness.

PRAYER.

O Lord God, let me so venerate the glory of Thy Divine Wisdom by the power of Thy Holy Spirit, that I may be sanctified according to Thine illumination, and glorify Thee according to Thy will; through Jesus Christ our Lord. Amen.

ILLUMINATION.

PRELUDE. i. *To give light.*

ii. The Son of Man making the Light of God to shine from His countenance.

POINT I. *Consider the illumination effected by the coming of Christ.*

    a. The darkness of religious speculation was changed into clearness of dogma, awakening the response of Love. The Being of God is made known in Personal relationship to us, instead of remaining a mere philosophical abstraction.

    b. The relationship of man to his fellow man is brightened by the revelation of truths affect'ng the whole race in its unity of life, past, present, and future.

    c. The acts of religious worship shine with sacramental brightness as means of grace, instead of being mere worthless acts by which man would seek after an unapproachable God.

POINT II. *Consider the illumination vouchsafed to the faithful departed of the Old Testament.*

    a. Christ made the Light of the eternal day to shine upon the dead. If they rejoiced to hope for Christ, how much more did they rejoice to see Him?

    b. The true Light hath now shined upon them, without even being veiled by the mortal flesh, as when His Presence was hidden from sight on earth during the time of His Passion.

    c. The Light of Christ's Presence enables them to see the purposes of God, which are still to us dark mysteries of the future.

POINT III. *Consider the Lamb of God illuminating the Heavenly City.*

    a. The Lamb of God shines with the brightness of the Divine Presence, an object of rapturous, joyous contemplation to the whole multitude of the redeemed.

    b. The Memorial of His Passion gives outward form to that manifestation of Light, as they see the blessed power of His Passion truly effecting our reconciliation with God.

    c. The Brightness of the illuminating Presence never ceases. Through endless ages it shines on with the exhaustless power of the Divine reality.

AFFECTIONS. Joy in Christ. Wonder at the work of redemption. Praise.

PRAYER.

Almighty God, grant that as we rejoice in the glorious Light of Thy Dear Son we may live worthy of that Light, and show forth the fulness of Thy transforming power, and that in the day of His Manifestation we may be found in Him and dwell in Thy Light for evermore; through the same Jesus Christ our Lord. Amen.

THE DARKNESS OF THE WORLD.

PRELUDE. i. *Them that sit in darkness and in the shadow of death.*

ii. A Light shining upon a multitude of sleepers.

POINT I. *Consider the extent of darkness in this sinful world.*

a. The power of seeing Light is not natural to fallen man. Darkness is again upon the face of the deep in man's soul, for we have forfeited our fellowship with God.

b. The darkness cannot be removed save by the restoration of communion with God. We do not want Light in order to see God, but we need to see God in order to have Light.

c. The whole race was in darkness; no moral or intellectual progress could, or ever can, remove the darkness.

POINT II. *Consider the abiding character of that darkness.*

a. Man cannot raise himself out of it. It must be now, as it was of old, the Word of God which alone can give Light to any. " God said, Let there be Light."

b. Even the Jewish law and its teachings were only a shadow of Truth, a colourless outline.

c. Now that Christ, the true Light, is come, yet the natural heart has no capacity for seeing Him. Hence the impossibility of demonstrating any Divine Truth to the natural heart.

POINT III. *Consider the helpless character of that darkness.*

a. Man in his darkness may feel his misfortune, but he has no desire for the True Light.

b. To receive the Light is to receive a new nature, and involves living according to that nature, and therefore in a manner at variance with the old nature.

c. The presence of the Light is a test of man's moral nature; for those who come not to the Light show that they are satisfied with the darkness of the world.

AFFECTIONS. Self-abasement. Dependence upon God. Expectation.

PRAYER.

O Lord God, Who knowest our darkness and pitiest our misery, grant that as Thou hast made Thy Light to shine upon us, we may welcome Thy face, and may seek to act in thankfulness to Thee Who alone canst deliver us from the darkness of our natural condition; through Jesus Christ our Lord. Amen.

THE DEADNESS OF NATURE.

PRELUDE. i. *To give light to them that sit in darkness and in the shadow of death.*

ii. The Powers of Hell like a cloud of evil spirits overshadowing the earth.

POINT I. *Consider the shadow of death covering the soul of man.*

   a. The whole of the present order of this world is created subject to death; for this world was created anew out of the darkness. Darkness is not God's work. It is sin.

   b. Man received the breath of life that he might triumph over death in the fellowship of the Divine Light.

   c. Having sinned, his soul fell under the shadow of death. Death came between him and the Light of God's Presence.

POINT II. *Consider the shadow of death hiding the Face of God.*

   a. Light is necessary to the natural creation, but much more is the Light of God's Countenance needful for our spiritual Life.

   b. Death, as Satan's Vicegerent, shuts us out from the sight of God. We also take the word as meaning that state of existence in which we are shut out from God our Life.

   c. Death not only impedes the radiance of the Divine glory, but hinders the intelligence from seeing God; for God cannot be known intelligently unless there be an experience of His Love quickening the nature with Divine Life.

POINT III. *Consider the shadow of death darkening the face of nature.*

   a. All nature is an insoluble problem to us, because we see it under the power of death. It is to us like a book to one who is in the dark.

   b. The origin of things, their mutual relation in this present world of strife, the issue of events, everything connected with the mystery of evil, its beginning and its endlessness, its toleration and its punishment, cannot be understood by us until the day when God shall show Himself.

   c. The workings of the world of grace underneath the surface of nature are hidden from our sight, so that in the world of death we can at the best only walk by faith.

AFFECTIONS. Patience. Desire for Christ's appearing.

PRAYER.

Grant, O Lord, that being in this world of death I may die to it by the power of Thy grace and live to Thee in the hidden fellowship of Thy Holy Spirit; through Jesus Christ our Lord. Amen.

MORAL PREPARATION.

PRELUDE. i. *To guide our feet into the way of peace.*
ii. S. John calling the Jews to newness of life.

POINT I. *Consider the feet of the soul.*

a. The understanding and the affections are the feet where-with the soul advances either for good or evil.

b. The understanding must be set free from the entangle-ments of worldly maxims and wisdom falsely so called.

c. The affections must be set free from all clinging to earthly objects.

POINT II. *Consider the preparation for direct intercourse between God and man.*

a. The way has to be made straight for God to come. Earthly hindrances must be removed, lest God in coming smite the earth with a curse.

b. God provides means of approach which are quite straight. Man must be made to walk straight in those straight paths. The difficulty of man's approach to God is in the uncertainty of his own footing.

c. S. John came, not merely to announce the coming Messiah, but to prepare the way for Him so that in coming He might find acceptance with man.

POINT III. *Consider the need of mutual approach.*

a. God must come to man by assumption of man's nature, if there is to be any real intercourse. The Incarnation is a necessity.

b. Man must be lifted up into fellowship with God by the communication of powers beyond that of nature. Sacra-mental renewal and elevation to God is a necessity.

c. The fellowship thus established is closer than that of mere local proximity. God is always close to us by His essence, but we need this moral proximity. Otherwise His Presence cannot affect us.

AFFECTIONS. Expectation of God: Preparation for Him. Thankfulness.

PRAYER.

O *God, Who comest near to us in the Person of Thine Only-begotten Son, and callest us near to Thyself by Him Whom Thou hast sent, grant us so to prepare ourselves for Thy manifestation, that we may rejoice in the fulness of Thy Love; through the same Thy Son Jesus Christ our Lord.* **Amen.**

DIRECTION.

PRELUDE. i. *To guide our feet into the way of peace.*

ii. S. John instructing those who came to him.

POINT I. *Consider wherein Divine direction consists.*

    a. By Providence God makes the way smooth.—2 Thess. iii. 11.

    b. By Instruction He suggests and inclines our hearts towards His holy will.—2 Thess iii. 5.

    c. By Regeneration He quickens us with power to live in holiness.

POINT II. *Consider wherein human direction consists.*

    a. The prophet, or spiritual guide, leads us to understand the purposes of Providence as estimated by outward events.

    b. He calls the heart to penitence, so as to put away the earthly idols which hinder the recognition of God's will.

    c. He counsels, so that the soul may rise to holiness in the power of the grace wherewith God quickens.

POINT III. *Consider the end of this guidance.*

    a. As the law was a schoolmaster to bring us to Christ, so is all guidance in this world. We need guidance because our union with Christ is as yet imperfect, that we may follow on to know the Lord more and more.

    b. The guidance even of the regenerate, as being now in an imperfect state, must thus be distinguished from their regenerate Life, which is perfect and needs no guidance, but rather is itself the unction which teacheth all things.

    c. Guidance is into the way of peace. Union is the perfection of that peace.

AFFECTIONS. Childlike docility. Desire of progress. Joy in the foretaste of union.

PRAYER.

O Almighty God, Who hast vouchsafed to regenerate me with Thy grace, grant me so humbly to follow on in the school of faith, that I may hereafter attain to the fulness of vision wherein Thine elect children shall rejoice before Thee; through Jesus Christ our Lord. **Amen.**

CHRIST THE WAY.

PRELUDE. i. *The way of peace.*

ii. Christ announcing Himself to His Apostles as the Way.

POINT I. *Consider that Christ is the only way of life.*

  a. There is no natural way out of this fallen world into the glory of God. We must be born again. Change of life does not bring us into the kingdom of Heaven. There must be a communication of new life.

  b. Christ is the highway promised by the Prophets. The wayfaring men, though fools, shall not err therein. We err when we think to walk by natural conscience in the way of grace, for in this way we can walk only by faith.

  c. Christ is the way of life, whereinto we are admitted by the Sacraments. Not even the teaching of John Baptist can put us in this way, though it points thither. We are brought into the way by being made members of Christ's Body.

POINT II. *Consider that Christ is the living way.*

  a. The way into the holiest is opened by the Blood of Jesus, for if that Blood becomes our life-blood, then we live with the life of heaven.

  b. We cannot walk in this way by our natural faculties. The faith whereby we walk therein is a fellowship with Christ, Whose members we are, exercising the supernatural powers which belong to Him.

  c. It is the way of life derived from on high, for grace is come by Jesus Christ, and the gracious gift of God is Eternal Life through Jesus Christ our Lord.

POINT III. *Consider that it is the way of truth.*

  a. Other ways may be preparatory, but this is the only way whereby the end can be attained.

  b. The law had the outline of good things to come, but in this way of life we have the true image of the things. The Sacraments of the Gospel are no longer empty signs, however significant. They contain what they represent.

  c. Men might err in the use of the empty symbols, but the grace which fills the way of life is a grace of personal loving guidance, the Presence of Christ Himself teaching the soul. If we err it is because we do not rise to the teaching of His Voice speaking therein.

AFFECTIONS. Faith in the personal Presence of Christ. Joy in the Holy Ghost. Desire of closer union.

PRAYER.

O God, Who hast given Thy Son to be the Way and the Truth and the Life, grant me so to walk in the way of life that I may experience the truth of Thy promises, accomplish the truth of Thy will, and attain to the truth of Thy manifestation; through the same Jesus Christ our Lord. **Amen.**

SUPERNATURAL LIFE IN CHRIST.

PRELUDE. i. *The way of peace.*

ii. The burdened soul seeking to be guided to Heaven.

POINT I. *Consider the purgative way.*

    a. S. John Baptist may be taken as personally symbolizing this way. It is the way *to* Christ.

    b. Herein we acquire a hatred of sin. We cannot come into the way of peace by any other approach.

    c. As long as we are in the flesh, we have need to be drawing near to Christ in the purgative way, for our whole nature must be brought to Him to be sanctified, and while we remain in the flesh there is much which needs to be purged in order to come to Him.

POINT II. *Consider the illuminative way.*

    a. The Ministry of Christ upon the earth represents this way of Life. It is the way *with* Christ.

    b. Herein Christ teaches us the will of God, giving us an example that we may follow His steps.

    c. We must seek this knowledge of Christ continually and increasingly; and yet it is not enough to know Christ after the flesh as a Companion and Guide. Those who rejoice to see Him in this way only may not "touch" Him, for He must "ascend unto the Father," not be held down any longer upon earth.

POINT III. *Consider the unitive way.*

    a. The Ministry of the Holy Ghost in the Church makes this way perfect for us, that hereby we may come to God. It is the Way *in* Christ. By this power of the Holy Ghost Christ *is* the Way.

    b. Herein we experience the consolation of Christ strengthening us so as to overcome every enemy. It is the way *of* the Cross outwardly, the way of suffering, and the way of triumph.

    c. Unless we are so using the sacramental powers of the Body of Christ as to walk in this way, we are stopping short of our true Christian calling. The Gospel of Christ is not the mere substitution of faith for works, of external light for external darkness, but it is the power of God unto salvation, whereby we are called to live with the righteousness of God.

AFFECTIONS. Humiliation for Sin. Joy in Divine Truth. Courage in serving God.

PRAYER.

O Lord God, grant me so to walk in the Spirit as befits our holy calling in Christ Jesus, that here I may show forth Thy glory in the world out of which Thou callest me, and hereafter may behold the fulness of the glory of that Love whereby Thou hast called me out of the world; through the same Jesus Christ our Lord. **Amen.**

2 F

THE WAY OF PEACE.

PRELUDE. i. *The way of peace.*

ii. The Heavenly Jerusalem shining with the glory of God.

POINT I. *Consider the peace re-established between God and man.*

    a. Righteousness and peace have kissed each other. Go d takes man into peace with Himself by giving His own righ teous- ness to man. The righteousness of faith is a Divine Life.

    b. Being justified by faith, and living in the exercise of this Divine gift, we have peace with God through Jesus Christ our Lord. The wrath of God is appeased and the rebellious- ness of nature is healed.

    c. Christ makes peace by the Blood of His Cross, which is a regenerating power for Jew and Gentile, so that we are all in the Body of Christ made to be one new man, the object of the Father's Love.—Eph. ii. 15.

POINT II. *Consider the peace of God, which passeth under- standing.*

    a. We are to have peace in Christ, and yet tribulation in the world. Christ did not come to send peace upon the earth, but to reveal the peace of Heaven in the hearts of those who will rise above the earthly life.

    b. If we are living in the peace of God, the world must hate us, even as it hated Christ, but the friendship of the world is enmity against God, and therefore we cannot desire to seek terms of agreement with it.

    c. The more we suffer with Christ the more do we experience this peace, for it is not a state of dreamy quiescence, but a Divine power that is felt in proportion as it is used.

POINT III. *Consider the Vision of Peace, which is the joy of the blessed.*

    a. Peace is in this world a hidden power, as a seed; but in the next world a manifest development of faithful energy, the consummation of righteousness in those who have laboured for God.—S. James iii. 18.

    b. The way of peace leads to the perfect Vision of Peace ; for as the faculties become conformed to God they acquire the power of seeing Him in His essential truth of love.

    c The Vision of Peace is an interior vision, whereby in the Holy City the indwelling of the Lord God glorifies the redeemed in the unity of the Body of Christ.

AFFECTIONS. Love. Joy. Desire of Perseverance.

PRAYER.

O most gracious God, Who alone canst give peace, delivering us sinners from the darkness of our fallen estate, grant that in the con- templation of Thy Love we may be so conformed to Thy Holy Will that in the accomplishment of Thy Holy Will we may experience the joy of Thy Love; through Jesus Christ our Lord. Amen

NOTES.

2 F 2

NOTES.

Note A, p. 360.

Many commentators understand the "Lord God of Israel" as intended to designate our Lord Jesus Christ: but it would seem that it must rather be the Eternal Father Who is here addressed. It is scarcely likely that a Jewish Priest would have so fully grasped the Truth of Christ's Incarnation as to acknowledge the yet unborn Saviour by this distinctive title. Of course the Holy Ghost might overrule his utterance so as to imply much more than he consciously apprehended. That is not only possible, but certain. We must, however, take his words as signifying primarily what would be the primary thought of his own mind. However much he may have been illuminated so as to recognize the Divine glory of Israel's hope, it would be naturally and rightly to the Eternal Father Who sent His Son into the world that he would give praise for that Advent.

In our Version there does appear to be some difficulty when wo ascribe redemption to the Lord God of Israel as having been effected by His Visitation, but in truth the words of Zacharias point onwards, for it is not the accomplishment of redemption but the Divine appointment of a Redeemer. "He hath made redemption for us, and hath raised up an Horn of Salvation in the House of His servant David." The Horn of Salvation is plainly distinct from the Person Who raises up that Horn.

It seems, therefore, most true to the context to refer the Divine Title here primarily to the Eternal Father, Who hath sent His Son to be the Saviour of the world.

Note B, p. 375.

The mention of the promise made to our forefathers causes somewhat of confusion in the interpretation of this verse. The promise did indeed include the expectation in which the prisoners of hope were content to die, the joyous anticipation of the Messiah coming into the world beyond the grave as their Deliverer. To us, however, the work of Christ on this side the grave is so much more apparent, that when we read of the promise made to our forefathers our thoughts may rest in the victory over Satan as achieved upon the Cross, and the future gifts of grace provided for Christ's Church. The intention of Zacharias, however, was to contrast the mercy which Christ at His coming would show to their forefathers, with the covenant of salvation in which He would gather His elect people to worship God in the time that was to come upon the earth.

He came to show mercy upon our forefathers, by His descent into Hell to effect their deliverance and bring them to that perfection which could not be until the Christian dispensation was begun. In Holy Scripture there is a constant reference made to the waiting spirits. As men of old died, they were spoken of as being gathered to their fathers. The society of the departed was constantly present to their minds, as the Parable of Dives and Lazarus indicates.

Their estate was a condition of imperfection, and they were in the region of darkness and death, until Christ the True Light went to them. True, indeed, they were comforted, but it was the comfort of expectation and alleviation, not of triumph or freedom.

As Christ came to institute a Covenant of regenerating grace for mankind upon the earth, so He came also to show mercy upon the faithful departed, by giving them the gifts necessary for their deliverance from death and their participation in the Kingdom of Heaven, which the ordinances of the Jewish Law could not bestow.

This Canticle, therefore, represents the coming of Christ as an act of grace by which the world of the departed was as truly transformed as was the world of our earthly pilgrimage. They whose trial was over were gathered by that Advent into the Light of Life and glory, and the bars of their prison-house were broken. We upon earth received the gift of regenerating grace, that we might serve God in a covenant which surpassed the Covenant of former time in glory ; for they who are made partakers of this Covenant of Life shall never come under the power of that death wherein they of the Old Covenant were forced to wait in bondage when their earthly course was run.

Note C, pp. 376-390.

It is important for us to have correct ideas of what is really intended by the Divine Covenant; and yet it is to be feared that few persons really do apprehend the meaning of that phrase. The Old and the New Covenant need to be distinguished. The points of similarity between the two often lead persons to a mistaken view of their identity. We ought however, by every point of similarity, to learn how better to appreciate their difference. The points in which their resemblance is most brought to light are just the points in which we ought especially to recognize their diversity.

Another cause of much misapprehension is to be found in the use of the two words Covenant and Testament, to translate what in the original Greek is one word ($\delta\iota\alpha\theta\eta\kappa\eta$). It is quite true that both these words are necessary for our language. The ideas which these two words convey are contained in the original Greek word, and it is used sometimes with reference to the one set of ideas, sometimes with reference to the other. The Greek word is in fact exactly our legal word Disposition, and it signifies sometimes disposition of property by way of living agreement, and at other times disposition of the same by way of testamentary appropriation.

This naturally leads to some precariousness of exegetical determination ; and the mind of the translator cannot but express itself with sharper distinctness than belonged to the original, because he has to choose one of the two words, altogether distinct as they are, which best suits his view of the passage.

Can we fix any principle by which to be guided in determining this matter ?

Here we come to an important inquiry. A covenant is between two parties, and a testament is made by one of two parties with reference to another. Are they then the same parties who are represented in Holy Scripture as linked together sometimes by a covenant, sometimes by a will ?

No ; they are not.

We shall find the best starting-point for our inquiry in those words of our Lord to His Apostles, I appoint (διατίθεμαι) unto you a kingdom, as My Father hath appointed (διέθετο) unto Me.—S. Luke xxii. 29.

Here the distinction is plainly stated. There is one disposition of the kingdom under which it is given by the Father to the Son. This is a Covenant. There is another disposition under which it is given by the Son to the Apostles. This is a Legacy. The Son received the kingdom by inheritance. The Apostles received it as a consequence of the Death of Christ, and could not receive it otherwise.

Persons shrink from recognizing the glorification of the Son of God in this kingdom as being the object for which it was instituted. They commonly treat the Incarnation as if it were merely subservient to the salvation of mankind. Holy Scripture, on the contrary, teaches us to regard the salvation of mankind as a secondary feature of this arrangement. The primary purpose of the kingdom is for the glory of the Son of God, the Incarnate Son, to Whom it has been given by an Eternal Decree of the Divine Love.

So S. Paul speaks of the Seed of Abraham, as the true Heir of the Promises ; and he explains to us that by that Seed of Abraham is meant Christ.

Christ then is the object of the Divine Promises. People commonly speak as if He were the thing promised ; and they are led into confusion, because this is in one sense true. In the primary Covenant, however, He is the receiver of the Promises, "To Abraham and his Seed were the promises made. He saith not, And to seeds, as of many ; but as of one, To thy Seed, which is Christ.—Gal. iii. 16.

Here, then, is the primary Covenant to Abraham and his Seed, or perhaps we should do well for clearness' sake to say, to the Seed of Abraham, and through Him to Abraham His forefather.

The Seed did not obtain the prerogatives of this Covenant by reason of Abraham, but Abraham received them by reason of the Seed which should be given to him.

This Covenant, conditioned through Abraham, was the manifestation of the Eternal Covenant which underlay the Creation of the Universe, by which all should be given eventually to the Son when Incarnate. All things were created by Him and for Him, and He is before all things, and by Him all things consist.—Col. i. 17.

Abraham was chosen of God to be the progenitor of this Heir of the world. "The promise that He should be the heir of the world was not to Abraham or to his seed through the law, but through the righteousness of faith."—Rom. iv. 13.

This Covenant was confirmed by an Oath of God; and what has been now said will help to understand what the Oath of God really meant.

We must not treat that phrase as if it meant nothing; and yet Commentators do not often attach to it more than a sort of rhetorical power. S. Paul plainly attached much more than a rhetorical power to it; for upon this he bases the great distinction between the Jewish and the Christian Priesthood. The one was with an oath, the other without one.

Observe, then, that God made a promise to Abraham first of all, and he believed God, and it was counted unto him for righteousness. But after this God required Abraham to give back to Himself that which was the very sum and substance of the promises—the life of Isaac. Abraham offered Isaac in obedience to God's command; and now God ratified the former promise with an oath. The promise was given when it is said, "Abraham believed God, and it was counted unto Him for righteousness." The oath was added when Abraham's faith was made perfect by his works, which S. James speaks of as fulfilling the Scripture, showing the truth of the benediction which the Scripture had enunciated with reference to his earlier faith.

Now what was this Oath? An oath amongst men is the giving of our word. Our word is our pledged honour. So the Oath of God is His Word. The earlier promise was a promise of Divine operation towards Abraham's unknown seed. The value of that promise was in some sort contingent. It would depend upon the seed to use it as it was intended. The fulfilment of the promise by oath was a promise of Divine operation not only towards Abraham's Seed, but in it. The Word of God should speak in Abraham's Seed. Not merely should the promise be fulfilled. It should be eternally perfected in the Life of God. The Son of God would Himself become Abraham's Seed.

A long period was indeed to intervene before the Seed should come. There should be many vicissitudes of the promise, vicissitudes which but for that Oath might have gone on for ever. The Oath necessitated the eventual removal of vicissitude. The honour of God was pledged to manifest itself in all its completeness in the Seed of Abraham.

During the interval which elapsed before the coming of this promised Seed, God provided the Covenant of the Law.

S. Paul contrasts this with the earlier Covenant of Promise, and shows that it could only exist in subordination to that higher and older Covenant. The law was given for the very purpose of fencing Abraham's descendants off from the rest of the world, that so they might be kept up with a view to the coming Seed. "The Law was a schoolmaster to bring them to Christ."

This legal Covenant was, however, organised by Divine revelation, so as in every point to exhibit some characteristic of the Heavenly Life which should belong to the Seed of Abraham when He Himself should come. It was an outline, a shadow, a silhouette, of the good things that were to come.

It was ordained by Angels in the hand of a Mediator.—Col. iii. 19. This important phrase of S. Paul has unhappily been made to aggravate the difficulty of understanding the two Covenants instead of relieving it. The mention of a Mediator seems to present points of agreement between the dispensation which preceded Christ and that which came after Him.

A Mediator there is in the Christian Dispensation, and there was a Mediator through whom the Jewish dispensation was instituted ; but that Mediator is mentioned just as the angels are, in order to show the difference between the two dispensations, not their identity. In many respects the Jewish Law had a shadow of glorious objects which should dignify the Christian Dispensation ; but the Mediator of the one was the Oath of God, already living, uttered, waiting to manifest Himself the Eternal Son. So S. Paul tells us, God mediated by an Oath.—Heb. vi. 17. The Mediation of Moses was merely the ministry of a servant for a temporary purpose. He would quickly give way to the Mediation of Aaron when the work of building was complete. The Mediation of Moses and Aaron both together would fall far short of representing the Mediation of our Lord Jesus Christ.

The law was given by angels. S. Paul again appeals to this as showing the inferiority of the Law to the Christian Church. " If the word spoken by angels was stedfast, and every transgression and disobedience received a just recompense of reward, how shall we escape if we neglect so great salvation, which at the first began to be spoken by the Lord?"—Heb. ii. 2.

Here is one great difference. The Word of God came then throug the ministry of angels, but did not take upon itself the nature angels. The Word of God has now come to us as by an Oath in the indissoluble Majesty of the Hypostatic Union.

The angelic nature was external to the law, and they administered it. Angels wait upon the Christian Church, but God hath not put into subjection to angels this " world to come ;" as S. Paul calls it, the Kingdom of Heaven. Here they are only servants to Christ, and to them that are heirs of salvation in Him.

But also the law was ordained in the hand of a mediator. It required some personage to inaugurate it. Not so the Christian Church. The Christian Church is not ordained in the hand of a mediator, but in the Person of Him Who is the Great Mediator between God and man. A Mediator He is, but in a sense widely different from Moses. Moses was a servant, entrusted with a work which he had to hand on. Jesus is the Son of God, inheriting a Life which he cannot hand on to any successor. He has it in Himself. He is Mediator because we obtain Life Eternal by being made members of His Body ; but He does not act between us and God as being Himself a third party like Moses. He is Himself the Receiver of the Kingdom from God for Himself ; and He gives it to us as members of Himself to enjoy in union with Himself. He mediates between God the Father and the members of His own Body; not, however, for the purpose of obtaining for them from God that which they need, but as the Head of the Body communicating to them what He has already received of the Father for Himself.

Now we come then to the New Covenant, or the New Testament, whereby Christ communicates to His people that kingdom which He has received of the Father.

As it is a Covenant belonging to another world, it could not be established within the limits of this world. He must die and pass out of this world, in order to take to Himself this kingdom. The Oath of God lives on through that death. God had not given merely a promise which might have been satisfied by the manifestation of Christ as an earthly Benefactor. The Oath of world-wide Benediction could never be withdrawn from the Seed of Abraham. The Blessing would show itself springing out of the grave of Christ, as it took its rise out of the grave—the seeming grave—of Isaac.

The Jewish ritual had contained symbols of the death whereby Christ should bring his people into the new Life, but the acts of the new kingdom were something much greater than arbitrary, even though Divinely appointed, symbols.

By dying Christ does not forfeit His hold upon earthly things. All that is His in the world remains Hypostatically united to His Ever-living Self. Only by means of death could He take it into the glory of Resurrection Life and Ascended Power. Before His Death He took His Apostles into fellowship with Himself, and made them heirs along with himself of His glory. He gave them no earthly inheritance which He would leave behind: but He gave them fellowship with Himself, that they might live in His glory. The Body and Blood which He left with them were not mere earthly gifts. Having died, He reassumed them in a mode of-Heavenly Life, and in that Heavenly Life His people come to live with Him by feeding on these gifts.

The New Covenant, therefore, is a Testamentary Covenant of Heavenly Life, whereby we are called to have fellowship with Christ in the glory of His Resurrection; and He is the Mediator of the New Testament, not merely as having obtained these gifts by His Death, nor as having instituted them by His authority, but as the living Head of the Body, the Church, that they which are called may receive the promise of Eternal Inheritance by union with Him, the Son of God. The New Covenant is a Testament, for it is the Communication from Christ Who died to the members of His Body,—the Communication to them of those gifts which He by eternal generation inherits from the Father.

Note D, p. 390.

Zacharias throughout this Canticle dwells upon the various names. The Horn of Salvation introduces the Name of Jesus, already announced by the Angels. His own name Zachariah, "The Lord remembereth," and Elizabeth, "The Oath of God," are linked together in that verse, "To remember His Holy Covenant, the Oath which He sware." The Name of the Child is indicated by " the tender mercies of our God." The allusion here seems to be to Exod. xxxiv. 6. The Lord merciful and gracious. And John means the grace of the Lord.

Note E, p. 432.

This clause is generally treated as if it were dependent upon the Dayspring from on high : but the grammatical form seems to make it parallel with the giving knowledge of salvation, as if John the Baptist were to prepare the ways of the Lord by a double action. (1) By proclamation of truth, intellectual preparation ; (2) By directing our feet, moral preparation. The way of peace is but another expression for the Dayspring from on high. It can scarcely be said that the one leads to the other. Christ is the Dayspring. Christ is the Way. The office of the child is to make Christ known, and to prepare men that they may come to Him.

Laus Deo.

London : Swift & Co., Printers, Newton Street, High Holborn W.C.

Lightning Source UK Ltd.
Milton Keynes UK
UKOW01f1919260717
306122UK00011B/596/P